Students and National Socialism in Germany

G EOFFREY J. G ILES

Students and National Socialism in Germany

PRINCETON UNIVERSITY PRESS

Copyright © 1985 by Princeton University Press

Published by Princeton University Press, 41 William Street,
Princeton, New Jersey 08540
In the United Kingdom: Princeton University Press,
Guildford, Surrey

All Rights Reserved

Library of Congress Cataloging in Publication Data will be
found on the last printed page of this book

ISBN 0-691-05453-3

Publication of this book has been aided by a grant from
The Andrew W. Mellon Foundation

This book has been composed in Linotron Trump

Clothbound editions of Princeton University Press books
are printed on acid-free paper, and binding materials are
chosen for strength and durability

Printed in the United States of America by Princeton
University Press, Princeton, New Jersey

To Jack and Frances Giles
for their encouragement and love

CONTENTS

CONTENTS

TABLES

ABBREVIATIONS

AFGNH	Archiv der Forschungsstelle für die Geschichte des Nationalsozialismus in Hamburg
ANSt	Arbeitsgemeinschaft Nationalsozialistischer Studentinnen (women's branch of the National Socialist Students' Association)
AStA	Allgemeiner Studenten-Ausschuss (local students' union)
BA	Bundesarchiv Koblenz
BAFM	Bundesarchiv Aussenstelle Frankfurt am Main
BDC	Berlin Document Center
BDM	Bund Deutscher Mädel (girls' branch of Hitler Youth)
CGD	Captured German Documents
CV	Cartell-Verband der katholischen deutschen Studentenverbindungen (the largest Catholic fraternity association)
DAF	Deutsche Arbeitsfront (German Labor Front)
DB	Deutsche Burschenschaft (the largest dueling fraternity association)
DDP	Deutsche Demokratische Partei
DNVP	Deutschnationale Volkspartei (German Nationalist Party)
DSt	Deutsche Studentenschaft (the national German Students' Union)
GStV	Gemeinschaft studentischer Verbände (national fraternity associations' interest group)
HB	Hochschulbehörde Hamburg (University Authority)
HIS	Hoover Institution on War, Revolution and Peace, Stanford University
HJ	Hitlerjugend (Hitler Youth)
IfH	Institut für Hochschulkunde, Würzburg
IfZ	Institut für Zeitgeschichte, Munich
KPD	Kommunistische Partei Deutschlands

KSCV	Kösener Senioren-Convent Verband (the most prestigious of the large fraternity organizations)
LC	Library of Congress, Washington, D.C.
MicAlex	Microfilms of captured German records, filmed at Alexandria, Virginia
NSAHB	Nationalsozialistischer Altherrenbund der deutschen Studenten (National Socialist Alumni Association of German Students)
NSDAP	Nationalsozialistische Deutsche Arbeiterpartei (National Socialist German Workers' Party)
NSDDOZB	Nationalsozialistischer Deutscher Dozentenbund (National Socialist German Lecturers' Association)
NSDStB	Nationalsozialistischer Deutscher Studentenbund (National Socialist German Students' Association)
NSS	Nationalsozialistischer Schülerbund (National Socialist Schoolboys' Association)
OP	Oberstes Parteigericht (Supreme Party Court)
REM	Reichserziehungsministerium (Reich Education Ministry)
RMdI	Reichministerium des Innern (Reich Ministry of the Interior)
RSF	Reichsstudentenführung (Reich Student Leadership)
RSFWü	Archiv der ehemaligen Reichsstudentenführung und des NSDStB, Universitätsbibliothek Würzburg
RSW	Reichsstudentenwerk (student financial aid organization)
SA	Sturmabteilung (the storm troopers)
SD	Sicherheitsdienst des Reichsführers-ss (the Party's secret police)
SS	Schutzstaffel
StA	Staatsarchiv Hamburg
StBO	Studentenbunds-Organisation (short-lived paramilitary arm of the National Socialist Students' Association)
UniHH	Archiv der Universität Hamburg
UniHH Phil	Files from the Philosophical Faculty of the University of Hamburg
VDSt	Kyffhäuser-Verband der Vereine Deutscher Studenten (extreme right-wing fraternity association)
ZStA	Zentrales Staatsarchiv Potsdam

xii

ACKNOWLEDGMENTS

My Cambridge University Ph.D. thesis, which formed the basis for this book, was made possible by major research grants from the Master and Fellows of St. Edmund's House Cambridge, the President and Fellows of Wolfson College Cambridge, and the *Stiftung Europa-Kolleg Hamburg*, to all of whom I am extremely grateful. Special thanks must go to my aunt, Mrs. Margaret Bird, for her financial assistance during the first year of the project. Visits to archives in West and East Germany were supported generously by St. Edmund's House, the Cambridge University Political Science Fund, the German Academic Exchange Service, the *Hamburger Wissenschaftliche Stiftung*, and the *Mildtätigkeitsstiftung Ferdinand und Emma Beit*.

Jonathan Steinberg, of Trinity Hall, supervised the research at Cambridge with the perfect combination of firm criticism and sincere enthusiasm. I benefited from the comments and encouragement of many other colleagues at Cambridge, Hamburg, Yale, and Florida. In Germany, the conscientious assistance and ready trust offered me by W. D. Hauptreif of the University of Hamburg registry and by H. D. Oppel, at that time the archivist of the *Archiv der ehemaligen Reichsstudentenführung und des NSDStB* at the University of Würzburg, more than compensated for the temporary frustrations that I sometimes suffered in my attempts elsewhere to gain access to sensitive material. The other archivists and librarians who helped me also deserve my thanks. I am particularly grateful to the East German authorities for allowing me the opportunity to work in the Central State Archives at Potsdam. The former students and professors at Hamburg who consented to my interviewing them added considerably to my understanding of the Nazi period, which they had experienced firsthand. I was heartened by the confidence of Professor Gustav Adolf Rein, who sent me a subjective but fascinating private memoir about his academic career less than a month before his death at the age of ninety-three in January 1979.

As my thesis was nearing completion, I was invited by Burton Clark to join Yale University's Institution for Social and Policy Studies. The four years I spent there as a member of the Yale Higher Education Research Group were exceptionally fruitful, spent in the detailed exploration of the characteristics of university systems throughout the world. This enabled me to put the present study into better focus. His penetrating mind (behind the disguise of his modest manner) made Burton Clark in every sense the intellectual leader of the group, but I should acknowledge the insights gained from the other members, especially the historians Robert R. Palmer and John Whitehead. Edward Shils also helped to sharpen my thoughts on the nature of academic institutions.

More than a decade after I had started the research for this project in Hamburg, the climate within the University had changed to the extent that a group of Hamburg scholars themselves felt able to begin examining the subject. Their work was prompted by the fiftieth anniversary of Hitler's seizure of power, and some preliminary findings were presented in an exhibition on the University of Hamburg under the Nazis, which I opened in November 1983, at the kind invitation of Vice President Huber. It was a delight to renew my friendship there with Albert Suhr, a former member of the White Rose resistance group, and to make the acquaintance of another opponent of National Socialism—Professor Wilhelm Flitner—who had lived through all those years as a faculty member. The research continues in Hamburg at the hands of some fifty scholars from a wide range of departments of the University, with a view to building up a composite picture of life in a German university under the Third Reich. The results, when completed, will present a more comprehensive analysis than for any other academic institution in Germany. Eckart Krause, the project coordinator, deserves praise for his efforts to persuade departments to open files that many would still rather keep closed. And I thank him for keeping me abreast of an endeavor that I have followed with close interest, albeit at a distance of several thousand miles.

The opportunity to revise my manuscript was provided by a faculty research award from the University of Florida. The Department of History gave positive support by relieving me of my teaching duties for a term. Discussions with my students at Yale University and the University of Florida have led me to explain a number of points more clearly in the text, and I thank them, too. Charles Sidman, David Colburn, Harry Paul, and George Pozzetta at the University of Florida generously gave of their time to read a longer version of the manuscript and made sensible suggestions for its improvement. My thanks are also due to Adrienne Turner, who managed to decipher an Englishman's strange handwriting and typed the draft of the manuscript with characteristic cheerfulness, intelligence, and efficiency; and to Steve Boyett and Tina Slick, who put the final version into the word processor.

Gainesville
June 1984

Students and National Socialism in Germany

INTRODUCTION

The German Students' Union was the first national organization to fall under Nazi control. This apparent endorsement of Hitler by a significant part of the educated elite was a source of great satisfaction to the Party, coming as it did fully eighteen months before Hitler succeeded in obtaining the chancellorship of Germany. Both seizures of power were made possible by electoral success at the local level. The fact that the National Socialists formed the strongest party in the Reichstag did not mean that Hitler would necessarily be offered the chancellorship, but victory in the local student elections did signify that a National Socialist would lead the national students' organization. Regional studies have been used to shed much light on the national success of the Nazi Party itself.[1] It is all the more instructive to examine the activities of an individual Nazi student group. No such study has been undertaken before in English.[2] The richness of the sources for Hamburg University make it a natural choice for such an inquiry. The meteoric rise of a small yet grimly determined group of activists is all the more remarkable in the face of the entrenched, well-organized phalanx of fraternity associations that wholly dominated student politics after the First World War.

[1] Two of the most useful are still Jeremy Noakes, *The Nazi Party in Lower Saxony 1921-1933* (Oxford, 1971), and Geoffrey Pridham, *Hitler's Rise to Power: The Nazi Movement in Bavaria 1923-33* (London, 1973).

[2] Some studies of local student unions have been undertaken in Germany, notably Manfred Franze, *Die Erlanger Studentenschaft 1918-1945* (Würzburg, 1972); Wolfgang Kreutzberger, *Studenten und Politik 1918-1933: Der Fall Freiburg im Breisgau* (Göttingen, 1972); and Peter Spitznagel, "Studentenschaft und Nationalsozialismus in Würzburg 1927-1933" (Ph.D. diss., Würzburg, 1974).

The rise of the National Socialist German Students' Association (NSDStB) overall, up to 1933, has been studied closely by Anselm Faust; the student body as a whole during the Weimar Republic has been analyzed and described with impressive thoroughness by Michael Kater.[3] Little attention has thus far been given to the student body in the Third Reich itself, especially during the Second World War.

The problems of the successful revolutionary are quite different from those of the pretender to power and usually immensely more difficult. Dissatisfaction with a regime can grow so great that its overthrow becomes an end in itself. Any reflections on future alternative policies are pushed into the background. In 1931 Nazi student leaders received word from Hitler in person that they should not sit around meditating on the nazification of scholarship: it was a time for action, not reflection. Consequently, when they appeared to have gained absolute power in 1933 with the backing of Nazi state authorities, they had little notion of what to do with it. The content of the "political education" programs was only vaguely perceived, and for the rest it was thought to be a relatively simple matter to draw up. The student leaders were so obsessed, however, with gathering all the students in teachable units that they never devoted much attention to the palatability of the ideological lessons.

The NSDStB was certainly not the only Nazi organization to suffer from this malady. The present work contributes to the history of National Socialism in a number of ways, but also to other areas of historical study. First, it reinforces recent studies of the organic structure of the Third Reich by showing how power was obtained and maintained. The polycratic nature of the student leadership after its "seizure of power" was typical of other areas of the Nazi state and so-

[3] Anselm Faust, *Der Nationalsozialistische Deutsche Studentenbund: Studenten und Nationalsozialismus in der Weimarer Republik*, 2 vols. (Düsseldorf, 1973); Michael H. Kater, *Studentenschaft und Rechtsradikalismus in Deutschland 1918-1933: Eine sozialgeschichtliche Studie zur Bildungskrise in der Weimarer Republik* (Hamburg, 1975).

ciety. Even the internal unification of the student leadership after 1936 did not herald a new, monolithic structure. W. S. Allen has called the competency battles between various agencies of the Party and state a "nonproblem": since no one ever challenged Hitler, the outcome is, he thinks, irrelevant.[4] In one sense, he is right: when Hitler went to war in 1939, there were few misgivings among the students. The student leaders positively clamored to enlist, but in marching off as cannon fodder they ruined any chance of success for the political education program. Their inexperienced replacements had no idea of what they should be doing. German universities in the Third Reich failed to produce intellectual ideologues for the new world empire. Whether Hitler ever intended the universities to accomplish this task is a moot point, but the NSDStB certainly believed that this was their mission. One of the central reasons for that failure was the struggle for influence. These battles, which were indeed often essentially trivial, filled the center stage for much of the time. They were quite simply the chief concern of the student leaders, and they therefore merit some discussion as well as the quite proper speculation over what the student leaders might have been doing.

What they ought to have been doing was constructing a coherent ideology, and that is the second major question that this study addresses. The main focus is not so much on the content of the ideology. For the Weimar period this has already been clearly set out in Kater's book; for the Third Reich the leaders produced little that was specifically tailored to a student audience. The emphasis is therefore on the presentation of the National Socialist ideas that the NSDStB desired to instill in the student body. After the fundamental change in the nature of the organization in 1934 from a mass movement to an elite cadre, efforts were repeatedly hampered by an ambivalence over the compulsory

---

[4] Cf. Allen's review of the second volume of Orlow's Party history in *Journal of Modern History* 47 (September 1975): 576-78.

or voluntary basis of its pedagogical programs. It was known that compulsion engendered hostility, but leaving to the individual the freedom to participate in Nazi activities brought the NSDStB up against the almost insuperable problem of apathy.

After the politicization of the student body, the NSDStB's principal ideological task was the nazification of scholarship. The importance that the Nazi Party appeared to attach to the achievement of these goals was emphasized by the high status accorded to the NSDStB within the Party structure. It was not merely one of the so-called affiliated organizations (*angeschlossene Verbände*) but one of only seven Formations (*Gliederungen*) of the Party alongside the *Schutzstaffel* (ss), the storm troopers (sa), and the Hitler Youth (hj).[5] It therefore held a position of much greater importance than Nazi professional associations like those for lawyers or physicians. The opportunity that the NSDStB presents for thorough investigation by the historian is rare indeed, for it is the only one of the Formations, apart from the ss, from whose headquarters comprehensive records survive. One is therefore able to examine closely the policies of the National Socialists toward a stratum of crucial importance to any modern society: the educated intelligentsia who would fill many of the leading positions in that society as teachers, lawyers, civil servants, and so on.

An examination of the Reich Education Ministry does not reveal such detail. Bernhard Rust, the quintessential schoolmaster, was more at home in the lower sectors than with the universities, which he largely left to his subordinates. As minister, he was scorned by other Party leaders, who quickly gave up any real hope that the nazification of Ger-

---

[5] It was elevated to this status on 29 March 1935 by a supplementary decree of the *Reichsgesetz zur Sicherung der Einheit von Partei und Staat.* Cf. Albert Derichsweiler, "Die rechtsgeschichtliche Entwicklung des deutschen Studententums von seinen Anfängen bis zur Gegenwart" (Diss. iur., Munich, 1938), p. 97.

man universities and German scholarship would be accomplished from this quarter. The National Socialist Lecturers' Association (*Nationalsozialistischer Deutscher Dozentenbund* or NSDDOZB), the faculty's counterpart to the NSDStB, was also awarded Formation status within the Party structure. Yet it, too, was directed by a weak leader, Walter Schultze, who never succeeded in winning decisive influence for his organization. By 1936, members of Himmler's Security Service, the *Sicherheitsdienst* (SD), one of whose concerns was the charting of the progress of nazification, realized that the only hope for accomplishing ideological orthodoxy in the universities lay with the NSDStB.

The traditional nature of the university as a center of critical thought posed a perennial problem. A third concern of this study is with the issue of opposition and collaboration in a broad sense. A marked institutional tenacity in the face of severe external pressures is just one feature that may be found in the universities of other countries at various times. Some of the similarities derive from the common oligarchical system of control that professors in many European and other countries secured in the nineteenth century. The mechanisms for combating political interference were well rehearsed by 1933. And yet overt dissent was not more clearly or forthrightly expressed than in other institutions in Nazi Germany. The professors and students fail to give the lie to the rather sorry record drawn up recently by Ian Kershaw. Universities are a vital part of any modern society, but they play a particularly prominent role in recent German history. Karl Dietrich Bracher has noted the unusual degree of reverence for its universities and professors that Germany has long displayed. An understanding of them is essential for any comprehensive analysis of Germany's modern history.[6]

---

[6] Ian Kershaw, *Popular Opinion and Political Dissent in the Third Reich: Bavaria 1933-1945* (Oxford, 1983); Karl Dietrich Bracher, *Das deutsche Dilemma: Leidenswege der politischen Emanzipation* (Munich, 1971), p. 131.

The first beginnings of real democracy, which the Weimar Republic ushered in, were perceived by academics as a threat. By retreating to a suprapolitical vantage point, they hoped to avoid the need to justify themselves. Claiming to stand above the mêlée of politics, they encouraged the view that theirs was a special institution for which democratic models were simply not appropriate. Such an attitude inclined them toward at least tacit support of right-wing groups and their ideologies. Not only did they perceive a fall in their own status within society, but serious overcrowding of the universities at the end of the 1920s led to a drop in academic standards and a loss of prestige for the institutions to which they belonged.

After March 1933 Hitler's government took hasty steps to reduce the numbers of students, which the faculty viewed as a positive sign (though it was completely offset shortly afterward by the purges of Jewish professors). Charles McClelland has recently written: "Given the contempt of the Nazis for the life of the mind, it is even remarkable that the universities were not abolished altogether."[7] German professors were well aware of this possibility, and it made them careful not to act in a totally uncooperative manner toward their new masters. It was a different matter when Nazi students brought their influence to bear on internal university affairs, which was considered to be an arrogant breach of the master-scholar relationship. In part, this was a generational problem that had been simmering since the end of the First World War. Soldiers returning from the front to study at a university refused to be treated like immature schoolboys any longer. It was partly this concern that led to the formation of students' unions.

The fourth area of inquiry to which this study contributes is the literature on student movements. The German student body of the late twenties displayed the common danger sig-

[7] Charles E. McClelland, *State, Society, and University in Germany 1700-1914* (Cambridge, 1980), p. 329.

nals. When the German Students' Union lost the official recognition of the Prussian and other federal states after 1926, its formal channels of communication with authority were closed. This made it much more difficult to insist that the state authorities should speedily meet the various demands expressed by the students over, for example, the dismissal of a number of pacifist professors (not to mention more complex subjects like the revision of the Versailles Treaty). The impatience typical of youth began to turn the students toward groups that offered radical solutions.[8]

Yet this did not inevitably lead them to the unlikely doctrine of National Socialism. An unparalleled dedication to political activism was needed on the part of the NSDStB in order to achieve that. One of the reasons why the National Socialist Students' Association seized power so early was precisely because they were students. Like the members of other student movements, they relegated lectures and study to a position of minor importance. Therefore, the students had an almost completely adaptable time schedule, a privileged position not shared by lower class radicals.

In order to discover the real impact of National Socialist control in the field of higher education, a thorough investigation at the local level is essential, and that is why the present book, while devoting considerable attention to national policies, also concentrates on a single city. The choice of Hamburg is uniquely favorable to the success of such a venture. The inability to discover until now the actual, limited impact of the NSDStB on the nazification of the German university is perhaps only to be expected in the absence of archival material from local groups. Their records, like those of other Nazi organizations, were ordered to be burned at the end of the war. The preservation of the almost-intact files of the Hamburg District Student Leadership (*Gaustu-*

---

[8] Cf. Edward Shils, "Dreams of Plenitude, Nightmares of Scarcity," in *Students in Revolt*, ed. Seymour Martin Lipset and Philip G. Altbach (Boston, 1970), pp. 1-31.

dentenführung) is therefore an exceptionally happy coincidence. These files, along with many belonging to the student leadership of the University of Hamburg, which shared the same offices, contain private letters as well as official correspondence, including confidential personnel files and secret papers. They were bundled together, clearly in a great hurry, in the autumn of 1944. At this time Hamburg lay virtually in ruins; the student leaders were finally abandoning even an attempt at their prescribed pedagogical tasks and were organizing the students and professors in the people's militia (*Volkssturm*) for the final defense of the Reich. Ten bulky parcels were sent off to the Institute for German Student History at Würzburg. (It appears that two of them never arrived.)

The Institute was officially inaugurated in April 1939, and had quickly managed with assistance from the Gestapo to acquire the libraries and archives of several disbanded fraternity associations. Its request for the old files of local NSDStB groups was, however, all but forgotten in the confusion following the outbreak of the war a few months later. It only managed to obtain a few from the University of Würzburg itself. When Party and government officials were burning their papers all over Germany at the end of March 1945, the inhabitants of Würzburg were still struggling to put out fires. Their town had been almost totally destroyed, along with most of its citizens, in a bombing raid on 16-17 March. The Institute for German Student History, however, was located in the old Marienberg fortress on a hillside above the town, and its holdings remained undamaged while the firestorms raged below.[9]

In Hamburg, a bonfire was lit under the few remaining

[9] Dibner confuses its location with the old Prussian castle, Marienburg. Ursula Dibner, "The History of the National Socialist German Student League" (Ph.D. diss., University of Michigan, 1969), p. 310. For an account of the Institute's development, see Günther G. Schulte, *Institut für Hochschulkunde an der Universität Würzburg: Werden und Wirken 1882-1982* (Würzburg, 1981), pp. 20-29.

student files, which came largely from the student aid organization, the *Reichsstudentenwerk*. There had been a negligible amount of paperwork in the District Student Leadership since the previous fall.[10] As the archives of the Reich Student Leadership, which were also sent to the Institute at Würzburg, barely stretch beyond 1939, the Hamburg files are of unique value in covering the entire period of the NSDStB's existence. No other opportunity exists to study the organization from its birth in 1926 right through to the end of the war.

Only for Hamburg do exact figures still exist for the membership of the NSDStB's political education groups, the *Kameradschaften* (literally "comradeships"). They and the reports of the local student leaders tell a sorry tale of apathy and failure and prove that the glowing reports of success that the national leadership published were grossly exaggerated. Since the NSDStB became an elite organization after 1934, it might be thought that it was thereafter less concerned with the mass of students. Yet the distillation of an elite leader corps for the Nazi state was only part of the NSDStB's aim. It quite definitely saw as its task the close supervision and control of the entire student body. There were several reasons for this. The student leaders shared in the professors' worries for the future of the university. They feared that if every graduate did not leave college as a staunch believer in National Socialism, the Nazi state would have an appropriate excuse for not tolerating the existence of the universities any longer. Hence it was necessary to monitor each student in order to test and reinforce his ideological orthodoxy and to weed out possible or actual dissenters. This would in addition provide a useful talent-spotting service for potential leaders. Finally, there was a financial incentive for bringing as many students as possible into the political education units: the participants of the *Kameradschaften* became pro-

[10] Information from former Acting District Student Leader Wilhelm Formel, who built the bonfire. Interview Giles/Formel, 7 March 1972.

bationary members of the NSDStB and were thus, unlike the minority of full members, liable for recurrent payment of fees. This was no small consideration for the NSDStB, which always considered itself poorly financed.

The archives of the University of Hamburg are almost completely intact for the period from its foundation in 1919 to the end of the Second World War. The University regrettably decided in conjunction with the Hamburg State Archives to destroy in 1966 a set of some dozen files on the relationships of the University with the Nazi Party (NSDAP) and its affiliated Formations, along with other material that was "no longer needed"or allegedly *"nicht archivwürdig."*[11] Fortunately the richness of documentary material that remains allows an accurate assessment of that question.

Hamburg is also a fortunate choice for study in that the records of the ministerial-level, governing body of the University, the University Authority, survive *in extenso*. As regards the files of the four Faculties of the University, I was told that those for Law, Medicine, and Mathematics and Natural Sciences had been lost. Fortunately it now appears that some still exist. I came across the files of the fourth, the Philosophical Faculty, myself in an attic of the University, and these include the files on doctoral dissertations during the Nazi period.

I profited enormously from the interviews that I conducted with former professors and Nazi student leaders. Corroboration from documentary sources was still necessary, but the information that I gleaned from these discussions greatly enriched my understanding of the period.

It is necessary at the outset to point out the ways in which Hamburg might not be typical of attitudes in the rest of the country. First, it was the second largest city in Germany after Berlin and therefore possessed a quite different envi-

[11] Correspondence between the University of Hamburg and the State Archives regarding this in the University administration's file 96-68.12 (new series).

ronment from many college towns that were very small and centered on the university. Hamburg was primarily an industrial and commercial city with an unusually large, working-class population. It was a traditional stronghold of the Social Democrats, a rather liberal city, and this was reflected in the University's constitution. The University was popularly regarded, even during the Third Reich, as something of a political "nature preserve" (*Naturschutzpark*) where National Socialism was not taken very seriously.[12] The same claims have been made for the Universities of Freiburg and Tübingen.[13] In fact, the present study demonstrates that this is simply a myth: the students in Hamburg did not differ significantly from those at other universities in their support of National Socialism before 1933. Similar reactions to the Nazi authorities during the Third Reich may be observed in other universities as well. If it is true that Hamburg's reaction to National Socialism lies nearer the norm than is widely assumed, then my argument for the essential failure of the NSDStB's political education program should have wider validity. It is to be hoped that it will lead to a closer examination of the albeit sketchy evidence at other universities, with a view to reassessing the success of the NSDStB there. Everything points, however, to the wider validity of the experiences recounted below. For all the distinctiveness of the University of Hamburg as an institution, the attitudes of the educated elite that filled its lecture halls and libraries were much like those that one might encounter from Kiel to Munich, from Cologne to Königsberg.

[12] Curt Eisfeld, *Aus fünfzig Jahren: Erinnerungen eines Betriebswirts 1902-1951* (Göttingen, 1973), p. 134.

[13] Gerhard Ritter, "The German Professor in the Third Reich," *The Review of Politics* 8 (April 1946): 248; Uwe Dietrich Adam, *Hochschule und Nationalsozialismus: Die Universität Tübingen im Dritten Reich* (Tübingen, 1977), p. 212.

CHAPTER ONE

A Political Fringe Group

Prior to the twentieth century, there was no such thing as student government as we understand it today. Although students in medieval universities had been able to dismiss their teachers, such power had long vanished. The modern European university saw its students as apprentices to their masters, the professors, who often laid down regulations for their private as well as their academic lives. Students did indeed form clubs and associations, where they could let off steam, but these rarely aspired to influence the internal workings of the university. That changed in Germany and elsewhere between the two World Wars. It is the purpose of this chapter to examine the increasing politicization of the German student body and to show how this new climate provided enough support to allow the most radical of right-wing groups, the Nazi Party, to gain a foothold in the universities.

Postwar Student Politics and the University of Hamburg

As soldiers streamed home at the end of the First World War, many thousands were eager to begin or resume their higher education. Despite the worldwide prestige of higher education in Germany throughout the nineteenth century, Hamburg, its second largest city, did not have a university. Only in 1908 had the municipal government been persuaded to support the foundation of a small college, the Colonial Institute. Though modest in scale it was well endowed and attracted a handful of distinguished academics, like the young Carl Heinrich Becker (later Prussian education minister).

German universities were hard pressed by the large, postwar influx of matriculants, and the Hamburg parliament agreed that the Colonial Institute should help to ease overcrowding by accommodating the considerable numbers of would-be students who were residents of Hamburg. The grateful Prussian education ministry, whose lead the other states generally followed, consented to recognize these courses during the spring of 1919 for credit toward its own degrees while stressing that Prussia was not conceding permanent university status to the Colonial Institute.[1] The number of students at the Institute grew rapidly from seventy to 2,000. Financial problems alone meant that most could not leave their homes so soon after the war in order to study at universities elsewhere in Germany. Following German tradition, they would want to attend other universities at a later stage and were perturbed to think that their studies in Hamburg would count for nothing if they registered for their final examinations in another state. The shrewd Senator von Melle therefore advised the students to call together a general meeting and to pass a motion calling on the legislature to undertake the formal foundation of a university in Hamburg. Knowing that this alone would not impress the city fathers, he recommended that the students collect as many signatures as possible for a petition. Von Melle's hopes were realized when the students' campaign led to the passing of a provisional bill setting up the University of Hamburg on 28 March 1919. Student numbers rose again to almost 3,000 within a year, continuing to a peak of 4,500 in the summer of 1923.

Ninety percent of the immediate postwar generation of students had participated in the First World War, and they claimed the right to express their opinions on political matters concerning the country that they had helped to defend. More than this, many of them played an active political role by joining the armed bands of the Free Corps and Student

[1] Carl Meinhof, "Hamburgische Universität," in *Das akademische Deutschland*, ed. Michael Doeberl et al., 5 vols. (Berlin, 1930), 1: 203.

Companies. Their occasional, fanatical excesses prompted professors to stress anew the incompatibility of politics and scholarship. The so-called Mechterstädt Workers' Slaughter, in which fifteen Communist workers were shot by members of the Marburg Students' Company, deservedly attracted adverse publicity. When students' unions were set up, they usually had to promise the university authorities that they would not engage in political activities. The Hamburg University Law of 1921 explicitly forbade party-political aims.[2] Despite countless reaffirmations of this, a concern with politics grew to become the principal occupation of student groups, and student welfare slipped into the background.

Anti-Semitism among students was not a peculiarly German phenomenon. It was widespread among American colleges in the 1920s, not least at the Ivy League institutions. President Lowell of Harvard proposed a quota limiting the enrollment of Jewish students in 1922, on the dubious grounds that this would prevent the growth of the anti-Semitism already evident in the student body.[3] It is no coincidence that anti-Semitism in the United States was most prevalent in the more socially exclusive student bodies. In German universities the social elite tended to congregate in student fraternities, and it was here that anti-Semitism was at its most virulent. Konrad Jarausch has described with convincing clarity the decline of the initial liberalism of the fraternities after 1848 and their rightward drift, until at the end of the Wilhelmine period a large number of them were actively engaged in nationalist and imperialist causes, which turned the most extreme groups into protofascist associations. There were so many different types of fraternity that it is almost impossible to characterize them in brief.[4] Not

---

[2] Hochschulgesetz, sec. 7, par. 33 (*Hamburgisches Gesetz- und Verordnungsblatt*, no. 17, 6 February 1921).

[3] Seymour Martin Lipset and David Riesman, *Education and Politics at Harvard* (New York, 1975), pp. 142ff.

[4] Overviews in German are given in Faust, *Studentenbund*, 1: 121ff., and

all were anti-Semitic; indeed, there were Jewish fraternities. Yet the overwhelming majority of fraternities did band together at the beginning of the Weimar Republic in an organization that openly espoused the *völkisch* movement's Greater German and anti-Semitic aims. This was the German University Ring (*Deutscher Hochschulring*), which quickly became the controlling force of student politics.

With very few exceptions, individual fraternities were affiliated with a national fraternity association (*Verband*). This provided entrée into similar fraternities when students moved from town to town in the course of their studies, and it often functioned as an employment bureau for graduating members. One can distinguish between three basic types of fraternity associations, according to their stand on the question of dueling. Apart from insisting that affairs of honor be settled with weapons, a large number of fraternity associations required their members to perform a fencing ritual (*Mensur*) both as a prerequisite of their official induction and thereafter on a regular basis as continued proof of valor. It was on these occasions that the prestigious facial scar was acquired. A second group of fraternity associations did not insist on the *Mensur* (while often encouraging it) but recognized the duel as the only means of obtaining satisfaction, even after the Weimar government had passed a law banning all dueling. The third group of fraternity associations rejected dueling altogether.

The first group contained the most prestigious associations. The elite of the fraternity world was to be found in the so-called Corps, above all in the *Kösener Senioren-Convent Verband* (KSCV), which retained an aristocratic air. The

---

Kater, *Studentenschaft*, pp. 24ff. One of the few detailed accounts in English of German fraternity life is Gordon Bolitho, *The Other Germany* (London, 1934), which focuses on the *Corps Saxo-Borussia* at Heidelberg. For a concise, informative account, see Konrad H. Jarausch, *Students, Society and Politics in Imperial Germany: The Rise of Academic Illiberalism* (Princeton, 1982), pp. 239ff. The most exhaustive contemporary coverage is provided by Doeberl et al., *Das akademische Deutschland*.

17

Corps based their membership criteria more on social than on racial grounds. Foreigners were occasionally admitted, at least as guest members. There were indeed very few Jewish members, but the *Kösener* acted entirely in character when it refused categorically (almost alone among fraternity associations) to break its ties with part-Jewish alumni in 1935.[5] The fraternal loyalty of the elite was stronger than what were perceived merely as the political considerations of the moment. The *Kösener* made its own rules and expected others to follow. Its influence was admittedly extensive: 20 percent of senior civil service positions in Prussia in 1928 were filled by *Kösener* alumni.

The largest fraternity association in Germany was the *Deutsche Burschenschaft* (DB), numbering 6,000 undergraduate members by 1919, and like most fraternity associations, more than doubling its membership by 1933. It had been aggressively nationalistic since its birth in 1817, and encouraged the maintenance among its members of the tradition of political activism. This self-assured group drew most of its recruits from the upper middle class. As the *Deutsche Burschenschaft* leaned toward the radical *völkisch* movement in the mid-1920s, its members became particularly susceptible to National Socialism, and they are to be found in the very first units of the National Socialist Students' Association.[6]

The second group of fraternity associations, which did not require regular fencing bouts, was nonetheless the ideological bedfellow of the first group. Its most persistent representative in *völkisch* extremism was the *Kyffhäuser-Verband der Vereine Deutscher Studenten* (VDSt). It was

---

[5] Geoffrey J. Giles, "Die Verbändepolitik des Nationalsozialistischen Deutschen Studentenbundes," in *Darstellungen und Quellen zur Geschichte der deutschen Einheitsbewegung im neunzehnten und zwanzigsten Jahrhundert*, ed. Christian Probst (Heidelberg, 1981), 11: 137.

[6] Members of the DB's *Bubenruthia* fraternity at Erlangen were already involved in National Socialist organizations in 1922 and 1923. Franze, *Erlanger Studentenschaft*, pp. 80-81.

specifically anti-Semitism that brought together its founding members in the early 1880s. The VDSt was the only fraternity association thought to be so objectionable that the French military authorities banned it in the Rhineland after the war. Gustav Adolf Scheel, the Reich Student Leader after 1936, chose a *Kyffhäuser* fraternity as an undergraduate.

The nondueling fraternities of the third group were dominated numerically by the confessional, and particularly the Catholic associations. The *Cartell-Verband der katholischen deutschen Studentenverbindungen* (CV) was second only to the *Deutsche Burschenschaft* in size, with some 4,400 members in 1919. The Catholic associations were supportive of Weimar democracy as long as other students did not impugn their nationalism. The leading Protestant associations, the *Wingolfsbund* and the *Schwarzburgbund*, were less dogmatic on religious matters and less active politically. The Jewish fraternities in the *Kartell jüdischer Verbindungen* and the *Kartell-Convent* were all but excluded from student politics.

Immediately after the foundation of the University of Hamburg, student fraternities sprang up there with surprising rapidity, about twenty-five of them in the first year. Not all the fraternities were entirely new foundations: the two most exclusive ones, the *Kösener Corps Suevo-Borussia* and *Franconia*, had moved *en bloc* from Berlin's Kaiser Wilhelm Academy for Military Medicine, closed down as a result of the Versailles Treaty. And no less than four Strassburg fraternities had emigrated from the now-French university to Hamburg. In fact, Hamburg had a smaller proportion of fraternity students than did most other universities. This was due not so much to the recent date of foundation[7] as to the fact that an unusually high percentage of Hamburg stu-

---

[7] The University of Cologne, also founded in May 1919, had over twice as many fraternity students. Doeberl et al., *Das akademische Deutschland*, 2: 896-908.

dents had their parental home in the city.[8] The cost of studying in Hamburg at this time was the highest in Germany,
for, although the university fees were the lowest, the average
rent was five times that of Tübingen, for example. In 1921,
a student at Berlin needed roughly 390 marks per month for
living expenses; in Hamburg he required 600 marks.[9] Problems of student welfare occupied a central place in the early
debates of student governments.

The first representative body of all students in Hamburg
was the general meeting (*Vollversammlung*). On 27 July
1919 a provisional constitution was passed and a committee
elected to draft a definitive version. At the same time the
Hamburg city parliament was in the process of placing the
provisional University Bill permanently on the statute book.
It was a period of much discussion on university reform in
Germany, and Hamburg's numerous socialists and liberals
saw a great opportunity for the city to lead the way by setting
up an institution of exemplary democracy. It was suggested
in committee that the university senate should have four
seats for student representatives, but this proposal was rejected by the professors and, surprisingly, by the students
themselves. Though they were to ask for just such representation after 1933, they now considered that a mere four
votes could play no decisive role. The students suggested
the formation of consultative committees at Faculty and
senate levels, composed of equal numbers of students and
professors. This plan gained the support of the faculty, as it

[8] Over 40 percent in Hamburg proper, but one must add to this figure the
residents of the suburbs of Wandsbek, Harburg, and Altona (until 1937 part
of Prussia). Hans Ochsenius, "Die Studentenschaft der Hansischen Universität zu Hamburg bis 1939 unter besonderer Berücksichtigung der gesamten studentischen Entwicklung im Altreich" (Ph.D. diss., Hamburg,
1941), p. 116.

[9] Helga Bauer, "Die studentische Selbstverwaltung und die studentischen
Gruppierungen an der Universität Hamburg 1919-1933. Organisation und
Entwicklung unter Berücksichtigung des Einflusses der wirtschaftlich-so-
zialen Verhältnisse der Freien und Hansestadt Hamburg" (Master's thesis,
Hamburg, 1971), p. 46.

left them with complete autonomy in the University senate, and was eventually accepted by the Hamburg city parliament.

By the winter semester 1920-1921 a student parliament had been set up to represent the wishes of the students "with regard to the running of the University, and for the self-government of the student body."[10] It consisted of thirty-six elected members, plus one student delegate from each of the four staff-student Faculty committees. The leadership was vested in a "general student committee," known then as today as the ASTA (*Allgemeiner Studenten-Ausschuss*), which was composed of five members chosen by the student parliament, and committee representatives of the four Faculties. The first ASTA had only a short term of office, for all nine members resigned in February 1921 as a result of a conflict over the rights of Jewish students. That anti-Semitism was rife in Hamburg from the very outset is underlined by the fact that the original umbrella association of almost all the fraternities (*Vertreterschaft der Hamburger Korporationen*), formed in 1919, admitted only those that expressly excluded Jews from membership.[11]

Through its successor, the Germanic University Ring (*Hochschulring Deutscher Art*), the fraternities in Hamburg (as elsewhere) were able to gain a decisive grip on local student politics from very early on, by dint of being much better organized than the so-called free students (*Freistudenten*). The fraternity-controlled ASTA passed a motion with the intention of depriving Jewish students of full voting rights, declaring that "national minorities at the University of Hamburg may only put forward representatives in proportion to their numbers. . . . Jews of Jewish-national persuasion, i.e. Jews for whom a real society of Jews exists or is

[10] Ochsenius, "Studentenschaft," p. 92.

[11] Hans Peter Bleuel and Ernst Klinnert, *Deutsche Studenten auf dem Weg ins Dritte Reich: Ideologien, Programme, Aktionen, 1918-1935* (Gütersloh, 1967), p. 145.

desirable, have the rights of national minorities."[12] The promulgation of the University Law on 4 February 1921 therefore marked a defeat for the ASTA, as it allowed for no such reservations, the city parliament regarding it as self-evident that all students of German nationality should be treated equally. In deference to this, the final version of the student constitution stated that "all students of German citizenship are members of the Students' Union."[13]

These developments were not peculiar to Hamburg. After the war, student parliaments were formed in all universities and came together in July 1919 at Würzburg as a national union, which from 1920 onward was called the German Students' Union (*Deutsche Studentenschaft* or DST). At first, most of the effective power lay in the *local* students' unions.[14] In order to consolidate this (and thus its own control) and to halt the spread of the anti-Jewish tendencies that the Austrian students' unions had already introduced into the DST, the Prussian Education Ministry officially recognized the local student bodies in September 1920 as unions of "all fully-matriculated students of German citizenship" at a university.[15] The necessity to grant Jews full membership brought no immediate protest from the ASTAS, for state recognition brought with it the right to levy compulsory fees from every student. Difficulties occurred only over the question of membership of the DST. The Prussian students' unions were allowed by the ministerial decree to join together with

---

[12] Quoted in Bauer, "Selbstverwaltung," pp. 21-22.

[13] Quoted in Ochsenius, "Studentenschaft," p. 95.

[14] The same was true in Britain, where, unlike Germany, apathy toward the national body increased markedly as the twenties wore on. Eric Ashby and Mary Anderson, *The Rise of the Student Estate in Britain* (Cambridge, Mass., 1970), pp. 68-69.

[15] Prussia deliberately specified membership of the state (*Staatsangehörigkeit*) as opposed to the racial group (*Volksangehörigkeit*). Most of the other states followed Prussia's example. *Verordnung über die Bildung von Studentenschaften an den preussischen Hochschulen vom 8.9.1920*, par. 1, quoted in Ulrich Kersten, *Das deutsche Studentenrecht* (Berlin-Zehlendorf, n.d. [1931?]), p. 155.

"corresponding" bodies at other German universities. Those in Austria, however, which the Prussian and other AStAs were anxious to include, differed in one important respect, namely, that of membership. They had effectively renounced the possibility of state recognition by insisting on a restricted membership: not only Jews, but also students "sympathetic towards the Jews or towards Marxism" were excluded.[16] The German students' unions tacitly supported this stipulation and saw no reason in it to prevent their Austrian counterparts from joining them, although a vociferous left-wing minority did seek to uphold the rights of the "non-Aryan," Austrian students. Attempts to write a clear statement of policy into the DSt constitution were glossed over in the final version of 23 July 1922, which permitted DSt membership to all students' unions of the German-language area. Since this apparently extended a hand to Austria, the maintenance of the state recognition of individual AStAs was henceforth dependent on the good will of the various education ministries.

In February 1924 the Hamburg AStA committee, upon which most of the power of student government had now devolved, asked the rector to support a constitutional amendment that would allow the students' union to apply for DSt membership. The democrats on the AStA (with five seats out of twelve) had previously managed to block this for fear of upsetting the Hamburg city parliament (a two-thirds majority was needed for any AStA decision). The fraternities took a seat from them in the AStA elections that month and pushed the motion through. The rector forwarded the request with his endorsement to the University Authority, the Hamburg government's equivalent of an education ministry.[17] This body ruled after consultation with

[16] Paul Ssymank, "Organisation und Arbeitsfeld der Deutschen Studentenschaft," in Doeberl et al., *Das akademische Deutschland*, 3: 365.

[17] In the city-state of Hamburg, the University did not come under the jurisdiction of an education ministry as elsewhere. It was supervised by a

23

the University senate that no constitutional amendment was necessary for the ASTA to take this step. Instead of accepting this as a green light, the ASTA came back to the University Authority, insisting that an amendment *was* necessary. Now looking into the question in greater depth, the Authority declared that a move to affiliate with the DST would probably cause serious disturbances within the student body. It also believed that this was incompatible with the spirit of the University, which did not discriminate on the basis of race or confession in accepting students.

When the Hamburg ASTA nevertheless sent delegates to the DST annual conference at Innsbruck in August 1924, they discovered that a formal application for membership was not really necessary, since all students' unions belonged to the DST automatically. This did nothing to smooth away the now-declared antipathy of the University Authority. Since further petitions brought no solution, the ASTA decided to send a letter of protest to the Authority in December 1924. In the New Year, it passed a motion stating categorically that "the Hamburg Students' Union is joining the DST" and sat back to await developments. The rector was therefore obliged to institute disciplinary proceedings against those committee members who had voted for the motion. The students were found guilty of a breach of academic discipline but were cleared in a subsequent appeal, which meant that the rector could no longer prevent DST membership. The Hamburg ASTA thereupon reaffirmed its intention in June 1925.[18]

Meanwhile a forceful left-wing element at the University of Heidelberg determined to raise the question of member-

---

special fifteen-man committee, the University Authority (*Hochschulbehörde*), of which the rector was also a member. On 31 May 1933 it became a mere department of the *Landesunterrichtsbehörde*, which in turn amalgamated on 1 October 1936 with the Authority for Church and Cultural Affairs to become the *Kultur- und Schulbehörde*. University of Hamburg Archives, Staatsarchiv Hamburg (UNiHH) B.4.

[18] Ochsenius, "Studentenschaft," p. 98.

ship again within the DST itself. By 1926 it found considerable support, albeit from a definite minority, at the DST annual conference. The whole matter was thus brought again into the open and could scarcely be overlooked by the Prussian Education Ministry. On 24 December 1926, Prussian Education Minister Carl Heinrich Becker called on his students' unions to alter their constitutions with a view to influencing the membership of the DST: either the latter must restrict itself to Imperial Germany, or, if it wished to include Austria in a Greater German union, then it must also accept the Jewish minorities. The Prussian ASTAS, having received five months' grace to negotiate with their Austrian counterparts, took no steps to meet with this ministerial request, and so Becker issued an edict on 23 September 1927 permitting the Prussian students' unions to amalgamate with other organizations only if they embraced all students of German citizenship under the same open terms of membership as his ministry had laid down for Prussia. They now had to decide, they realized, whether they would continue, "as state-recognized constituent parts of the university, to conduct the business of academic politics strictly neutrally in the sense and spirit of the present state, or whether, as an ideological group, they would now promote national-political activity in the service of the Greater German concept of the future, as they understood it."[19] A referendum, held among all Prussian students, encouraged the ASTA to refuse compliance with the edict. They thus lost their state recognition and their steady source of income in Prussia, though they continued to function as "Free Students' Unions" on a voluntary basis.[20] At the national level, the DST suffered as well: not only was it now denied students' fees from Prussia, but most other states froze the contributions of their students' unions for

[19] Ssymank, "Organisation und Arbeitsfeld," p. 369.
[20] An account of the dispute between Becker and the Prussian students' unions is given in Erich Wende, *C. H. Becker—Mensch und Politiker: Ein biographischer Beitrag zur Kulturgeschichte der Weimarer Republik* (Stuttgart, 1959), pp. 257ff.

the next five years. These actions created a background of resentment against which those who wished truly to radicalize the student body could act out their exaggerated grievances with plausible sincerity. National Socialist students used the issue especially adroitly, as will be seen, to show themselves as the true champions of the independence of student self-government.

The Formation of National Socialist Student Groups

Some students had been attracted to the Nazi movement even in its early days. Rudolf Hess claimed to have formed a Nazi student group while studying at the University of Munich in 1921; certainly by the end of 1922 there is concrete evidence of the setting-up of a separate student group.[21] This was the SA Student Company, mustered by Hess as part of the Munich SA Regiment. More general appeals to students were given, too, as when Hitler spoke in Munich's *Löwenbräukeller* in February 1923 on the subject: "German Workers and German Students: The Bearers of the German Future."[22] Hitler was well received among right-wing fraternity students, particularly when he spoke for the first time in Erlangen on 17 May 1923. Although the Erlangen students preferred the paramilitary *Bund Oberland* to the NSDAP, most of the fraternity students acceded to Hitler's request that they should participate in the march-past before him at a nationalistic rally, the *Deutsche Tag*, at Nuremberg on 2 September 1923 as a separate unit in the uniforms of their fraternities. So many students joined the Nazi Party as a result of this rally that a National Socialist Student Group was formed in October with some 120 Erlangen students.

[21] Cf. Hans Volz, *Daten der Geschichte der NSDAP*, 10th ed. (Berlin and Leipzig, 1939), p. 16: "Rudolf Hess ... 1921-1923 Führer der NS-Hochschulgruppe in München."

[22] This was to become a common theme. Cf. Hitler's speech with the same title in February 1925. Leaflet in Bundesarchiv Koblenz (BA) Sammlung Schumacher 279.

The group stood ready for action on 8 November 1923, though no orders reached it until the Beer Hall Putsch had already failed. The Munich students, on the other hand, played an active part in the Putsch. Arms were handed out on the evening in question not only to the SA students but to some fraternities as well. They also participated in the protest march on 9 November. Indeed, a fraternity member, Karl Laforce, was among the sixteen Nazi "martyrs" killed at the *Feldherrnhalle*. Subsequent pro-Hitler demonstrations by Munich students forced the rector to close the university for several days until peace was restored.[23]

The Reich Chancellery expressed its concern about the strong influence of Hitler upon students, and on professors as well, though there is little evidence of widespread support at this time. It seems that the only repercussions in Hamburg were when some very drunken fraternity students made their nocturnal way home through a noted Communist area of the city singing "the Hitler song."[24] It was not the singing of "inappropriate songs," however, but the subsequent letting-off of fire extinguishers that led to disciplinary action by the University.[25] A couple of Nazi student groups were active even after the ban on the NSDAP. The Erlangen group (under a false name) gained twelve out of twenty-five seats in the ASTA elections, which happened to take place there just after the Beer Hall Putsch, on 20 November 1923.[26] It was only in May 1924 that a National Socialist group was formed in Heidelberg, but its concentrated activity brought it three seats out of fourteen in the July 1924 ASTA elections there, including the position of chairman.[27] These groups all but fizzled out toward the end of 1924, largely as a result of

---

[23] Faust, *Studentenbund*, 1: 27.

[24] I am grateful to Reginald Phelps of Harvard University for the suggestion that the song in question may have been Dietrich Eckart's "Sturmlied."

[25] Disziplinarakte Hamburger Studentenhilfe e.V. contra Mitglieder der Burschenschaft Hansea, UniHH Di-Alt-42.

[26] Franze, *Erlanger Studentenschaft*, p. 84.

[27] Faust, *Studentenbund*, 1: 29.

the muddled leadership of the banned Party while Hitler was still in prison. Furthermore, the First World War veterans who were fiercely interested in politics had now left the universities. The new generation seemed rather uninterested in the ASTA, and political groups found it difficult to maintain their membership. Students were attracted more to the club life of the fraternities. Not until the "Becker dispute" were political hackles raised again over the membership criteria of the DST.[28]

The Party leadership had no plans for the foundation of a separate student branch of the NSDAP, and the initiative came from two Munich law students, Wilhelm Tempel and Helmut Podlich. After a meeting with Hitler and Hess in December 1925, they received permission to found National Socialist student groups in universities and colleges, though Podlich played no further active role. The National Socialist German Students' Association (*Nationalsozialistischer Deutscher Studentenbund* or NSDStB) was officially founded, according to later Nazi publications, on 26 January 1926,[29] but the first mention of it came during a local meeting of the Schwabing branch of the Munich NSDAP on 4 February 1926, in which Tempel announced that "yesterday the National Socialist Students' Association was formed with the main task of bringing together manual and intellectual workers, and of helping to alleviate social need."[30] The first general public announcement in the Nazi Party newspaper, the *Völkische Beobachter*, was printed on 20 February 1926, urging Nazi students to band together and form NSDStB groups.

[28] Wolfgang Zorn, "Student Politics in the Weimar Republic," *Journal of Contemporary History* 5 (1970): 135; Franze, *Erlanger Studentenschaft*, p. 95.

[29] Cf. Volz, *Daten*, p. 21. An isolated Nazi student group had been founded at Leipzig in November 1925 and later claimed to be the very first NSDStB group, but there was no plan for a national organization at this time. Dibner, "History," p. 4; Michael Stephen Steinberg, *Sabers and Brown Shirts: The German Students' Path to National Socialism 1918-1935* (Chicago, 1977), p. 74.

[30] Faust, *Studentenbund*, 1: 36-37.

By June 1926 there were probably about ten local groups, and by mid-December twenty-one groups existed, claiming a total membership of 290. Most groups had some ten members, though Munich, Dresden, Leipzig, Frankfurt am Main, and Vienna had around twenty-five. Hamburg lagged behind, second from the bottom, with only three members.[31] Tempel's deputy, Hans Glauning, summed up the situation by stating that "it is all a question of personality. Those groups work well in which the leader works well." Hamburg's early difficulties certainly stemmed from problems with its leaders as much as from a general lack of interest of the students in the NSDStB.

The first attempt to start a group in Hamburg in the summer of 1926 failed. Karl-Albert Coulon volunteered his services to Tempel but warned that he knew of only one other Nazi Party member at the University, who was far too busy to help.[32] No further move was made until mid-November, when Alfred Freudenhammer dispatched a similar letter, stating that to his knowledge Fräulein Ella Kroglin was the only other student Party member. At Freudenhammer's suggestion, a notice was printed in the *Völkische Beobachter*, urging Party members at the University and others interested in forming an NSDStB group at Hamburg to contact him. To his disappointment, not a single student did so. He put the blame partly on the general crisis of confidence that had arisen locally as the result of an internal Party feud.[33]

[31] Tempel to Organisationsleitung der NSDAP, 13 January 1927, BA Sammlung Schumacher 279.

[32] Coulon to Reichsleitung NSDStB, 10 June 1926, Archiv der ehemaligen Reichsstudentenführung und des NSDStB in der Universitätsbibliothek Würzburg (RSFWü) II*5 α 461. The signature is almost illegible: Bauer, "Selbstverwaltung," p. 98, reads it as "Pg. Albert Conlon"; a list of former Hamburg leaders drawn up in 1937 somehow makes it two separate names, "Karl Alberg" and "Coulon." Aufstellung für das RSF-Archiv von Pg. Schmauser, 6 July 1937, BA NS 38/2.

[33] This got so out of hand that the Hamburg *Gauleiter* was deposed and the Hamburg *Gau* demoted to an *Ortsgruppe* on 1 November 1926. Helga Anschütz, "Die NSDAP in Hamburg: Ihre Anfänge bis zur Reichstagswahl vom 14. September 1930" (Ph.D. diss., Hamburg, 1955), p. 94.

Freudenhammer only managed to persuade one other student to join, but he hoped that greater interest would be roused by a speech delivered by Gottfried Feder. His supposed economic expertise made Feder a frequent speaker among Hamburg Nazis. Freudenhammer secured the assistance of the SA in publicizing the meeting in the University and stationed himself at the entrance of the hall in which Feder was speaking in order to keep a lookout for students whom he might recruit for the NSDStB. But according to Albert Krebs, Feder's dull lecturing style often drove away, rather than attracted, new Party members.[34] On this occasion Freudenhammer picked up only two recruits. With this handful of five members, the group successfully applied to the rector on 20 January 1927 for inclusion in the University's register of societies.[35]

The constitution submitted to the rector differed from those of most other NSDStB groups in that no mention was made of the exclusion of Jews. The constitution of the Darmstadt branch, for example, stated specifically that "Jews or persons of Jewish ancestry cannot become members."[36] This condition was concealed in Hamburg in the requirement that all members join the NSDAP, which did not, of course, admit Jews. It was probably not stated openly for fear of antagonizing the University authorities, whose efforts to guarantee the rights of Jewish students in the students' union were well known. The constitution was dictated in outline by Tempel, and although it reflected his "social-revolutionary" concerns, no conclusions can be drawn about the thinking of the Hamburg members at this very early stage. What is clear is that anti-Semitism was present from

[34] William Sheridan Allen, ed., *The Infancy of Nazism: The Memoirs of ex-Gauleiter Albert Krebs 1923-1933* (New York, 1976), p. 257.

[35] Freudenhammer to Rektorat der Universität Hamburg, 20 January 1927, UniHH 0.30.6.

[36] Faust, *Studentenbund*, 2: 151-52, and Satzungen des Nationalsozialistischen Deutschen Studentenbundes, UniHH 0.30.6.

the start. Freudenhammer wrote to national headquarters in February 1927: "There is an *exceptionally strong* Jewish influence at the University of Hamburg. It is impossible to complete one's studies here without attending classes given by Jewish professors."[37] This was an exaggeration, but evidently some of Hamburg's NSDStB members needed to fulfill certain academic requirements through classes taught by Jews. Three out of the five members were unable to move away from Hamburg to another university, probably for financial reasons. Freudenhammer was not so dogmatic as to forbid them to take these courses.

Despite the fact that official university recognition now permitted the group to display a notice board within the University, there was little activity or propaganda to show of its existence. NSDStB headquarters became dissatisfied with the lackluster leadership of Freudenhammer, so when Georg Reuss, the leader of the quite successful Jena branch, moved to Hamburg in February 1927, he was requested to admonish Freudenhammer for the infrequency of his reports and to look into the running of the Hamburg NSDStB. Matters did not improve, and by the end of the summer semester Reuss had become thoroughly disillusioned: ". . . for as long as I have been in Hamburg, the same notice has been hanging on the NSDStB board (just once there was an invitation to the Goebbels' meeting). I have never seen anything of leaflets or newspapers distributed."[38] It was only Tempel's personal request, when they met at the Party Rally in Nuremberg, that persuaded him to withdraw his resignation from the NSDStB altogether. Three months later he was moved to write to NSDStB headquarters again with the complaint that there was no evidence whatsoever of any activity on the part of the NSDStB. Tempel discovered that he had received neither reports nor membership lists, nor, most important of all,

[37] Freudenhammer to Reichsleitung NSDStB, 17 February 1927, RSFWÜ II*5 α 461.

[38] Reichsleitung NSDStB to Reuss, 21 February 1927, and Reuss to Tempel, 20 July 1927, ibid.

subscriptions for months past, simply because Freudenhammer had departed for Kiel without telling anyone.[39] Reuss
was appointed leader and set to work with a vengeance to
put the group on its feet again.

The first issue that he tackled went straight to the hearts
of most Hamburg students. Reuss demanded to know,
though in the politest of terms, why the university refectory
could not remain open on Sundays, as was the case at most
other universities, to provide subsidized hot meals for students. In the event, Reuss's first political battle was a non-
event, for the perfectly reasonable request was readily conceded; it did no harm, however, to remind the student body
that it was thanks to the Nazis that they were able to eat
Sunday lunch, for the refectory was the only place where
many of them could afford to eat at all.[40] Outside the university, Reuss latched onto the activities of the Nazi Party.
He began by obtaining half-price concessionary tickets for
students wishing to attend a local NSDAP meeting at which
Hitler was to speak.[41] He advertised this particularly among
the fraternities, but although Reuss managed to sell more
than eighty tickets, thus demonstrating the potential inter-

[39] Reuss to Reichsleitung NSDStB Amt Presse und Propaganda, 26 November 1927, ibid. Freudenhammer was dismissed from the NSDStB but not
from the NSDAP. The Party wanted to reserve dismissal as the ultimate
disgrace, and Freudenhammer's inactivity had not caused actual harm to
the Party itself. Tempel to Parteileitung NSDAP, 3 December 1927; Buch
Uschla NSDAP to NSDStB, 12 December 1927; Buch to Freudenhammer, 21
December 1927, RSFwü II*5 α 461. Klinger to NSDStB Kiel, 5 December 1927,
BA Sammlung Schumacher 279. See also Michael H. Kater, "Der NS-Studentenbund von 1926 bis 1928: Randgruppe zwischen Hitler und Strasser,"
Vierteljahrshefte für Zeitgeschichte 22, no. 2 (April 1974), p. 178.

[40] NSDStB to Hamburger Studentenhilfe, 8 December 1927; Hamburger
Studentenhilfe to NSDStB, 20 December 1927, Staatsarchiv Hamburg (StA)
NSDAP 35 vol. 1.

[41] The meeting was arranged by the Gau Schleswig-Holstein but had to
be held inside the Hamburg boundary because of the ban on public speaking
imposed on Hitler by the Prussian government (March 1925-September
1928). Gaugeschäftsstelle Schleswig-Holstein NSDAP to Reuss, 1 December
1927, ibid.

est in the Nazi Party, the hoped-for increase in NSDStB membership did not come. As a follow-up, the fraternities were invited to a meeting to hear about the current DST situation in the light of the Becker dispute from the DST Area Leader, Dr. Joachim Haupt, an excellent speaker who also happened to be a prominent Nazi and leader of the Kiel NSDStB.[42]

Reuss received attentive help from his colleagues in Kiel in his concerted effort to gain a seat on the ASTA. Although the NSDStB group still only numbered four members, they had all managed "by clever maneuvering" to be co-opted onto the ASTA advisory council.[43] The foremost need was for financial coverage of the election campaign expenses, which, it was estimated, would reach 120 marks. As usual the Nazi students had to dip into their own pockets. No financial support ever came from their impoverished national headquarters: initially Tempel mailed propaganda material to Hamburg only on a cash-on-delivery basis.[44] Reuss's campaign was organized for him almost entirely by the Kiel group leaders, Joachim Haupt and Reinhard Sunkel, who formulated the text and design of both the poster and the election leaflet to be used. They particularly urged Reuss to use bright red posters, which were rather expensive, but

[42] The students' unions in the DST were grouped in ten Areas (Kreise), each of which elected an Area Leader. The latter formed the so-called Central Committee (Hauptausschuss) of the DST, which met between the Annual Conferences, at least twice yearly, to review the work of the three DST chairmen. It enjoyed certain executive powers itself and had the right to call an Extraordinary Conference, or to postpone the Annual Conference for a year. These rights enabled the NSDStB to foil the fraternities' attempts to prevent their seizure of the DST in the summer of 1931; see below, chap. 2. Satzung der DST, pars. 10 and 12-14, quoted in Kersten, Studentenrecht, p. 164.

[43] The ASTA advisory council (Beirat), a committee of twenty-five, could ratify or reject decisions of the ASTA itself, but it was seldom called on to do so, since its political composition usually corresponded with that of the ASTA. Ochsenius, "Studentenschaft," p. 97; Bauer, "Selbstverwaltung," p. 39.

[44] Cf. Freudenhammer to Reichsleitung NSDStB, n.d. (mid-December 1926), RSFWü II*5 α 461.

"unfortunately in our experience more depends on the external appearance than on the actual content of the poster." A late and sudden appearance in the campaign was strongly recommended, keeping the platform of the Nazis a closely guarded secret until then, so that their opponents would not have time to prepare a counterattack.[45]

By the mid-twenties, the contestants for Hamburg AStA elections had crystallized into three factions. Twenty-nine fraternities had joined forces as early as the autumn of 1920 to form the Germanic University Ring (*Hochschulring Deutscher Art*) in Hamburg, and most other universities saw similar developments. The Ring sought to promote among the students the *völkisch* movement in Germany and to oppose "the destructive forces of internationalism of whatever complexion."[46] It envisaged the struggle by no means as a purely intellectual battle: in the summer of 1922 the Breslau branch was banned by the Prussian authorities when it transpired that its recent "Sport and Hiking Course" had taken the form of a military exercise with machine guns.[47] As the efficient association of the equally well-organized fraternities, it quickly became the controlling force of the DSt.

The Hamburg left wing—a motley crowd of socialists, democrats, Jews, Catholics, and pacifists (a mere eight societies plus the Markomannia and the Jewish Kadimah fraternities)—united under the name the German Students' League (*Deutscher Studentenbund*).[48] The aim of this Hamburg coalition was to keep politics out of the University, to support the Weimar Republic, and to cripple the *völkisch* movement by its opposition to the Germanic University

[45] Sunkel to Reuss, 25, 28, and 31 January 1928, StA NSDAP 35 vol. 1.
[46] Satzung des Hochschulrings Deutscher Art zu Hamburg, par. 1, UniHH 0.30.5.204.
[47] Rundschreiben Preussischer Staatskommissar für öffentliche Ordnung, 24 July 1922, ibid.
[48] Constituent groups listed in *Mitteilungsblätter des Deutschen Studentenbundes*, February 1927, p. 8 (eight groups listed); and Matthewes to Blunck, 4 May 1927 (ten groups), UniHH 0.30.5.108.

Ring. Since it did represent such a wide spectrum of opinion and interest, the German Students' League succeeded as a combined front in gaining a considerable number of votes in the ASTA elections. It was the fact that Hamburg's left-wing factions formed a cohesive group for the purposes of elections that gained the University the reputation of being a left-wing stronghold. In 1922, 1923, 1927, and 1928, as Appendix 1 shows, the German Students' League actually won the same number of seats as the fraternities (five out of twelve). Since a two-thirds majority was needed for any ASTA motion, it was able to block any decision with which it disagreed.[49] In 1927, for example, it succeeded in halting the payments of Hamburg student funds to the DST, a move that the Hamburg University Authority supported with an edict the following year, despite the protests of a large number of students.[50]

Between those two blocs, and tipping the balance to the right, stood the *Deutsche Finken*, representing the nonfraternity students. Between 1922 and 1931 they regularly gained two seats on the Hamburg ASTA. But despite its claim to impartiality, the group was little more than an adjunct of the Germanic University Ring, working hand in glove with the fraternities on most issues.

During the year 1927 the NSDStB began to make its presence felt nationally in the German Students' Union, noisily if not yet effectively, for although only the ASTA delegates could vote, any student society was free to attend and speak at the DST Annual Conference. Since the Nazis would now clearly be participating in most of the local ASTA elections, the DST Chairman, Schmadel, suggested that they might join the fraternity lists.[51] Tempel realized that this was an at-

[49] Bauer, "Selbstverwaltung," Table 2, Sitzverteilung ASTA Hamburg.

[50] "Eine Abfuhr Beckers in Hamburg," *Mitteilungen des Nachrichtenamtes der DSt* 10 (18 November 1927), Bundesarchiv Aussenstelle Frankfurt am Main (BAFM) DB HPA 1927 BIV4 4545.

[51] The list system was used in ASTA elections, whereby one voted for a party list, not for individual candidates. The ranking of candidates was

tempt to place the NSDStB under the thumb of the fraternities, but in order to show his willingness to cooperate with
the DSt he wrote to his groups instructing them to enter into
coalitions for the AStA elections while secretly hoping that
they would not.

The subtleties of the situation were beyond Reuss and his
associates in Hamburg, and the order led to considerable
confusion and resentment against NSDStB headquarters for
almost spoiling the campaign.[52] In fact, the Hamburg group
set up virtually its own list, not under its own name but
with the appellation *Völkisch* Ring. Although it had combined with a minor right-wing group, the *Völkisch* Free Students' Union (*Völkische Freistudentenschaft*), Reuss was
certain that the new list would at best poll only enough
votes to give it one seat, and he himself held first position
on the list: "If we win a seat, it will be a victory for the
NSDStB; if we don't, then it's a defeat for the *Völkisch* Ring.
In either case, however, the student body will realize by our
presence and propaganda that we are there and have to be
reckoned with."[53] In fact, the *Völkisch* Ring drew 151 votes,
and Reuss won his seat. A contributory factor may have been
the dishonest behavior of the fraternities, who attempted to
set up an entirely fictitious, supposedly left-wing list, the
Progressive University Bloc (*Fortschrittlicher Hochschul-
block*), in order to split the left vote and possibly gain an
extra seat for themselves under false pretenses. The machinations were uncovered in time, however, and provided welcome propaganda to damage the credibility of the fraternities.[54] Support for the Nazis was also increasing in Hamburg
at large, albeit gradually: in the elections for the city parlia-

---

decided by each party, and it was not likely that the NSDStB would be given
a very high place on the fraternity lists.

[52] Glauning to Reuss, 29 January 1928; Reuss to Tempel, 2 February 1928,
RSFWü II*5 α 461.

[53] Reuss to Tempel, 28 January 1928, ibid.

[54] Disziplinarakte Universität contra Möller/Eggert/Göbelhoff, UniHH Di-
Alt-67.

ment ten days after the ASTA election, a third seat was added to the two (out of 160) already held by them since the previous October.[55]

Yet in spite of such a promising start to the year, no further progress was made. Reuss was at the end of his studies in Hamburg, and already before the ASTA elections he had written a circular letter to other NSDStB groups outlining his predicament: four of the group's six members were leaving Hamburg, and the other two would be too busy with exams to remain active. He urged the Nazis at other universities to transfer to Hamburg.[56]

The response was minimal, and though the group had slowly increased to eleven members by August, this was scarcely due to the efforts of the new leader Auerswald, under whom it remained rather dormant. It is likely that any new members were culled from the weekly seminars on National Socialist ideology and political thought run by the Hamburg *Gauleiter*, Dr. Albert Krebs.[57] The NSDStB group attended these regularly, but it held only three of its own meetings during the entire summer semester. Auerswald jus-

[55] The NSDAP had increased its share of the poll from 1.5 percent and 9,754 votes on 9 October 1927, to 2.15 percent and 14,760 votes on 19 February 1928. Werner Jochmann, *Nationalsozialismus und Revolution: Ursprung und Geschichte der NSDAP in Hamburg 1922-1933. Dokumente* (Frankfurt am Main, 1963), Appendix 5: Election Results in Hamburg from 1919 to 1932.

[56] Reuss to Hochschulgruppen des NSDStB, 27 January 1928, STA NSDAP 35 vol. 1.

[57] The seminars were held at the *Fichte-Hochschule* (known from 1930 as the *Nationalpolitische Hochschule Hamburg*), under the aegis of the *Deutschnationale Handlungsgehilfen-Verband*. It was Krebs's position as a leading official of this organization that resulted in this private arrangement, which "made it difficult for the Education Authority to issue a ban." The NSS also held its meetings here. Hildegard Milberg, *Schulpolitik in der pluralistischen Gesellschaft: Die politischen und sozialen Aspekte der Schulreform in Hamburg 1890-1935* (Hamburg, 1970), pp. 347 and 529. Cf. also the brochure of courses offered in winter 1929-1930 in STA NSDAP 35 vol. 1. Dr. Krebs had close contact with the Hamburg NSDStB from the very beginning and was a frequent speaker. Allen, *Infancy*, p. 91.

tified this by declaring that the students at large generally imagined the group to be about forty strong, and he did not wish to destroy this favorable impression by actually holding public meetings! He left Hamburg in the autumn to study at Leipzig on the depressing note that "unfortunately no one here is in a position to take over the leadership."[58]

Although one or two groups were in fact flourishing, Tempel's position as national leader was fraught with difficulties. On his move to Leipzig in the winter semester 1926-1927 he forfeited much that "nearness to the throne" might have brought. In the first place, he received no financial support whatever from NSDAP headquarters at Munich. This placed him at a strong disadvantage to other political groups with regard to the volume of propaganda that he could afford. He complained to Party headquarters that in all other political parties the student section was incorporated into the party leadership and was in some cases subsidized with enormous sums of money. Yet the Party did not come to Tempel's aid.[59] This should not be too readily grasped as an example of the anti-intellectual attitude of the NSDAP at this time; it was just that no clear policy on the question of support for the NSDStB had been formulated. The NSDStB was too small for Hitler to be bothered with, and Tempel did not have personal access to Hitler; indeed, he scarcely dared write to him directly.[60]

Tempel also had to contend with discord in his own ranks. The NSDStB leader at the University of Berlin set about undermining Tempel's position with the support of Gauleiter Goebbels. Criticizing the NSDStB as being too much a de-

[58] Auerswald to Reichsleitung NSDStB, 4 August 1928, RSFWü II*5 α 461.

[59] Tempel to Parteileitung NSDAP, 6 November 1927, BA Sammlung Schumacher 279. With adequate financial support, other political groups were able to waive subscriptions for membership, unlike the NSDStB. Cf. the constitution of the Student Group of the German National People's Party (DNVP), at Hamburg, sec. 4, par. 9, UniHH 0.30.5.106.

[60] Kater is right in suggesting that Hitler was waiting for the NSDStB "to prove itself." Kater, "Der NS-Studentenbund," p. 177.

bating club and too little an action group, he removed his group from the central organization and placed it in Goebbels's hands, whereupon the groups at the other two Berlin colleges followed suit.[61] The Dresden NSDStB had to be closed down for a time, owing to similar insubordination, and in the spring of 1928, the Halle group refused to subscribe to Tempel's newspaper, "The Young Revolutionary" (*Der Junge Revolutionär*), or to carry out any of Tempel's orders.[62] But it was at the University of Kiel that Tempel saw his most serious threat. Dr. Joachim Haupt had been an active Nazi since 1921, long before Tempel himself, and was well acquainted personally with Hitler (and Goebbels). He had been an important figure in the North German Nazi group, the *Nationalsozialistische Arbeitsgemeinschaft*, during Hitler's imprisonment and the Party's ban.[63] A shrewd thinker and single-minded leader, Haupt showed scant respect for his superior, Tempel. The Kiel group operated in an altogether unorthodox way: applications for membership were dealt with by a democratically functioning Standing Committee. Whereas Tempel was anxious to win as many members as possible and frequently urged NSDAP headquarters to order that every student Party member must also join the NSDStB, Haupt was concerned with quality and reliability and was not prepared to accept every applicant—even Party members—without question. Imitating the Berlin procedure, Haupt formally severed links with NSDStB headquarters and placed his group under the jurisdiction of the Schleswig-Holstein Party leadership in December 1927.[64]

Tempel hoped to clear the air and shore up his authority at the conference of NSDStB leaders arranged for February, which Hitler had promised to attend. But Hitler's speech

[61] There were also groups at the *Technische Hochschule* and the *Handelshochschule*.

[62] For a discussion of the NSDStB press organs under Tempel, see Kater, "Der NS-Studentenbund," pp. 167 and 182.

[63] Noakes, *Nazi Party*, pp. 53ff. and p. 204 n. 1.

[64] Faust, *Studentenbund*, 1: 64.

was so typically vague that each of the rival factions believed its attitudes substantiated, and opposition to Tempel became more open than ever. To Tempel's surprise, Hitler refused to accept his proffered resignation, pressing him "to keep up the good work." Tempel continued for another semester, but Hitler's promise of political and financial support was not followed by any noticeable improvement, and having failed his law degree examinations, he did ultimately resign in June 1928.[65]

Since Tempel did not exercise his right to appoint a successor, the unusual step was taken of holding an election among the individual groups, though Hess stressed that the winner must live in Munich or move there. This was recognized by some to be a hint toward the candidacy of the Munich NSDStB leader, Baldur von Schirach, who had recently been advocating the necessity of placing NSDStB headquarters in Munich, the home of the Party headquarters. Schirach was known to be something of a protégé of Hitler's and to enjoy close personal relationships with the Party leadership in general. A cultured, grand-bourgeois aesthete, he was the complete opposite of the social revolutionary Tempel. Displaying a total lack of understanding for the problems of the NSDStB at the time when Tempel was literally counting pfennigs, Schirach drew up plans for a clubhouse for the Munich NSDStB group comprising reception room, library, office, ladies' room, bedroom, kitchen, bath, and servants' room, which he envisaged as "a cultural center of Munich academic life" and which would incidentally serve as his own apartment![66]

A total of five candidates was proposed by the various groups in the election, and Baldur von Schirach gained six out of seventeen votes. Though he gained more votes than anyone else, it was anything but a decisive mandate. He was certainly not recommended by the majority of the groups,

[65] Ibid., p. 66.
[66] Ibid., pp. 105-106.

as he was soon claiming. Indeed, some of Tempel's associates on the left wing of the NSDStB had polled a surprising number of votes. Hitler's decision to confirm Schirach in office nonetheless has been taken by Anselm Faust to be a sign that the Party leader wished to halt the socialistic leanings of Tempel and steer the NSDStB on a new course. Michael Kater suggests that Hitler may not have had any strong feelings on the choice of Tempel's successor but admits the possibility that the appointment may be linked with Hitler's attempts to develop closer ties with the upper middle class and the generally noticeable right turn of the Party after the 1928 Reichstag elections.[67] The choice of Schirach rather than Joachim Haupt, whom Hitler actually preferred (according to Hess), may on the other hand be just as much a question of personality. Little attention has been paid to the influence of Hess in the matter. Faust lends credence to the report (in Schirach's notoriously unreliable memoirs) that Hess argued with Hitler that Schirach was too young for the post (he had just turned twenty-one).[68] It seems much more likely that Hess, given a choice between the independent-minded Haupt and the fawning and faithful Schirach, picked the latter. In his attitude of passionate submission toward Hitler, Schirach was Hess's twin. The fact that Schirach spent his spare time writing adoring poems about Hitler confirmed that he would be a reliable lieutenant. Haupt was far less predictable.[69] Hess certainly acted in a similar fashion in 1934 when he rejected Education Minister Rust's nominee for the position of Nazi student leader, Andreas Feickert.[70] The Party was not interested in the sort of schemes that Feickert had devised to bring together students and manual workers. More important, he might spoil the

---

[67] Kater, "Der NS-Studentenbund," pp. 188-89.

[68] Faust, *Studentenbund*, 1: 66.

[69] "Dr. Haupt was a much too independent thinker and personality for Hitler to tolerate in such a key position" (as successor to Schirach). Allen, *Infancy*, p. 264.

[70] See below, chap. 5.

chances for support from the middle class and upwardly mobile fraternity students, which the Party needed in 1934, just as it was beginning to realize it might need this support in 1928.

Fraternity students were important, even in places like Hamburg where there were proportionately fewer, because it was they who overwhelmingly controlled student politics through the local ASTAs and the national German Students' Union. The DST was to the Nazi students what the *Reichstag* was to the Nazi Party. By 1928 the realization was dawning, though with Tempel all too slowly, that real influence in this body would never be achieved by the uncompromising opposition of the insignificant NSDStB to the fraternity associations. If Nazis were ever to be elected to a majority of student representative seats, it could only be with the votes of fraternity students, not against them. Some rapprochement was necessary. Tempel was temperamentally incapable of this, and the aristocratic von Schirach was a better candidate than Haupt, who was inclined to view the Youth Movement as a more fertile recruiting ground for the NSDStB than the fraternities. The Youth Movement was certainly one of the nurseries of *völkisch* thought in the old Empire, and it was still perhaps the more committed to it ideologically, though it was not active in student politics. For it was the fraternity associations who were responsible for the acceptance of *völkisch* doctrines as the official policy of the German Students' Union and for the radicalization of the student body in the confrontation with Becker. This was very welcome to the Nazi students in a sense, for it meant that they had not so much to win over fraternity students to their ideology as to harness them. Yet it was not that simple.

Since the NSDStB shared ideological common ground with the fraternities, it was up to the Nazis to justify themselves by offering something either greater than or different from the latter. The fraternities had no need of a group of socially unacceptable demagogues to urge them to beliefs that they

42

already held. The NSDStB had to do more. In 1928 it was failing in this respect. Tempel had certainly set the new branch of the Party on a firm footing, but it seemed to be stagnating. There was little of the extraordinary dedication and activism manifested a year or so later. Tempel was in fact such a marginal figure that Schirach is still often taken to be the actual founder of the NSDStB, a myth that Schirach himself did little to discourage.[71] It was still a very minor fringe group in both student politics and in the Party. Baldur von Schirach, for all his unpopularity within the NSDStB, soon changed that.

[71] Karl Dietrich Bracher, *The German Dictatorship: The Origins, Structure and Effects of National Socialism* (New York, 1970), p. 139, for example, suggests as much. And Schirach's obituary in *The Times*, 9 August 1974, states: "Hitler was swift to realise his special gifts and was also flattered by his open worship. As a result, when he was barely of age, Schirach was permitted to form the Nazi *Studentenbund*."

CHAPTER TWO

The Struggle for Power

Five and a half years after its insignificant, almost pathetic beginnings, the National Socialist Student Association captured the prize that had thus far eluded even Hitler himself: national office. Indeed the Nazi Party had to wait another eighteen months before Hitler's chancellorship. How was it that young Nazi students, who seemed more often than not to scandalize most of the university, could bring the national students' union under its control as early as July 1931? This chapter looks at the crucial period of Baldur von Schirach's stewardship between 1928 and 1931, and weighs the relative importance of his policies and of the activities and initiatives of the individual, local NSDStB groups.

The Emerging Role of the NSDStB

On assuming office as national leader of the NSDStB, Baldur von Schirach gave no immediate indication of a change of course. Only after the semester had begun did he turn his attention to the leadership vacuum in Hamburg and ask the NSDStB there to elect a new leader as soon as possible.[1] There were now some twenty-five members, but a number of these came from the Hamburg State Technical Institute, where there was sufficient interest for the NSDStB to consider forming a separate unit.[2] Tempel had been quite willing to found groups outside the universities. There was evidently considerable potential in the nonuniversity sector, but Schirach wanted to grant membership in his organization only to university students: the Technical Institute therefore

[1] Schirach to Klüwer, 9 November 1928, RSFWü II*5 α 461.
[2] Schröder to Reichsleitung NSDStB, 21 June 1927, ibid.

formed a unit of the Party (*Ortsgruppe*) in November 1929 with some fifteen members.[3] This reflected well the shift by Schirach away from Tempel's deliberate identification with the broad mass of the working class toward the elitist values of the middle class.

Under Schirach's leadership, efforts continued to gain control of local ASTA committees. In 1929 the Hamburg Students' Union election was fought by the NSDStB without the assistance of their comrades in Kiel. While groups elsewhere campaigned openly as the National Socialist Students' Association, the group in Hamburg felt it necessary to keep the nomenclature of the *Völkisch* Ring for the NSDStB list. They feared that a former member—now dismissed—would set up his own list with this name in order to rob them of some of the votes of the Youth Movement, which had previously always supported the *Völkisch* Ring.[4] When they discovered that Joachim Haupt had persuaded Hitler to come and speak to the Kiel students, the leaders tried to persuade Hitler to stop on his way through Hamburg to talk there as well, but without success. The NSDStB emerged from the election with virtually the same proportion of votes as it had the previous year. The constellation of the Hamburg ASTA changed little overall, the only significant feature of the election being the loss of a seat by the left-wing coalition, the German Students' League, to the "free students" (*Finken*). The steady erosion of the power that the German Students' League had thus far held through compact alliance had now been set in motion by the defection of the Socialist Students' Group. The NSDStB's poll of 13 percent of the votes did not deviate

[3] By early December membership had risen to twenty. Koeberle to Schirach, 8 December 1929; Meyer to Reichsgeschäftsstelle NSDStB, 24 February 1930, ibid.

[4] NSDStB Hamburg to Reichsleitung, 3 January 1929, RSFwü II*5 α 461. For the receptivity of the Youth Movement to *völkisch* thought and their susceptibility to National Socialism, see Peter D. Stachura, *The German Youth Movement 1900-1945: An Interpretative and Documentary History* (New York, 1981).

45

from the average of 13.1 percent that the Nazi scored at other universities, and it gives the lie to the assertion that Hamburg was especially resistant to National Socialism.[5]

The main concern of the Hamburg NSDStB during the winter semester 1928-1929 lay outside the University. The students were diligently engaged in setting up, on their own initiative, a new Nazi organization for older pupils in Hamburg's high schools, which already boasted 100 members by the end of January 1929. This was the first group of what was to become the National Socialist Schoolboys' Association (*Nationalsozialistischer Schülerbund* or NSS).[6] The NSDStB members held their work in this area to be an excellent training in organization, leadership, and public speaking. It was also in keeping with their elitism that they restricted their efforts to high schools (*höhere Schulen*), whose pupils tended to come from the upper middle class. The justification for this was that they were on the lookout for potential NSDStB members: it was from these schools that university freshmen came.

Franz Koeberle, leader of the group in the summer semester of 1929, took an entirely different view of the role of the NSDStB and clashed with many of its members. He

---

[5] The national average would be 14.4 percent if one includes Erlangen, but I have omitted it here because of the unusually high support for the NSDStB there (33 percent of the votes). See Appendix 1, and also Baldur von Schirach, *Wille und Weg des Nationalsozialistischen Deutschen Studentenbundes* (Munich, 1929), p. 13.

[6] Meyer to Schirach, 27 January 1929, RSFWü II*5 α 461. Hans-Christian Brandenburg, *Die Geschichte der HJ: Wege und Irrwege einer Generation* (Cologne, 1968), p. 49, believed the earliest reference to the NSS to be at the Nuremberg Rally in August 1929; Daniel Horn, "The National Socialist *Schülerbund* and the Hitler Youth 1929-1933," *Central European History* II (December 1978): 358, claims that groups were formed in both Hamburg and Berlin during April 1929; Albrecht Tyrell, *Führer befiehl . . . Selbstzeugnisse aus der Kampfzeit der NSDAP: Dokumentation und Analyse* (Düsseldorf, 1969), p. 358, correctly refers to the Hamburg group as the first but puts the date of its foundation as March 1929; Volz, *Daten*, p. 27, confirms the organization's foundation in Hamburg but gives no exact date.

demanded categorically that everyone join the SA, and he declared it the central task of the members to attend local branch meetings of the Party. Indeed, in an effort to curry favor with the new *Gauleiter*, Karl Kaufmann, Koeberle wanted to place the group under the exclusive jurisdiction of the Hamburg District Party headquarters. He denied the necessity of a separate identity for the student group and described such demands as "class arrogance." When Koeberle made known his intention of turning the Hamburg NSDStB into an "SA University Group," he met with strong protest.[7] At the same time, his opponents discovered that he was not a full-time student at all but an elementary school teacher, and they forced his resignation. The Nazi Party in Hamburg was beset with problems at this time that were subsequently attributed to the predominance of a coarse element. The District Secretary (and for a while temporary *Gauleiter*), Hüttmann, was a prime example. His vulgar but forceful personality attracted many criminals to the Party, and he adversely affected overall recruitment. His eventual dismissal by *Gauleiter* Kaufmann led to a marked improvement in support from the middle-class circles the Party was seeking to attract.[8]

The conflict within the Hamburg NSDStB brought out a weakness in Schirach's leadership: after a year in office he had still not made it sufficiently plain what the political role of the NSDStB ought to be. The Hamburg students assumed that the very existence of the association signified that there were special tasks beyond support of the Party: "namely academic politics and an examination of National Socialist ideas in a form corresponding to the education and mental ability of the academic, *alongside* the work of the student

[7] Meyer to Reichsleitung NSDStB, 11 June 1929, RSFWü II*5 α 461. Kaufmann was appointed as *Gauleiter* on 15 April 1929.

[8] Anschütz, "Die NSDAP," pp. 113 and 129. It was Hüttmann who encouraged Koeberle, after his dismissal from the NSDStB, to found a unit of the Party at the Hamburg State Technical Institute and appointed him leader of it. Koeberle to Schirach, 8 December 1929, RSFWü II*5 α 461.

in the Party."[9] Other groups, too, believed that they were a cut above the ordinary Party member.[10] Despite the harsh economic realities of the Weimar Republic, university students enjoyed an elevated social status. The Hamburg NSDStB members received little respect from Koeberle's brutish storm trooper associates. This must have been painful for them, following the adulation that they doubtless received as leaders of the Nazi schoolboys' groups.

The Hamburg students received an indirect response to their query in the form of a recommendation to read Baldur von Schirach's recently published booklet, *The Will and the Way of the NSDStB*. In it he pandered to just the sort of elitist feeling that had surfaced in Hamburg. He attached, for example, much importance to a remark of Hitler's that he wanted the Students' Association to be not only an organization for the dissemination of National Socialist thought in the universities but also the "leader-training school of the NSDAP." Schirach defined the task of the NSDStB as a threefold one: the endowment of National Socialism with scholarly credentials, the spreading of Nazi propaganda within the university, and the training of leaders for the Party. For the rest, the goals were "identical with those of the NSDAP." From this, one would deduce that NSDStB members would have something to do with the Party only inasmuch as they were preparing to lead it. This was precisely the impression Schirach intended to create, and one in which, with his unthinking self-confidence, he possibly even believed himself. Yet it did not correspond with the intentions of the Party leadership. Schirach stressed the similarities between the elite dueling fraternities and the political elite of the NSDStB while pointing out that the latter was not as detached and aloof from the common people because of its roots in the all-embracing party. He chided the fra-

[9] Meyer to Reichsleitung NSDStB, 11 June 1929, ibid.

[10] Kater discusses the widespread incidence of this feeling of superiority in his chapter, "NS-Studentenbund und NSDAP: Die Unüberbrückbarkeit sozial fundierter Gegensätze." Kater, *Studentenschaft*, pp. 173-97.

ternities for having lost all touch with the lower classes, whereas in the SA "workers and students march side by side as fellow warriors of a great future."[11] Yet despite fine words about solidarity with the rank-and-file storm troopers, Schirach was suggesting that the universities themselves and the DSt must be the prime concern of the NSDStB.

Schirach began now to mount a number of campaigns in order to increase the public visibility of the NSDStB. Golo Mann has described his father's novel *The Magic Mountain* as "a stage on which everything was discussed and nothing decided."[12] The analogy might well be applied to the way undergraduates felt about student politics. The Becker dispute had helped tip the balance toward *völkisch* radicalism— though by no means toward violent action—by forcing the DSt to decide whether it would retreat into purely academic affairs (e.g. student meals and welfare) or take issue with ideological matters as well. The NSDStB had drawn attention to itself through Tempel's resolve to stand firm against Becker. Schirach made sure that it remained noticed by initiating a nationwide series of AStA motions on the restriction of student admissions (*numerus clausus*) and on rearmament, again expressing aloud what most students were really thinking. Nazi students entered the limelight dramatically in June 1929 by defying a specific ban on demonstrations against the Versailles Treaty. In the course of a Nazi brawl with left-wing students, the Berlin police opened fire on the rioters, and subsequent student unrest forced the closure of Berlin University for several days. In the Berlin AStA elections the following week the Nazis' share of the votes rose to 20 percent.[13] Moving beyond mere words, they had discovered the campaign value of action.

The winter semester 1929-1930 heralded for the NSDStB in Hamburg, under yet another new leader, Gerd Reitz, the

[11] Schirach, *Wille*, pp. 10-12.
[12] Golo Mann, *Deutsche Geschichte des 19. und 20. Jahrhunderts* (Frankfurt am Main, 1966), p. 723.
[13] Faust, *Studentenbund*, 1: 98.

49

unfolding of a period of activism more intense than ever before. Whereas only in July the University administration had noted that the NSDStB had not so far given rise to any difficulties, the group was henceforth constantly in trouble, above all over the tone of the notices displayed on its board, a large number of which were removed by the University syndic (attorney).[14] Contrary to the practice at many other universities, where restrictions on the content of notices were not generally imposed, the standing orders for the fraternities and societies at Hamburg permitted the display only of "straightforward and tasteful" announcements of meetings. Tendentious comments about other societies, the University, or the government—such as the NSDStB now made a habit of displaying—were altogether forbidden.[15]

Offensive notices usually led to a summons before the syndic, but until an official letter to this effect arrived, the NSDStB often thought that their student opponents, rather than the authorities, were stealing them. When an announcement of a talk on "National Socialism and the Middle Class" vanished, notices threatening violent retaliation were put up, and these were also confiscated by the syndic.[16] The Communists under similar circumstances were no less exasperated. Their poster for a talk on the "Ideology and Methods of European Fascism," displaying photographs of Mussolini together with the Social Democrat Police Commissioner of Berlin, Karl Zörgiebel, was swiftly removed, as were the two others announcing the same meeting.[17]

[14] As well as his proctorial or disciplinary function vis-à-vis the students, the syndic acted as the university attorney. He served also as secretary to the University senate. Cf. Hochschulgesetz vom 6. Februar 1921, sec. 7, par. 30. Syndic to Rector of Tübingen University, 9 July 1929, UniHH 0.30.6.I.

[15] Richtlinien für die Vergebung von Hörsälen in der Universität und von Räumen im Studentenhaus an eingetragene studentische Vereinigungen, 25 November 1931, UniHH F. 10.15.

[16] Notices in UniHH 0.30.6.I.

[17] The three posters in UniHH 0.30.5.252.

A particular source of friction was the fact that the University senate had in 1929 elected a Jewish rector, the philosopher Ernst Cassirer.[18] This positively encouraged the NSDStB members to be provocative. By early December, their behavior led to the summoning of Reitz before the rector to answer for the group's continual contravention of the regulations about notices. Cassirer was especially upset by the rubric "Jews not admitted" on the announcements of some meetings. A poster commenting on the NSDStB's election success at Frankfurt University described the town as "heavily populated by *Jews and Marxists.*" Reitz disclaimed personal responsibility but admitted that it was "of course unfitting and excused it with the excesses of some of the younger members, whose outbursts of feeling the leaders did not always succeed in restraining." In shocked innocence, the Nazis asked why two policemen had been present inside the University during a recent NSDStB talk by Dr. Krebs. The University syndic supposed in a similarly innocent tone that they had been sheltering from the rain, but he added that it was to be welcomed if the police were standing by at meetings where disturbances might be expected.[19] Cassirer made it plain enough that although he was reluctant to summon the police against students, he would immediately do so if he were no longer able to guarantee "the freedom of lectures, the peace of the University, and the personal safety of its members." Specifically, this would be the case if fighting broke out within the University building.[20]

Reitz promised to abide by the existing regulations but kept his word for a few hours only, for that very evening he ended an NSDStB meeting in the University, at which A. E. Günther had lectured on "The Origins of Judaism," with

[18] For a discussion of Cassirer's rectorship, see Geoffrey J. Giles, "The Academic Ethos in the Face of National Socialism," *Minerva* 18 (Spring 1980): 171-79.
[19] Aktennotiz Syndikus, 29 November 1929, UniHH 0.30.6.I.
[20] Aktennotiz Syndikus and Rector, 10 December 1929, ibid.

three cheers for Adolf Hitler.[21] Thereupon the syndic denied permission for NSDStB meetings inside the University, particularly as the group had appeared in uniform, another offense against the regulations designed to ensure the neutrality of the university.[22] The ban did not seriously hamper the Nazi students, for they were able to meet a short distance away in the students' union building, which did not lie within the rector's jurisdiction. The NSDStB, however, lost its privileges even here in January 1932, after preventing Jews from attending its meetings.[23]

Membership of the NSDStB was becoming more than a casual spare-time activity. The "program" had become a "duty plan," and demands on the students' time were heavy.[24] Apart from special lectures, there were the weekly Monday evening meeting of the group for talks and discussions, the short Tuesday morning gathering at the club bulletin board, and the additional work performed by some of the members in the proto-Nazi youth groups or the SA.[25] Attendance at local Party meetings took up not a little time. Furthermore, a "sport section" was set up in the autumn of 1929 for the physical training of members, and the NSDStB

[21] This is not the well-known Professor of Racial Studies, H.F.K. Günther, as Bauer assumes, but a lecturer at Hamburg's *Fichte-Hochschule*. Bauer, "Selbstverwaltung," p. 108; cf. also Jochmann, *Nationalsozialismus*, pp. 269ff.

[22] Aktennotiz Syndikus, 14 December 1929, UniHH 0.30.6.I.

[23] Kümmel to Feickert, 27 January 1932, RSFwü V*2 α 511.

[24] Rundschreiben Reitz, 29 November 1929, StA NSDAP 35 vol. 1. A report from the NSDStB group at Heidelberg illustrates the frequency of the meetings there. *Die Bewegung*, no. 9, 1 July 1930, clipping in Zentrales Staatsarchiv, Potsdam (ZStA) Reichsministerium des Innern (RMdI) 26108.

[25] *Der Jungsturm, Die Schilljugend*, and *Die Geusen* were all forerunners of the Hitler Youth and for some years existed alongside it. Cf. Brandenburg, *Die Geschichte*, pp. 22ff. and 36, and Peter D. Stachura, *Nazi Youth in the Weimar Republic* (Santa Barbara and Oxford, 1975), pp. 96ff. The Hamburg NSDStB leader, Gerd Reitz, was attached to the *Schilljugend*, whereas his successor also held the position of *Geusenkanzler der Nordmark*. All three youth groups had links with the Hamburg NSDStB. A joint letter to Cassirer complains about the presence of the police in the University, 4 December 1929, StA NSDAP 35 vol. 1.

now produced its own newspaper.[26] Even during the vacation there was a weekly meeting for those still on campus. As if all this were not enough, the Nazi students often put in an appearance at meetings of their opponents, the other political students' groups.

In the country at large, the Nazi campaign had received a great fillip from the acceptance of the NSDAP as equal partners in the fight against the Young Plan by the "respectable" German Nationalist Party (DNVP) and the veterans' organization, the *Stahlhelm*. Many people laid aside earlier misgivings about Hitler and his Party. Moreover, in the light of the evident splitting-up of the Nationalists after December 1929, more serious popular attention was given to the apparently cohesive and purposeful NSDAP. In many students' union elections during the winter semester 1929-1930, the NSDStB made significant, and sometimes spectacular gains. At Erlangen and Greifswald the Nazis won an absolute majority of the votes.[27] Although one may examine such local differences as the size of the fraternity population or the confessional profile of the students,[28] it is extremely difficult to make a significant comparison between the ASTA election results, for they took place at different times over a period of six months against a volatile background of political and other developments.[29]

---

[26] The *Akademische Warte: Kampfschrift für den nationalen Sozialismus* appeared as a monthly supplement to the *Hamburger Tageblatt*, the local Party organ, and was distributed free to students. Cf. Allen, *Infancy*, p. 91. Unfortunately, only two copies remain in existence, Archiv der Forschungsstelle für die Geschichte des Nationalsozialismus in Hamburg (AFGNH), NSDStB miscellany, and UniHH 0.30.6.I.

[27] Tyrell, *Führer befiehl*, p. 381.

[28] Spitznagel, for example, suggests a connection between the rise of the NSDStB's popularity and an influx of Protestant students into the predominantly Catholic University. Peter Spitznagel, "Studentenschaft," p. 308.

[29] A comparison of support for the NSDStB in ASTA elections during 1929-1930 and 1930-1931 in Karl Dietrich Bracher, *Die Auflösung der Weimarer Republik: Eine Studie zum Problem des Machtverfalls in der Demokratie* (Villingen, 1955), pp. 147-48.

53

Overall, however, the results from universities were alarming enough to prod the Ministry of the Interior into a national survey of National Socialist support in students' unions. The results confirmed the ministry's suspicions. Even at those colleges where the NSDStB had not campaigned before, they had often done remarkably well in recent months. Where this had been a second or third campaign, there was not a single instance of decline in support. Rather the NSDStB was everywhere becoming a force to be reckoned with (see Table 1).

This was alarming to the government in the light of the

TABLE 1. Percentage of Votes Polled by National Socialists in Students' Union Elections, 1928-1930

School	1928	1929	1930
Erlangen University	22.1	32.1	56.0
Köthen Trade School	—	—	44.1
Kiel University	—	33.4	39.1
Leipzig Commercial College	—	—	38.2
Giessen University	—	—	36.9
Königsberg University	—	—	33.8
Göttingen University	—	13.3	29.0
Würzburg University	8.7	19.6	28.9
Halle University	—	12.8	28.9
Leipzig University	6.8	7.9	25.7
Mannheim Commercial College	—	13.4	21.7
Hamburg University	9.7	12.8	18.9
Munich Technical University	—	11.0	18.9
Freiburg University	4.1	8.4	17.4
Munich University	6.5	9.7	16.4
Friedberg Polytechnic	—	—	16.1
Darmstadt Technical University	7.0	8.3	14.8
Bonn University	—	—	9.4

Note. The dash indicates data not available.
Source: Calculated from voting figures in a table drawn up by the Reich Ministry of the Interior in April (?) 1930, zStA RMdI 26108. The figures are incomplete and not always accurate, as for Erlangen, Freiburg, Würzburg, and Hamburg, but the broad trend demonstrated was correct, and this was what the ministry wanted to find out. Cf. also the list drawn up by Schirach, giving the percentage of *seats* (rather than votes) gained in various student governments, which the ministry also noted. Tyrell, *Führer befiehl*, pp. 380-81.

NSDStB's violently expressed opposition to the state. One Nazi student leader, Reinhard Sunkel, had been quoted as commenting in a speech at Erlangen that the destruction of the present state was the supreme law for every conscientious German. Other incidents turned public attention toward the NSDStB. Prussian Education Minister Becker had been wantonly insulted in Marburg in January 1930. The former Bavarian Commissioner Kahr, hated by the Nazis for his failure to support the Beer Hall Putsch in 1923, was also ostentatiously insulted at a university celebration in Munich. Baldur von Schirach, who had brought the Nazi students to attention for the entry of the academic procession, deliberately stood them at ease when Kahr, a guest of honor, passed by. Finally, the ministry noted the violent disruption of meetings of other political groups by the NSDStB in Heidelberg, Giessen, and Munich.[30]

Although in Hamburg the NSDStB's share of the poll increased from the previous year's 13 percent to only 19 percent, the group in fact rose from fourth position out of five lists (with 199 votes) to come second only to the fraternities (with 366 votes). The Nazis gained the secretary's post on the ASTA executive.[31] No longer had the campaign been fought under the misleading rubric, *Völkisch* Ring: the list was openly described as the NSDStB. The left-wing German Students' League split up still further before these February 1930 elections into three lists: the Working Party on Academic Politics (*Hochschulpolitische Arbeitsgemeinschaft*),[32] the Socialists, and the Revolutionary Socialists.

[30] Vortrag Regierungsrat Kuntze "Über die Entwicklung der NSDAP," gehalten auf der Deutschen Nachrichtenkonferenz am 28./29. April 1930, ZStA RMdI 26108.

[31] The figure quoted in Bracher (see above, n. 29) for the 1930 election (16.6 percent) is incorrect. The ASTA executive consisted of two chairmen, a secretary, and a treasurer.

[32] Not to be confused with the *national* umbrella organization set up in September 1932 by a number of fraternity associations and whose headquarters were raided by Oskar Stäbel in April 1933.

They forfeited much by this break, and between them gained only three seats out of twelve on the new ASTA (the Socialists two, the Working Party one), with the result that their share in the power was minimal.

The propaganda efforts of the Nazis far surpassed those of the other candidates. The NSDStB was handing out leaflets before the other groups had even thought of beginning their campaigns, and three days before the elections it took the unheard-of step of carrying placards up and down in front of the University—much to the alarm of the rector. The Political Police were contacted, but they admitted that there was little they could do. The police could not, they claimed, confiscate a placard that was being carried in a public street; neither did an individual need special permission in order to display one.[33] The election campaign was an all-out effort that the NSDStB could not afford in financial terms. Four thousand copies of their newspaper supplement, the *Akademische Warte*, were distributed. Expenses for posters and leaflets came to almost 100 marks, half of which Reitz was forced to pay out of his own pocket.[34] It was characteristic of the Nazis to take the whole affair with such an intense seriousness that they even considered overspending. Other groups were slow to grasp this new earnestness that the NSDStB brought into student politics. The result of their zeal was that the Hamburg Nazi students were widely thought to be more numerous than was actually the case. Although membership remained below two dozen, the Hamburg police estimated their strength at around 120 members.[35]

The Nazis took less notice of the Hamburg University administration the more they realized how far they could go with impunity. In the summer semester 1930 so many provocative statements had appeared on the NSDStB's bulletin board that the leaders were again summoned before the

---

[33] Bausch to Bertram, 11 February 1930, UniHH 0.30.6.I.
[34] Ochsenius, "Studentenschaft," p. 130.
[35] Polizei-Behörde Hamburg to RMdI, 12 August 1930, ZStA RMdI 26108.

syndic for a dressing-down. Since the new semester had again brought new leaders, they were able to plead ignorance of the regulations. The new syndic, Dr. Kurt Niemann, was altogether more tolerant toward the right-wing student groups and merely made them promise to abide by the rules in the future. When two further offensive notices appeared the very next week, no action was taken beyond explaining once more the reasons for the removal of the notices.[36] The NSDStB took to carrying placards as an alternative method of displaying its propaganda, which brought the culprits before the syndic again a few days later, following a complaint by a member of the Socialist Student Group. When it was put to them that they knew full well the ban on the display of placards in the University, one of the students replied that he had merely fastened his poster to a board inside the building and was in the process of carrying it outside into the street in order to walk up and down with it there! The syndic ruled that even this was not permissible "and explained . . . that if this happened again, disciplinary action might *possibly* have to be taken" [emphasis added].[37]

The fact that no punishments worse than the occasional oral or written reprimand were meted out by the syndic might lead one to believe that he was sympathetic or deliberately lenient toward the Nazis. A report written in 1946 accused him of just that.[38] Niemann's attitude was very similar to that of the rector for the academic year 1930-1931, Professor Brauer. The Nazi student leaders, however, found them tiresome and overly pedantic. They could not openly attack them as they had done with Cassirer because these professors always paraded their nationalism.[39] Niemann's

---

[36] Aktenvermerke Niemann, 4 and 10 July 1930, UniHH 0.30.6.I.

[37] Aktennotiz Niemann, 15 August 1930, ibid.

[38] Erklärung Wolff, 29 July 1946, Hochschulbehörde Hamburg (HB) personnel file Niemann.

[39] Friedrich Schorer and Heinz Riecke, "Nationalsozialismus als Geist und Organisation in der Hamburger Studentenschaft der Jahre 1930-33," *Hamburger Universitäts-Zeitung* 15, no. 7 (8 February 1934), p. 117.

interventions usually followed the posting of abusive or inflammatory notices. He removed them and often cautioned the student leaders. But there is just as much evidence of confiscated notices in the files of the Socialist and Communist student groups, and he does not appear to have discriminated between the two sides at all in this respect. There are indeed more confiscated notices in the University's file on the NSDStB than anywhere else, but this is almost certainly because the Nazi Students' Association dared to post a greater number of offensive notices than did other groups. Probably the syndic was reluctant to take any firm action for such minor offenses and risk charges of authoritarian repression from the student body at large. The Erlangen University authorities behaved in a similar manner toward the NSDStB there, yet they harassed the Republican Students' Association with disciplinary proceedings.[40] The tolerance of Nazi excesses was not universal. Some ten NSDStB groups were banned during 1930, including those at Cologne and Frankfurt Universities. The ban was generally ineffective, since the groups merely continued their activities under another name as university sections of the local Party, but at least a gesture of firmness was made.[41]

Although the NSDStB was progressing quite satisfactorily across the country, many of its members felt that gains were not due to Reich Leader Baldur von Schirach. Directions or advice on policy matters were seldom forthcoming. Matters were brought to a head at the annual conference of the German Students' Union in July. Most of the National Socialist AStA delegates had arrived at Breslau intending to press strongly for a motion demanding a *numerus clausus* on university places for Jewish students. They had not been informed at all that Schirach had promised that the NSDStB would, in return for its own freedom of action in questions

[40] Franze, *Erlanger Studentenschaft*, p. 139.

[41] Bericht Reichsministerium des Innern, "Nationalsozialistische Studentenvertretungen an den Hochschulen," 15 May 1930, ZStA RMdI 26108.

of national politics, support the official DST line in the field of academic politics. This was currently a moderate one, in the hope of securing the release of accumulated but frozen DST funds at Bavarian universities through a show of good behavior.[42] When, therefore, Schirach's representative, Walter Lienau, spoke out at the Conference against the *numerus clausus* motion, the other Nazis were as surprised as they were annoyed. This ill feeling prompted Reinhard Sunkel and Ernst Anrich to prepare detailed memoranda criticizing Schirach.[43]

Hamburg was happy to join the thirty other groups backing them, for Schirach had never made much impression there. During one talk he gave to the Hamburg students, his lyrical remarks about soldiers in the trenches of the First World War were so obviously far from the truth that Dr. Krebs, who, unlike Schirach, had seen active service, was moved to correct the young Reich Leader after the meeting had ended. Placing his hand on Krebs's shoulder, Schirach insisted: "Believe me, my dear Dr. Krebs, it *really* was just as I described it!" and he was quite perplexed at the mocking laughter that greeted his remark.[44] Schirach was similarly scorned elsewhere. Area Leader Gerhard Krüger later claimed that he did everything possible to try to prevent Schirach from ever appearing as a public speaker, though personal animosity had much to do with this.[45]

On 31 March 1931 Anrich and Sunkel brought their petition to the Brown House in Munich and managed to deliver it to Hitler in person, who, however, refused to read a word of it. Concerning himself as usual only when a crisis loomed,

[42] Although the Bavarian Education Ministry had not derecognized its students' unions, as Becker had in Prussia, it did temporarily withhold the DST subscriptions collected along with other students' fees. Kersten, *Studentenrecht*, pp. 110-11.

[43] Faust, *Studentenbund*, 1: 153ff.

[44] Allen, *Infancy*, p. 299.

[45] Gerhard Krüger, "Memoiren im Schnellverfahren," *Burschenschaftliche Blätter* 83, nos. 1 and 2 (January/February 1968), p. 17.

Hitler appeared at a meeting of all NSDStB group leaders called by Schirach on 2 May 1931, and made an emotional speech praising his devoted follower as having always acted exactly as he (Hitler) had wished. He stressed that Schirach was right to concentrate on winning more members for the Movement; as for studying ideology, ". . . later on, yes, when we've come to power . . . ," but now there was just no time to devote to elaborate intellectual training. Although this made nonsense of what most of the leaders present probably believed the role of the NSDStB to be, the opposition was completely deflated on the receipt of these *ipsissima verba*, and Sunkel publicly apologized there and then. He and others had to resign themselves to the fact that Schirach could apparently not be deposed.[46]

In Hamburg, links with the Party's District headquarters were much stronger than those with NSDStB national headquarters and increased during 1930. The Hamburg NSDStB leader was now invited to meetings of District Party leaders, and the District headquarters showed an active interest in the AStA elections, even voluntarily giving financial support to the Students' Association.[47] This was due to the determination of *Gauleiter* Karl Kaufmann to bind together all the units in his District into a strong, cohesive organization under his personal control, an effort in which he was remarkably successful right through to 1945. At the end of 1930, the NSDStB group was able to report that fourteen members (half the group) were in the local SA and one in the SS, two members were leaders of NSS groups, and two of HJ groups. Moreover, five students offered their services as speakers for local Party meetings, and one member worked six hours daily for the local Party newspaper.[48] Yet all this

---

[46] Faust, *Studentenbund*, 1: 162-63.

[47] Rundschreiben no. 16 Kaufmann, 7 May 1930, StA NSDAP 35 vol. 1. Von Allwörden to NSDStB Hamburg, 6 December 1930 and 12 January 1931, ibid. Ochsenius, "Studentenschaft," p. 130, mentions the good relations with the Party at this time.

[48] Schorer to Kaufmann, 1 January 1931, StA NSDAP 35 vol. 1.

involvement in the local Party was not considered to be the only or the most important work of the NSDStB. The members of the group, encouraged by local Party thinkers like Dr. Krebs, did try to find time to examine the "Intellectual Foundations of National Socialism," which they believed it their task to elucidate and strengthen.[49]

The Nazis' call for action compared favorably with the excessive intellectuality of the other purely political groups. Andreas Feickert, who became leader of the group in the autumn of 1931, explained to the author how he first came to join the NSDStB in 1930. On his way home from the University every day he used to pass more and more groups of unemployed men standing on street corners and was sometimes drawn into conversation with them. Feeling that something must be done to help them, he decided to join a political group, which he saw as the only effective means of achieving anything. He attended meetings of various student groups, the Communists, the Socialists, and the Democrats but found them to be little more than debating clubs with elaborate, theoretical discussions: "Half the time I couldn't even understand what they were talking about." But the direct, straightforward nature of the NSDStB talk that he attended, indeed of the Nazis themselves, impressed him. More than anything there was the promise of action: he was immediately offered the job of propaganda organizer and became a member without further ado.[50] It was this absence of social elitism, this impression that the individual mattered and could be trusted with important work, that marked off the NSDStB from its rival political associations. The local loyalties that it was able to foster were crucial to its success nationally. As the next section will show, the 1931 AStA election campaign in Hamburg was fought against a back-

[49] Title of a lecture by Krebs on 18 November 1930. The AStA executive complained afterward to the rector about the presence of a squad of policemen in the University during the meeting. Heesch to Brauer, 20 November 1930, RSFWü V*2 α 516.

[50] Author's interview with Dr. Andreas Feickert on 27 September 1973.

ground of an important, specifically local, issue, in addition to the broader ones that influenced elections at universities throughout Germany that winter. Not until victory had been gained in a majority of these local ASTA committees could the Nazis risk their bid for power in the national union.

The Seizure of the German Students' Union

If everyday manifestations of the weakness of the national government tended to make students more alive to politics in general, the apparent meddling of the Hamburg authorities in strictly student affairs was a much more inflammatory issue that took a central place in the local ASTA election campaign of 1931. The Becker dispute in Prussia had led to the assumption in the city parliament that the Hamburg Students' Union would either forego its state recognition or disaffiliate from the DST. But neither step was taken, and so the Hamburg city parliament amended the University Law on 15 May 1929 with a clause that required the Students' Union constitution to state that affiliation would only be sought with bodies of similar membership specifications to its own (i.e. that included all German citizens).[51]

When the ASTA nonetheless still refused to amend its constitution, a legal problem arose. The left-wing deputies maintained that the very amendment of the University Law was tantamount to an effective alteration of the Students' Union constitution in the desired sense. But whereas in all the other federal states the students' constitution could be changed by a straightforward decree, the Hamburg student body's constitution enjoyed unique protection by dint of the reference to it in the University Law. The University Authority came to the conclusion that by instructing the ASTA to alter the constitution (as a result of the recent University Law amendment), they were acknowledging that such a step

[51] Gesetz zur Änderung des Hochschulgesetzes, *Hamburgisches Gesetz- und Verordnungsblatt* 40 (19 May 1929): 195.

could be taken only by the student body itself. The latter, still refusing to cooperate, now expected its official recognition to be withdrawn. It found to its surprise that "the Hamburg University Authority intended to be careful not to make the same mistake as the Prussian Education Ministry," which would have brought it much adverse publicity.[52] The Authority planned to uphold state recognition of the Students' Union, thereby forcing the students (so it thought) to leave the DSt.

The ASTA Chairman made it clear that the student body would not give in. It became known that the University planned therefore to discuss a further amendment to the University Law, whereby the Students' Union constitution would after all become alterable by decree.[53] The prospect of losing permanently their specially privileged position was considered by the ASTA to be too high a price to pay. They proposed to amend the constitution in the required manner, but with the additional clause: "The University Authority may permit exceptions to the aforementioned requirements in particular cases." In this way permission for affiliation with the DSt could be given at some future date when the left-wing majority of the parliament (and thus of its subordinate committee, the University Authority) changed more to their favor, "in particular through the gains of the National Socialists." Baldur von Schirach condemned this procedure, accusing the Hamburg students of "capitulation to the Marxists" and stressing that it was a question of principles, not tactics. He instructed the NSDStB to have nothing to do with the compromise.[54] Without the Nazi vote in the

[52] The remark was attributed to Senator de Chapeaurouge, the chairman of the University Authority. Heesch to Schulz, 9 December 1930, RSFWü II*5 α 461.

[53] Through the good offices of the new rector, Professor Ludolf Brauer, the actual discussion of this by the University Authority, which had been planned for early November, was delayed until mid-December. This gave the ASTA time to plan in advance the steps it would take. Ibid.

[54] Schirach to Schorer, 12 December 1930, ibid.

ASTA, the right-wing block did not have a two-thirds majority to adopt its desired amendment, and so the University Authority was left to implement its threat.[55]

These tensions with the Authority were a major issue in the Hamburg ASTA elections of February 1931. Now that the Nazis in Hamburg had been ordered by Schirach to stand by their principles, opposing the quasi-conciliatory attitude of the fraternities, there arose a very similar situation to that of the national one at the time of the Becker dispute. Then it was the NSDStB alone (under Tempel) that had stood firm in its contention that no concessions should be made to the Prussian government. The fraternities had suggested that the German Students' Union drop its political emphasis and concentrate on cultural and social work. Little improvement in relations with the government was seen after several months, and the fraternities came round with a grudging respect to the NSDStB's view by the summer of 1928. Honor was the guiding light of the fraternities, and the NSDStB had stood by its convictions more steadfastly than they. The fraternities looked on the NSDStB with a new respect.[56] Similarly, many Hamburg students now sympathized with what appeared to be the NSDStB's firm stand. The fact that it had been completely willing to go along with the fraternities did not matter, for the majority of students did not know this, and to those who did, the sudden volte-face of the Nazis would make them appear even more praiseworthy as they responded to the last-minute call of duty.

[55] The proposal still had to come before the Hamburg city parliament for the long-winded process of actually amending the University Law before it might take effect.

[56] At the national level, Schirach's promulgation of a Code of Honor for the NSDStB on 1 July 1930 had been a very important step in this direction, for it laid the way for the exchange of challenges to duels between fraternity students and NSDStB members. Text of "Ehrenordnung des Nationalsozialistischen Deutschen Studentenbundes" in Faust, *Studentenbund*, 2: 153-54. Steinberg is inconclusive on the success of Schirach's policies for winning over fraternity students: he claims variously that the NSDStB was successful in attracting them and that it failed to attract more than a minority. Steinberg, *Sabers*, pp. 74 and 82.

The NSDStB received 39.5 percent of the votes in the 1931 Hamburg AStA election and increased the number of seats it held from two to five (out of twelve).[57] It thus became the strongest group in the Students' Union Committee. It appears to have been from the previous supporters of the fraternities and the *Finken* that the NSDStB gained their extra votes rather than from the mobilization of previous nonvoters. The proportion of students voting crept up only slowly from 58.9 percent to 62.6 percent in the years 1929-1931.[58] The tremendous activism of the NSDStB in recent months had brought the Nazis to the attention of the students at large. Their youthful, zestful idealism contrasted favorably with the pedestrian pace of student politics under the control of the fraternities and in the hands of either alumni or examples of "the eternal student" (*der ewige Student*). A recent case of corruption had further damaged the credibility of the old-timers. The deputy chairman of the Hamburg Students' Union, Adolf Bachmann, was charged in the autumn of 1930 with the embezzlement of 2,000 marks from student funds and was subsequently found guilty. This student was forty years old![59]

Actual membership of the NSDStB was still low, and most meetings enjoyed only modest attendance. But attention was directed toward the Nazis by the spectacular gains of the September 1930 *Reichstag* elections and, nearer home, by the rise from zero to thirty-two seats (out of 120) in the Bremen parliamentary elections (30 November 1930). Hitler had sworn an oath at the Leipzig Reichswehr Trial in September that he would only attempt to achieve power by legal means, and the soft-pedaling of the Hamburg NSDStB during the first part of this winter semester must have reassured

---

[57] The figure of 41.7 percent given in Bracher, *Auflösung*, p. 148, is again incorrect. Dibner's assertion that "only Hamburg was an exception, considered a stronghold of the Social Democrats," is neither correct nor supported by the evidence she presents elsewhere. Dibner, "History," pp. 82 and 301ff.

[58] See below, Appendix 1.

[59] Copies of court proceedings in UniHH Di.B.1.

the students about this. The Nazis kept away from the Communists' meetings in order to escape the charge of rowdy provocation,[60] and they avoided wearing uniforms at university ceremonies.[61] They seemed concerned to persuade on academic terms by participating in the discussions of other groups with coherent arguments rather than facetious interruptions and by arranging serious public lectures themselves. Earlier in the year they had not always been very well prepared for serious discussion. Their heckling in a meeting in February 1930 was stopped short when a Reichstag deputy, the Democrat Gustav Ehlermann (DDP), countered their objections with quotations from Hitler himself.[62] By December 1930, the German Nationalist Students' Group reported that the National Socialist students had participated in a "lively discussion" following a lecture, but there were no complaints about their behavior, which in any case would have been less vituperative than in a left-wing students' gathering.[63] When NSDStB meetings were disturbed by Socialist students, the Nazis made an ostentatious display of righteous indignation, asking: "Who, then, are really the disturbers of the peace, National Socialists, or Marxist student rowdies?"[64]

In the weeks leading up to the Students' Union elections, the NSDStB began to attract fairly substantial audiences. The

[60] The Party District Leadership ordered this in the summer, mainly to escape the risk of awkward questions about the Otto Strasser controversy. Rundschreiben no. 20, NSDAP Gau Hamburg, 15 July 1930, StA NSDAP 35 vol. 1.

[61] Although the NSDStB Leader, Fritz Schorer, had intended to order that uniforms be worn by members at the induction ceremony for the new rector on 10 November 1930, the group was forbidden to do so by Gauleiter Kaufmann. Aktenvermerk Niemann, 4 November 1930, UniHH 0.30.6.I; Kaufmann to Schorer, 5 November 1930, StA NSDAP 35 vol. 1.

[62] "Ehlermann gegen den Nationalsozialismus. Rede vor den Hamburger Studenten," Demokratischer Zeitungsdienst, 19 February 1930, clipping in ZStA RMdI 26005.

[63] "Studentenschaft, Republik und Drittes Reich," Hamburger Nachrichten, 5 December 1930.

[64] "Provokation marxistischer Studenten!" Hamburger Nachrichten, 21 November 1930.

average attendance at the meetings of the group between 5 November 1930 and 28 January 1931 was twenty-eight. Three public meetings with outside speakers, held just before the election, drew a larger crowd. Between 150 and 200 people attended a lecture on "The Question of German Defense" on 24 January 1931; there were 75-100 people in the audience three days later to listen to a talk by a National Socialist lawyer on the reform of criminal justice, and Hamburg's popular Albert Krebs spoke on 5 February 1931 to 250-300 students on "East and West."[65] Students were becoming increasingly interested in National Socialism, if not in actually joining the NSDStB, and were growing more willing to have the Nazis represent them in student government. Furthermore, the growing Nazi victories at other universities, many of whose student elections were held in the earlier part of the winter semester, were a good advertisement for the Hamburg NSDStB. And better than any propaganda that the Hamburg group could have arranged itself, the theatrical walk-out of the 107 Nazi deputies from the *Reichstag* (10 February 1931) was the major news item in everyone's mind when the Hamburg students went to the polls two days later.

As a result of the election, Heinz Haselmayer became the first Nazi chairman of the Hamburg AStA. Despite their protests, Haselmayer ensured that none of the three Socialist members on the committee received an executive post. He was particularly anxious to deny them that of treasurer, which they claimed as their right, for this would give them some control over the spending of accumulated student fees.[66]

During the previous months the right wing (fraternities, Nazis, and *Finken*) had succeeded in removing the Socialists from all committees on which students sat: financial, disciplinary, consultative, and grant-awarding.[67] Haselmayer believed that Schirach's insistence on principles was quite

---

[65] Attendance figures in Ochsenius, "Studentenschaft," p. 131.

[66] With as many seats as the fraternities had, they did indeed expect an executive post. Protokoll AStA-Sitzung, 23 February 1931, RSFWü V*2 α 514.

[67] Haselmayer to Schirach, 9 December 1930, RSFWü II*5 α 461.

misplaced and feared that if the ASTA persisted in its refusal to amend the Students' Union constitution, the entire right-wing faction might eventually be dismissed by the rector for their breach of academic discipline and their committee posts transferred to the remainder, namely, the Socialists. This would undo the years of work of the right in gaining almost total control of student affairs.[68] But Schirach remained adamant that "all the tactical advantages . . . do not bear any relation to the sacrifice needed, that is, the forfeit of a principle."[69] The Hamburg parliament accepted the proposals of the University Authority in July 1931, thus allowing the latter to issue the decree amending the student constitution.[70] The ASTA did not immediately react, and by the time the new semester had begun, the Nazis had scored another election success and were the second strongest party in the Hamburg city parliament.[71] The student leaders felt safe enough now to issue a defiant statement: "The Hamburg Students' Union notes the amendment of its constitution by the University Authority without recognizing therein any occasion for declaring its withdrawal from the DST."[72]

At the national level, the Nazi students also had power within their grasp. After the NSDStB success in the ASTA elections of the winter semester 1930-1931, it was clear that the fraternity associations would not be able to choose the chairman of the DST in the summer, for now the majority of voting delegates at the annual conference would be NSDStB members. Each university had one vote per 1,000 (or part thousand) students at the DST conference. Although this meant

---

[68] Haselmayer to Schirach, 30 March 1931, ibid.

[69] Schirach to Haselmayer, 18 April 1931, ibid.

[70] Gesetz zur Änderung des Hochschulgesetzes, 1 July 1931, *Hamburgisches Gesetz- und Verordnungsblatt*, 3 July 1931, p. 169.

[71] In the elections of 27 September 1931, the National Socialists received 26.2 percent of the votes and 43 seats (out of 160). The Social Democrats still remained the strongest party with 46 seats. Jochmann, *Nationalsozialismus und Revolution*, Anlage 5, Wahlergebnisse.

[72] Protokoll ASTA-Sitzung, 27 November 1931, RSFWü V*2 α 514.

that there were about three votes for each students' union, there was no general rule on the distribution of these votes among all the parties in the ASTA committee. In practice, the majority group often appointed its own members alone as official voting delegates.[73] There was no doubt that the NSDStB would follow this precedent. Schirach had decided already in March 1931 that Walter Lienau, a DST Area Leader and Nazi, should become the new Chairman.[74] At Lienau's suggestion Gerhard Krüger was to be nominated as his deputy, and the second deputy's position would be left to the fraternities. Even though both Lienau and Krüger were former fraternity students, this was not good enough for the fraternity associations, who wanted their own nominee as the first deputy chairman. Notwithstanding the electoral support for the Nazis, the NSDStB still only numbered some 4,000 members, whereas the 79,000 fraternity students represented over 60 percent of the student body. The fraternity associations pleaded with Hitler in vain for the deputy chairmanship. They called on the Erfurt Agreement, signed in January by the NSDStB and the dueling fraternities, by which they had promised to share executive posts equally without regard to the electoral majorities, in return for mutual support against the Left.[75]

[73] Satzung der DST, Stück 9, quoted in Kersten, *Studentenrecht*, p. 164. Cf. also Dieter Fricke, *Die bürgerlichen Parteien in Deutschland: Handbuch der Geschichte der bürgerlichen Parteien und anderer bürgerlicher Interessenorganisationen vom Vormärz bis zum Jahre 1945*, 2 vols. (Leipzig, 1968), 1: 594: "Each ASTA appointed its delegates as it thought fit, and could thus completely exclude the minorities from representation at the Annual Conference." Steinberg cites no evidence to support his claim that there was a "traditional" gentlemen's agreement, providing for proportional representation of all groups among the delegates. Steinberg, *Sabers*, p. 111.

[74] Lienau, a student of agriculture at Munich, had become a DST Area Leader in May 1930, and the corresponding NSDStB Area Leader the following autumn, following Schirach's policy of uniting the posts wherever possible in preparation for the takeover of the German Students' Union. Faust, *Studentenbund*, 2: 18ff.

[75] The Erfurt Agreement undoubtedly helped the NSDStB in gaining their

Just when it seemed that the fraternities had lost their struggle, the Darmstadt National Bank collapsed on 13 July 1931, giving rise to the panic closing of all banks on the following day. The retiring DST leaders at once seized the opportunity of canceling the annual conference, due to start two days later, "in the light of the desolate economic and political situation."[76] They were afraid of student demonstrations, which might get out of hand if the student leaders were away. In any case the expense of holding a conference, in distant Graz at that, seemed unjustifiable in the midst of the crisis. The decision to cancel a conference, however, could only be taken by the Central Committee, composed predominantly of the Area Leaders. The majority of these were now Nazis, and they hurried to Berlin to chastise the Executive and reverse the cancellation.[77] The Nazis could not bear the thought of losing the huge propaganda victory that was now so nearly in their grasp.

Once in Graz, where the conference finally began three days late, the fraternity associations declared it intolerable that the candidates did not include a representative of the 49,000 dueling fraternity students on the Executive. They suggested that Gerhard Krüger's nomination as deputy chairman be dropped in favor of the lesser known Harald Askevold (who belonged to both the NSDStB and a dueling fraternity). Baldur von Schirach, brimming over with self-confidence and strutting everywhere with an SS Guard of Honor, stubbornly refused even to consider the idea. The fraternities threatened that if Krüger were not replaced, they would withdraw altogether from the DST. Since this move would ruin the promised propaganda success of the Nazi victory,

---

victory in Hamburg's elections a fortnight later. Text in Faust, *Studentenbund*, 2: 155-56.

[76] Rundschreiben DST, 15 July 1931, quoted in ibid., p. 19. Dibner curiously describes this determined move as "a weak attempt." Dibner, "History," p. 93.

[77] It was also the Central Committee's task to propose officially the slate of nominations for the incoming Executive to the Conference.

Schirach reluctantly, and with considerable loss of face, accepted the fraternities' proposal. As expected, the Conference delegates agreed unanimously with the Central Committee's nominations for new officers, and the DSt fell formally under Nazi control. "You have no idea how much this means to me," Hitler told Schirach on the telephone that night, "now that I am able to say in the coming negotiations: the majority of the young intelligentsia stands behind me."[78] True to form, Nazi propagandists outdid one another in eulogizing this "historic event."

It was the electoral success of the local NSDStB groups that made the Nazi takeover of the German Students' Union possible. By 1931, with a majority of AStA committees in Nazi hands, this became inevitable, and it was left to Schirach only to negotiate the best possible terms for the transition. His irrepressible arrogance almost spoiled the success of the coup, yet it was he who reaped most of the praise. In October 1931 he was given the title of Reich Youth Leader, with responsibility for the National Socialist Schoolboys' Association and the Hitler Youth, as well as the NSDStB. Yet Schirach was not directly responsible for the Nazi seizure of the German Students' Union: the appeal of National Socialism to the voters in AStA elections was. Kreutzberger's explanation of the early date of the Nazis' victory in the student sector (a full eighteen months before Hitler's accession to the chancellorship) has much merit: he points out that although the Nazi Party appealed predominantly to middle-class groups and to younger groups, the student body was more middle-class and more youthful than the Party mem-

[78] Steinberg, *Sabers*, p. 112, claims that Schirach was in jail for the duration of the DSt Annual Conference, though he remained "in close postal contact with the Nazi leaders on the scene." In fact, Schirach makes it clear in his memoirs (not consulted by Steinberg) that, although arrested on 2 July 1931 in Cologne at a student rally, he was released in time to travel to Graz. Baldur von Schirach, *Ich glaubte an Hitler* (Hamburg, 1967), pp. 94ff. Dibner, "History," p. 85, incorrectly places the whole incident in March 1931, though she bases her account on Schirach's memoirs.

bership as a whole, and therefore more readily susceptible to National Socialist propaganda.[79] This is true, yet a strict comparison between the two "seizures of power" cannot be made on this basis. In 1931 there was none of the backstairs intrigue that subsequently maneuvered Hitler into the chancellorship. The first Nazi leader of the German Students' Union was elected into office, whereas Hitler very definitely was not. The NSDStB made such extraordinary gains in the ASTA elections in such a short time, primarily because of the unparalleled single-mindedness and dedication of its members. In this they were similar to the rank-and-file Party members of the period. Nonetheless Baldur von Schirach had coordinated the policy of the local groups on a number of important issues. In calling their tune for them, he had ensured a consistency that, as is evident from Hamburg's disagreements with him, would otherwise have been lacking. Schirach must then be given some credit, if only in second place. He certainly did not even approach Hitler in political acumen, and, annoyed at the widespread opposition to his leadership within the NSDStB, he now turned away from student affairs. The larger problems of building up the Hitler Youth began to occupy his attention. Just as the local NSDStB groups had played the major role in obtaining power, so now it was left largely to them to exploit it.

[79] Kreutzberger, *Studenten und Politik*, p. 106.

CHAPTER THREE

The Difficulties of Consolidation

It was a great victory, to be sure, but was it a decisive one? The Nazi students could not be certain that the antagonism they had aroused among some of the fraternities might not yet combine to rob them of their prize at the next annual conference of the German Students' Union. They had to broaden the basis of their support. In a sense, this period of consolidation is more interesting to the historian of student movements than the struggle for power. There was much that the NSDStB had wanted to destroy while in opposition. Now it had to prove that its ideas had a constructive side to them as well, and that it had the will and the means to make them work. The difficulties of the NSDStB in office will engage us for the remainder of the book. The period that this chapter covers, from July 1931 to January 1933, were trying times for Germany, as rising unemployment, mounting street violence, and growing disillusionment in the power of parliament or cabinet to cope with the exigencies of the depression pushed the Weimar Republic further toward collapse. NSDStB members were required to play an active part in the Nazi Party's national bid for power, often in violent ways. Yet they also had to demonstrate their trustworthiness as leaders of student politics at the campus level and in the national union. The turmoil and competitiveness of this increasingly fluid period made that a demanding task, one that the Nazis did not altogether succeed in accomplishing. It was a reaction to their fears that their grip was slipping, as much as an expression of Nazi doctrine, that the authoritarian "leader principle" was introduced into the DSt executive at the 1932 annual conference, thus doing away with any future democratic election. If the fraternity associations did not endorse this very warmly, it was not for want of effort on the NSDStB's part in seeking their support.

The Credibility of the Nazi Student Leadership

Having gained control of the Hamburg Students' Union, the Nazi students there did not rest on their laurels but worked harder than ever, in order to eliminate any challenge to their running of student affairs. The leading local figure at this time was not so much the NSDStB Leader, Fritz Schorer, as the Nazi ASTA Chairman, Heinz Haselmayer, although he was nominally Schorer's subordinate. The founder of the Würzburg NSDStB group, Haselmayer had moved to Kiel in the summer of 1930 after a semester at Hamburg, but he had caused such a scandal there in leading a demonstration against a pacifist professor that the University of Kiel had refused to allow his matriculation.[1] Although the University registry had been particularly warned to look out for him, he was readmitted to Hamburg "inadvertently" (so the rector later claimed).[2] A fortnight later he was summoned before the rector, who, stressing that he did not wish to discuss the events in Kiel, "which do not require any

[1] Haselmayer had taken over the leadership of the NSDStB at Kiel for the summer vacation and circulated a leaflet denouncing Professor Baumgarten, who was to preach the sermon at the Bach Festival there, as a "traitor, philosemite and pacifist." As a result, the University of Kiel withdrew its official recognition of the NSDStB. Rector Kiel to all rectors, 16 October 1930, UniHH Di.H.1. For Haselmayer's activities in Würzburg, see Spitznagel, "Studentenschaft," pp. 11ff. Haselmayer continued his involvement in educational affairs during the Third Reich. His 1932 doctoral dissertation, "A contribution to the question of the sterilization of the feeble-minded," had an appropriate ideological slant from the National Socialist point of view, and in March 1933 he was appointed as the director of the Hamburg Community College (*Volkshochschule*), where he lectured on "racial studies." He was excluded from the NSDAP on 2 May 1936 after having made an official speech in Haarlem in a state of apparent drunkenness. Cf. *Das Deutsche Führerlexikon 1934/35* (Berlin, 1934), and personnel files in the Berlin Document Center (BDC).

[2] Protokoll des Universitätssenats, 15 May 1931, UniHH C.20.4.

justification," asked Haselmayer to give him his hand and promise "to behave quietly and unobtrusively for the rest of his time in Hamburg."[3] Despite the fact that he broke this pledge by campaigning at the head of the Nazi list for the ASTA elections, no further steps were taken by the rector for the rest of the year. Haselmayer even closed a public meeting with a threefold "Sieg Heil" for Hitler, but the usual plea of ignorance of the regulations was accepted by the syndic.[4]

Haselmayer quickly set about restructuring the Hamburg NSDStB group. He persuaded Schorer to appoint him as "Organization Leader" and then created wide powers for the new post, including the personal authority to appoint junior leaders (*Amtsleiter*).[5] He attached great importance to the departmental student groups (*Fachschaften*). These had existed since the foundation of the University, but they had been largely dormant bodies, called together only for the sake of arranging departmental dances and parties. Haselmayer saw promising possibilities for the spread of National Socialist propaganda here, for the ASTA was empowered to make available substantial sums of money to the groups. It was important for the departmental student committees to be in Nazi hands in order to ensure that the money was spent in the desired way.[6] This was not yet everywhere the case, notably in the Education Department, where three of the four committee members were Socialists.[7] The Nazis hoped

[3] Aktenvermerk Brauer, 18 November 1930, uniHH Di.H.1.

[4] Aktenvermerk Niemann, 2 February 1931, uniHH 0.30.6.I.

[5] This post existed at the local level in the Party but not in the NSDStB. "Aufbau des Bundes," Bundeskorrespondenz, n.d. (ca. April 1931), stA NSDAP 35 vol. 2.

[6] The money was disbursed to the departmental committees by the ASTA treasurer. Angry exchanges took place during the first ASTA meeting following the 1931 election, at which the allocation of executive posts was negotiated, but the NSDStB prevailed over the Socialist Students' Group in securing the post of treasurer for Fritz Schorer. Protokoll ASTA-Sitzung, 23 February 1931, RSFWü V*2 α 514. Steinberg, *Sabers*, p. 93, claims that the NSDStB did not bother about such "politically unimportant offices."

[7] Haselmayer to Reichsleitung NSDStB, 16 March 1931, RSFWü II*5 α 461.

first to impress the student body by their commitment to university reform. When they had gained control of the committees, they intended to spend the money available for the departmental groups on the provision of lectures and propaganda for National Socialist causes.[8] In order to prepare for this, NSDStB study groups were formed to draw up plans for the nazification of various academic disciplines.[9]

In his own medical faculty Haselmayer aimed for something more ambitious: a national organization for medical students. The central task was to be the examination of various problems of "racial studies, such as the determination of the hereditary nature of certain superior and inferior qualities and the consequences of this for our policies (sterilization, castration, selection principle, heredity in general) . . . ."[10] The proper National Socialist attitude to Freud, homosexuality, and abortion would be discussed. Haselmayer also desired to have lists drawn up of all doctors, medical professors, and lecturers who were Jewish in order to plot their dismissal.[11] The cool response from Halle was typical:

The departmental student committees were elected by the students whose major field of study lay in a particular department.

[8] Haselmayer listed some fifty topics for lectures that the group might hold. Unfortunately, there is no evidence that the group ever used more than a handful of them. Steinberg, *Sabers*, p. 93, suggests that Haselmayer's comprehensive plans on paper were translated into "an extensive program." His claim is even more extravagant than that of Haselmayer, who writes to Schirach of possibilities, not accomplishments, in the letter on which Steinberg bases his assessment. Haselmayer to Schirach, 30 March 1931, RSFWü II*5 α 461.

[9] Arbeitsplan des Fachamtes des NSDStB Hamburg, 25 April 1931, StA NSDAP 35 vol. 2. Again, there is unfortunately no evidence of the results, if any, of these deliberations.

[10] Haselmayer to all Hochschulgruppenführer des NSDStB, 26 March 1931, ibid.

[11] Schirach had already prepared some statistics for publication, viz. "Die Zurückdrängung des deutschen Volkstums zugunsten des Judentums im Ärztestande," in Schirach, *Wille und Weg*, p. 14. Cf. Kater's excellent analysis of the misleading nature of these statistics and others in Kater, *Studentenschaft*, pp. 147ff.

the majority of the NSDStB members there already had four or five evenings a week taken up with NSDStB or SA meetings; a further weekly meeting seemed scarcely possible.[12] Above all, Baldur von Schirach believed that the scheme might easily lead to separate organizations for every faculty and a "dangerous undermining" of the NSDStB itself. He ordered Haselmayer to discontinue his efforts at once.[13]

To add to his disappointment, Haselmayer was now involved in a scandal within the University, caused by his unauthorized "reorganization" of the students' reading room. Situated in the new Students' Union building since 1928, the reading room provided a selection of newspapers for students, to which a collection of books was added in 1929. It did not come under the jurisdiction of the Students' Union but was administered by an independent faculty-student committee. There had been a number of student complaints about the "one-sided, Marxist coloring" of the books (most of which were the gifts of professors), and the Nazis, once in charge of the AStA, submitted to the reading room committee a long list of book recommendations "with a very marked National Socialist tendency."[14] At the end of April 1931 during the librarian's absence through sickness, Haselmayer seized the opportunity to conduct a purge. Hurriedly summoning several Nazi students by telegram to assist him, he announced his intention to close the reading room for several days in order to remove a number of newspapers and magazines that he considered superfluous. When warned of the inadmissibility of his action by a member of the reading room committee, he brusquely declared that as Students' Union Chairman, he could do what he liked in the Students' Union building. Not only did he remove some fifty items from the shelves, but he also destroyed the corre-

[12] Blümel to Haselmayer, 18 January 1931, StA NSDAP 35 vol. 2.
[13] Schirach to Haselmayer, 13 May 1931, RSFWü II*5 α 461.
[14] Böhler, "Bericht über die Herausgabe des Buchkataloges," 10 May 1931, UniHH Di.H.1.

sponding catalogue cards, leaving no trace of what was missing.[15]

Surprisingly, the rector did not institute formal disciplinary proceedings against Haselmayer even after this blatant transgression of the bounds of his authority. Brauer claimed that he did not wish to anticipate any decision on the matter by the University senate in its meeting of 15 May. Furthermore, the ASTA appeal committee (*Spruchhof*) had been asked by the fraternity representatives on the Students' Union committee to investigate the matter, and there was provision under the Union constitution for Haselmayer's dismissal if he lost his case there. Brauer probably also feared that he would unleash Nazi demonstrations if he disciplined Haselmayer. In the event, his counsel for temporary inaction proved wise, for the whole affair was cleared up within the student body itself.

During the ASTA committee meeting of 4 June 1931, the National Socialists tried to dissolve the appeal committee for the purpose of appointing their own members to it. Since this body had only met once in the lifetime of the University, they had not bothered to fill its seats with NSDStB members, and this now left Haselmayer susceptible to attack. When their attempt failed, the Nazis proposed another motion that combined formal disapproval of Haselmayer's action with retroactive endorsement. This motion was rightly viewed as an attempt to prejudice, if not invalidate, the appeal committee's proceedings and was rejected by the ASTA (in which the Nazis still only held five out of twelve seats).[16] It was clear that only Haselmayer's resignation would prevent an ignominious dismissal.

Just as the Nazi Party instituted a regional reorganization to allow its districts (*Gaue*) to coincide with the Reichstag

[15] Bericht Böhler, "Vorfälle im Lesesaal der Akademischen Lesehalle," 10 May 1931, ibid.
[16] Protokoll ASTA-Sitzung, 4 June 1931, RSFWü V*2 α 514.

electoral districts in order to facilitate the coordination of propaganda, so too the NSDStB introduced in October 1930 an intermediate level of leaders to duplicate the ten areas (*Kreise*) into which the DST was divided. The NSDStB Area Leaders (*Kreisleiter*) were appointed additionally for the purpose of surveillance over the individual units in their area, following the first wave of dissent at Breslau against Schirach. The NSDStB Area Leader for North Germany was the Hamburg student, Reinhold Schulze, who was also a member of the Hamburg Students' Union Committee.[17] He was embarrassed that the Hamburg NSDStB group had joined the revolt against Schirach's authority. Although officially the senior Nazi student in Hamburg, he was clearly not in control.

On 13 May 1931, Schulze called a meeting of NSDStB leaders in which he insisted on Haselmayer's resignation as AStA Chairman. Fritz Schorer, the Hamburg group's leader, claimed that this was *his* right alone as Haselmayer's immediate superior, but that he had no intention of dismissing Haselmayer. Area Leader Schulze irately banned Schorer from the NSDStB altogether.[18] Peace was temporarily restored by a visit from Schirach on 20 May 1931, but the defeat in the AStA was used by Schulze to force Haselmayer's retirement. In order to give himself cover for a behind-the-scenes change, Schulze staged a walk-out from the AStA meeting, aping the 107 Reichstag deputies' gesture of February 1931, declaring that the Nazis regarded the defeat as a general vote of no-confidence, and therefore as an insult.[19] A mass meet-

---

[17] Dibner, "History," p. 93, lists the names of the ten *Kreisleiter* at this time but incorrectly refers to Rudolf, not Reinhold Schulze, as the *Kreisleiter Norddeutschland*. Schulze was a Reichstag deputy from November 1932 to March 1933, but he suffered a nervous breakdown during the spring. In September 1933, he was appointed as head of the DST's *Hauptamt für Grenz- und Aussenpolitik*.

[18] Aktenvermerk, "Konflikt des Kreisleiters Pg. Schulze gegen Pg. Haselmayer und Pg. Schorer," n.d., StA NSDAP 35 vol. 2.

[19] Protokoll AStA-Sitzung, 4 June 1931, RSFWü V*2 α 514.

ing was hurriedly arranged with *Gauleiter* Kaufmann as the main speaker in order to present the Nazis as the injured party.[20]

On 12 June 1931 Haselmayer called on the rector to inform him that "he had heard that he had apparently made a promise after his matriculation that he would not engage in any political activity for the duration of his studies in Hamburg." In light of this, he intended to step down and devote himself to his academic work.[21] Meanwhile, Schulze negotiated with the fraternity representatives for the smooth handover of office to a new Nazi chairman, Wolff Heinrichsdorff, skillfully stage-managed so that it would appear that Haselmayer was leaving voluntarily.[22] The appeal committee by now, however, had found him guilty of abusing his office, and he would have found it difficult to continue in any case.

Within the Hamburg NSDStB, the inner turbulence resulting from the constant change of leaders now subsided. Wolff Heinrichsdorff remained ASTA Chairman until the end of 1933. A good public speaker and a smooth talker in committees and negotiations, he gained the respect of rectors and professors by his urbane manner and did much to help the image of the NSDStB in the University.[23] Schulze also made a wise choice in the appointment of Andreas Feickert as NSDStB Group Leader, whose diligence in building up the Voluntary Labor Service later brought national publicity to

[20] Haselmayer also spoke on "Warum wir auszogen." Cf. leaflet announcing the meeting, and "Die Protestversammlung der Studenten. Die Versammlung vollkommen überfüllt," *Hamburger Tageblatt*, 12 June 1931, UniHH Di.H.1.

[21] Aktenvermerk Brauer, 12 June 1931, ibid.

[22] Heesch to Schulze, 19 June 1931, RSFWü V*2 α 511. A resigning member of any students' union committee had the right to name a successor to stand until the end of his term of office.

[23] Heinrichsdorff subsequently enjoyed a distinguished Party career. He became director of the Institute for the Study of the Jewish Question (part of the Propaganda Ministry) on 1 April 1939, and advanced to the position of personal advisor to Goebbels in July 1944. This appointment was reported in *Die Bewegung*, July 1944.

Hamburg.[24] Feickert was the first person to remain leader of the group for two full semesters, before he left Hamburg in 1932 to take up an appointment at the headquarters of the German Students' Union in Berlin.

It was an important time for the group to have credible leaders as representatives to the University authorities, for during 1931 violence erupted in the student body. On the evening of 2 July 1931, the police reported to the Press that armed National Socialists had attacked a group of Jews returning from a religious service. The Nazis' version was that a single member of their group had been set upon by thirty Communists wielding knives, crowbars, and truncheons, and that an SA unit, alarmed by a fortuitously passing SS cyclist, had gone to the rescue.[25] During an NSDStB meeting a couple of weeks later on "Hitler or Stalin?—The Bankruptcy of Bolshevism," the awkward questions of several Communist students were terminated when storm troopers marched up and positioned themselves around the podium. These strong-arm tactics brought protests from the audience, whereupon the storm troopers began hurling chairs, and general fighting broke out.[26] On 23 July 1931, Nazis beat up members of the Socialist Student Group who were distributing leaflets about the SA attack, and again a week later they tried to provoke a fight.[27] The University brought no disciplinary charges against the student participants, for the police had made arrests, and the usual practice was to suspend university action until criminal proceedings had been completed. When they were, it transpired that only a single defendant was a student, and he was acquitted (like the others) on grounds of insufficient evidence.[28]

---

[24] Even within the NSDStB, the retirement of Schorer was made to appear voluntary. Cf. Bundeskorrespondenz, n.d. (July 1931), RSFWü V*2 α 510. ASTA Chairman Heinrichsdorff temporarily headed the NSDStB group as well until Feickert's appointment in mid-September.

[25] Several press cuttings in UniHH 0.10.3.5.

[26] Press cuttings collected by Feickert in RSFWü V*2 α 523.

[27] Press cuttings in StA HI2h.

[28] Aktennotiz Niemann, 27 January 1932, UniHH Di.K.6.

It was clear which student society had been involved. Under the Disciplinary Code of 1925 there was provision for university action against "acts that disturb or endanger the customs and order of academic life."[29] Disciplinary proceedings might not have been successful in this particular case because the offenses did not occur on University territory. The NSDStB meeting had been held in the Students' Union building, which was controlled not by the University but by an independent body, the Hamburg Students' Aid (*Hamburger Studentenhilfe e.V.*); the scuffles on 23 July occurred in the Moorweide park adjacent to the University (students were not allowed to distribute leaflets *inside* the University buildings). The Disciplinary Code, however, permitted the rector to sidestep formal proceedings completely and still withdraw academic recognition from a society.[30] The complete absence of official reaction does, then, strongly suggest an attitude of indulgence toward the Nazis and indifference to the intimidation of their opponents.

On his assumption of office, Feickert was faced with what was now becoming a common problem. His members were supposed, as university students, to be acquainted with Nazi ideology in greater depth than the normal Party member, yet most of them had so many Party commitments or SA drill evenings that little time remained to come to grips with the relevant literature. An attempt to send out his students as instructors to Nazi groups of manual workers showed clearly "that only a few NSDStB members are fitted for this task."[31] Undeterred, he called on Dr. Krebs to assist in the teaching of National Socialist ideology.[32] Feickert was eager

[29] Disziplinarordnung für die Hamburgische Universität (17 February 1925), sec. 1, par. la, UniHH 0.20.1.

[30] Ibid., sec. 3, par. 31.

[31] Bericht über die Arbeit des NSDStB, 16 November 1931, StA NSDAP 35 vol. 2.

[32] Although Krebs was always willing to hold seminars with the group, he refused Feickert's request on this occasion to write a brief on foreign policy from the National Socialist point of view. He believed such "training

to hold a meeting "in a particularly red part of Hamburg," with the theme "National Socialist Students and Workers."[33] He hoped for some good publicity from this and the achievement of "that which the Students' Association still rather lacks today: a welding together through shared action and danger."[34] Such a meeting was finally held on 2 February 1932 with considerable success "in one of the reddest districts in Hamburg." Some 380 people were in the audience, including forty students who were not NSDStB members.[35] This provided the group with some useful propaganda on the solidarity of the Nazi students with workers just as the ASTA election campaign was getting under way.

Andreas Feickert introduced to Hamburg the idea of joint camps of workers and students under the Voluntary Labor Service scheme. After the First World War considerable though fragmented support arose for the introduction of a compulsory program of labor service for all youths, as a substitute for military service, or in order to encourage civic consciousness. In Hamburg a small, private society, called the German Association for Compulsory Labor Service, was formed in 1921.[36] Even the endorsement of such important organizations as the *Stahlhelm* brought such groups little support. On the other hand, there was considerable interest

---

notes" (*Schulungsbriefe*) to be worthless, as they invariably contained just "superficial chatter" as a result of their brevity. Feickert to Krebs, 17 October 1931, and Krebs to Feickert, 19 October 1931, RSFWü V*2 α 512.

[33] The slogan for the semester was: "Jeder Student wirbt einen Arbeiter." NSDStB headquarters urged each of its members at this time to try to recruit a worker for Party membership. Feickert to Krebs, 17 October 1931, ibid.

[34] Bericht über die Arbeit des NSDStB, 16 November 1931, StA NSDAP 35 vol. 2. This was an attempt to duplicate the *"Fronterlebnis"* of the First World War, which this generation of students had heard so much about but had not shared.

[35] The remainder of the audience was reported to be divided between Communist Party (KPD) members and storm troopers. Semesterbericht NSDStB Hamburg, 4 March 1932, ibid.

[36] Wolfgang Benz, "Vom freiwilligen Arbeitsdienst zur Arbeitsdienstpflicht," *Vierteljahrshefte für Zeitgeschichte* 16 (October 1968): 318.

nationally in the idea of voluntary labor camps, particularly among Youth Movement organizations. The first camp held by students was arranged by *Wandervogel* members at Easter 1925 at Schloss Colborn near Hanover. Other camps followed, and in 1928 a mixed camp was held with students and young industrial and agricultural workers in Silesia. The experiment was viewed as such a success that students at other universities, still largely members of the Youth Movement, organized their own camps during the next two years.

The discussions about a compulsory labor service were revived against a background of sharply rising unemployment in 1931. A government commission decided that little would be done to ameliorate the overall job market by such a measure. The commission warmed to the idea of a voluntary scheme, however, and the government provided financial support after June 1931 for participants who were unemployed or under the age of twenty-one. The Nazi Party at first stood aloof from the undertaking, partly from a lack of genuine interest and partly because Hitler's commissioner for labor service questions, Colonel Konstantin Hierl, inclined toward compulsion. For him, labor service was a question not of performing useful work but of training character in the ideologically unsound. Volunteer camps would merely preach to the converted. This was not the view of all members of the Nazi leadership. Gregor Strasser managed to persuade Hierl to support one or two voluntary camps to train future leaders for the time when the Party could introduce a compulsory scheme.[37]

In the student body there were no reservations about starting camps as soon as possible, especially from those who had already participated in one. The Hamburg NSDStB Leader, Andreas Feickert, had attended a student camp in Stuttgart and helped lay the road leading up to Schloss Solitude.[38] He

[37] Ibid., pp. 329-30.
[38] Feickert to Wigand, 4 May 1932, UniHH 0.10.2.3.I.

was much impressed by the format. Earlier student camps in Silesia had severely restricted the work component. Even later ones arranged by the Kiel students' union had entailed only four hours' manual labor per day; the afternoons and evenings were taken up entirely with discussion groups and lectures. In Stuttgart the working day was extended to between six and seven hours, leaving just the evenings for discussions.[39] Feickert began to plan a camp for Hamburg students immediately after his assumption of office.[40] The first, which opened in May 1932, involved the reclamation of marshy land outside Hamburg. The participants were all between the ages of nineteen and twenty-two, and comprised five students and seventeen unemployed, skilled and unskilled workers and sailors. Accommodation was provided in an abandoned brickworks. In order to cover the expenses of food, tools, and protective clothing, the local labor office paid 2 marks daily for each unemployed person, and the Hamburg Students' Union matched this amount for each student.[41]

Apart from encouraging the socialistic experience of worker-student contacts in such camps, Feickert also sought, through the unusually active Hamburg program, to focus attention on the question of settlement. In particular, he wished to promote the thoroughly *völkisch* cause of resettling the areas of Eastern Prussia where German speakers were in the minority.[42] The inherent elitism of the student body showed through in this question. The expanding East Prussian communities would require leaders, and the promise of such a role, which the home job market made so

[39] Andreas Feickert, "Warum freiwilliger studentischer Arbeitsdienst?" *Hamburger Universitäts-Zeitung* 15, no. 2 (15 May 1932), pp. 25-27.

[40] Feickert to Reichsleitung NSDStB, 6 October 1931, quoted in Kater, *Studentenschaft*, p. 170.

[41] Bericht Feickert, "Abteilung Freiwilliger Arbeitsdienst der Hamburger Studentenschaft," n.d., UniHH 0.10.2.3.I.

[42] Rundschreiben Feickert, Wigand, Kümmel, 12 July 1932, ibid.

elusive, was held out to the students. The experience gained in the camps of actual contact with workers in a rural setting would help prepare students to step forward later as the civic, educational, and intellectual leaders of larger communities of settlers.

In August 1932, Feickert staged a far more ambitious venture with 100 participants who lived on a converted barge, working to reclaim marshland in the vicinity of Hamburg.[43] Simultaneously, he opened two land-based camps with fifty participants each. The camps were warmly supported by the rector, and several professors came out to give lectures on such topics as the German minorities question, geopolitics, racial research, and defense studies.[44] The only concerted opposition to the camps came from local Communists, who saw voluntary labor service as a step toward forced labor. They believed that a "fascist work army" would be employed as a strike-breaking force against the working class. The camp in May was actually attacked by a group of Communists, who were brutally repulsed by the Nazis, armed with sticks and spades.[45]

A major problem was the financing of these work camps. Before August 1932 it was not possible to pay for the upkeep of student participants from government funds, which were earmarked solely for people eligible for unemployment or welfare payments. By the winter of 1932-1933, however, the Hamburg organizers were relatively well off. They had collected 2,361 marks from local alumni and siphoned off another 1,400 marks from students' union funds. On top of

[43] The flag designed for this camp (two crossed spades on a black background) became the *Traditionsfahne* of the Hamburg NSDStB, an especially cherished memento that was still brought out years later on special occasions. Cf. "Im Geiste des 'Kahnlagers von 1932.' Eindrucksvolle Kundgebung der Hamburger Studentenschaft," *Hamburger Anzeiger*, 15 July 1943.

[44] Ochsenius, "Studentenschaft," pp. 148-49.

[45] Draft article, "Der freiwillige studentische Arbeitsdienst," RSFWü V*2 α 535.

this the Reich government now began to contribute a per capita grant of 2 marks for each day that a student worked.[46] At the end of 1931, the head of the national student financial aid organization (*Deutsches Studentenwerk*), Reinhold Schairer, had proposed a scheme for a compulsory "work year" for all prospective students before admission to university, by means of which he hoped to lessen the overcrowding problem.[47] The immediate suspension of a whole year's freshman intake, some 30,000 students, would provide immediate but not lasting relief. Schairer assumed, however, that many would decide not to study after their work year. The German Students' Union, now radicalized under Nazi control, did not wish control of a national labor service scheme to rest with another organization in which they had little influence. Therefore the DST annual conference in August 1932 set up an Office for Labor Service in order to draw up plans of its own. Andreas Feickert seemed the natural choice to head the new body. The DST leaders were anxious to be prepared for government approval of a general labor service scheme in order that they might try to take over its operation themselves. If they were successful, they would undoubtedly gain favorable publicity and possibly promote a more benevolent attitude from the Education ministries toward the German Students' Union. Although the DST seemed well on the way to realizing its plan, the government rejected on 14 December 1932 the comprehensive proposals that Feickert had put forward, largely for financial reasons.[48] A general and compulsory scheme could not therefore be

[46] Ochsenius, "Studentenschaft," p. 146.

[47] The *Deutsche Studentenwerk* was formed in 1921 to distribute financial aid to students in the form of monetary grants, catering subsidies, medical insurance, and so forth. A short history is given in Deutsches Studentenwerk, eds., *Deutsches Studentenwerk 1921-1961: Festschrift zum vierzigjährigen Bestehen* (Bonn, 1961).

[48] Cf. Faust, *Studentenbund*, 2: 95. Feickert confirmed the rivalry with Schairer's office when he was interviewed by the author. Interview Giles/Feickert, 27 September 1973.

put into practice, but plans went ahead to conduct it on a voluntary basis, and support was sought among the future school-leavers of Easter 1933.[49]

Of central importance in Feickert's labor service concept was so-called defense sport" (*Wehrsport*). The idea of this surreptitious military training through pack marches, orienteering exercises, and shooting contests had found warm general support in professorial circles for several years. It represented a further cause for concern in the Reich Ministry of the Interior during the summer of 1930 over the growing right-wing radicalization of the student body. The Ministry was alarmed by the increasingly militaristic nature of the activities of a number of organizations in which students participated. Not only the National Socialists, but other Youth Movement groups, including the Boy Scouts, were training in ways that were certain, if discovered, to rouse the suspicions of foreign governments. The declared purpose of one Nazi camp, "to work and fight, to create the possibility mentally and physically of destroying our slavery," which was considered to be typical of the outlook of similar organizations pursuing defense sports, gave the ministerial officials pause. If it was more than an empty slogan, they reasoned, there were only two possible interpretations: if slavery referred to the terms of the Versailles Treaty, then the matter could "become very unpleasant" for the German government abroad; if, on the other hand, the restrictions and the cautious attitude of the government at home were considered hyperbolically to be "slavery," then the exercises were nothing less than preparation for treason.[50]

Any moderating influence that the government would have liked to inject was neutralized by professorial approval. In Hamburg, an invitation to join a "Society for the Military Strengthening of Germany" evoked a positively enthusiastic

---

[49] Merkblatt für Abiturienten. Freiwillige Meldung zum Werkhalbjahr 1933, UniHH 0.10.2.3.

[50] Interior Ministry report, "Wehrbewegung in der rechtsradikalen Studentenschaft," 25 June 1930, ZStA RMdI 26108.

response from Rector Wigand and a promise to canvass his colleagues for support. He was proud to report that the University of Hamburg now gave a regular course in military studies, ostensibly an historical study of the First World War, "which, however, also covers contemporary and future problems."[51] Indeed, secret officer-training courses were held in the University during the winter semester 1931-1932. Under the aegis of the University Authority, some ninety students received army instruction in questions of organization, weaponry, and tactics, held night exercises, and even took part in the army's autumn maneuvers on Lüneburg Heath. The true content of this "Civil Air Defense" course (as it was misleadingly called) was revealed in a leaflet pinned to the Socialist Students' Group's bulletin board in May 1932. Details of the dates, times, venues, and content of the courses were given.[52] The student posting the leaflet was apprehended by a member of the *Stahlhelm* Students' Group, and the syndic immediately called in the police to arrest him. Further arrests of members of the Socialist and Communist Students' Groups followed. Evidently there was some substance in the revelations of the leaflet, for the students were charged with the "betrayal of military secrets."[53] When they were acquitted under the political amnesty of 20 December 1932, the syndic was still anxious for the University to discipline the students but reluctantly decided to drop the proceedings in order not to "endanger the necessary secrecy of the incidents involved in this case."[54]

A preoccupation with military matters was a direct contravention of the Versailles Treaty, which stated that "educational establishments . . . must not occupy themselves with any military matters. In particular they will be forbidden to instruct or exercise their members, or to allow them

---

[51] Wigand to Otto, 14 January 1932, UniHH A.70.1.663.

[52] Anonymous leaflet, "Die schwarze Reichswehr lebt," UniHH Di.A.3.

[53] Untersuchungsrichter des Reichsgerichts to Syndic (Geheim), 13 August 1932, ibid.

[54] Aktenvermerk Niemann, 8 April 1933, ibid.

to be instructed or exercised, in the profession or use of arms."[55] Far from being ignorant of this, or concerned about the misdemeanor, the students made little attempt to conceal their defense sports activities and almost flaunted them as an expression of their hostility toward the Treaty. When the Students' Union invited General von Metzsch to speak on "Military Sovereignty and Rearmament of the German Empire," the rector himself graced the occasion by his presence. Indeed, whereas his predecessor had banned a proposed Anti-Versailles Rally, Rector Wigand now spoke in person to an enthusiastic audience, declaring that opposition to the Versailles Treaty was *above all* the affair of the universities. It was their task especially, he claimed, to keep alive the spirit of national honor and military-mindedness; it was no coincidence that the Versailles Treaty had made special mention of the German universities, for they were certain to resist the Treaty with every means.[56] Only the previous week the Students' Union journal had published articles promoting defense sports and recommending textbooks on small-arms, as well as such monthly periodicals as *The Art of War in Words and Pictures (Kriegskunst in Wort und Bild)*. If, the students were assured, they read these and carried out ostensibly innocuous physical exercise as private individuals, they could not be accused of transgressing the Treaty stipulations. "It should be clear to everyone," they were reminded, "that omission and neglect are graver faults than error in the choice of means."[57]

[55] *The Treaty of Peace between the Allied and Associated Powers and Germany, and other Treaty Engagements, signed at Versailles, June 28th, 1919*, London H.M.S.O. 1920, Article 177. The contraventions of the military provisions of the Treaty, which occurred from the very start, are discussed by Hans W. Gatzke, *Stresemann and the Rearmament of Germany* (Baltimore, 1969).

[56] The main speaker at the meeting on 19 January 1932 was A. E. Günther from the Hamburg Fichte Society. Press cuttings in uniHH 0.10.3.5.

[57] From the *Ausbildungsvorschrift für die Infanterie*, I, 33, 2, quoted and recommended by Helmut Gause, "Wehrsportliche Notwendigkeiten," *Hamburger Universitäts-Zeitung* 14, no. 3 (15 June 1932), p. 47.

Student Disillusionment with the NSDStB

The German Students' Union's annual conference in July 1932 reflected deliberately the current emphases of the Nazi leadership. It took place at Königsberg in East Prussia in order to focus attention on the putative problems of the frontier areas. The delegates marched in formation from the docks where they had disembarked to the soldiers' barracks in which they were to be accommodated. Militarism pervaded the entire conference, which culminated in the passing of a sort of enabling act. The overwhelming majority of voting delegates this year were again National Socialists, and they supported a motion to abolish parliamentary procedures. From now on the annual conference would have no decision-making powers but would merely function as a political rally, with training sessions for student leaders. The Nazi leader principle would henceforth apply to appointments from the top downward: retiring leaders would name their own successors rather than calling an election.[58]

There were protests about the way things were going. Already in June, the leaders of the *Deutsche Burschenschaft* had formally condemned the NSDStB as an unsatisfactory representative of National Socialism, which as an ideology they applauded.[59] But having long advocated more authoritarianism themselves, there was not much that they could say when the Nazi students put these ideals into practice. All in all, Baldur von Schirach seemed to have student politics well under control. Aware of this, and having by now lost interest in the NSDStB, Schirach relinquished its top post in June 1932 (a month before the DSt annual conference) to Gerd Rühle, who had been one of his few consistently loyal followers. Rühle possessed impeccable National Socialist credentials. He had come to the Nazis in 1924, during Hitler's imprisonment, as a member of the *Grossdeutsche Volksgemeinschaft* in Munich. He joined the reconstituted

---

[58] Faust, *Studentenbund*, 2: 34ff.
[59] Ibid., p. 36.

NSDAP shortly after his twentieth birthday, receiving the extraordinarily low (and thus prestigious) membership number 694. His SS membership number, 290, was no less impressive, though an addiction to cigarettes and the contraction of gonorrhea made him slightly less than the model SS man.[60] A member of the Munich NSDStB group since its foundation in 1926, he became the first Nazi chairman of a students' union in May 1927 at the University of Frankfurt. He had proved a good organizer, and all his intelligence was needed for the situation in which the NSDStB now found itself. Despite its grip on the reins of student government, the NSDStB was steadily losing the confidence and support of the students at large and even of some of its own members. This was caused partly by a certain impatience for Hitler to join the Reich government, which was also reflected in the several national elections in 1932, and partly by the high-handedness of the Nazis in attempting to shut out the fraternities from all participation in student government. A third reason was the organization of defense sports.

The NSDStB was disappointed to find that it was not the only organization to take an active interest in the promotion of military sport, and it could not succeed in gaining principal control over the activity. The fraternities organized similar programs, and many NSDStB fraternity members preferred to carry out training in the more subdued atmosphere of their fraternities rather than under the auspices of local storm troopers: many students thought that the bloody street brawls in which the NSDStB involved them were beneath their dignity.[61] As in many other places, it was the *Stahlhelm* veterans' organization that, with the encouragement of the fraternities, gained the upper hand in Hamburg in the provision of sports facilities. The state, too, was anxious to keep control of these increasingly popular pursuits

[60] SS Officer's file and other personnel files on Rühle in BDC.

[61] Engelken to Schulze, 31 October 1932, RSFWü V*2 α 520; Engelken to SA-Untergruppe Hamburg, Standartenführer 76, 22 November 1932, RSFWü V*2 α 523.

from the Nazis. Since 1930 at the latest, when the Reich Ministry of the Interior had begun to realize that the paramilitary training of the Nazis might constitute preparation for civil war, plans had been mooted to attract the youth of Germany away from National Socialist organizations. Defense Minister Groener was the first to explore the possibilities of an enormous state-controlled umbrella organization for defense sports. His successor, General Schleicher, set up in September 1932 a state body for the training of defense sports instructors from all youth organizations (*Reichskuratorium für Jugendertüchtigung*).[62] The NSDStB now saw a steady drain of its membership to other organizations. This was serious because the local Students' Union elections were approaching. Despite the introduction of the leader principle by the national union, the DSt leaders had no power to abolish the elected AStA committees at individual colleges. The danger existed that if the NSDStB lost control of a number of these during the winter semester 1932-1933, their hegemony would be threatened in the national union.

A National Socialist edict requiring all NSDStB members to enlist also in the SA (or SS) was quickly issued to prevent possible further losses of members to rival organizations.[63] During a student's first semester he would not be required to attend NSDStB meetings but would be fully at the disposal of the SA. After this, he would transfer back to the NSDStB, which now set up its own paramilitary section, the *St.B.-Organisation* (stBO), modeled on the SA. After two years' active service in the stBO, the student would return to active service in the SA. Although it was necessary to call on the SA to undertake the military training, for which the NSDStB was not equipped, the latter held that an exclusive claim to

[62] Gordon A. Craig, *The Politics of the Prussian Army 1640-1945* (Oxford, 1955), p. 442; Faust, *Studentenbund*, 2: 98ff.

[63] Verfügung Röhm/Schirach/Rühle, 12 September 1932, RSFWü V*2 α 527.

93

the students for four whole semesters was essential if they were to accomplish successfully the special high-level ideological training that members needed in order to take their places as the "intellectually skilled fighters" of the Party.[64] For it was admitted yet again that largely because of the many conflicting commitments of other Nazi organizations to which most NSDStB members belonged, it had "so far *never* been possible to carry out even approximately" the necessary ideological training.

Above all, the heavy demands on the time of Nazi students adversely affected support for the NSDStB during 1932. Participation in every activity was mandatory: the Hamburg NSDStB leader Feickert warned that merely two unexcused absences would lead to instant dismissal.[65] In fact, the leaders were so extraordinarily busy that they had no time to check such things. At the end of October 1932, the new NSDStB leader at Hamburg University, Albrecht Engelken, reported that he had no idea how many members there were in the group. On paper there were 120, but the most recent check on active members (in July) had revealed only fifty-five names.[66] Andreas Feickert, occupied with national planning for a student labor service in Berlin, was careless enough to let his NSDAP membership lapse, a fact brought out later with relish by his opponents, who accused him of abandoning the Party during its most difficult struggle.[67]

Although it may be assumed that membership was rather higher earlier in the year, the national total at the beginning of November 1932 showed some 7,600 students in the NSDStB. A Party edict issued at this time, which required all students in the NSDAP to join the NSDStB also, raised the

[64] Actually, the SA and SS were not well equipped either, as the NSDStB leader had ruefully to admit. Denkschrift Rühle, "Die Neuorganisation des NSDStB," n.d. (October 1932), ibid.

[65] Rundschreiben Feickert, 5 December 1931, StA NSDAP 35 vol. 2.

[66] Engelken to Schulze, 31 October 1932, RSFWü V*2 α 520.

[67] See below, chap. 5.

figure to 8,800 members by December 1932.[68] The National Socialist Students' Association was still small, compared with the tens of thousands of students in fraternities, yet it had now become, on the eve of the Third Reich, the third largest student association, after the *Deutsche Burschenschaft* and the Catholic cv.[69] Over half the NSDStB members must already have belonged to the SA; so the new measures cannot have placed a significant number of SA units at the disposal of the Party in absolute numbers. More important, it was a disaster in the university context.[70] A year earlier, SA Chief of Staff Röhm had admitted that regular SA duty was "a scarcely feasible burden" for a student, and he conceded that there were more arguments against setting up student units than there were for them.[71] Now that this had been introduced after all, the fraternity associations complained that their Nazi members no longer had any time left for the fraternity.[72] Already in September 1931 one of the Hamburg NSDStB members had had to give up his seat on the Students' Union committee since, as the leader of two SA units, he was unable to cope with the work.[73] The main complaints came from within the SA itself: the units grumbled at losing some of their best members to the new StBO;

[68] Figures given in Faust, *Studentenbund*, 2: 91.

[69] According to Steinberg, the DB had 12,634 members in 1933, and the cv 10,282. Steinberg, *Sabers*, p. 45.

[70] Kater, *Studentenschaft*, p. 165, believes that the scheme decisively "took the wind out of the sails" of the NSDStB's rivals in the field of defense sports. Dibner, "History," p. 112, is impressed by the fact that "uniforms and badges were designed in minute detail (and) a rigid rank system was worked out," though this differed minimally from the regular SA. She also attaches too much importance to the existence of the StBO. The plan per se was as catastrophic as its execution proved to be, and no amount of extra "effort, time and money" could have made it any more successful, as Dibner claims. Steinberg, *Sabers*, p. 126, while referring incorrectly to the new organization as the "Studentenbund (St.B.)," at least recognizes that it was a failure.

[71] Rundschreiben Röhm, 17 July 1931, BA Sammlung Schumacher 279.

[72] Faust, *Studentenbund*, 2: 101.

[73] Wilkens to Heinrichsdorff, 28 September 1931, RSFWü V*2 α 511.

students were reluctant to be torn away from their nonstudent comrades just as they had succeeded in building up friendships. As Röhm had foreseen the previous year, the special student SA units of the STBO were "unfavorably regarded by the rest of the SA men as a division (that) completely contradicts the principles of the Party, which, after all, aim primarily at bringing the intellectual and manual workers as close to one another as possible."[74]

The NSDSTB Area Leader, Reinhold Schulze, found great antipathy toward the STBO precisely because of this "psychological difficulty of an ostensible separation of students and workers." He spent an entire month visiting all the SA leaders in his North German Area to convince them of the necessity of the new set-up. This tour was financed partly by the modest expense account that he had been allowed for the first time in October, partly by "financial manipulations that I refuse to perform again." The result was that he had no money left to forward to the individual groups the circulars sent to him from headquarters in Munich. Repeated appeals for financial support had proved disappointing: "Towns like Kiel, Hamburg, Bremen, Lübeck, Wismar, Rostock are utterly dependent upon shipping, and there is a degree of distress here quite unlike that of Nuremberg or Chemnitz. The Party got their hands on those who still have any money long ago; the rest of the wealthy people reject the autarchic plans of the Nazis."[75] Schulze's personal situation soon improved when he became a Reichstag deputy. With his free railway pass, he was able to establish much better contact with the groups under his supervision, which spread over a wide area from the Dutch border to Western Pomerania. Schulze spent much of his first Reichstag deputy's salary on setting up an office for himself in Hamburg, only to be surprised by a demand from Munich for 150 marks

[74] Rundschreiben Röhm, 17 July 1931, BA Sammlung Schumacher 279. Spitznagel, "Studentenschaft," pp. 203ff., describes the ill feelings that the new arrangements caused in Würzburg.

[75] Schulze to Rühle, 6 November 1932, RSFWü II*146 α 79.

toward NSDStB headquarters funds.[76] National and Area headquarters had to exist on a shoestring budget right up to 1933, and the local groups, while they were still small, needed all the money they could raise for their propaganda.[77]

Although there did exist some internal discontent, coupled with a drop in support, the NSDStB had obtained for itself by the end of the Weimar Republic a secure place in the universities from which to leap into absolute power. It now possessed wide experience of the limits of the university's tolerance, which were extremely elastic. The Nazis in Hamburg had received benevolent treatment from Rector Brauer in the face of mounting violence, and in Professor Wigand they saw "*the* rector of the University who paved the way for the Nazi era."[78] The meteorologist Wigand, an expert on the dispersal of fog, appeared to have a less clear view of Nazi aims than did some of his colleagues. He was chastised for his evident support of the Nazi student body by Professor Emil Wolff, who reminded him that "their openly declared goal is the destruction of the intellectual autonomy of the university and its replacement by the primacy of their Party ideology." Wolff felt that the rector's behavior made it extremely difficult to give "a firm and resolute response to the challenging and arrogant attitude" of the right-wing students.[79] Wigand defended himself by claiming that he was trying to meet the students halfway in order to prepare the ground for benevolent guidance on his part; the effects of this would be much better than detached, authoritarian censure, "which is of course easier, but

[76] Schulze to Rühle, 9 January 1933, ibid.

[77] There is no information on the size of the membership subscription in Hamburg. NSDStB members in Munich during 1930 apparently had to contribute RM 12.—per month, plus another RM 3.—to the Party. Cf. Pridham, *Hitler's Rise*, p. 211. In January 1933, Schulze did institute a monthly fee of RM 1.—from all NSDStB members to cover the expenses of the Area Leader's office. Pfeifer to NSDStB groups, 23 January 1933, RSFWü V*2 α 527.

[78] Schorer and Riecke, "Nationalsozialismus als Geist," p. 120.

[79] Denkschrift Wolff, 15 February 1932, UniHH C.10.12.

must needs be fruitless, as the example of Halle recently showed."[80]

The mention of Halle betrays a strong reason behind Wigand's willingness to condone Nazi excesses: he feared repercussions from the students if he upset them. The Halle senate had banned the NSDStB there in the hope of arresting its campaign against Günther Dehn, a professor of theology who had spoken out against the glorification of war, but the agitation simply escalated.[81] There were similar incidents at many universities besides Halle. It was not as though the machinery of defense did not exist. There was every reason for the rector to suspend or ban the NSDStB after it had brought outright violence onto academic soil. It was quite within the provisions of the University's disciplinary code to take such action against students (or societies) who committed "disturbances of the peace or order, or breaches of good conduct in the university buildings or grounds."[82] Were official recognition withdrawn from the NSDStB, it would automatically be deprived of its AStA mandates, which would then be shared by the remaining members. That such a measure was a real possibility is demonstrated by the fears within the Students' Union committee during the altercations with the University Authority over the student constitution. In August 1932, Wigand acted in such a manner when he "took pains to strike out pacifist student organizations from the societies' register of the University on formal grounds," namely, the German Pacifist Students' Association and the Republican Students' Association.[83] Like the University Authority earlier, the rector and the syndic did not want to make the mistake of Becker and risk demonstrations, which, abetted by official tolerance, were becoming increasingly

---

[80] Denkschrift Wigand, "Grundsätzliches zur Universitätspolitik: Eine Antwort," 26 March 1932, ibid.

[81] Faust, *Studentenbund*, 2: 62.

[82] Disziplinarordnung für die Hamburgische Universität (17 February 1925), sec. 1, par. 2/5, UNIHH 0.20.1.

[83] Ochsenius, "Studentenschaft," p. 139.

violent. In Halle, the faculty had feared the complete inca-
pacitation of the university following a mass student boycott. This had already happened at Hanover. When 200 nationalistic students were disciplined for their disruptions of
the classes of Dr. Theodor Lessing, a full 1,200 students (out
of a total of 1,500) abandoned the college and transferred to
the Technical University in Brunswick.[84] The specter of a
possible closing of the young Hamburg University had been
and always remained a vivid and alarming one. Almost any
sacrifice of principle (and academic freedom was the central
feature of the German university) seemed justified if it could
avert that danger. If "it was not by chance that the University
of Hamburg remained calm, while at other universities in
the country disturbances flared up again and again," the relative quiet must be seen in light of these fears.[85]

Like the fraternities, the professors also misjudged the
Nazis. Their student leaders seemed respectable—Heinrichsdorff, the urbane negotiator, a model of bourgeois respectability;[86] Feickert, the earnest young quasi-socialist
with his Labor Service, widening the horizons of academic
youth through contact with workers, and at the same time
strengthening their *völkisch* nationalism through political
lectures. They both seemed, and undoubtedly were, sincere
young men who were able to persuade the professors of their
honorable intentions. Many of the professors reassured
themselves that these moderate leaders could and certainly
would try to tone down the excesses of their subordinates
once the political conflict had been resolved. This was similar to the widespread and misguided view that Hitler himself was really a moderate. The notion that the Nazis' ap-

[84] Bleuel and Klinnert, *Deutsche Studenten*, pp. 125ff.

[85] Obituary by Heinrichsdorff, "Zum Tode Professor Wigands," *Hamburger Tageblatt*, 23 December 1932.

[86] It is interesting that Heinrichsdorff seems to have had a counterpart
as the leader of the NSDStB's AStA delegation in Tübingen, whom Adam
describes as being, "with his literary interests, completely alien to the
typical Nazi student rowdy." Adam, *Hochschule*, p. 27.

parent freedom to commit violence with impunity might positively encourage them later to yet greater trials of strength, attacking the very heart of the university, was one that was too painful to contemplate, for it would signify a complete renunciation of the professors' self-respect and their belief that they could still influence the students for the good. It would be tantamount to an admission of failure as a teacher. The self-confidence, and often the self-importance, that characterized the German professor bolstered his optimism and kept such thoughts at bay.

CHAPTER FOUR

The Political University

Hitler's appointment as German chancellor was the event for which all National Socialists had long been waiting. It marked the ultimate bestowal of trust on Hitler by the German establishment. It semed to be a recognition of the responsibility and maturity of the core of the Nazi movement. In any case, it offered National Socialists everywhere, the students included, a great opportunity to prove themselves. Especially after the passage of the Enabling Act, the Nazis were well and truly in power. How would they use that power? That was the question that exercised not only the opponents of National Socialism but also its sympathizers. In higher education, everyone knew that the politicization of the German university was on the program. But few foresaw the chaotic fashion in which this would be attempted. Conversely, the Nazi students did not imagine that they would meet with quite the subtlety of resistance that the professoriate swung into play, after they had recovered their breath from the initial heavy blows of 1933. This chapter examines the bungling progress of the Nazi students during the first eighteen months of the Third Reich. This was the period of burning books, purging, and cleansing, but it did not result in the nazification of the university in short order, as many contemporary observers outside Germany believed. There were two major problems: the Nazi student leaders could not agree among themselves exactly who should direct the operation; neither had they really been able to decide precisely what constituted the nazification of the university. The professoriate on the one hand, and the large number of students in fraternities on the other, had very clear and strong ideas on what should be retained as integral parts of German academic life.

The Purging of the University

In nearly every local student election in the winter semester 1932-1933 support for the NSDStB dropped, if only
slightly. This cannot be explained simply in terms of the
national trend in the November *Reichstag* elections. Faust
suggests that the sharp rise in violence had alienated some
students, who had been quite willing to sympathize with
Nazi rhetoric until they saw ostensibly vague threats turn
increasingly into stark and ugly reality.[1] Another reason is
that the Nazi students were so involved now with their local
SA and Party duties that there was simply less time for the
organization of student election campaigns. The Hamburg
Area Leader bemoaned the absence of Party support for the
release of students for the ASTA campaign, as well as a shortage of money for propaganda.[2] Hamburg had particular difficulty in obtaining speakers for its student election campaign, which fell in the early part of February 1933. Following
Hitler's accession to the chancellorship, urgent engagements
caused three Nazi speakers to cancel their visits, and the
only replacement sent was so poor that the NSDStB begrudged
him his rail fare.[3]

Nonetheless, the elections did bring favorable results to
the NSDStB, which in Hamburg marginally increased its lead
(from 43 percent to 45 percent of the poll).[4] It took one seat
from the fraternities, which, plagued by disagreements about
tactics, fought an extremely confused campaign. Even the
fact that one of the fraternity groups, the Greater German
Ring, was headed by the former Freiburg NSDStB leader did
nothing to lessen support for the official Hamburg NSDStB

[1] Faust, *Studentenbund*, 2: 114-15.

[2] Rundschreiben Schulze to Hochschulgruppenführer, January 1933,
RSFWü V*2 α 527.

[3] Engelken to Propagandaabteilung der Bundesleitung NSDStB, 18 February
1933, ibid.

[4] See Appendix 1. Faust incorrectly gives an increase from 45.5 percent
to 50 percent for Hamburg. Faust, *Studentenbund*, 2: 111.

slate.[5] The left-wing groups, too, failed to pull together. The Socialist Students' Group's proposal to the Revolutionary Socialists to join forces for the "decisive battle against Fascism" was turned down as a result of a petty personal squabble.[6] With such a muddled campaign conducted by all factions, the voting patterns did not change greatly from the previous year, and the Nazis remained squarely in power.

The months following 30 January 1933 saw the NSDStB busy in the confident flush of success. Although the Nazi students did not test the full extent of their power until after the March *Reichstag* elections, violent excesses occurred even before then. The persecution of their opponents reached a new peak. The leader of the StBO unit at Hamburg, now numbering fifty students, still tried to present the Nazis as the underdog in his report for the month of February. Among its activities was the successful wrecking of a performance by a communist actors' collective. Ten Nazis protested against the "shameless and treasonable presentation." The audience, about 250 strong, attacked them with chairs, but they allegedly emerged with only light injuries. Thereafter the Nazis staged daily scuffles with their supposed opponents outside the University. A number of Jewish students were beaten up in this way.[7] Although the Nazis found electoral support, this sort of behavior did not attract new members.[8] There were forty-three members on 1 December 1932;

[5] Engelken to Krüger, 19 February 1933, Captured German Records microfilmed at Alexandria, Virginia (MicAlex), T-81/259/5051138.

[6] Confiscated notice, 27 February 1933, UniHH 0.30.5.404.

[7] Monatsbericht Studentenbunds-Sturm, 1 March 1933, RSFWü V*2 α 520. In Würzburg, the houses of two Jewish fraternities were raided by the SA at the end of June. Spitznagel, "Studentenschaft," pp. 276-77.

[8] Bracher claims that the *majority* of students supported the excesses and even encouraged further brutalities. Bracher, *Das deutsche Dilemma*, p. 138. This is probably an exaggeration—of the same order as Kater's claim, based on a few isolated reports—that disturbances and violence by Hitler Youths were "everyday occurrences" in schools through to the war years. Michael H. Kater, "Hitlerjugend und Schule im Dritten Reich," *Historische Zeitschrift* 228 (1979): 574. All the evidence concerning the University of

TABLE 2. Growth of NSDStB in Hamburg Colleges, July-December 1933

College		Number of members			
	July	Beginning winter semester	October	November	December
Hamburg University	266	250	321	366	412
ANst* (female members at University)	42	43	50	63	63
College of Fine Arts	15	31	31	31	39
Merchant Marine School	61	46	46	48	63
State Technical Institute	89	56	101	148	159

* Arbeitsgemeinschaft Nationalsozialistischer Studentinnen
Source: Stärkemeldungen des Kreises Nord des NSDStB, RSFWü II*146 α 79. Figures not available for other Hamburg colleges.

by the end of February 1933 there were only forty-two in the Hamburg University NSDStB group (see also Appendix 2). Hitler's appointment as chancellor had no effect whatever on membership figures. On the other hand, the March *Reichstag* elections were followed by a rush of recruits, particularly at the University, as the above table shows (see Table 2). The old guard certainly celebrated wildly. Oskar Stäbel, the new national leader, hastened to warn NSDStB members of the damage caused by their drunken rowdiness in public.[9] The impression of National Socialist asceticism was being ruined.

Hamburg indicates that the violence abated by the middle of 1934 at the latest. Even beforehand, disruptions were perpetrated only by the members of Nazi organizations or by isolated students with a grudge against a particular professor.

[9] Rundschreiben Stäbel, 8 June 1933, RSFWü V*2 α 524. See also Geoffrey Giles, "Student Drinking and the Third Reich: Academic Tradition and the Nazi Revolution." Paper presented at the Social History of Alcohol Conference, Berkeley, January 1984.

In February, however, the NSDStB was not yet so jubilant. The ASTA was still functioning, and so the more radical demands the Hamburg Nazis were shortly to make were set aside for less contentious policies. Heinrichsdorff requested the introduction of compulsory medical examinations.[10] The University senate's response to this was typical of its largely national-liberal professors. Although it would welcome the extension of the University Medical Service in order to promote a rise in the general standard of health, it disliked the idea of making university admission contingent on physical perfection.[11] The senate was less hesitant over the question of compulsory sport, which was ordered by Prussian Education Minister Bernard Rust for all students of that state, starting in the summer semester 1933. It agreed to support a similar measure for Hamburg.[12] The Students' Union thereupon pressed once more for a medical examination on the grounds that this was essential prior to a rigorous program of physical activities. The senate agreed that this would be advisable but believed that anyone in doubtful health would be sensible enough to request an examination.[13] In the light of their helpless reaction to faculty dismissals (as described below), the senate should not be viewed here as striving to preserve the freedom of the individual; their action probably represents resistance to new bureaucratization, which became, however, an unavoidable feature of the Third Reich. By the summer semester 1934, admission to all universities depended on a certificate of good health.[14] The syphilis ex-

[10] The demand was made on the day before the ASTA elections. Heinrichsdorff to Raape, "Denkschrift der Hamburger Studentenschaft zur Frage der Pflichtuntersuchung," 9 February 1933, RSFWü V*2 α 516.

[11] Protokoll Universitätssenat, 10 February 1933, UniHH C.20.4.

[12] Protokoll Universitätssenat, 28 July 1933, ibid. Erlass Rust UI no. 65629, 29 April 1933, UniHH M.30.2.

[13] Protokoll Universitätssenat, 28 July 1933, UniHH C.20.4.

[14] Cf. the booklet published by Hamburg University in the summer semester 1934, *Was hat der Student bei der Einschreibung und beim Belegen der Vorlesungen zu beachten?* University of Hamburg Registrar's Office reference library.

pert, Professor Wirz, the Party's Deputy Commissioner for Higher Education, was a prime mover behind this stipulation and was doubtless responsible for the proviso that any prospective or current student found to have venereal disease would be permanently debarred from study.[15]

The Hamburg University senate was also ambivalent in its attitude toward compulsory Labor Service: while welcoming the advantages this might bring for the nation, it could not bring itself to support an obligatory scheme, for it foresaw little pedagogical success unless participation was voluntary.[16] The senate clung to the traditional German concept of the freedom of learning (*Lernfreiheit*), and not unwisely, for the NSDStB leaders themselves often had to admit later that force produced the worst results.

During April the Reich government hurried to introduce various measures to placate the nationalistic majority of students. The Law on the Formation of Students' Unions at Universities and Colleges of 22 April 1933 restored official recognition by the state, thereby allowing the unions to collect fees once more.[17] At the beginning of April the leader of the Hamburg Students' Union sent a letter to the rector, demanding the immediate introduction of a *numerus clausus* for Jewish students.[18] The University's response was overtaken by the promulgation on 25 April 1933 of the national Law against the Overcrowding of German Schools and Universities. This stipulated that no more than 1.5 percent of freshmen could be "non-Aryans," and only then if the

[15] Cf. Protokoll Reichstagung NSDStB in Frankfurt am Main, 12 May 1935, RSFWü II* φ 319.

[16] Beschluss des vom Universitätssenat zur Prüfung der Pläne betr. die Einrichtung eines akademischen Werkjahres eingesetzten Ausschusses, 13 December 1932, UniHH 0.10.2.3. In fact, compulsory labor service was introduced in the summer of 1933 for all prospective students two years before the general scheme began.

[17] Gesetz über die Bildung von Studentenschaften an den Wissenschaftlichen Hochschulen, 22 April 1933. Text in Joachim Haupt, *Neuordnung im Schulwesen und Hochschulwesen* (Berlin, 1933), p. 17.

[18] Heinrichsdorff to Raape, 1 April 1933, UniHH N.20.1.

total number of non-Aryan students did not exceed 5 percent of the student body.[19] In Hamburg this was not the case: only 4.6 percent of the students in the summer semester were Jews. The pressures against Jewish students steadily reduced their numbers from 102 at this time to nine in the summer semester 1938 (or twenty-one if one includes the so-called part-Jews).[20] The Hamburg students also demanded that, in the future, appointments of Jews to the faculty should not even be considered, and that all requests for student aid by Jewish students should be rejected out of hand. On these two points there was no national legislation, but the new Nazi head of the Hamburg University Authority agreed to endorse the proposals at once with an appropriate decree.[21]

Of the greatest importance to the student leaders was the promulgation of a new Prussian Student Code on 12 April 1933, which formally abolished the ASTA committee system of student government and placed all power in the hands of the Students' Union Leader. The Hamburg government immediately copied this provision.[22] The important constituency of fraternity students was not forgotten either. Although the Weimar ban on dueling, imposed in 1925, was

---

[19] Gesetz gegen die Überfüllung der deutschen Schulen und Hochschulen, 25 April 1933 (and Erste Durchführungsverordnung). Texts in Haupt, *Neuordnung*, pp. 10ff.

[20] Denkschrift Statistisches Landesamt Hamburg, "Volkszugehörigkeit der im Sommersemester 1933 an der Hamburgischen Universität eingeschriebenen Studierenden (d.h. der Inländer sowie der Ausländer deutscher Muttersprache)," 6 July 1933; Universität Hamburg, "Verzeichnis der im Sommersemester 1938 eingeschriebenen inländischen jüdischen Studierenden," 12 November 1938, UniHH N.20.1. The latter list was drawn up in response to a telegram from the Education Ministry authorizing the Rector to bar Jewish students from entering the University following the *Reichskristallnacht*. Telegram Zschintzsch to rector, 12 November 1938, ibid.

[21] Protokoll Universitätssenat, 5 May 1933, UniHH C.20.4.

[22] Preussische Studentenrechtverordnung, 12 April 1933. Text in Haupt, *Neuordnung*, pp. 17ff. Cf. Satzung der Studentenschaft der Hamburgischen Universität, 1 May 1933, UniHH N.20.1.4.

not rescinded, the Prussian government announced at the beginning of April that it would no longer press charges in cases of fraternity dueling. In fact, the Prussian authorities had already been turning a blind eye to these fraternity rites for some time. Hamburg students had been crossing the city boundary into Prussia for the last seven years to perform their fencing rituals out of reach of the city police. They continued to do so for sentimental reasons, as if relishing the furtiveness, although a similar policy of leniency was quietly introduced in Hamburg, too.[23]

Students' Union Leader Heinrichsdorff and NSDStB Leader Albrecht Engelken now worked hand in glove with the new president of the Hamburg University Authority, Senator Ofterdinger, who appeared willing to cede to all their requests without consulting the rector or the University senate. On 5 April 1933 Ofterdinger banned all "communist, Marxist (social-democratic) and pacifist organizations at the University."[24] On 10 April 1933 the contentious clause preventing the Hamburg student body's membership in the German Students' Union was deleted from the University Law.[25] The legal justification for the dismissals of faculty was provided on 7 April by the national Law for the Restoration of the Career Civil Service. Although this was primarily aimed at the exclusion of Jews, the law also provided for the dismissal of all those whose previous political activity did "not offer security that they [would] act at all times and without reservation in the interests of the national state." A later gloss explained that this referred particularly to members of parties or organizations promoting the aims of communism, Marxism, or social democracy, but the vagueness of the def-

[23] "Keine Strafverfolgung studentischer Mensuren in Preussen," *Hamburger Tageblatt*, 7 April 1933; "Auf der Mensur," *Hamburger Fremdenblatt*, 18 May 1933.

[24] Protokoll Universitätssenat, 5 May 1933, UniHH C.20.4.

[25] Gesetz zur Änderung des Hochschulgesetzes, 10 April 1933, *Hamburgisches Gesetz- und Verordnungsblatt*, no. 34, 22 April 1933.

inition allowed the net to be cast very widely indeed.[26] Afraid that universities would turn the tables and use this imprecision to protect their faculty, the German Students' Union sent an internal memorandum, dubbed the "espionage decree," to its local leaders on 19 April, asking for lists of undesirable professors. The *Vossische Zeitung* managed to obtain a copy of the order and caused a worldwide stir by publishing it on 28 April. Professors who had merely insulted the National Socialists, or who displayed a liberal or pacifist attitude, were to be added to the blacklist.[27]

The Nazi students in Hamburg needed no prompting from the national union. Already on 11 April the NSDStB leader, Albrecht Engelken, had sent a letter to Senator Ofterdinger, the president of the University Authority, hinting that he would not discourage violent demonstrations if his demands for dismissal were not met. They were few in number but contained names of international stature. Engelken made a show of indignation that these Jewish professors had not already been suspended. The list contained the names of the economists Eduard Heimann and Theodor Plaut, the historian Richard Salomon, the psychologist William Stern, the art historian Erwin Panofsky, and the professor of Nordic literature Walter Berendsohn. The student leader called in addition for the gradual replacement of the remaining Jewish lecturers by German teachers.[28] This highlighted a problem caused by the purges: fully qualified replacements for sacked scholars could not be conjured up out of thin air. If every

[26] *Gesetz zur Wiederherstellung des Berufsbeamtentums*, 7 April 1933, here sec. 4. Text (in English) in Jeremy Noakes and Geoffrey Pridham, *Documents on Nazism 1919-1945* (New York, 1974), pp. 229-30.

[27] Quoted in Eduard Spranger, "Mein Konflikt mit der nationalsozialistischen Regierung 1933," *Universitas* 10 (May 1955): 459. Cf. also "Hitlerite War on Professors. Students' Black List. Ability a Minor Consideration," *The Daily Telegraph*, 28 April 1933.

[28] Heinrichsdorff to Ofterdinger, 12 April 1933, RSFWü V*2 α 523. Of the six professors named, Plaut emigrated to England, Berendsohn to Sweden, and the other four to the United States. Schulbehörde Hamburg, Hochschulabteilung to Rektor, 8 November 1948, UniHH A.1.6.

undesirable professor were dismissed without delay, the students would suffer as well, for teaching would come to a standstill in some areas. The naming of only six individuals was clearly prearranged with Ofterdinger. A confidential gloss accompanying the letter admitted that "the other Jews functioning at the University have a less pernicious influence, besides which some of them are for the moment the only lecturers in their field, so that they would have to be replaced by new appointments."[29] It was already clear that filling vacancies with reliable National Socialists might demand a difficult search.

The University senate accepted the suspensions without protest or comment. Admittedly, the corporate solidarity of the teaching body did become more visible, as always when outside intrusion caused indignation, but essentially the professors were reluctant to raise objections lest they, too, should fall from favor.[30] The senate was afraid that if it did not toe the line, the University might be closed altogether. This fear was naturally aggravated by the pronounced anti-intellectualism of the Party. Official denials did little to quell the distress. *Gauleiter* Kaufmann authorized Engelken to issue the following statement during the ASTA election campaign: "The NSDAP will not consider closing the Hamburg University just because the Social Democrats have no joy in this National Socialist stronghold any more. Rather the NSDAP will oppose all attempts in this direction in the strongest possible fashion."[31] When the DST's "espionage decree" was announced in the press the fears of the rector and

[29] Heinrichsdorff to Ofterdinger, 11 April 1933, RSFWü V*2 α 523. At the University of Tübingen a similarly cooperative partnership existed between the student leaders and the Ministry of Culture: the rector tried in vain to make an appointment with the Minister, whereas the student leaders had no difficulty whenever they wished to speak to him. Adam, *Hochschule*, p. 51.

[30] The question of the faculty's reaction to the National Socialist regime is discussed in Geoffrey J. Giles, "University Government in Nazi Germany: Hamburg," *Minerva* 16, no. 2 (Summer 1978), pp. 196-221.

[31] Engelken to Krüger, 20 January 1933, MicAlex T-81/259/5051117-19.

deans of Faculty were renewed. They sped to meet with the president of the University Authority the very next morning to ask for his protection. He promised them that he would condemn disruptions of lectures and would receive future complaints about professors only through the leader of the Students' Union. He also agreed to consult with the rector before making further dismissals under Civil Service Law.[32] The most that could be said about the reassurances was that they came better late than never. Most of the initiatives of the Nazi students were negative in nature, but they did make some effort toward filling the void that they were creating. It took the form of a search for a sympathetic professor who might act as the herald of the National Socialist revolution among the faculty. In Hamburg there was little doubt who that might be.

Adolf Rein and University Reform

Throughout the spring of 1933 the Nazi students worked hard to promote to a position of influence the man whom they considered to be the most well-disposed toward their aims: Adolf Rein, professor of modern history. As early as 1931 he had invited NSDStB members to his private "Political Round Table," at which one of the subjects for discussion had been university reform. At the beginning of 1933, Rein's essay *The Idea of the Political University* (*Die Idee der politischen Universität*) appeared as a pamphlet.[33] The timing of its publication was particularly fortunate, for the Nazis took it up immediately as the work of a pioneer. As so often, more people knew of it than actually read it, and the title alone sufficed as a fashionable slogan.

[32] Aktenvermerk Raape, 29 April 1933, UniHH A.I.6.

[33] For a discussion of several proposals for university reform at this time, see Geoffrey J. Giles, "Die Idee der politischen Universität: Hochschulreform nach der Machtergreifung," in *Erziehung und Schulung im Dritten Reich. Teil 2: Hochschule, Erwachsenenbildung*, ed. Manfred Heinemann (Stuttgart, 1980), pp. 50-60.

For most of the Third Reich, with the possible exception of the war years, Adolf Rein was quite simply the leading light, the *spiritus mentor* of Hamburg University. Even after the collapse of the Third Reich, people, reflecting on the University in the Nazi period, would think of Adolf Rein. Boldly ambitious and self-confident, he readily grasped the opportunities for self-advancement that came his way. Trained as a student of history, he was no political fool concerning the maintenance of power, and he shrewdly made a point of cultivating Hamburg's *Gauleiter* so cleverly that his enemies within the Nazi movement were often reduced to impotence. Since Rein's figure looms so large, it will be instructive to ponder for a moment on the intellectual background of the man in order to examine how a highly educated, well-traveled, and intelligent academic could allow himself to be persuaded of the acceptability and viability of the doctrine of National Socialism. At the end of the day, we must inevitably come back to Rein's careerism, but only via a tortuous route of intellectual self-deception that may reflect the thinking of other professors in Nazi Germany. It bears consideration in some detail.

Adolf Rein's family background provided the fuel for his burning interest in political education. His father, Wilhelm, was professor of education at the University of Jena and became involved with the leading Christian social reformer of the time, Friedrich Naumann. In 1896 Wilhelm Rein became a co-founder of Naumann's National-Socialist Union and a member of its steering committee, with special responsibilities for educational policy. The young Adolf had met Naumann as a guest in his family home and had as an enthusiastic eighteen-year-old campaigned on behalf of the local National-Socialist candidate in the 1903 *Reichstag* elections.[34]

[34] Much of the biographical information in this section comes from a well-documented private memoir sent to me by Professor Rein a couple of weeks before his death in January 1979. It was not intended for publication, and he requested me not to quote directly from it.

Adolf Rein's academic career received a setback when his doctoral dissertation was rejected by the faculty at the University of Leipzig. It was a work of cultural history titled "The beginnings of the individual literary portrait in German historiography and the beginnings of autobiography." Although Rein's supervisor, the distinguished historian Karl Lamprecht, had given the dissertation his blessing, the majority of the faculty considered the topic itself unsuitable for a history dissertation, and the thesis was returned to Rein for extensive revision. With remarkable (yet typical) self-assurance the doctoral candidate declared that such a compromise of his scholarly integrity was out of the question, and instead he set to work on a new dissertation with the title, "The participation of Sardinia in the Crimean War and public opinion in Italy." This time he passed with flying colors, and the work was promptly published in a series edited by Lamprecht.[35] Having been caught in the cross fire of what was essentially a departmental squabble, Rein was not enamored of the academic life and left to become a political correspondent in England. The feeling that negative criticism overrode positive idealism in the world of journalism brought him more disillusionment. A conversation with the historian, Professor G. P. Gooch, in 1911, finally convinced him to turn back to history and to write a book on the political historian, Sir John Seeley. Rein's study of Seeley's work, and of his philosophy, was crucial to his subsequent championing of the political role of the university. The Universities of Cambridge and Oxford produced the leaders of British imperial power, and Rein's visits to these institutions made a deep impression on him.[36] In seeking to

[35] Adolf Rein, *Die Teilnahme Sardiniens am Krimkrieg und die öffentliche Meinung in Italien (Beiträge zur Kultur- und Universalgeschichte, Heft II)* (Leipzig, 1910).

[36] Rein's father had also visited these universities as a guest lecturer on a number of occasions. Cf. *Geschichte der Universität Jena 1548/58-1958: Festgabe zum vierhundertjährigen Universitätsjubiläum* (Jena, 1958), 1: 476.

learn from their success, Rein came upon Seeley and his efforts to incorporate contemporary history and political science into historical teaching at Cambridge. Seeley described in his inaugural lecture as Regius Professor the pride of place that history ought to have: "If it is an important study for every citizen, it is the one important study for the legislator and ruler." He saw Cambridge University as "a great seminary of politicians" and historical study as "the school of statesmanship."[37] Rein's own "Political Round Table" was surely modeled on the similar "Conversation Classes" that Seeley held at his home for interested students (among them G. P. Gooch), in which he strove to build up a science of politics.[38]

During the academic year 1912-1913, Adolf Rein taught history at Syracuse University in the state of New York. He found American academic life to be a far cry from Cambridge and Oxford; there was little interest in and shocking ignorance about European affairs among the students. The offer of a position as assistant professor for European history at the University of Wisconsin, Madison, did not tempt him, and Rein returned to Germany and the University of Strassburg, where he became a *Privatdozent*.

The outcome of the First World War was doubly painful for Rein, as Strassburg University reverted to the French. In trying to explain the German defeat, Rein concluded that much of the blame must be placed on the Germans' attitude toward politics. In an article published in 1919, he wrote that the outcome of the World War had shown the Germans to be an unpolitical people. Germany had failed to provide proper political training for its citizens, especially regarding other countries. Their cultures had been studied rather thor-

[37] Sir John R. Seeley, "The Teaching of Politics: An Inaugural Lecture delivered at Cambridge," in his *Lectures and Essays* (London and New York, 1895), p. 328.

[38] G. P. Gooch, "The Cambridge Chair of Modern History," in his *Maria Theresa and Other Studies* (London, 1951), p. 319.

oughly, but not their "politics and the essence of (their) political life."[39]

The offer of a post as *Privatdozent* at the new University of Hamburg in 1919 was especially welcome, then, because of the city's strong links with other countries and the interest at Hamburg in colonial and international studies. Rein's mentor at Strassburg had been Professor Martin Spahn, who became in 1924 a German Nationalist Reichstag deputy and was long a popular speaker among student groups. It was he who formed in Berlin in 1920 a so-called *collegium politicum*, an informal group of students and faculty for the discussion of political matters. Rein was spurred on by this idea to develop his own thoughts on political education in the 1920s. He took a similarly elitist approach and sought to nurture a "political aristocracy." Eschewing the predominant concern with domestic affairs of most political parties and associations, Rein gathered students about him to discuss international politics and to inform themselves through the reading of foreign newspapers. Through his own scholarly endeavors, he was appointed to a new Extraordinary Chair of Colonial and Overseas History in 1926.

About 1931, he allowed the focus of the group to turn more toward German politics, but still with a view to the international arena. Politically, Rein's goal was to contribute to the restoration of Germany as an equal partner in Europe and an important factor in world affairs. Parties that promised to accomplish this drew his sympathetic attention. His invitation to National Socialist students to attend his "Political Round Table" evenings did not signify his approval of their party.[40] Rein did not support the NSDAP. Yet he thought he recognized kindred spirits in the handful of

[39] Adolf Rein, "Illusion und Politik," *Deutsche Politik* 4, no. 35 (August 1919), p. 277.

[40] The discussions during 1931 had examined the content of the nationalism and conservatism of a number of parties. Schorer and Riecke, "Nationalsozialismus als Geist," p. 116.

NSDStB leaders who came to him with their desire to politicize the university and to make students strive for the sovereignty of Germany in the concert of nations once more. The willing students he found in them were not typical of their fellows. It has been seen above that National Socialists in this period had little time for academic pursuits. But this, after all, was Rein's "political aristocracy," and if he could exercise some benign influence on them, then perhaps they in turn would have some civilizing effect on the brutal mob element in the Nazi organizations.

On 10 November 1932 Rein gave a lecture on "The Idea of the Political University" to the Hamburg Students' Union. It was evidently a success, for the author was invited to deliver it again in Göttingen on 16 December. In Hamburg, the president of the University Authority requested a copy of the text, and the rector asked Rein to lead a discussion with the faculty of the University on 13 January 1933. A lively, not to say stormy, evening ensued, which was attended by some eighty professors, an indication of the interest Rein's topic commanded. Ernst Krieck, the education professor in Heidelberg, wanted to publish the paper, but by this time it was already in press in Hamburg.

Rein's work seems to have been the best received of several contemporary tracts on university reform, perhaps because of its more philosophical tone and apparent profundity. The *Schwarzburgbund* fraternity association, for example, distributed free copies to all its fraternities and made it required reading.[41] In his book, Rein distinguished between three types of university. The pre-eighteenth-century "theological university" sought primarily to combat heresy by teaching the absolute truth of religious dogma; in the "philosophical-humanistic" university of the eighteenth and nineteenth centuries reason superseded faith as the driving force. At the time he was writing, however, people had lost some of their respect for philosophy and learning. Many now believed,

---

[41] Rundschreiben Janisch, 23 May 1933, BA R130/89.

particularly in the light of the increasing democratization of the Weimar Republic, that competence to lead or govern society did not depend on a university education.[42] Rein, as much concerned as the students by the loss of status of the academic world, was eager to restore the university (and more particularly professors of history) to a position of prestige. He claimed that what was called for was the "political university," dedicated not to universal concepts like faith or reason but to its finite environment: "Its core must be conditioned not transcendentally, but historically."[43] Its goals were to be "the recognition, the assertion of the Absolute in German form: German power."[44] He wished to make the university the servant of the state and yet remain somehow independent of it. His inability to resolve the contradiction, which remained as a rather unclear muddle, laid him open to misinterpretation and misunderstanding by the Nazis.

There were plenty of phrases to be found in the book that were music to the Nazis' ears. "Freedom *per se* is anarchy and therefore barbarity," he wrote. Calling down Fichte, Hegel, and Nietzsche to support him, Rein asserted that "the idea of false tolerance, the admissibility of all and everything, can be no more justified in the political university than [it was] in the theological or the true philosophical university."[45] The leaders of the nascent totalitarian state could find further succor in his insistence that "strictness and discipline in everything must be the characteristic of a political university geared to the reality of the state."[46] Such sentiments won him support among the students, who did

---

[42] Fritz K. Ringer, *The Decline of the German Mandarins: The German Academic Community 1890-1933* (Cambridge, Mass., 1969), pp. 44ff. and 66-67.

[43] Adolf Rein, *Die Idee der politischen Universität* (Hamburg, 1933), p. 10.

[44] Ibid., p. 11.

[45] Ibid., pp. 24-25.

[46] Ibid., p. 36.

not see clearly enough that Rein did not wish for outside influence on the affairs of the academic community but held that the disciplinary power was to be wielded by the professors themselves. In this sense university and state were to be no more closely linked than before. On the one hand, Rein emphasized that "the universities should have no share in the government of the state, not even the political universities"; but on the other, "scholarship cannot be ordered about, either from above or below."

How, then, did Rein see the special relationship between state and university? The nearest he came to explaining it is this: "When we bind scholarship to the principle of power, it is not, of course, to 'power,' insofar as it is arbitrary violence, but to 'power as spiritual essence,' as 'idea,' as 'creative principle,' as 'creative will,' and then it is of course scholarship which gives form to the spirit, the idea, the creative principle, the creative will of the state by raising all this to the level of consciousness and proving it to be reasonable."[47] The double occurrence of "of course," a device often used to mask an author's doubts, serves to make one suspicious that Rein feared he had not previously made it clear what he meant by "power." Nor do the vague terms of this passage help much, but Rein was in fact suggesting that it is the task of scholarship to support and justify the state. It is hard to imagine how a mathematician *qua* mathematician, or a mineralogist, might do this.

Rein's concept really applied only to the humanities. Within them he left no doubt as to where the state should primarily turn for support and which subject would therefore become the prince of disciplines: "History will again become politicized."[48] Although it is by no means clear, Rein's true position may be defined as one of support for the state when this is justified. But he never said this in so many words, and he indeed rejected the notion of the dependence of sup-

[47] Ibid., pp. 30-32.
[48] Ibid., p. 36.

port on the whim (more correctly, judgment) of the individual scholar as being precisely what was intolerable about the parliamentarian Weimar Republic. Like the majority of his professorial contemporaries, he wanted to be authoritarian and liberal at the same time but failed to find the balance between the two.

During the Easter Vacation 1933, Rein invited a handful of Hamburg Nazi student leaders to stay with his family on the island of Sylt, and further discussions took place on the changes that might be introduced at Hamburg.[49] The enthusiastic leaders saw in Rein one of the few professors to take a direct interest in their opinions, the most likely person to carry out sympathetic reforms in the University. They therefore made representations to Senator Ofterdinger to have him appointed executive head of the University Authority. Although Senator Ofterdinger was the titular head, as *Präses*, it was the executive head (*Regierungsdirektor der Hochschulbehörde*) who acted on behalf of the University Authority in most instances. His office was in the University itself rather than in the city hall, and it was he who usually made decisions on academic appointments and dismissals. To place Rein more centrally in the limelight, the student leaders tried to persuade him to make the main speech at the Nazi May Day celebration at the University. Heinrichsdorff informed the prorector that he held it to be "absolutely necessary in the present critical situation for the University of Hamburg to produce a revolutionary representative of National Socialist ideology." He particularly requested that the speech should be made by Rein, "who enjoys the quite special confidence of the Hamburg student body."[50] When Heinrichsdorff threatened demonstrations if his proposal were not followed, it was agreed that Rein, although not a member of the University senate, ought to speak.[51]

[49] Schorer and Riecke, "Nationalsozialismus als Geist," p. 120.

[50] Heinrichsdorff to Brauer, 27 April 1933, uniHH A.170.8.15. Sitzung Universitätssenat, 27 April 1933, uniHH C.20.4.

[51] Vermerk Rein, "Anteil an den Vorbesprechungen zur Feier des 1. Mai,"

An appointment of Rein as executive director of the University Authority presupposed the removal from office of his predecessor, Professor von Wrochem. Wrochem had already angered the Nazi student leaders by refusing to permit the hoisting of the swastika flag over the University. This took courage on Wrochem's part, for in Heidelberg Professor Alfred Weber was dismissed after ordering the flag's removal from his institute, and in Tübingen the university authorities left the illicit flag flying, precisely in order to avoid violent demonstrations by the Nazi students.[52] In Hamburg, the students did not intend to let Wrochem get away with such an affront. They determined to manufacture another insult by making it appear that Wrochem had ostentatiously absented himself from their May Day celebrations. To this end they planned to kidnap him. Wrochem was warned about the impending abduction by the more moderate Students' Union leader, Heinrichsdorff, and sensibly stayed away from the event.[53] His conspicuous absence gave Ofterdinger the excuse to dismiss him the following day, citing

27 April 1933, UniHH A.170.8.15.

[52] Adam, *Hochschule*, p. 33. Adam mistakenly refers to Weber as the rector of the University of Heidelberg at this time, but cf. Reinhard Bollmus, *Handelshochschule und Nationalsozialismus. Das Ende der Handelshochschule Mannheim und die Vorgeschichte der Errichtung einer Staats- und Wirtschaftswissenschaftlichen Fakultät an der Universität Heidelberg 1933-1934* (Meisenheim am Glan, 1973), pp. 54 and 66. Wrochem was apparently persuaded by the rector to change his mind. Heinrichsdorff to Raape, 9 March 1933, UniHH R.60.4. When the NSDStB wished to fly its own flag over the University in November 1937 for a "Langemarck celebration," Rector Rein consented, but the petition was refused by the *Staatsamt* of the city government. It based the decision on a ruling of the Reich Ministry of the Interior that only the national flag might fly on public buildings. Shortly afterward, Frick did give permission for the flag of the NSDStB to be flown on special university occasions only, provided that the national flag was hoisted as well. Rein to Kultur- und Schulbehörde, 3 November 1937; Niemann to rector, 9 November 1937; Zschintzsch to Reichsstudentenführer, 24 January 1938, UniHH R.60.4.

[53] Testimony of Frau Heinrichsdorff (in 1933 Fräulein Frank, the students' union typist), 28 March 1953, AFGNH Box 3752.

"a lack of confidence by the majority of the teaching staff and by the entire student body."[54]

Ofterdinger's measure shook the University senate to its foundations, disturbing its members far more than the dismissals of the Jewish professors. For Professor von Wrochem had worked with enormous efficiency and diligence and was unanimously regarded by them as the ideal man for the position. Their reaction, however, was typically ineffectual: *after* planning a farewell dinner and a collection for a gift, they drafted a letter of protest to Ofterdinger, stressing that they had never displayed the slightest lack of confidence in Professor von Wrochem; neither did the senate believe that isolated student action signified a general dissatisfaction on the part of the students. The rector registered his protest without suggesting that the dismissal be withdrawn.[55] The very same day Rein was appointed "Consultant on University Reform" to the University Authority, receiving promotion to executive director just over a month later, by which time he had expediently joined the Nazi Party.[56]

Something had to be done. The faculty was in a state of siege. Any student with a grudge against a professor was seizing the opportunity to make mischief. By the middle of May, Heinrichsdorff felt compelled to issue a proclamation calling on the students to refrain from instigating unofficial demonstrations and from writing anonymous letters and pamphlets.[57] Some of these activities were having grave consequences: Professor Kestner's house was raided by the po-

[54] Wrochem to rector, 5 May 1933, uniHH B.2.

[55] Raape to Wrochem, 10 May 1933, ibid. Protokoll 209. Sitzung Universitätssenat, 6 May 1933, uniHH C.20.4.

[56] Rein's NSDAP membership dated from 1 May 1933 (though such dates are not always accurate). Rein himself wrote that "Senator Ofterdinger, who at the end of April repeatedly asked my advice on university affairs . . . held it desirable for the continuation of my advisory capacity that I join the Party." Statement appended to questionnaire for Military Government of Germany, 21 June 1945, HB personnel file Rein.

[57] Heinrichsdorff, "Aufruf an die Studentenschaft der Hamburgischen Universität," n.d., uniHH 0.10.3.5.

121

lice, "on the grounds of (his) alleged communist sympa-
thies," as was that of Professor Salomon, "apparently
because of a false accusation."[58] The response of the senate
to all this was that it had better take positive steps on the
reform of the University, for "in the light of the present
situation firm and concerted action is necessary. This action
must be in the hands of the rector and senate."[59] Lengthy
discussions led to the adoption of a plan to introduce an
interdisciplinary "Political Faculties Group" (*Politische
Fachgemeinschaft der Fakultäten*), which had formed the
one concrete proposal of Rein's book. Indeed, the senate had
little choice but to give the scheme a trial run, for it now
enjoyed national acclaim, and Rein himself had recently
urged its introduction in Hamburg in the students' newspaper.[60]

The implementation of Rein's plan would be a useful response to the charges that professors were actually hindering
the realization of the "political university" for which the
students had been fighting. Heinrichsdorff had no illusions
about the lack of enthusiasm toward National Socialism on
the part of most professors, and his May Day speech contained remarks of an insulting nature.[61] This arrogant tone
alienated even some of the otherwise sympathetic profes-

[58] Protokoll Sitzung der Philosophischen Fakultät, 6 May 1933, Akten
der Philosophischen Fakultät der Universität Hamburg (UniHH Phil); Protokoll Universitätssenat, 15 June 1933, UniHH C.20.4.

[59] Before amendment, this minute had read rather unrealistically: "This
action must remain, now as before, in the hands of. . . ." Cf. copy of minutes
in UniHH A.1.6; Protokoll Universitätssenat, 27 April 1933, UniHH
C.20.4.

[60] Adolf Rein, "Die Gestalt der politischen Universität," *Hamburger
Universitäts-Zeitung* 15, no. 2 (22 May 1933), pp. 17-20. The whole issue
was devoted to "The Political University." Moreover, Rein had been elected
on 12 April to the Commission for University Reform of the German Rectors' Conference. Protokoll Sitzung der Philosophischen Fakultät, 29 April
1933, UniHH Phil.

[61] Draft of Heinrichsdorff's speech in UniHH A.170.8.15. Some of the
harsher remarks were removed at the rector's insistence, but others crept
in.

sors. Professor Degkwitz—an early, though lapsed, Party member who had participated in Hitler's "Beer Hall Putsch" in 1923—complained to Heinrichsdorff the following day. He resented being marked down as a second-class patriot simply because he did not "wear a Party badge and [stood] at a place where different weapons [were] demanded." Students still had the duty to listen to people like him.[62] Degkwitz, like other professors, wanted to regain the confidence of the students. The majority of them had simply no idea how this might be accomplished. Only a very small number, like the education professor Gustaf Deuchler, curried favor with the students by donning a storm trooper's uniform and "surround[ing] himself with sa men, whose jackboots resounded through the corridors of the Education Department."[63] Most felt that university reform could be achieved without prostituting themselves in such an ostentatious and undignified manner. A similar conservatism regarding the master-scholar relationship may be seen at the University of Rostock, where the rector announced that all National Socialists, faculty and students alike, should address each other as "comrade" and use the familiar "du." The shocked professors forced him to rescind the order at once.[64] In Hamburg, the "political university" scheme, widely represented

[62] Degkwitz to Heinrichsdorff, 2 May 1933, UniHH A.1.6. Rudolf Degkwitz had served in the 18th Bavarian Reserve Infantry Regiment with Rudolf Hess. He participated regularly in early meetings of the Nazi Party but did not join after the Beer Hall Putsch. He became well known in the University of Hamburg during 1933 for his scurrilous remarks against the regime. On 19 June 1933 he was suspended by Ofterdinger for six months, "arising from complaints handed in about political remarks." At the same time, the Party rejected his application for membership, as it did again in 1937 and 1940. Aktennotiz Rein, 19 June 1933; Urteil Volksgerichtshof, 24 February 1944, HB personnel file Degkwitz. See also below, chap. 7, n. 140.

[63] Gutachten Flitner über Deuchler, 10 November 1950, HB personnel file Deuchler.

[64] Ruth Carlsen, "Zum Prozess der Faschisierung und zu den Auswirkungen der faschistischen Diktatur auf die Universität Rostock 1932-1935" (Ph.D. diss., Rostock, 1965), p. 111.

as the very thing the new age demanded, offered itself as a solution. If this were set up successfully in Hamburg, the professors would not only bask in the gratitude and admiration of the Nazis, but they would be hailed as trailblazers in the educational world. During the summer the preparations for Rein's Political Faculties Group began in earnest. Rein wanted the Group to have the status of a Faculty in its own right, and though it never achieved this, its classes and seminars were planned and controlled by a quasi-Faculty committee of (usually) twelve professors, whose chairman was referred to unofficially as the Dean and even had an appropriate chain of office.[65]

The lecture list for the winter semester of 1933-1934 made a show of the lectures provided within the Group, but the vast majority of these were the regular courses of the Faculties, listed separately under the heading of "general political lectures." There were, however, three special courses given by the Group: (1) The Policies of National Socialism, (2) Studies of the German Culture and *Volk*, and (3) The Political and Economic Problems of Asia. These were not normal public lectures, for the students had to apply at the Political Education Department of the Students' Union to be enrolled. The courses were to be counted as an integral part of the ideological indoctrination of the student, and records of participation were kept.[66] The student leaders ad-

[65] The registrar's office of the University still has the medallion, which bears the inscription "Hansische Universität. Politische Fachgemeinschaft" around a large swastika. The University was given the "Hanseatic" epithet at the end of 1935 to underline its overseas and colonial concerns. Cf. Rein's speech, "Bismarcks Stellung zur Kolonialpolitik," 30 January 1936, UniHH A.170.6.15.

[66] In some states "political" lectures were compulsory. Students in Baden were obliged to spend not less than five hours per week in lectures on German culture, war studies, and racial studies. Rundschreiben Kultusminister Baden A 30736, 3 November 1933, UniHH C.51.1. For the course offerings in Hamburg, see Universität Hamburg (ed.), *Verzeichnis der Vorlesungen, Wintersemester 1933/34* (Hamburg, 1933), pp. 57ff. For the difficulties of drawing conclusions about content from the mere titles, see Giles, "University Government," pp. 211ff.

mitted again that "in the NSDStB a regular and systematic schooling has not been achieved" because they had been bogged down with purely administrative tasks.[67] The initiative of the University was therefore welcomed by them. The professors themselves were eager to "cooperate in the political education of the students," or rather they saw themselves as the only people suitable and qualified to supervise this task.[68] To allay suspicions that the faculty were trying to exclude student influence, Rein willingly met the request of the NSDStB leaders that they be included in the planning of the political education courses, and he set up another body, the Political College (*Politisches Kolleg*) to coordinate ideological training. The student leaders were delighted with this fillip of a faculty-student consultative committee, though in fact it only met twice.[69]

The Political Faculties Group seemed soon to forget its prime concern with students and became more introspective. The fear still lingered that universities in general might be closed down by the Nazis and replaced by training camps on the one hand, and entirely separate research institutes on the other, if the universities could not prove their worth by demonstrating the importance of their contribution to the education of the youth in Nazi Germany.[70] After February 1934, the Group concentrated its efforts increasingly on faculty seminars, in which lecturers read papers to show how "relevant" they were making their subjects. The responsibility for student instruction was passed gradually back to the Faculties.

Apart from the apparent concession offered to the students

[67] Protokoll Sitzung Politisches Kolleg, 15 December 1933, UniHH C.51.1. The sentiment that the NSDStB was "no more than an office" (*"eine blosse Geschäftsstelle"*) was also expressed in the previous meeting. Protokoll Sitzung Politisches Kolleg, 21 November 1933, UniHH C.51.

[68] Bericht über die Bildung der "Politischen Fachgemeinschaft," n.d., UniHH C.51.

[69] Protokolle Sitzungen Politische Fachgemeinschaft, 3 and 13 November 1933, UniHH C.51.1.

[70] Auszug aus den Verhandlungen der 1. wissenschaftlichen Sitzung der Politischen Fachgemeinschaft, 16 February 1934, ibid.

in the form of the Political Faculties Group, which was in reality a professorial attempt at self-assertion, the student leaders found that they were not able to have their way as much as they had hoped. "Their" executive director, Adolf Rein, was not prepared to support them against senate or Faculty opposition. Heinrichsdorff demanded in October 1933 that he be consulted over appointments in the Medical Faculty, stressing that this was "an absolutely unequivocal and irrevocable" standpoint of the Students' Union.[71] But his strong words were to no avail. The NSDStB became furious when all attempts to push its candidate, Dr. Blotevogel, into the vacant Chair of Anatomy failed. Rein, who probably already had his eye on the rectorship, refused to intercede and risk upsetting the majority of the professoriate, even after "the most urgent representations" of the Student Leader and the Nazi Lecturers' Leader. He dampened the now-proclaimed enmity of the Nazi students with further concessions. In the University Law of 19 January 1934, he gave the Students' Union leader (along with one other student representative) membership of the University senate.[72] They would be allowed to attend senate meetings only in particular instances to be specified subsequently, but nonetheless the student leaders were delighted by this step forward.[73] They were also gratified by the constitutional an-

[71] Heinrichsdorff to all medical professors, 16 October 1933, stA Uq 3/1.2.

[72] It was generally acknowledged that the law was almost solely the work of Rein. Gesetz über die Neuordnung der Universität vom 19. Januar 1934, Hamburgisches Gesetz- und Verordnungsblatt, no. 15, 21 January 1934, par. 10. Cf. par. 15 for the similar arrangement regarding Faculty meetings.

[73] Since the senate was no longer the governing body of the University but merely an advisory council for the rector (cf. par. 11), the restriction seems petty. In fact, a student leader was not to take part in a meeting of the senate until 10 February 1937. This was the second of the only two meetings Rein called during his four years as rector. Cf. also Adam, Hochschule, p. 50, for the restrictions applied in Tübingen. During the war, the Reich Education Ministry found it necessary to remind rectors that they ought to invite student representatives to Faculty meetings, at least "in

choring of the Political Faculties Group in the text of the University Law. A further encouraging note was that the rector would in the future be appointed by the University Authority (effectively by Rein himself) and no longer chosen by an election of the senate. This held out promise to the students of a sympathetic and progressive "leader" of the University, as the rector was now to be.[74] Once he was in charge of the University Authority, Rein's *Extraordinariat* was converted into an *Ordinariat*—as a full professor he now became eligible for the rectorship himself.

Another conciliatory measure toward the Nazis at the national level was the publication, in the autumn of 1933, of a declaration by university teachers in support of Hitler and the plebiscite of 12 November, which called for an endorsement of the behavior of the Nazi government. It contained messages from the rectors of several universities, translated into four languages for circulation among the academic communities of the world, in order to demonstrate to them that the policies of the new regime, in particular its withdrawal from the League of Nations, were endorsed by the academic world in Germany.[75] One of the contributions was submitted by the newly elected rector of the University of Hamburg for 1933-1934, the law professor, Eberhard Schmidt, and consisted largely of a lamentation of the injustice of the Ver-

---

those cases where student matters are on the agenda." (Emphasis in original.) Mentzel to rectors, WA 690, 19 July 1944, uniHH 0.10.2.1.

[74] The powers of the senate first passed to the rector in Prussia, in accordance with Prussian Education Minister Rust's edict of 28 October 1933, "Temporary Measures for the Simplification of University Government." See Hellmut Seier, "Der Rektor als Führer: Zur Hochschulpolitik des Reichserziehungsministeriums 1934-1945," *Vierteljahrshefte für Zeitgeschichte* 12, no. 2 (April 1964), p. 105.

[75] A similar, though much shorter appeal was published just before the March Reichstag elections. "Erklärung von 300 deutschen Universitäts- und Hochschullehrern," *Völkischer Beobachter*, 4 March 1933. Cf. Anselm Faust, "Professoren für die NSDAP: Zum politischen Verhalten der Hochschullehrer 1932/33," in Heinemann, *Erziehung*, p. 40.

TABLE 3. Faculty Endorsement of Statement of Support for Hitler

Faculty	Percentage of whole Faculty supporting	Full professors	Tenured associate	Untenured associate	Privat-dozenten	Others
Law	36	6	1	0	3	2
Medicine	51	14	2	21	14	5
Philosophy	53	14	2	9	9	6
Mathematics and Natural Sciences	66	12	2	13	7	6
Percentage of each rank supporting		69	54	54	56	47

Source: *Bekenntnis der Professoren*; Universität Hamburg (ed.), *Verzeichnis der Vorlesungen, Wintersemester 1933/34* (Hamburg, 1933).

sailles Treaty.[76] In the list of signatories at the end of the booklet, Hamburg University had a clear numerical lead over all the other institutions. The 168 signatures represented some 60 percent of the Hamburg teaching faculty. The following table shows the signatories by Faculty and rank (see Table 3). This does not seem to be simply a case of careerism at play. What is immediately striking is the large proportion of full professors represented. Their names of course carried more weight and were intended to make the document more impressive for both the domestic and the international audience. But as Frederic Lilge points out, we cannot attach too much importance to the document, since "it is not known how these signatures were obtained, what exactly the signees agreed to, and whether they actually saw the text of the statements."[77] Certainly there is no mention whatever

---

[76] *Bekenntnis der Professoren an den deutschen Universitäten und Hochschulen zu Adolf Hitler und dem nationalsozialistischen Staat*, ed. NS-Lehrerbund (Dresden, n.d. [1933]; here the English section), p. 45.

[77] Frederic Lilge, *The Abuse of Learning: The Failure of the German University* (New York, 1948), p. 167. Assel took both statements at face value as a spontaneous expression of loyalty. Hans-Günther Assel, *Die Perversion der politischen Pädagogik im Nationalsozialismus* (Munich,

of the publication in the minutes of the University senate, the Philosophical Faculty, or the Political Faculties Group; nor is there evidence of any correspondence elsewhere in the archives. As the book was clearly produced in a great hurry (between the dissolution of the *Reichstag* on 14 October and the plebiscite on 12 November), it may well be that Schmidt or Rein alone drew up a list of names, eschewing the time-consuming task of gaining prior consent from so many people.

Factionalism in the Student Leadership

To the faculty it may have seemed that the University was trapped on the predetermined path of the inflexible Nazi juggernaut. In fact, the course of the Nazi revolution in the universities was characterized by confusion. The dualistic structure of the student leadership, where the German Students' Union was responsible to the state and the NSDStB to the Party, brought with it rivalries from the start. "Institutional Darwinism" pervaded the student world no less than any other sector of the Third Reich.[78] On 1 February 1933 Gerd Rühle had been unceremoniously dismissed and blamed for the disorder that had accompanied the stbo scheme (which was soon abandoned). His replacement as national leader of the NSDStB was Oskar Stäbel, who had been consistently loyal to Schirach when others had opposed

1969), pp. 114-15. Kater has recently followed suit. Cf. Michael H. Kater, "Die nationalsozialistische Machtergreifung an den deutschen Hochschulen: Zum politischen Verhalten akademischer Lehrer bis 1939," in *Die Freiheit des Anderen: Festschrift für Martin Hirsch*, ed. Hans Jochen Vogel et al. (Baden-Baden, 1981), pp. 64-75.

[78] David Schoenbaum, *Hitler's Social Revolution: Class and Status in Nazi Germany 1933-1939* (New York, 1967), p. 196. An important contribution to the literature on this infighting is Gerhard Hirschfeld and Lothar Kettenacker (eds.), *Der "Führerstaat": Mythos und Realität. Studien zur Struktur und Politik des Dritten Reiches* (Stuttgart, 1981).

him.[79] Dr. Stäbel now surmised that the NSDStB at last had the opportunity to concentrate all its efforts on the political education of the student body. DSt Leader Gerhard Krüger, however, believed that *his* organization should properly direct this.

The DSt kept secret its notorious campaign against "un-German" books until the very last moment, not merely from the public but also from the NSDStB. Only the day before the scheduled start did Stäbel send out an express letter to his NSDStB leaders, instructing them "not only to support this campaign but of course to take over the leadership as well."[80] Two days later the DSt posted in Berlin its "Twelve Theses against the Un-German Spirit" to prepare the way for the book-burnings. These included a call for "vigorous steps against the misuse of Gothic print," which only Germans ought to be permitted to use. The most offensive passage served as a public reminder of the enduring anti-Semitism of the student leadership, as it claimed that "the Jew can only think in a Jewish way. If he writes German, then he is lying." It went on to demand that the works of Jewish authors should be printed only in Hebrew. If a German Jew did publish something in German, then the piece was to be designated as a translation.[81]

Immediately, a conflict developed with the university authorities in Berlin. The rector, Professor Kohlrausch, found

[79] Stäbel had joined the Landsmannschaft Suevia fraternity in 1920 as a student at the Technical University in Karlsruhe. His Party membership dated from 16 October 1929 (membership no. 191919), though he had already been appointed as leader of the NSDStB in Karlsruhe during 1928. BDC, SA officer's file Stäbel.

[80] Quoted in Hans Wolfgang Strätz, "Die studentische 'Aktion wider den undeutschen Geist' im Frühjahr 1933," *Vierteljahrshefte für Zeitgeschichte* 16 no. 4 (October 1968), p. 358.

[81] Text in Herbert Michaelis and Ernst Schraepfer (eds.), *Ursachen und Folgen: Vom deutschen Zusammenbruch 1918 und 1945 bis zur staatlichen Neuordnung Deutschlands in der Gegenwart. Eine Urkunden- und Dokumentensammlung zur Zeitgeschichte* (Berlin, n.d.), 9: 486-87.

the text not only objectionable but absurd. He termed some of the statements "exaggerations, which are of such a nature that the struggle against the un-German spirit will be discredited rather than advanced. Furthermore, they are (even if unintentionally, as we were assured) testimonies of a disdain for one's fellow men, whom one may oppose but should not defame." Kohlrausch ordered the student leaders to remove the notices from the university. DST headquarters countered with a false announcement of the resignation of Rector Kohlrausch, causing considerable confusion.[82]

Stäbel, unwilling to sit back while the rival DST gained publicity at the expense of his organization, carried out a raid on the Berlin head office of the fraternity associations' interest group (*Hochschulpolitische Arbeitsgemeinschaft*) in imitation of Schirach's occupation of the central offices of the German youth organizations.[83] It was the German Students' Union, however, and its campaign throughout the country that remained the center of attention. In Hamburg the Students' Union obtained a warrant from the chief of police empowering the students to seize "harmful" literature from public and private libraries, such as the works of Freud, Marx, and Erich Maria Remarque. The blacklist also included works by John Dos Passos, Ernest Hemingway, Jack London, Upton Sinclair, and Jaroslav Hasek. The NSDStB, inexperienced in cultural matters, borrowed the list from the head of a committee of librarians whose purge of Berlin's libraries ("literary brothels") had been underway since February. The police themselves actually assisted in the raids in Hamburg; in other places, such as Halle and Würzburg,

[82] "Ein Konflikt an der Berliner Universität: Eine Erklärung des Rektors Kohlrausch. Die 12 Thesen 'wider den undeutschen Geist,' " *Frankfurter Zeitung*, 26 April 1933.

[83] The raid took place on 26 April 1933. Peter Stitz, *Der CV 1919-1938: Der hochschulpolitische Weg des Cartellverbandes der katholischen deutschen Studentenverbindungen (CV) vom Ende des ersten Weltkrieges bis zur Vernichtung durch den Nationalsozialismus* (Munich, 1970), p. 128.

a police official accompanied the students on their rounds.[84] The confiscations therefore occurred peacefully; in fact, many of the owners of lending libraries had already withdrawn the offending authors from circulation. The book-burning itself did not take place on 10 May in Hamburg, as ordered by DST headquarters. The event was not held until five days later. This may indicate some disagreement in the Hamburg student leadership, for it is significant that the Students' Union Leader Heinrichsdorff did not make even a short speech at the bonfire.[85] Rather, the NSDStB and DST Area Leader Schulze and the NSDStB alumnus Wolf Meyer spoke to the assembled crowds, the latter claiming the event to be "not empty folly, but an academic tradition hallowed by blood, the origin of which stretches back to the act of Martin Luther."[86] The Hamburg professors were apparently

[84] This would seem to point to an order from a higher authority, perhaps from Interior Minister Frick, whose support Krüger for the moment enjoyed. Strätz does not investigate this possibility and concludes that the DST alone was involved in the execution of the plan. Strätz, "Die studentische 'Aktion,' " pp. 363 and 348.

[85] Steinberg notes that one of the student leaders at Hamburg reported that it was "impracticable" to carry out the campaign there, which brought down the charge of sabotage. A letter from another leader the following day, however, stated that 1,000 volumes had already been collected. Steinberg, *Sabers*, p. 139.

[86] "Am Scheiterhaufen des undeutschen Geistes: Feierliche Bücherverbrennung am Kaiser-Friedrich-Ufer," *Hamburgischer Correspondent*, 16 May 1933. The fiftieth anniversary of the book-burning spawned a number of essays: Anselm Faust, "Die Hochschulen und der 'undeutsche Geist': Die Bücherverbrennungen am 10. Mai 1933 und ihre Vorgeschichte," in *"Das war ein Vorspiel nur . . ." Bücherverbrennung Deutschland 1933: Voraussetzungen und Folgen*, ed. Hermann Haarmann, Walter Huder, and Klaus Siebenhaar (Berlin and Vienna, 1983), pp. 31-50; Joachim-Felix Leonhard (ed.), *Bücherverbrennung: Zensur, Verbot, Vernichtung unter dem Nationalsozialismus in Heidelberg* (Heidelberg, 1983); and Stephan Füssel, " 'Wider den undeutschen Geist': Bücherverbrennung und Bibliothekslenkung im Nationalsozialismus," in *Göttingen unterm Hakenkreuz: Nationalsozialistischer Alltag in einer deutschen Stadt. Texte und Materialien*, ed. Jens-Uwe Brinkmann and Hans-Georg Schmeling (Göttingen, 1983), pp. 95-104.

not convinced by this, for they are conspicuously absent in the newspaper reports of the Hamburg ceremony, whereas their presence in most other towns was eagerly seized upon by the press. Recalling the reaction to the Nazi student leader's book purge in 1931, one may assume that they were as shocked by this as by any of the excesses of the Nazi students. Although they hesitated to show active opposition, they were not sufficiently intimidated to feel obliged to associate themselves with such activities, particularly since Adolf Rein had taken over the helm at the University Authority on 10 May.[87] Over the country as a whole, the campaign was a huge success, which redounded to the credit of the DST and Gerhard Krüger, for he had often been able to involve in the campaign not merely the NSDSTB but also a large part of the student body, including the *Stahlhelm* student groups and many fraternities.

Nevertheless, Stäbel soon gained the upper hand in formal terms through the creation a few weeks later of the Reich Organization of Students at German Universities and Technical Colleges (*Reichsschaft der Studierenden an den deutschen Hoch- und Fachschulen*), which combined the DST with a new body, the German Technical Students' Union (*Deutsche Fachschulschaft*). The latter was merely a device to gain control over (and collect fees from!) the approximately 27,000 technical students without wounding the elitism of the university students through a dilution of the DST.[88] The *title*, Reich Organization of Students (for there was in reality no organization behind the name), was a piece of pseudosocialist propaganda to give the nonuniversity stu-

[87] Strätz, despite his extremely detailed study of the affair, sheds no light on the reasons for faculty participation or absence. He merely guesses that the motive of the supporters of the campaign was either a fear of retaliation or an exaggerated nationalism. Strätz, "Die studentische 'Aktion,' " p. 371.

[88] A similarly elitist attitude prevailed in Britain at this time. Students in institutions of further education were excluded from membership of the National Union of Students until 1937. Ashby and Anderson, *Student Estate*, p. 63.

dents the appearance of equality of status with their university counterparts in the DST. Stäbel, as leader of the new umbrella organization, became Krüger's immediate superior. Yet the latter refused to be cowed and announced to his DST leaders at the Annual Conference at Aachen in July 1933 his own political education plans for the following semester. In the future all freshmen were to be assembled in residential communities (to be known as *Kameradschaften*) for the purpose of intensive ideological training. The "free students" would live in DST houses, whereas fraternity students would remain with their fraternities, whose houses would consequently be brought under DST control (with the designation *Wohnkameradschaften*).[89] The outcry of the fraternity associations over this unsubtle attack was only to be expected. Yet it was Baldur von Schirach who directly brought about Krüger's downfall.

Although Schirach had backed away from direct involvement in student politics after 1931, he still wished to exercise overall control. He was particularly annoyed by Krüger's refusal to kowtow to him. Krüger on his own authority appointed Werner Trumpf as his successor, as he was indeed permitted to do under the new Prussian Student Code. Immediately Schirach complained to Interior Minister Frick that the leader principle was being violated, since Frick had not been consulted about the appointment, though he was Krüger's superior.[90] Frick was persuaded to sack Krüger and make Stäbel the leader of both student organizations. Indeed Schirach succeeded in raising the ire of the Interior Minister so thoroughly that Frick ordered the Berlin Police President to arrest Krüger for insubordination. Stäbel, an SA officer, provided the assistance of an SA unit for this dramatic gesture. Krüger, who had been warned of his impending arrest, sent word to Ernst Röhm. The SA chief was so furious with

---

[89] Stitz, *Der CV*, pp. 223-24.

[90] Until the creation of the Reich Education Ministry on 1 May 1934, the Ministry of the Interior had certain responsibilities for national education policy in the Third Reich, including the appointment of the leader of the German Students' Union.

Schirach's machinations that he arrested Stäbel, called out two brigades of Berlin storm troopers, and threatened to occupy the Interior Ministry if Krüger were not immediately released. Only the hurried return of Hitler to Berlin prevented Frick's resignation and further unpleasantness.[91] The situation was no less tense at the Berlin University student offices, where rival factions faced each other with drawn pistols.[92] The impasse was resolved by a mutual exchange of prisoners and their subsequent release. Stäbel emerged from the battle as the head of both the DST and the NSDStB.

In Hamburg there were also feuds, though of a rather different, more personal nature. The radical but nonviolent Heinrichsdorff rejected the extremism of the SA students and found himself as leader of the Hamburg Students' Union at the head of a revolution, some of the methods of which he could not bring himself to condone. Whereas he had turned a blind eye to excesses before the seizure of power, he now became concerned that many possible supporters would be alienated by irresponsibility that appeared to be officially sanctioned. He first put himself on a bad footing with the SA students by dismissing one of the "old guard," Wolf Müller, from his post as ASTA Treasurer in April. The ASTA budget had been overspent by 2,400 marks due to the negligence of the officers. Although the highly embarrassed Heinrichsdorff tried to place all the blame on Müller's carelessness, the general feeling was that Heinrichsdorff himself should have been more vigilant and ought to share the responsibility. Several months of fierce arguments followed, which also involved the fraternities.[93] It took a special trip

[91] Letter of Gerhard Krüger to author, 2 December 1981; Gaustudentenbundsführer Gross-Berlin to Gau-Uschla Berlin, 4 February 1935, BDC Parteikorrespondenz Krüger. Also interview Giles/Feickert, 27 September 1973.

[92] Anonymous pamphlet, "Die sozialistische Revolution," 3d semester, no. 4, May/June 1935, ZStA Reichserziehungsministerium (REM) 872.

[93] Engelken, the NSDStB leader, was eager to replace Heinrichsdorff with an NSDStB member who also happened to belong to the fraternity *Niedersachsen* in order to win favor with the fraternities. Engelken to Schulze, 8 April 1933, RSFWü V*2 α 523.

to Berlin in November by the rector, who begged the national student leaders to find a formula to end the petty bickering in Hamburg, before Heinrichsdorff was prepared to go.

First Attempts at Indoctrination: The Kameradschaft Scheme

During 1933 the Hamburg student leadership lost itself in trivialities. No agreement could be reached on a plan for the consolidation of the victories gained. It is surprising that any advances were made in the training program that was the declared aim of the student leaders, and indeed progress was embarrassingly slow. Heinrichsdorff was beset with financial difficulties in trying to set up the *Kameradschaft* House, the residential community proposed by Krüger.[94] The plan to charter a ship for the purpose had to be abandoned, but eventually a house of more modest dimensions was acquired with the financial assistance of the University, albeit not in time for the start of the winter semester.[95] The goal was to accommodate from fifty to sixty students here, but the scheme was made voluntary, and by mid-December only "about 26 students had shown sufficient interest to enroll."[96]

The *Kameradschaft* (comradeship) idea was an extension of the Labor Service scheme.[97] Feickert and Krüger had now, with ministerial backing, turned the latter into a compulsory prerequisite for university entrance.[98] They thus ensured

[94] Heinrichsdorff to Feickert, 18 August 1933, RSFWü V*2 α 575.

[95] Protokoll Universitätssenat, 27 October 1933, C.20.4.

[96] "Einweihung des Kameradschaftshauses," *Hamburger Anzeiger*, 15 December 1933.

[97] According to Andreas Feickert, the term "Kameradschaft" was suggested by the Nazi philosopher Alfred Baeumler during a train journey that they shared when returning to Berlin from a meeting in Leipzig during 1933. Interview Giles/Feickert. For Baeumler's longstanding interest in such a scheme, see his speech dating from 1930, "Das akademische Männerhaus," in *Männerbund und Wissenschaft*, by Alfred Baeumler (Berlin, 1934), pp. 30-44.

[98] Rundschreiben Frick III 3382/30.5. II. Ang., 7 July 1933, UniHH 0.10.2.3.

136

that all freshmen would arrive at the university with the benefit of some ideological training. The DST leaders saw the risk in releasing their charges into the free-thinking world of the university. They feared rows of empty seats if students were merely exhorted to attend ideological lectures, and they strove toward compulsion as soon as this was practicable. This question of the compulsory or voluntary nature of ideological training was the most crucial problem for all the Nazi student leaders, and the failure to solve it satisfactorily contributed to the ultimate collapse of the political education program.[99]

Many people, like Rein, looked to the colleges of Oxford and Cambridge, which demonstrated to the Germans "the immense value [of] communal education," and the University senate itself debated whether to introduce a college system at Hamburg, during its deliberations on university reform.[100] One reason for this admiration of Oxford and Cambridge, apart from their output of political and other leaders, was betrayed in the spring of 1933 in J. W. Mannhardt's book on university reform: "The manifest proof of [their] success was shown by the World War. There the College men only needed a technical training in weaponry in order to provide without further ado excellent officers for the British Army, which without them would not have been so easily set on its feet, by any means."[101]

It was realized that the *Kameradschaften* would have much to learn from the fraternities, most of which had, if not directly educated their members, instilled an unshakable

---

[99] Cf. Geoffrey J. Giles, "The Rise of the National Socialist Students' Association and the Failure of Political Education in the Third Reich," in *The Shaping of the Nazi State*, ed. Peter D. Stachura, (London and New York, 1978), pp. 160-85, esp. pp. 180-81.

[100] "Kameradschaftshaus der Studenten," *Hamburger Tageblatt*, 27 October 1933. Protokoll Universitätssenat, 26 May 1933, UNIHH C.20.4. Rust also stressed his admiration for Oxbridge. Protokoll Konferenz Studentenschaftsführer im Reichserziehungsministerium, 26 May 1935, ZStA REM 868.

[101] Johann Wilhelm Mannhardt, *Hochschulrevolution* (Hamburg, 1933), p. 42.

TABLE 4. Occupancy of Hamburg University *Kameradschaft* Houses, Summer Semester 1934

House	Residents
Owned by students' union	
Bruno Reinhardt House (men)	43
Karin Göring House (women)	28
Owned by fraternities	
Burschenschaft Alemannia	12
Hamburger Burschenschaft Askania	10
Corps Franconia	8
Burschenschaft Germania	10
Landsmannschaft Hammonia	5
Burschenschaft Hansea	10
ATV Hegelingen	12
Corps Irminsul	5
Turnerschaft Niedersachsen	4
Turnerschaft Slesvigia	6
Verbindung Schauenburg	8
Corps Suevo-Borussia	5
Verbindung Thuringia	9
Verein Deutscher Studenten Strassburg-Hamburg	5
Landsmannschaft Wartburgia	8
Hamburger Wingolf	8
Total	196
Total number of students in first three semesters	514

Source: Rein to REM, 5 July 1934, ZStA REM 871.

nationalistic ethos in them. The Nazis hoped to harness these to their own educational program. Despite the initial ill-feeling caused by Krüger's clumsy advances, seven fraternities in Hamburg offered to set up fraternity *Kameradschaften* for the winter semester 1933-1934.[102] By the following summer sixteen were cooperating in the scheme, catering for some 120 students. Together with the seventy-one students in the Students' Union's own houses, they represented 38 percent of the students in their first three semesters, for whom the *Kameradschaften* were intended (see

[102] Heinrichsdorff to Feickert, 18 August 1933, RSFWü V*2 α 575.

138

Table 4). A typical day's program is revealed in a contemporary report:

6:30 a.m. Defense sports exercises
7:30 a.m. Tidying and housework
8:00 a.m. Communal breakfast, followed by march to the university
1:30 p.m. Communal lunch
2:15-3:00 p.m. Afternoon nap, absolutely essential because of the heavy demands of defense training
3:00-4:30 p.m. Study period
4:30-5:30 p.m. Free time
5:30-7:00 p.m. Ideological training
After 7:00 p.m. Special functions of the local students' union, the SA University Office, or the *Kameradschaften*[103]

One of the most important features of the student's education was paramilitary physical training. This fell under the exclusive control of the SA in September 1933. Hitler created the SA University Office to take over the duties of the Reich Organization of Students for a standard "physical and mental [training] in the spirit of the vanguards of the German revolution."[104] All students in their second and third semester were to undergo instruction, and a whole new bureaucracy was brought into being, in order to issue and control certificates of attendance.[105] In Hamburg office space was provided in the University for the local leader, Adolf

[103] Stitz, *Der CV*, p. 230.
[104] Verfügung Hitler, 9 September 1933, UniHH 0.10.25. Regular, nonmilitary sport had already been made compulsory for all students in their first two semesters in the spring of 1933.
[105] As well as full-scale military exercises, the basic training covered small-arms shooting, grenade throwing, and pack marches. Erlass Preuss. Kultusministerium, UI no. 67051, 28 December 1933, UniHH 0.10.25.

Puls, and his staff. Although they were officially students, they requested that their fees be waived because they would not have time to attend more than one lecture per week.[106] Cooperative as Rein was with the SA, he refused to allow Puls a seat on the senate, as had apparently been granted at most other universities, on the grounds that his Political College was now "much more important and significant than the University senate, since the latter is no longer the governing body of the University, but merely an occasional advisory council for the rector."[107] Despite the further insistence of Brigade Leader Bennecke, the Reich SA-University Office Leader (*Reichs-SA-Hochschulamtsführer*), on this symbolic gesture, Rein remained adamant and merely granted Puls membership in the Political College.[108]

Once the organizational framework had been established, the work of the SA University Office was stepped up considerably.[109] The Reich Ministry of the Interior announced in March 1934 that students would not be allowed to reregister after the summer semester 1935 without the requisite SA course certificates. It seemed that SA service was assuming greater importance than study. In working out its timetable for the summer semester 1934, the University had kept Wednesday afternoons and evenings free of classes, in accordance with the wishes of the local SA Brigade. It was therefore annoying to be told, just before the lecture list was going to press, that the SA had decided, after all, to use Thursday for student training. Despite the inconvenience, Rector

[106] Puls to Schmidt, 9 December 1933, ibid.

[107] Bennecke to Landesunterrichtsbehörde Hamburg, 21 December 1933; Rein to Bennecke, 3 January 1934, STA Uo 3. This statement from Rein came before the actual promulgation of the new University Law of 19 January 1934.

[108] Bennecke to Rein, 12 January 1934, ibid.

[109] It operated on an annual budget of 6 million marks. Cf. Albert Derichsweiler's remarks in Entwurf Etat NSDStB für 1935, 13 December 1934, ZSTA REM 907.

140

Schmidt decided that "no other course is open to the University than to move to Wednesday all those lectures and classes planned for Thursday afternoon and evening."[110] He realized that lecturers would otherwise be faced with empty classrooms.

Complaints about the demands of SA training arose from both students and lecturers, and in June the University Authority asked the Faculties to report on the difficulties experienced. It was discovered that students were frequently missing from classes because of early morning sport or attendance at special courses. Even when they were present, the training represented "such a physical strain that their mental efficiency is seriously affected."[111] Many students had missed so much work that they were obliged to postpone examinations, and moreover, a general drop in academic standards was observed. Stäbel himself admitted in the autumn of 1933 that "the past semester . . . brought a quite catastrophic drop in academic standards." He knew full well that the main reason was the endless round of extracurricular duties that the student was expected to perform, but Stäbel aggravated the problem rather than solving it: "The young student's time was so taken up, he was so overburdened, that he did not really get round to his proper task, his studies, at all."[112] One law professor reported: "In most of my two-hour seminars last semester I spoke almost alone, so little did the participants contribute to the discussion. In past years this would happen only very rarely. It seems therefore that on the whole either knowledge or interest has declined, and a certain lassitude plays a role with some of them."[113] In the course of the reorganization of the NSDStB

---

[110] Schmidt to all faculty, 9 February 1934, UniHH 0.10.25.

[111] Schmidt to Hochschulbehörde, 16 August 1934, ibid.

[112] Stäbel's speech, "Unser Weg: Entwicklung und Ziele des NSDStB," n.d. RSFWü II* φ 48.

[113] Eisfeld to rector, 31 July 1934. UniHH 0.10.25.

that summer, Hess found a welcome pretext in the purging of the sa (following the murder of Röhm) to dissolve the sa University Office altogether. By this action he tacitly acknowledged its failure, if not the harm that it was causing.

There were fewer reservations about the student Labor Service, probably because it did not interfere directly with academic work during term time. In part, it duplicated the work of the sa University Office in paramilitary training. Two weeks after Hitler had proclaimed his intention, on May Day of 1933, to introduce a general compulsory labor service before the year was out, Prussian Education Minister Rust declared labor service to be obligatory for all college students forthwith.[114] Students in their first four semesters were initially affected. All school-leavers from Easter 1934 onward had to carry out four months' labor service and six weeks of paramilitary exercises before they were allowed to matriculate at university.[115] Because of staffing difficulties— the North German district alone already had thirty-eight camps for male students and seven for women operating in the summer of 1933—the emphasis on political education sessions dropped somewhat in favor of military training.[116] The warm interest in the camps on the part of students from other countries led the Hamburg student leaders to designate a model camp, which foreign visitors could be shown, where the military aspect was played down. It was not, however,

[114] See above, n. 98. Text of Rust's speech in Berlin in Paul Meier-Benneckenstein (ed.), *Dokumente der deutschen Politik* (Berlin, 1935), 1: 247-51.

[115] An exception was made for prospective students of Catholic theology, who were viewed with the utmost suspicion throughout the Third Reich and subjected to various kinds of discriminatory treatment. Their participation in the Labor Service was left optional in the hope that they would not take part and thus provide fuel for further vituperation. Jewish or foreign students were simply not allowed to participate, even if they wanted to. Rundschreiben Reichsminister des Innern, II 3447/13.2, 34 February 1934, uniHH 0.10.2.3.

[116] Bericht Müller, 16 July 1933, rsFwü V*2 α 575.

entirely absent, and the leaders once observed that it was a good thing that two visiting British students understood little German.[117] Another reason for the neglect of ideological training was that the physical exhaustion of the camp participants made them not uncritically receptive to propaganda but often unreceptive to anything. A report from Halle noted sadly that the men could barely keep awake during the radio broadcast of Hitler's May Day speech![118]

The camp training was the student leaders' first brush with the problem of compulsion. The camps had worked well when they comprised a small group of enthusiastic volunteers. The members really had embraced National Socialist ideology readily and keenly. There was little sign of that now. As for encouraging students to become idealistic settlers in the rural frontier areas, there were no indications that labor service, even in Eastern Prussia, was having any such effect. The student leader there saw only self-seeking opportunists on the one hand and "proper little bolshevists" on the other who had developed "in their hearts a secret, deep hatred of the 'system.' "[119] It was a great disappointment to the student leaders to admit that the DST had not succeeded in making the labor service "the melting-pot of the German people." Though the Nazis held the reins of power ever more tightly, they did not produce from one day to the next the masses of sincere converts for which they had hoped. "Scarcely one of those who are now coming out of the labor service has become a socialist; they are all still bourgeois who have but one wish and see only one task for themselves: to finish their studies as quickly as possible and

[117] Frank to Feickert, 1 July 1933, ibid. Müller to Rein, 7 August 1933, UniHH 0.10.2.3.

[118] Baum to SA-Hochschulamt Berlin, 18 September 1933, BAFM DB Pol.Amt 1933-34 BIV16.

[119] Otto to Drescher, 21 August 1934, Library of Congress, Washington, D.C. (LC), Captured German Documents (CGD), RSF 489.

begin their career."[120] When the introduction of the general labor service came in 1935 with its own bureaucracy, it was without many regrets that the disillusioned student leaders relinquished their own responsibility and turned their efforts fully toward the *Kameradschaft* as the vehicle for political education.

Although the SA University Office had represented yet another authority claiming the right to educate the student body, there was every hope of a resolution of the chaos within the student leadership after Stäbel's appointment to the joint leadership of DST and NSDStB. The Party organization, it was thought, would now formally control the state body. Yet the duality was maintained in the new DST Constitution, proclaimed in the presence of Hitler himself on 7 February 1934.[121] Admittedly, on the central point of political education, the constitution indicated direct control. This was to be carried out within the framework of the German Students' Union (which alone had jurisdiction over *all* students) but was "entrusted to the NSDStB."[122] The appointment of the DST Leader lay in the hands of the Minister of the Interior, whereas the NSDStB Leader was to be chosen by the Party.[123] This arrangement was soon to have far-reaching consequences. For the moment Stäbel saw no danger

[120] Otto to DST-Amtsleiter für Arbeitsdienst, n.d. ibid.

[121] The constitution had been largely drafted by Krüger while he was still in office. The date of its promulgation had been postponed in order to secure the attendance of Hitler. Naturally, an amalgamation was the last thing that Krüger wanted in the summer of 1933, when he was striving to promote the independence and superiority of his organization. Interview Giles/Feikkert. Rust had supported the independence of the DST in a letter to Frick on 13 July 1933, quoted in Steinberg, *Sabers*, p. 143.

[122] Text of the DST constitution and the similar one for the *Deutsche Fachschulschaft* in Wilhelm Frick, *Student im Volk: Völkische Aufgaben der Hochschulen* (Langensalza, 1934), pp. 20ff.

[123] The leader of the Reich Organization of Students was also appointed exclusively by the Minister of the Interior now. Ibid., p. 19. Stäbel's appointment as *Reichsschaftsführer* had been made, however, by Frick and Hess jointly.

because the combination of offices in his own person was reflected at the local level as well. Since it became clear that one of the main hindrances to the training program was the sheer volume of paperwork to be completed, he even went so far as to order a splitting of the DSt and NSDStB at the local level so that the latter might be free from all the bureaucratic drudgery to carry out its pedagogical tasks: "The danger of an overlapping of particular tasks and the usual concomitant arguments between two departments—as was previously common at the universities before the takeover of the DSt by the Reich Leader of the NSDStB—is for the following reasons no longer possible: the former squabbles resulted from the presence of two supreme offices, the DSt and the NSDStB leadership, which were more or less independent of each other, and showed no concern for each other in the publication of orders. This central reason is removed for the future by the combination of offices. . . ."[124] The marriage, however, was not yet permanent.

On 1 May 1934, a Reich Education Ministry was formed with Prussian Education Minister Rust at its head, and Stäbel immediately ran into difficulties. He failed to establish the good working relationship with Rust that he had enjoyed with Frick. Rust, in securing areas of influence for his brand-new ministry, clearly viewed unwillingly the *de facto* Party suzerainty over the student body, which left him personally with little effective control. Stäbel was forced to hand over the DSt leadership to his deputy, Heinz Zähringer, on 26 May 1934, and Rust forbade the former to meddle any further in DSt affairs.[125] It was now discovered by Zähringer that Stäbel had been misappropriating an estimated 1,900 marks per

---

[124] Denkschrift Stäbel, 16 April 1934, MicAlex T-81/236/5020685-87.

[125] Horst Bernhardi, "Die Göttinger Burschenschaft 1933 bis 1945: Ein Beitrag zur studentischen Geschichte in der nationalsozialistischen Zeit," in *Darstellungen und Quellen zur Geschichte der deutschen Einheitsbewegung im neunzehnten und zwanzigsten Jahrhundert*, ed. Paul Wentzcke (Heidelberg, 1957), 1: 214.

month from DST funds to maintain his lavish life style.[126] Stäbel already had a monthly income of 600 marks as a Reichstag deputy. He seems to have reveled in the power of his high office, tyrannizing his staff with frequent threats to send them to a concentration camp. One of his assistants was constantly interrupted in his student government work and obliged to chauffeur Stäbel's wife round Berlin.[127] In the light of this unfortunate evidence, and not wishing to leave the split in the Reich leadership that had proved so damaging in the past, Hess deprived him of his leadership of the NSDStB in July 1934. He appointed a "University Commission of the NSDAP" to reorganize the NSDStB completely while he searched for a new joint leader.[128] Another reason for dropping Stäbel was that he had made virtually no progress with political education. He had also upset the fraternity asso-

[126] There were several instances of corruption during this early period of the Third Reich: the Nazi student leaders at the University of Berlin had treated themselves to seven (!) automobiles out of students' fees. Steinberg, *Sabers*, p. 143. Dr. Heinrich of the Reich Education Ministry later spoke of another case where three automobiles had been acquired. Protokoll Konferenz Studentenschaftsführer im Reichserziehungsministerium, 26 May 1935, ZStA REM 868. A chance, private remark in 1933 quickly led to the circulation of wild rumors about embezzlement by Gerhard Krüger at the time of his arrest by the Gestapo. Gaustudentenbundsführer Gross-Berlin to Gau-Uschla, 4 February 1935, BDC Parteikorrespondenz Krüger.

[127] Steinberg, *Sabers*, p. 143, from which he has omitted the spicier details given in his thesis. Cf. Michael Stephen Steinberg, "Sabers, Books and Brown Shirts: The Radicalization of the German Student 1918-1935" (Ph.D. diss., Johns Hopkins University, 1971), p. 746. After his resignation, Stäbel was put in charge of educational matters in the *NS-Bund Deutscher Techniker* and was made a director of the *Verein Deutscher Ingenieure*. On 17 August 1936 he was named "Reich Expert Speaker No. 1 for techno-political questions." Karl-Heinz Ludwig, *Technik und Ingenieure im Dritten Reich* (Düsseldorf, 1974), p. 130; and BDC SA Officer's file Stäbel.

[128] The *Hochschulkommission der NSDAP* was set up by Hess on 10 July 1934. Unfortunately its records have not survived. For more information on its foundation see Reece C. Kelly, "National Socialism and German University Teachers: The NSDAP's Efforts to Create a National Socialist Professoriate and Scholarship" (Ph.D. diss., University of Washington, 1973), pp. 194ff.

ciations, who found that they were no better off under Stäbel than they had been under Krüger, for the former also announced that the DST would take over control of their houses in order to supervise the obligatory *Wohnkameradschaften*. Many fraternities resisted Stäbel successfully, though in the face of his threats to have them suspended by the university authorities (over which he in fact had no control), many did decide to form a *Wohnkameradschaft*.

In Hamburg, peace was not restored by the appointment of Karl Minnich as Student Leader. The leadership split ordered by Stäbel did not take place in Hamburg, but there was neither harmony nor progress. Andreas Feickert, although now busily and efficiently overseeing the organization of the student Labor Service at DST Headquarters, commuted frequently between Berlin and Hamburg and maintained the close links that he enjoyed with the student leadership and the University, particularly with Professor Rein, who had involved Feickert from the start in the Political College. In the spring of 1934 Rein gave him an official academic appointment, "for the strengthening of the creative revolutionary spirit in the University" as "Secretary" of the Political Faculties Group.[129] Rein was especially keen to use Feickert's experience in the development of the *Kameradschaft* House at Hamburg.[130] The *Kameradschaft* House had, of course, nothing to do with Rein but was the direct responsibility of the *student* leadership. It was a typical attempt by Rein to gather every strand of control into his own hands. At the same time, Wolf Müller was given the post of DST and NSDStB Area Leader, with the support of Rein but against the advice of Feickert, who perceived that he would have a freer hand with the *Kameradschaft* House if he were the Area Leader himself. Wolf Müller was to cause untold trouble because, as Rein came to realize, Müller and

[129] Rein to Allwörden, 8 February 1936, HB personnel file Rein.

[130] Denkschrift, "Aufgaben eines ständigen Unterleiters des politischen Kollegs und der politischen Fachgemeinschaft," n.d. and unsigned (but with penciled heading "Feickert"), UniHH C.51.1.

147

Feickert were "as a result of the . . . internal student conflicts of 1933 such bitter enemies as I did not believe it possible for two young National Socialists to be." Müller soon ousted Minnich and made Wilhelm Dansmann Student Leader at the University, who very soon was also at loggerheads with Feickert. Rein commented: "To my horror I had to experience once again how enmity between National Socialist students almost completely crippled the work of the reshaping of student life."[131]

Müller did not endear himself to Rector Schmidt in his first major speech, in front of the *Gauleiter* and the entire University, by stressing how little the professors had contributed to the struggle for a National Socialist university and claiming that "almost none of the professors are National Socialists yet."[132] Further embarrassment was caused when the guest of honor, *Gauleiter* Kaufmann, noticed some students creeping out as soon as the meeting began and the attendance control was lifted. Kaufmann delivered them a stern warning and complained that 80 percent of the students were not yet National Socialists.[133] The following day the rector penned a letter underlining the intensive work being carried out by "an ever-growing circle of professors, whose concern it has been since the summer semester of 1933 to realize the plan of a political university, as conceived by our colleague, Rein, in a National Socialist way." He

---

[131] Rein to Allwörden, 8 February 1936, HB personnel file Rein. It is probable that Müller strove to preserve the joint leadership of the NSDStB and the students' union because he feared that a separate leader of the latter, such as many universities now appointed, would be played off by Feickert (at DST headquarters) against the NSDStB leader.

[132] "Arbeiter und Student: Ein Wille, ein Weg, ein Ziel. Ein hinreissender Appell des Reichsstatthalters an Hamburgs Studenten," *Hamburger Tageblatt*, 15 May 1934.

[133] Draft article "Altes und neues Studententum," RSFWü V*2 α 517. Kaufmann later complained that "not 10% of the students participate actively," in a speech to students on 23 May 1935. Quoted in Günther Weisenborn (ed.), *Der lautlose Aufstand: Bericht über die Widerstandsbewegung des deutschen Volkes 1933-1945* (Hamburg, 1953), p. 94.

contrasted their reforms with the "destructive personal squabbles" of the student leaders.[134]

The NSDStB national leaders admitted that since January 1933 they had gained little more than "rubber stamps and headed notepaper," conceding that "intrigues were legion in the student organizations for a year and a half."[135] The dualistic structure of the Reich leadership (with the added complication of the SA University Office) was undoubtedly the cause of strife at this level.

In Hamburg the fighting was of a different nature. It was a question not so much of which office should have which tasks but of how the revolution should be conducted. This became in the first instance a contest between the moderate "civilian" Heinrichsdorff and the extreme "military" SA group. The SA was employing physical violence for swift attainment of its ends. The SA leader recorded gleefully that one Communist was "repeatedly thrown out of every institute of the University of Hamburg by us SA-students . . . during the purging of the University of Marxist student leaders by the SA-students."[136] Heinrichsdorff placed more faith in constructive than destructive work. But it was Heinrichsdorff who proved to be wrong (and eventually he himself was virtually run out of town by the storm troopers);[137] violence brought fast results and did not, as Heinrichsdorff had feared, turn the rector and the senate completely against the student leadership.

It had still been considered appropriate to discipline an NSDStB member for a disturbance of the peace of the University for shouting "Heil Hitler" on the day following Hitler's appointment as chancellor.[138] But the professors were soon rushing with unseemly haste to endear themselves to

---

[134] Schmidt to Witt, 15 May 1934, UniHH 0.10.3.5.

[135] NSDStB-Reichsführer Albert Derichsweiler's first speech to his junior leaders at Rittmarshausen, 22 August 1934, RSFWü II* φ 319.

[136] Protokoll Vernehmung Minnich, 23 February 1934, UniHH Di.M.9.

[137] Interview Giles/Feickert, 27 September 1973.

[138] Protokoll Vernehmung Schoof, 1 February 1933, UniHH Di.Sch.3.

the students by granting their request for a political university. Many hurried to make some (usually superficial) effort at personal *Gleichschaltung* in order to represent their contribution to the new era in the best light and to ensure their self-preservation. One should perhaps not expect them, in the face of the rumored closure of the universities, to be anything but conciliatory toward the demands of a radical student body that had come to enjoy official government support. They no doubt convinced themselves of the sincerity of their rationalization of this as a desire to retain *some* influence on the academic youth, to guide and teach them as before. Adolf Rein was certainly sceptical of leaving political education to the squabbling Nazis. But although utterly intransigent on some matters, he was willing to share, or at least to appear to share, educational control with the Nazis: indeed, it was the latter concession that made possible the former firmness. At the end of the day the concessions by the university saved it, a shadow of its former self perhaps, but nonetheless still functioning.

An irreconcilability between Nazi doctrine and practice led the Nazi movement to function so chaotically: for the leader principle taught that power, to be effective, must not be shared but must derive from one source. Yet the dualistic structure of state and Party control continued throughout the Reich. The Third Reich opened up undreamed-of opportunities of high authority for many young people. In the scramble for position, in which there were far more frustrated leaders of society than there were influential posts to be filled, it was the most ambitious who survived the Darwinian struggle to reach the top. They were the very people likely to be most jealous of their areas of influence and most eager to extend their control at the expense of others. While these rival factions were busily trying to destroy one another the university, standing apart from the conflict, was able on the whole to hold its own, despite the setbacks that resulted from occasional partisan interventions.

Professor Rein (at right in top photo) at an "academic camp" of the Political Faculties Group at Schloss Kalkhorst in February 1936.

Daily sport (bottom) formed an integral part of *Kameradschaft* training. These students are members of the elite ss house in Hamburg.

A happy snapshot (top) of the DSt Leaders at Rittmarshausen in 1934, before their battles with the NSDStB began. Oskar Stäbel is standing ninth from right.

Derichsweiler's moment of triumph (bottom): Hitler comes to speak in person to NSDStB members at their 10th anniversary celebrations in January 1936.

Self-government by students ended in 1936 when Dr. Gustav Adolf Scheel (bottom) became Reich Student Leader, succeeding both NSDStB Leader Albert Derichsweiler (top left) and DSt Leader Andreas Feickert (top right).

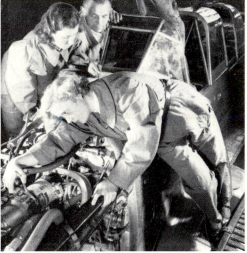

Female students contributing to the war effort both as air raid wardens (top) and as workers in an aircraft factory (bottom).

CHAPTER FIVE

Gown or Brown Shirt?

The purging of the sa in the summer of 1934 signaled the official denouement of the Nazi revolution. Hitler called for an end to the violent excesses of the *Gleichschaltung* period, in the hope of preventing further alienation of the moderate Right. But if an albeit uneasy peace returned to some sectors of German society, this was not true in the universities. The next two years saw the most bitter battles yet.

The students, once the vanguard of the Nazi seizure of power, were now lagging behind in their program of nazification. The fraternities were proving especially tiresome in refusing to submit to external control. The faculty were no better: behind the warm professions of loyalty to the regime, a devious regrouping seemed to be taking place. All that this really amounted to in both cases was a desire to act independently, within National Socialist guidelines if need be. The official Nazi organizations with the university could not allow this, for such autonomy would in their eyes undermine their *raison d'être*: leadership. At the student level, progress was further crippled by the struggle over which of the student organizations, the DSt or the NSDStB, would actually lead the students. A similar contest occurred between the state and Party representatives for the faculty leadership. The altercation between the Hamburg rector and the Nazi Lecturers' Leader typifies the relations between gown and brown shirt at this time.

The Effects of Nazi Polycracy on University Autonomy

A month after both the *Gauleiter* and the Student Leader had publicly complained of the lukewarm attitude of faculty and students toward National Socialism, the Hamburg University senate met to recommend a new rector to the University Authority. Rein's University Law had deprived the senate of its power to elect the rector, leaving it only the right to make suggestions to the Authority, which would appoint him without being "bound to the recommendation [of the senate]."[1] In a secret ballot, all thirteen members of the senate proposed Adolf Rein himself for the rectorship.[2] There is no evidence that they received any prompting from the Authority or from the outgoing rector prior to the vote, though the widely differing political views of the thirteen make their unanimity surprising. They probably believed that Rein would have more scope to realize his plans for a "political university" if he were the actual head of the University. By nominating him they displayed public support for the idea, regarding this outward politicization as the ultimate defense against the threat of closure, which always hung over the University. The appointment was a definite blow to the Nazi student leaders: Müller and Dansmann were trying to have the leader of the Nazi Lecturers' Union, Professor C. A. Fischer, appointed. Rein had already proved to be insufficiently cooperative. Their efforts proved fruitless, for Fischer had to leave Hamburg following an attempted sexual assault on a boy in the Hitler Youth.[3] Rein had provoked the antipathy of the Nazi students and lecturers by his refusal to give Dr. Blotevogel a full professor-

---

[1] Gesetz über die Neuordnung der Universität, *Hamburgisches Gesetz- und Verordnungsblatt*, 21 January 1934, par. 5.

[2] After the election, the handwritten voting slips were put under sealed cover, bearing the seal of the University, which remained unbroken until opened by the author. UniHH C.10.1.1. and C.20.4.

[3] Fischer's personnel file, the contents of which probably followed him after his move to the University of Königsberg, consists of a single memorandum noting his arrest there two years later by the Gestapo for a homosexual offense. A letter by Rein notes laconically: "Prof. C. A. Fischer left Hamburg at this time [autumn 1934] for various reasons." Rein to Allwörden, 8 February 1936, HB personnel file Rein. Further details were given to the author in his interview with Professor Rudolf Sieverts, 7 December 1971.

ship. He now arranged, in order to smooth things over, that the latter be appointed Fischer's successor as the local leader of the Lecturers' Union, a body from which he felt no threat.[4]

All seemed set for a peaceful start to Rein's term of office when, a fortnight after his appointment on 1 October 1934, a clash occurred during his first senate meeting, typifying professorial attempts at reassertion. Rein was determined to set the tone for his rectorship by demonstrating who was in charge. A discussion was underway about exactly who should wear academic dress at the rector's installation ceremony. The University possessed only a limited number of gowns for use on such occasions. Professor Mühlhausen, a representative of the Lecturers' Union, suddenly declared that "he would either appear in his SA uniform or not at all."[5] Rein refused to allow this, since it would destroy the appearance of corporate unity. Besides, if one or two members wore Nazi uniforms, it would appear that they were the only Nazi sympathizers on the faculty. A heated exchange followed in which Party members accused Rein of trying to suppress the wearing of the brown shirt. But the new rector stood his ground and insisted that, since this was to be an academic occasion, academic dress must be worn. Two days before his induction Rein discovered that Blotevogel, who had himself remained silent during the discussion, had issued orders to Nazi professors to appear in uniform. Two hours before the ceremony he found out that lecturers had been instructed by telephone that morning to absent themselves, on orders from the Berlin headquarters of the Lecturers' Union. Only a dozen of them obeyed these instructions, and the ceremony took place without incident.[6]

Only afterward did Rein receive an express letter containing the refusal of Dr. Lohmann, the national leader of the Union, "to appear at an event at which the warriors of the

---

[4] Rein to Allwörden, 7 February 1936, HB personnel file Rein.

[5] Protokoll Universitätssenat, 15 October 1934, UniHH C.20.4.

[6] Bericht Rein über Vorgänge betr. Talar- und Uniformfrage beim Rektorwechsel, 14 November 1934, UniHH C.10.13.

Movement are obviously unwelcome. There can be no discussion or compromise for the German Lecturers' Union in this matter. It will make certain that in the University of Hamburg, too, the honored uniform of National Socialists is accorded the respect it deserves."[7] Rein, never easily intimidated, armed himself with the support of the University Authority, the Reich Education Ministry, the Party's district headquarters, and the assurance from the local SA chief, Brigade Leader Fust, that he would in the future ban the wearing of SA uniforms on academic occasions. He dismissed Blotevogel as leader of the Lecturers' Union and demanded that Lohmann withdraw his slanderous remarks.[8]

No sooner had Blotevogel lost his post than an independent Nazi Lecturers' Association (*Nationalsozialistischer Deutscher Dozentenbund* or NSDDOZB) was set up, and Lohmann immediately gave him the leadership of the Hamburg branch.[9] In an arrogant letter expressing hope for mutual cooperation, Blotevogel now regarded himself "as the representative of the Party (in the University)," the equal of Rein, who was "the representative of the State."[10] The rector, pointedly neglecting to send a letter of congratulation, brushed aside the offer of Dr. Lohmann that the NSDDOZB would bury the hatchet if Rein reinstated Blotevogel as leader of the Lecturers' Union.[11] For the moment Rein was correct in judging that he had little to fear from the NSDDOZB, a body that, even by the following summer, could only boast

[7] Risse to Rein, 5 November 1934, ibid.

[8] Rein to Lohmann, 4 December 1934, ibid. Rein to NSDDOZB, 6 December 1934, UniHH T.10.7.

[9] Rundschreiben Reichsleiter des NS-Lehrerbundes, 1 December 1934, UniHH T.10.7.

[10] Blotevogel to Rein, 11 December 1934, ibid. Rein expressed surprise that Blotevogel was appointed as the local NSDDOZB leader on 30 November, although the organization was not even called into being until the following day.

[11] Rein to Allwörden, 8 February 1936, HB personnel file Rein. Also corroborated in author's interview with Professor Rein, 30 November 1971.

154

ten members out of an active teaching staff of over 250.[12] He had demonstrated to his colleagues that it was by no means essential to accede to every demand of the Nazi bullies. Rein's attitude set what the Lecturers' Association considered to be a mischievous example, but at the same time he enhanced his standing among the majority of the professors as a firm and responsible leader of the University.

The Nazis were late in forming a professional association for academics. The German Lecturers' Union, formed in 1934, was not comparable to the German Students' Union (DST). It began as a lobbying group for nontenured college teachers, although full professors were permitted to join. Like the DST, it fell under the jurisdiction of the Reich Education Ministry. There was no Party organization paralleling the NSDStB until the National Socialist German Lecturers' Association (NSDDOZB) was founded on 1 December 1934 as a subdivision of the National Socialist Schoolteachers' Association (NS-Lehrerbund). It became independent on 24 July 1935, rising above the Schoolteachers' Association to the status of a fully fledged Formation (Gliederung) of the Party, like the NSDStB. Hellmut Seier ascribes the NSDDOZB's relative lack of influence in Munich to its late start, but the choice of the exceptionally inept Walter "Bubi" Schultze as its national leader must be seen as the main reason.[13] Following his appointment, Schultze requested local student leaders to send him reports on the officials of the Lecturers' Association. Hellmut Nöldge replied from Hamburg that, although the work of the ten NSDDOZB members had not "extended beyond writing reports on professors and lecturers," he was anxious that the leader, Mühlhausen, should keep his appointment and that a new rector be found.[14] Schultze soon persuaded the Reich Education Ministry to recommend Mühlhausen for a full professorship.[15] Rein at

[12] Nöldge to Schultze, 3 August 1935, RSFWü V*2 α 573.
[13] Seier, "Der Rektor als Führer," p. 135.
[14] Nöldge to Schultze, 3 August 1935, RSFWü V*2 α 573.
[15] Nöldge to Schultze, 14 October 1935, ibid.

once realized that the purpose behind this was to make Mühlhausen eligible for the rectorship. He convinced both *Gauleiter* Kaufmann and the Education Senator von Allwörden that such an appointment was not financially viable for the Hamburg state, since Mühlhausen's post as Director of the Library of Commerce was not a teaching position and did not attract student fees. It is probable that the offer to Rein of a Chair at Königsberg at this time (which he refused) was prompted by Schultze in order to remove him from Hamburg.[16] At a national conference in October 1935, Schultze made scathing comments about Rein and openly plotted his downfall. When this reached Rein's ears, he had Mühlhausen summoned before the president of the Hamburg Education Authority, Karl Witt, who declared the unqualified support of *Gauleiter* Kaufmann and the city senate for Rein. They regarded him "as an excellent and reliable National Socialist, of selfless, upright and impeccable character."[17] Both Mühlhausen and Nöldge were ordered to halt their plotting.

It was not only Rein who had cause for grievance over Schultze's behavior at the NSDDOZB conference in October. The representatives of the Reich Education Ministry, led by Professor Franz Bachér from the Ministry's higher education department, felt directly affronted. Schultze, posturing as the

[16] Rein's refusal of the job offer brought an immediate increase in his salary—this *was* financially viable for the Hamburg state! Mühlhausen had apparently been earmarked by some Nazis for the post of executive director of the University Authority in 1933. It had proved possible to prevent this because he lacked the status of a tenured civil servant (*Beamter*), and Rein received the job instead. Cf. Nöldge to Allwörden (drafted January or February 1936, but never sent—there was no point in dispatching this long and bitter tirade against Rein after Mühlhausen's dressing-down on 24 February), RSFWÜ V*2 α 546.

[17] Mühlhausen to Reichsamtsleitung NSDDOZB, 24 February 1936, RSFWÜ V*2 α 546. This official declaration by the governor and city senate was prompted by fears that Education Minister Rust would be unable to ignore the constant criticisms of Rein "unless he received support from a definitive political source." Protokoll Senat, 12 February 1936, HB personnel file Rein.

ultimate authority in the field of higher education, claimed that it was the task of the state organs (i.e. the Ministry) to execute the decisions of the Party. He accused the Ministry of dilatoriness and threatened liberal use of his riding whip in the future in order to ensure compliance. Not only did Schultze refuse to withdraw this remark, but he subsequently confirmed in writing that the implication was indeed that he would horsewhip Rust's civil servants. The four ministerial officials at the conference were furious.[18] They wanted their minister to insist on a personal apology from Schultze, but Rust was lying sick at this time. They considered resignation but thought that such a gesture might aggravate the Minister's illness (probably his heart ailment[19]). They complained to Himmler, but he did not react. Three months elapsed before Rust returned to his desk in January 1936, and there is no evidence that he pursued the matter further, despite the urgent entreaties of his staff.[20] In fact, by April 1936 Rust had agreed that the NSDDOZB leader at each college should also head the Lecturers' Union: the new "Lecturers' Leader" (*Dozentenführer*) would be responsible both to him and to Schultze.[21]

Both the NSDDOZB and Schultze were very much the creation of the Nazi Party's "Commission on Higher Education" (*Hochschulkommission der NSDAP*). This was formed by Rudolf Hess on 10 July 1934 as a means of influencing educational policy. It was directed by Gerhard Wagner, a nature healer, and his deputy, a Munich specialist for venereal diseases, Professor Franz Wirz. Their penchant for medical quackery doubtless led Hess, who was fascinated by such things, to them. "Bubi" Schultze had treated Hitler's dislocated shoulder following his putsch attempt in 1923,

[18] Bericht, "Vorfälle bei der Führertagung des NSDDOZB und NSDStB in Alt Rehse am 11. und 12. Oktober 1935" (probably by Bachér), zStA REM 11887/2.

[19] Cf. Krebs, *Infancy*, p. 293.

[20] Vermerke Bachér to Rust, 13 and 16 January 1936, zStA REM 11887/2.

[21] Kelly, "University Teachers," p. 235.

and this was enough to give him a lifelong reputation as a medical expert, though he was in fact totally incompetent as a physician. He became the Bavarian State Commissioner for Public Health in 1933, on the strength of which he was appointed to an honorary professorship in public hygiene at Munich University the following year.

One of the Reich Education Ministry's criticisms of the Commission on Higher Education was this strong medical bias. It thought that the Commission generalized too much from its experience of medical education, which operated in a different way from other university Faculties.[22] Yet the main reason was that it meddled actively in the Ministry's own provinces. Since Gerhard Wagner was also busy as overlord of Germany's physicians (under his hat as *Reichsärzteführer*), Wirz was the driving force in the Commission. And Wirz was an extraordinarily vicious intriguer, even for the Third Reich. He tried to have the rector of Munich's Technical University, Professor A. W. Schmidt, dismissed because he had dared to propose a vote of confidence for Rust at the rectors' conference in May 1935. Informants were placed in university senates and Faculties, and pressure was applied to try to prevent professors from accepting commissions from the Reich Education Ministry or from adhering to some of its edicts. Wirz lambasted the work of the Ministry as "un-National Socialist" and encouraged the view that "things will not get better until Rust has gone."[23] Wirz's scheming went too far when he took up arms against the original head of the Lecturers' Union, Heinz Lohmann. The latter countered by bringing up before a Party Court the sensitive issue of Wirz's former marriage to a Jewish woman in 1928. The case dragged on for three years and almost ended in Wirz's dismissal from the Party.[24] By this time the role

[22] Bericht, "Hochschulkommission und Hochschule" (draft for Rust to Hess), n.d., zsta rem 11887/2.

[23] Ibid. and Vermerk Bachér to Rust, 6 December 1935, ibid.

[24] Kelly, "University Teachers," pp. 210ff.

of the Commission was fading because Hess had decided to operate through the NSDDOZB to influence higher education.

The Reich Education Ministry, then, was under siege almost from its inception, with various Party agencies seeking to trespass on its territory. Yet the lame-duck reputation that the Minister deservedly acquired obscures the frequent successes of his higher education staff in protecting their bailiwick. This is particularly true of their reclamation of the authority of the rector in 1935 from the importunity of the Nazi student leaders. An edict of 1 April 1935 emphasized that the leader of the student body at each university was not a free agent but was answerable to the rector.[25] The disciplinary code promulgated on the same day placed the rector squarely in charge of proceedings so that there would be no chance of arbitrary recriminations by the Nazi student leaders, who dearly wanted a monopoly of disciplinary powers over all students.[26] The record keeping that the DST had performed since 1933, filling out detailed cards on the membership of each student in Nazi organizations and on his progress in political education, was taken over by the university registrars in the interest of greater objectivity.[27] Furthermore, the Ministry ordered on 15 May 1935 that all student newspapers must be submitted to the rector before publication. Rust hurriedly explained that this should not be understood as censorship, but the aim of the measure was clearly to halt the accusations and insults that the student leaders had made a habit of leveling at the professors.[28]

[25] Erlass Rust, "Richtlinien zur Vereinheitlichung der Hochschulverwaltung," 1 April 1935, UniHH 0.10.3.4.

[26] Erlass Rust, "Strafordnung für Studenten, Hörer und studentische Vereinigungen an den deutschen Hochschulen," 1 April 1935, UniHH 0.20.1.1.

[27] Cf. Protokoll Konferenz Studentenschaftsführer, 26 May 1935, ZStA REM 868.

[28] Rundschreiben Kunisch, 25 June 1935, UniHH 0.10.14.1. Cf. also Bachér to Universitätskurator Bonn, 18 July 1935 (copy in Wiener Library, among press cuttings on German universities), in which the Ministry ordered that all news items about universities for release to the press must in the future

Although the Third Reich was not a monolithic state, its internal structure did not represent a straightforward two-way struggle between Party and state agencies. The situation could not be as simple as that, where there were several agencies claiming to represent the Party or the state. In Hamburg, for example, Rector Rein had succeeded in asserting his authority in the face of all-out opposition from the branch Formations of the Party because of the great confidence he enjoyed with the local head of the Party itself, Karl Kaufmann.

This is an indication of the dominant position of Kaufmann within the Hamburg District. The various *Gauleiter*, having fought so hard before 1933 to gain the reins of power, now wished to wield it unhampered by all external agencies.[29] Kaufmann was naturally suspicious of self-sufficient (and perhaps rival) organizations like the NSDStB and the NSDDOZB, which entertained direct links with their own headquarters in Munich, thus bypassing his own overall control.[30] It cannot have been too difficult for Rein to strengthen these fears in the eyes of the *Gauleiter*. Eager for as much independence as possible from Berlin's ministerial control, both of them saw that it was to their mutual advantage to support each other. Rein did not encourage membership of the Nazi Lecturers' Association, yet when the NSDAP began accepting new members again in 1937, he raised no objections to the applications of 160 University faculty and administrative staff—this was a profession of faith for Kaufmann, under whose direct leadership as *Gauleiter* the new

be relayed through the rector's office in order to put a stop to the "frequent, incorrect reports about events at the universities."

[29] Peter Hüttenberger, *Die Gauleiter: Studie zum Wandel des Machtgefüges in der NSDAP* (Stuttgart, 1969), pp. 107ff.

[30] Kelly asserts that the loyalties of the local NSDDOZB leaders lay more with their college than with their national headquarters. For Hamburg, at least, the opposite is true. Kelly, "University Teachers," p. 297.

party members would come.[31] It seems probable that this local cohesiveness of allegiance was stronger than elsewhere, in the mighty yet compact Hanseatic unit that was city-state and *Gau* all in one. Other universities that were not at the seat of a Party district would have experienced further atomization of loyalties.

Not all the applicants for membership in the NSDAP in 1937 were accepted. Nevertheless, a large proportion of the faculty were Party members. Adam notes that only about 31 of 160 faculty members at Tübingen after the war had not belonged to the NSDAP.[32] The profile of the Hamburg faculty is similar. Information was not available on 39 faculty members (18 percent) when lists were drawn up for the local denazification boards, but only a further 37 of them (17 percent) had definitely not been Party members, whereas 136 professors (64 percent) had. The differences among the Faculties are striking. NSDAP members represented in each case at least 41 percent of the Philosophical Faculty, 57 percent of the Faculty of Mathematics and Natural Sciences, 66 percent of the Faculty of Law, and an overwhelming 80 percent of the Faculty of Medicine.[33] It would be unwise to jump to conclusions about the success of the ideological contamination of the faculty on the basis of these figures. The majority of these professors were merely the

---

[31] Liste der das Hochschulwesen betreffenden Anträge auf Aufnahme in die NSDAP, n.d. (July 1937), StA Pa 4.1. Letters of consent were solicited, but many were less than enthusiastic. Professor Sieverts wrote dutifully that "if the Governor should come to the conclusion that I am worthy of initiation into the NSDAP and my assistance within the Party is desirable, and therefore my acceptance as a member should be proposed, then I shall of course be at his disposal." Sieverts to Kultur- und Schulbehörde, 11 May 1937, ibid. Another applicant, an official with the Education Authority, pointed out that even if he were accepted, his periodic attacks of gout might make it impossible for him to take part in parades and marches! Rabe to Kultur- und Schulbehörde, 10 May 1937, ibid.

[32] Adam, *Hochschule*, p. 153.

[33] Calculated from the lists in UniHH D.10.10.

Karteigenossen[34] who added a little prestige to their local Party unit and brought a little credit to the University but were otherwise quite inactive. After the war, the new deans of the Faculties, often former Social Democrats, were vindictive toward the true exponents of National Socialism in the University. But the notations in the denazification lists refer to only a few of their colleagues as "fanatical National Socialists." Many members of the Party were characterized as "not a National Socialist" and even in some cases as a "resolute opponent of National Socialism." Although one should not naïvely accept postwar apologies at face value, it does seem probable that a number of professors faced pressure from deans to enlist in the Party for the good of the University. Even if defined in terms of professional dedication, some personal opportunism undoubtedly played a part in the willingness to become a wearer of the Party badge (popularly known as a "safety pin").[35] Whatever the motives of these academics, the fact remains that by their acceptance of Party membership they offered a public affirmation of the regime and of the policies of Hitler. One might also argue that those who remained inactive in the Party were no less reprehensible than the fanatics, for they wasted an opportunity to exercise whatever moderating influence they might have brought to bear, at least in the local setting, by asserting their beliefs.

Factionalism in the Student Body

Rein's relations with the NSDStB at the time of the "gown or brown shirt" dispute were no less strained than those with the Nazi faculty leaders. Students had participated in his induction ceremony, and indeed forty-six members of

[34] This was a pun common in Party circles on the official title of all Party members, *Parteigenosse* (Party comrade). *Kartei* is a card index file, the only place where the membership of such people was apparent.

[35] Edward Y. Hartshorne, *German Youth and the Nazi Dream of Victory*, no. 12 in the series America in a World at War (New York, 1941), p. 31.

the *Kameradschaft* House had marched in brown shirts with the academic procession to the podium (a fact that Rein pointedly communicated to the Lecturers' Union headquarters as evidence of his good will).[36] Yet NSDStB Leader Dansmann had written a sympathetic letter to Blotevogel promising that the student body would boycott future events where similar disputes arose.[37] This alone was enough to incur Rein's displeasure, but there was now a much more serious bone of contention between them, centering again on the *Kameradschaft* House.

At the beginning of 1934, the student Hans Leitner had been specially matriculated in mid-semester at the request of the German Students' Union (probably through Feickert) in order to assist the *Kameradschaft* House leadership.[38] The SA University Office discovered in the summer semester 1934 that he had signed an ASTA election list in support of a Communist student group in 1932, and this led to his dismissal.[39] Leitner had become extremely popular among the members of the *Kameradschaft* House, however, and they came out in open defiance against his removal. A picture of Bruno Reinhardt, after whom their house had been named, was removed and replaced by a sign saying "Hans Leitner Hall," and the Nazi flag was relegated to the lavatory. NSDStB Leader Dansmann attempted to restore order by closing down the house.[40] But thirty-four of the members moved *en bloc* to the fraternity *Niedersachsen*, which set itself up as a fraternity *Kameradschaft*.[41] Dansmann ordered that fraternities could not accept closed groups of students from the

[36] Telegram Rein to Deutsche Dozentenschaft, 6 November 1934, UniHH C.10.13.

[37] Dansmann to Blotevogel, 5 November 1934, ibid.

[38] Schmidt to Hamburger Studentenschaft, 11 January 1934, RSFWü V*2 α 516.

[39] Engelbrecht to Gestapo, 4 July 1935, RSFWü V*2 α 573.

[40] Kreisgericht Winterhude, Beschluss gegen Rolf Thiede, 12 April 1937, RSFWü V*2 α 571.

[41] Arbeitsbericht des Kameradschaftshausführers Ochsenius, 22 January 1935, RSFWü V*2 α 537.

Kameradschaft House, "for then the danger continues to exist that a new cell directed against State and Party would be formed."[42] He was frustrated by Rein, who, armed with the latest edict of Minister Rust stating that no force was to be used in the question of *Kameradschaft* membership, supported the students' freedom of choice. Rein lost his last shred of confidence in Dansmann as student leader on discovering that he had even called in the Gestapo to try to concoct charges of "Marxist agitation." "I do not," remarked Rein, "consider this to be the proper way for young academicians to settle differences among themselves."[43]

Dansmann thereupon shut down the *Kameradschaft Niedersachsen.* Undaunted, its members formed themselves into an *SS-Mannschaft.* These were special residential groups of students under the direct jurisdiction of the ss rather than the student leader. Their members regarded them as sanctuaries from the tiresomeness of the other Party agencies. With some arrogance they also believed that they, not the NSDStB, would form the true student elite.[44] After the mass walk-out, the official *Kameradschaft* House struggled in vain to find new members.[45] With a mere twenty-two places filled, the House was losing 600 marks a month and therefore had to be closed down at the end of the winter

---

[42] Dansmann to Rein, 26 November 1934, UniHH C.10.14.

[43] Rein to Roosch, 4 December 1934, ibid.

[44] Wilhelm Formel told the author that the *SS-Mannschaft* that he had joined in Cologne at this time consisted exclusively of former Youth Movement members who had deliberately formed the ss unit in order to escape the control of the NSDStB and the Party. Interview Giles/Formel 7 March 1972. The members in Hamburg regarded themselves as an elite in social as well as racial terms. In April 1939 they decided that it befitted them to take riding lessons, and they requested a subsidy from the University (which was refused). Hinrichs to Gundert, 19 April 1939, UniHH 0.10.15.

[45] The House leader, Ochsenius, complained of the "egoistic indolence" of the students in general. Arbeitsbericht Ochsenius, 22 January 1935, RSFWü V*2 α 537. The *Kameradschaft* House at the University of Berlin was likewise only half full at this time and was suffering from the considerable loss of income from rent. Studentenschaft Universität Berlin to Reich Education Ministry, 22 November 1934, ZStA REM 871.

semester. Ironically, it was the new *SS-Mannschaft* that now bought the house from which Dansmann had struggled so hard to expel the group.

With the continued incidence of such pettiness among the students, Rein's unfavorable reports to the *Gauleiter* ruined their credibility. The close relations that the "smooth diplomat" Rein enjoyed with the leaders of the city administration were irksome in the extreme to the leaders of both the Nazi Students' and Lecturers' Associations, who at this stage simply did not have the *Gauleiter*'s ear.[46] The rector was concerned above all with the success of the University, and he believed that it would be disastrous for too much influence to be entrusted to the incompetent hands of the NSDStB and NSDDOZB. In his eyes the members of the latter had dubious academic credentials (they were *"nichtarrivierte Gelehrte"*[47]). Yet the scholarly success of the University was a very important matter of prestige for the city, particularly in its attempts to establish Hamburg as Germany's sole "gateway to the colonies" when the time came, not only as a port but also as the training center for colonial service.[48] The NSDStB and NSDDOZB manifestly lacked a clear concept for the future development of the University, and thus it was not difficult to justify their exclusion from uni-

[46] "Not a man of honest, open words, but a smooth diplomat" was the characterization of Rein given by Dr. Werner Burmeister, a lecturer in the History of Art. Burmeister was peeved at his slow advancement in the University, having expected Erwin Panofsky's chair when the latter was forced to emigrate to the United States. Burmeister made a number of slanderous remarks about Rein's leadership of the University, which only made matters worse for him. Protokoll Vernehmung Burmeister durch Staatsanwaltschaft Hamburg, 25 November 1937, UniHH personnel file Burmeister.

[47] Interview Giles/Rein 30 November 1971.

[48] Hamburg's rivalry with Bremen and Lübeck is described in Henning Timpke (ed.), *Dokumente zur Gleichschaltung des Landes Hamburg 1933* (Frankfurt am Main, 1964), pp. 147ff. See also "Das permanente Kolonialinstitut: Die kolonialistische und 'politische' Kontinuität der Hamburger Universität," *Das permanente Kolonialinstitut: 50 Jahre Hamburger Universität* (Hamburg, 1969), pp. 26ff.

versity governance. Rein could always fall back on the Nazis' own doctrine of the "leader principle." The NSDDOZB later complained that "in the conduct of his rectorship [Rein] showed himself, in spite of all the external charm (especially with higher authorities), to be strongly egocentric and autocratic."[49] In other words, he got his way, he *led* the University, he pursued those policies that he believed to be correct.

The student leadership was divided again at the national level after the search for a replacement for Stäbel as joint NSDStB and DSt Leader came to nothing. Rust was anxious to have a supporter of a strong German Students' Union, and his choice fell on Andreas Feickert, the former Hamburg NSDStB Leader and head of the DSt Labor Service department. He had just won his intellectual spurs, in Rust's opinion, with his book *Students Attack! National Socialist University Revolution*, a manifesto of Nazi students' aims published in June 1934. Feickert hoped to politicize the university by careful indoctrination of the next generation of lecturers (now students), for he realized that it was futile to try to make Nazis out of the majority of current professors. He regarded this as important not merely for the future of the universities themselves but in a much wider sense: "If the university wants to have National Socialist freshmen, it needs a National Socialist school; if the school wants to teach in a National Socialist way, then it must have National Socialist teachers; these in turn can only come from a National Socialist university."[50] It was the vital task of the Students' Union's *Kameradschaften* to break through this vicious circle. His ambition was to halt the already noticeable shift of preeminence toward the Party's own training colleges and to restore the universities to their position and responsibility for producing "the future class of leaders for

[49] Reichsdozentenführung to Härtle, 2 April 1942, Institut für Zeitgeschichte, Munich (Ifz) MA-116/13/Rein.

[50] Andreas Feickert, *Studenten greifen an! Nationalsozialistische Hochschulrevolution* (Hamburg, 1934), p. 38.

Germany."[51] This promising vision clearly looked attractive to Rust.

The Reich Education Ministry had been formed in the first place to try to improve the noisy but lukewarm *Gleichschaltung* of the universities, and the Minister would earn much praise if he were able "to imbue the university and its members with National Socialist spirit and National Socialist will," winning back "the confidence of the German people in the universities."[52] Feickert seemed to have sound ideas to help him achieve this. Mindful of the bother caused by previous divisions of the student leadership, Feickert made his acceptance of Rust's offer of the DST post contingent on his appointment to head the NSDStB as well. The Minister sent him to Munich to be interviewed by Hess and Gerhard Wagner, who were at this time consulting with the NSDStB Area Leaders over Stäbel's successor.[53] Wagner rejected Feickert absolutely. Seeing through the Party's attitude toward the intelligentsia, Feickert was advocating a dangerous independence of mind for the student elite.

Rust did not wait to hear the outcome of the interview in Munich but assured Feickert over the telephone that all would be well, and he immediately released a press announcement of his appointment as DST Leader. By this means he perhaps hoped to force Hess to accept Feickert as NSDStB

---

[51] Ibid., p. 17.

[52] Otto Graf zu Rantzau, *Das Reichsministerium für Wissenschaft, Erziehung und Volksbildung* (Berlin, 1939), p. 236.

[53] In light of their mutual enmity, Area Leader Wolf Müller undoubtedly painted Feickert's name black. On the other hand, Ernst Horn, another Area Leader who was being tipped for the leadership of the NSDStB, recommended Feickert for the post. Pesta to Feickert, 24 July 1934, RSFWü I*02 ɸ 382. Both Feickert and Derichsweiler, in interviews with the author, spoke of Gerhard Wagner as a kind of grey eminence behind Hess in higher education matters. Feickert recalled that, during this particular meeting, Hess sat unnervingly corpse-like before him and did not utter a word, leaving all the questioning to Wagner. Interview Giles/Feickert, 27 September 1973; interview Giles/Derichsweiler, 12 March 1973.

Leader as well.[54] But Rust had miscalculated the effect of this slight completely. Although both sides agreed that a joint leadership was essential, Hess refused to be bullied into accepting a leader unsuitable from the Party's point of view, or worse still, likely to heed Rust more than him.

Hess and Wagner next drew up plans for a reshaping of the NSDStB, according it special tasks and boosting its prestige in order to make it indisputably the premier organization within the student leadership. Hess acknowledged that the NSDStB in its past form had "failed completely" and was led by Wagner into projecting it as "a sort of intellectual ss," a new elite order under his command that would provide the Party with a sound National Socialist philosophy and with National Socialist guidelines for economic, home, and foreign affairs.[55] Despite the fundamental antipathy of the Party toward intellectuals, who were viewed as dangerous critics, Hess seemed to hope that a fresh start in the NSDStB might improve the credibility of Party ideology. Like Rust, he no doubt had ambitions to gain credit for the nazification of the universities, too.

He entrusted the NSDStB national leadership to Albert Derichsweiler, a former Area Leader, and summoned Rust to Munich to establish boundaries of influence.[56] On 30 July 1934 Hess announced that "in the future the NSDStB alone

[54] Feickert telephoned Rust in Berlin after the interview in order to report on how it had gone, though he was left puzzled as to the Party's probable decision. Rust insisted that he promise over the phone to accept the leadership of the German Students' Union, and he assured him that he would shortly have control of the NSDStB as well. Interview Giles/Feickert, 27 September 1973.

[55] This seems a more appropriate translation of "eine geistige ss" in this context than "a spiritual ss," as Steinberg renders it. Steinberg, *Sabers*, p. 215. Baldur von Schirach lost out altogether in the reorganization. The NSDStB was removed from the Reich Youth Leadership and placed under the direct control of Hess. Bekanntgabe Hess 18 July 1934, MicAlex T-81/236/5020698-9.

[56] For Derichsweiler's role in the *Gleichschaltung* of the Catholic CV fraternity association, see Stitz, *Der CV*, pp. 220ff.

168

is responsible for the entire ideological, political and physical training of the student body."[57] It was difficult to imagine any activity that might not come under this rubric—Rust's knuckles had been sharply rapped.

Unfortunately, Hess had overlooked the problem of finance. The NSDStB was to take over a vast training program with its bank balance already 8,000 marks in the red, whereas the DSt, condemned to little more than administration, received annually several hundred thousand marks from student fees.[58] Clearly there would have to be a redistribution of funds, especially since Hess had now ordered that NSDStB members should no longer pay membership subscriptions.[59] Derichsweiler's view that "if our people do the work, the others can jolly well pay for it"[60] found the support of the Party Treasurer, Franz Xaver Schwarz, who approved the NSDStB Leader's budget of 29 August 1934 and wrote to Rust, instructing him firmly to authorize a per capita sum of RM 2.50 to be transferred from the semester's fees of 6 marks that it received from each student.[61] The Education Ministry refused to make any such concession. The evidence that had recently been revealed of the *nouveau riche* life style of Stäbel and his staff, who had squandered thousands of marks on cars and expensive hotels, made the Ministry altogether unwilling to hand out large sums of money to the student leaders. It started by putting its own house in order: the German Student's Union was instructed to revert to the practice of having nonsalaried officials. The DSt budget for the winter semester 1934-1935 was rejected with an order

[57] Erlass Hess, "Aufgaben der neuen Studentenorganisation," 30 July 1934, UniHH 0.30.6.
[58] Rede Derichsweiler, Ordensburg Crössinsee, August 1936, RSFWü II*A29 α 477.
[59] Probationary members were still to pay 6 marks per annum, which brought in a substantial sum. Rundschreiben Derichsweiler, 28 September 1934, RSFWü II* φ 312.
[60] Vortrag Derichsweiler, Rittmarshausen, August 1934, RSFWü II* φ 319.
[61] Schwarz to Rust, 15 September 1934, RSFWü II* φ 312.

to submit a balanced one, based on the income from student fees and requiring no subsidy from the Ministry.[62]

This put the Ministry in a much better position for turning down Derichsweiler's budget of well over one million marks for the year 1935. The NSDStB Leader pestered the Education Ministry for monetary help again and again, making a final pre-Christmas call on 19 December 1934 to repeat that he still did not have the money to begin his task of political education. Derichsweiler pleaded for 400,000 marks without delay in order to set up training camps for his junior leaders.[63] Rust's officials informed the Minister that this was unthinkable and tore apart the NSDStB budget. The student leaders had not even added it correctly. The individual budget items totaled almost 3,000 marks less than the NSDStB indicated. One item specified 1,000 marks monthly as maintenance and running costs for a car, whereas 300-400 marks was considered in the Ministry to be the maximum amount needed for even the largest car. It was noted that Derichsweiler was giving himself and other leaders the salary of a senior civil servant, as well as an enormous expense account. No wonder the NSDStB leaders were able to travel second (instead of third) class on the railways, thereby already provoking criticism in student circles![64] In fact, the whole budgetary estimate for administration was grossly inflated. Since the Ministry would scarcely get away with paying nothing, the officials recommended Rust to give no more than 1 mark per student (rather than the RM 3.50 now requested).[65] In March 1935, a sum of 70,000 marks was finally paid over from DSt funds, though the Ministry took pains to stress that this was not a per capita sum (which might set a precedent

[62] Kunisch to DSt, 17 January 1935, ZStA REM 907.

[63] Vermerk Kunisch, 19 December 1934, ibid.

[64] Vermerk Heinrich, 1 February 1935; Etatentwurf des NSDStB für das Kalenderjahr 1935, 13 December 1934, ibid.

[65] Vermerke Heinrich to Kunisch, 17 January 1935; Kunisch to Vahlen, 25 January 1935, ibid.

for the future) but merely a one-time payment to help the NSDStB out of present difficulties.[66]

The 70,000 marks did not go very far, and less than two months later Derichsweiler was writing to Party Treasurer Schwarz, insisting that he obtain 700,000 marks from the Ministry for his training camps. This, he claimed, was vital for the whole selection process with which Hess had charged the NSDStB. He could only work effectively in camps, not only because of the "genuine community" that they promoted but also because of the possibilities offered for surveillance and selection.[67] Schwarz was impressed, but Derichsweiler made no progress with Ministry officials. Then on 15 July 1935, the NSDStB leader confronted Rust in Hitler's presence with his failure to support the political education program, and he solicited the Minister's meek consent to pay for the camps.[68]

A week later Derichsweiler arrived at the Ministry again, cap in hand, only to hear its officials insist that Rust had promised neither to cover the entire cost of the camps nor to make over a fixed per capita amount.[69] He was sent away empty-handed. Dr. Heinrich, the official responsible for student affairs, reported that the Ministry should not pay a penny while Derichsweiler continued to claim 1,000 marks monthly in car expenses and to draw a monthly salary of 600 marks ("That is a scandal!" Professor Bachér happily noted—it had been bad enough in the 1935 budget proposal at 470 marks).[70] It was again unlikely, however, that the Ministry could give nothing, and another one-time payment of 60,000 marks was grudgingly discussed and finally ordered by Rust at the end of September 1935.[71]

---

[66] Rust to Schwarz, 28 January 1935; Pempeit to REM, 19 March 1935, ibid.

[67] Derichsweiler to Schwarz, 3 May 1935, MicAlex T-81/236/5020725-8.

[68] See below for the importance of this meeting.

[69] Vermerk Kunisch, 24 July 1935, ZStA REM 907.

[70] Vermerk Heinrich to Bachér, 6 August 1935, ibid.

[71] Vermerk Burmeister, 13 September 1935, ibid. This and other memos

The niggardliness of the Ministry and the outrage of Derichsweiler and the Party Treasurer continued through 1936.[72] The NSDStB viewed this as deliberate sabotage of its efforts toward the complete nazification of the university. This was not the aim of the Education Ministry. A commentary on the apparent ponderousness of the officials illuminates the prevailing attitude very well: "We are not being bureaucratic but fundamental . . . , in order to point up and maintain the contrast between our methods and the frivolous thoughtlessness of other people. We wish to present and preserve a bit of Prussiandom."[73] The Ministry might have loosened its grip on the purse strings a little if it had been convinced that the money would be spent wisely. Yet Derichsweiler showed clear signs of "frivolous thoughtlessness": apart from trying to cripple the work of Feickert and the DST, he seemed recklessly impolitic in his treatment of the fraternity associations. For the time being, therefore, the NSDStB had to rely on additional finance from Party funds. The monies of the student financial aid organization, the *Reichsstudentenwerk* (RSW), were also increasingly channeled toward the NSDStB: by 1936 it was paying for the meals of members of *Kameradschaft* Houses.[74]

Although Derichsweiler's long-term aim was "the basic political schooling of the entire student body," there were just not enough qualified leaders in the NSDStB to carry out this ambitious plan at once. Derichsweiler realized that rushing the matter would only end in the chaos that had accompanied the SA University Office. He proposed to reorganize the political education program with a thoroughness that had previously been lacking. In the first instance,

---

argue against any payment, but on 27 September a terse marginal note recorded: "Herr Minister has ordered the payment!"

[72] Cf. Schwarz to Rust, 28 January 1936; Schwarz to Rust, 14 April 1936, ibid.

[73] Krebs, *Infancy*, p. 296.

[74] REM to RMdI, 14 September 1936, ZStA REM 893.

the District Student Leaders (*Gaustudentenführer*) and the individual college Student Leaders were to be trained in a three-week camp during the summer of 1934. These leaders would then be able to set up their own training camps for other members of the NSDStB, whose detailed political training would be pursued during the winter semester 1934-1935. Enough ideological teachers for the whole student body might then be available by Easter of 1935. Derichsweiler was eager to inaugurate his plan as speedily as possible, for he had been warned of the introduction of conscription and was particularly anxious to try to make National Socialists out of the students before they fell into the hands of the Army.[75] But on top of his financial problems came disruption from another quarter.

Feickert made a sudden, bold attempt to reassert the power of the German Students' Union and unexpectedly produced on 20 September 1934 the so-called Feickert Plan, by which *all* freshmen would henceforth live in *Kameradschaft* houses provided by the DST or the fraternities, and all would even wear a standard uniform to emphasize the strict militaristic discipline that was to prevail.[76] After the failure of both his predecessors, Krüger and Stäbel, to introduce compulsory residence in *Kameradschaften*, and the ill-feeling stirred up by them, this was an extraordinarily gauche move. Predictably, the fraternity associations were soon up in arms again. They now chose as their champion the president of one of the associations, State Secretary Lammers. As head of the Reich Chancellery, with direct access to Hitler, he was able to broach the subject with him personally and telegraphed Hitler's disapproval of the compulsory nature of

[75] Vortrag Derichsweiler, Rittmarshausen, August 1934, RSFWü II* φ 319.

[76] "Die Kameradschaftserziehung der Deutschen Studenschaft," *Völkischer Beobachter*, 21 September 1934; "Neugestaltung der studentischen Erziehung," *Völkischer Beobachter*, 22 September 1934. Cf. also Stitz, *Der CV*, pp. 315ff.

the scheme to Feickert on 27 September 1934.[77] The leaders of the fraternity associations gathered in Berlin on 8 October, where Feickert tried to pacify them while Derichsweiler assured them that the DST Leader was overstepping his authority. After Rust had himself consulted with the fraternity leaders on 25 October 1934, he cabled to all universities that *"Kameradschaft* education" would in fact be voluntary, although he would welcome it if as many students as possible could live in *Kameradschaften*.[78] The matter appeared to be settled at last when suddenly Hitler decided that he did not approve of the students' actually *living* together at all. A generation that passed through the male seclusion of the Labor Service camps and a (planned) year in the Army, as well as a further year or eighteen months in the barracks-like discipline of a *Kameradschaft*, would run the risk, he argued, of predominantly homosexual orientation. Hitler, probably more concerned with population figures than morals, considered that the students should have a certain freedom at the university to develop relations with the opposite sex.[79]

The announcement of this extraordinary decision to the exclusively male fraternities would have been a difficult task for Rust. A considerable number of them had by now considered it desirable or expedient to undergo costly conversions of their houses into the large dormitories requested by

---

[77] Steinberg, *Sabers*, p. 160. Since letters of protest were sent to Hitler personally, Lammers was able to bring up the matter in his official capacity. Cf. Lammers's own account in Niederschrift Verbändesitzung am 8. Oktober 1934 im Studentenhaus Berlin, RSFWÜ I*02 γ 27.

[78] Aktennotiz Winter, 25 October 1934, BA R128/1008; Funkspruch Rust (durch Polizeibehörde Hamburg), 25 October 1934, UNIHH 0.1.4.

[79] Derichsweiler to Hess, 22 July 1936, BDC Oberstes Parteigericht (OP) Derichsweiler/Hoffmann; Protokoll Reichstagung NSDStB in Frankfurt am Main, 11 May 1935, p. 22, RSFWÜ II* φ 319. Derichsweiler did not make either of these later references to Hitler's fears in public. At the time, Rust did discuss "Paragraph 175" in this context with fraternity leaders without attributing the matter to Hitler. Cf. Protokoll Bundesamtssitzung Schwarzburgbund, 2 November 1934, BA R130/126.

174

successive student leaders. Now they had to be told that their money had been spent in vain. Rust had already appeared confused and indecisive at the meeting on 25 October, and he now determined to withdraw entirely and leave the explanations to Derichsweiler. He released Feickert and the DST from any co-responsibility for political education suggested by the DST constitution and declared the NSDStB to be entirely responsible for it.[80] Derichsweiler was now officially the supreme overlord of the student body, though neither Feickert nor the fraternity associations were willing to accept this wholeheartedly, and a long and exceptionally bitter struggle between them and the NSDStB ensued.

The Destruction of the Fraternity Associations

The fraternities could not fathom what Derichsweiler really wanted of them. In May 1934 he had declared that he was determined to destroy any fraternity that did not form a so-called residential *Kameradschaft* (*Wohnkameradschaft*), but then later he had taken sides with them against the compulsion of the Feickert Plan.[81] Finally he announced in November 1934 that there would henceforth be only one *Kameradschaft* proper in each town, the *Kameradschaft* House of the NSDStB. Fraternities with NSDStB members could form study groups (*Arbeitsgemeinschaften*), but they would no longer be accorded any special recognition: "The Students' Association refuses to judge fraternities on whether they have set up residential *Kameradschaften* or not." And yet he also warned: "Should fraternities show themselves to be hotbeds of reaction, the Students' Association will spare no efforts to *eradicate* those elements, dangerous to *Volk* and nation, from German university

[80] Rust to Feickert, 14 November 1934, quoted in Derichsweiler, "Die rechtsgeschichtliche Entwicklung," p. 118.

[81] In a radio broadcast speech to students in Cologne. Cf. the report in the *Kölner Zeitung*, 16 May 1934, MicAlex T-81/236/5021028.

life."[82] Hitler's complete rejection of residential communities was unknown to them, and Derichsweiler's comments led to speculation about what exactly his own intentions were. Most fraternities were by now anxious to cooperate to some extent, in the interests of self-preservation, but they were puzzled as to how to win favor from the NSDStB.

The fraternity associations split into two camps, the first willing to renounce all their tradition and independence in order to fulfill "the demands of the times," and the second, while embracing National Socialism, wishing to retain their autonomy and former character. In October 1934, the largest fraternity association of all, the *Deutsche Burschenschaft*, broke away from the *Allgemeine Deutsche Waffenring* (the corporate grouping of dueling fraternity associations) because of the vacillating attitude of some of the other associations toward Nazi policies, in particular the Aryan question. It formed the *Völkische Waffenring* at the beginning of December together with another four associations, which accounted for about half the dueling fraternity members.[83] The others, not wishing to lag behind in negotiating strength, banded together on 12 January 1935 in the Student Fraternity Association Group (*Gemeinschaft studentischer Verbände* or GStV).[84] In fact, by dint of selecting State Secretary Lammers for its presidency, the GStV soon won the superior position, and on 12 March 1935 it was recognized by the Party and the NSDStB as the only official representative of all fraternity associations with which business would be conducted.[85] The *Völkische Waffenring* promptly dissolved

[82] Rundschreiben Derichsweiler, "Richtlinien für die politische Erziehung (Kameradschaftshausfrage)," 26 November 1934, RSFWü II* φ 312.

[83] The DB practiced the strict Aryan membership requirements of the NSDAP itself and fully supported the compulsion of the Feickert Plan. Schwab to Lammers, 26 October 1934, BA R128/1008. The other associations joining the DB were the *VC der Turnerschaften*, the *Deutsche Sängerschaft*, the *Naumburger Thing*, and the *Deutsche Wehrschaft*.

[84] Lammers to rector, 7 February 1935, UniHH 0.30.2.1.

[85] Vereinbarung Wagner/Derichsweiler/Lammers, 12 March 1935, ibid.

176

itself, and its members moved into Lammers's camp. By April 1935, Lammers had succeeded in drawing together seventeen associations with a total membership of 180,000 students and alumni; only some 40,000 were not represented by him.[86]

Despite the appearance of a good working relationship, Derichsweiler revealed to his NSDStB leaders that he absolutely rejected the national fraternity associations. On the other hand, he saw some advantage in the preservation of the individual, local fraternities with a view to transforming them into NSDStB training cells.[87] While the fraternity association leaders were shaking their heads and wondering why their gentlemen's agreement at the national level with the Students' Association was not producing "an agreeable relationship with the [local] student leaders" NSDStB headquarters was collecting evidence of misdemeanors with relish. The *Palatia* fraternity at Tübingen, for example, had used the portrait of Hitler hanging in their house for fencing practice "so that the picture which reached Party headquarters . . . showed our Führer with his face slashed."[88] Relations grew steadily more strained.

In Hamburg there was little open hostility on either side, though the fraternities cooperated only as much as absolutely necessary. By and large they tried to maintain the autonomous exclusivity of fraternity life, "seeing in National Socialism and the NSDStB a '*Gesellschaftsspielverderber*,' "[89] as a Hamburg NSDStB leader put it.[90] The District Training Leader of the NSDStB tried to form classes in Ham-

[86] Erklärung Lammers, 23 April 1935, ibid.

[87] Protokoll Reichstagung NSDStB in Frankfurt am Main, 11-12 May 1935, RSFWü II* φ 319.

[88] Reichsamtsleitung NSDStB, "Bericht über das Verhältnis des NSDStB zu den studentischen Vereinigungen," 27 May 1935, RSFWü II* φ 90.

[89] This is an untranslatable pun: *Gesellschaftsspiel* normally means a parlor game, but here it is rather "the game of getting on in society"; *Spielverderber* means "spoilsport."

[90] Semesterbericht Ochsenius, 3 July 1935, RSFWü V*2 α 537.

burg to instruct two members from each of the fraternities in the GStv in the teaching of political education, but only after repeated requests did he succeed in gathering them together. When he had done so they acted with enthusiasm and made promises to order all their freshmen to become NSDStB members (though doing little to translate the promise into fact).[91] The Hamburg students seemed to be awaiting developments elsewhere.

They were soon to come. On the evening of 21 May 1935 all Germans were supposed to be at their wireless sets, listening to Hitler's Reichstag speech. The members of the Corps *Saxo-Borussia* at Heidelberg were, however, at the same time celebrating the initiation of some freshmen and left the fraternity house before the end of the speech in order to go to a local bar. Their noisy entry, with one of their number whistling down an empty champagne bottle, provoked an admonition from the landlord that the *Führer* was still speaking, and they sat down and listened to the rest of his speech in silence. A few days later the members were eating asparagus at a restaurant in town, and a jocular remark was made as to whether one should more properly eat asparagus with one's knife and fork or with one's "paws." One student suggested that to be certain of being correct, one would have to ask the *Führer* how he ate asparagus. This comment on the structure of the Nazi state carried with it the unspoken and opposite implication that in fact Hitler had no table manners.

Thanks to the initiative of District Student Leader Gustav Adolf Scheel, disciplinary proceedings were instituted by Heidelberg University,[92] based on these two trivial occurrences, and the Nazi press unleashed an unparalleled campaign of vituperation against "the incredible behavior of reactionary corps students," which it extended to the

[91] Semesterbericht Nöldge, 8 July 1935, ibid.

[92] Details of the incidents in Urteil des Akademischen Disziplinargerichts der Universität Heidelberg gegen Corps Saxo-Borussia, 3 July 1935, BA R128/73.

fraternities in general.[93] The disciplinary court of the university was unable to find firm "evidence of intent to defame the *Führer*," although Scheel had even mobilized the Party's secret police, the SD, to provide the required kind of evidence.[94] The lack of proof did not dampen the press campaign, and cartoons of the white-tied, champagne-guzzling Saxo-Borussians abounded. Despite the protests of alumni, fraternity students everywhere were now likened to the "Heidelberg asparagus eaters."[95] Baldur von Schirach denounced "the brutality, licentiousness, and abysmal meanness of a small clique of coarse students who row and drink while Germany works." On 6 July 1935 he forbade any Hitler Youth member to belong to a fraternity.[96]

The fraternities were given further cause for unrest. On 25 June 1935 Derichsweiler had issued instructions for the ideological training of fraternity students. Each fraternity that was prepared to cooperate with the NSDStB was to send three members to training camps during the summer vacation.[97] Derichsweiler was trying to avoid upsetting the fraternities by allowing their own members to conduct the eventual training rather than imposing on them instructors from outside.[98] Yet the fraternities saw no attempt at appeasement here. In the first place, they held that they were

[93] Headline in *Völkischer Beobachter*, 6 July 1935.

[94] Kraaz to Lammers, 12 July 1935, BA R128/73.

[95] Stellungnahme der Altherrenschaft des Corps Saxo-Borussia zu den Vorfällen am 21. and 26. Mai 1935 in Heidelberg, 18 July 1935, ibid. Months later Nöldge reported a conversation in Hamburg with the president of the *Deutsche Landsmannschaft*, Dr. Huth (also deputy *Staatspräsident* of Danzig), in which Huth had deplored the "eternal comparison with the asparagus eaters in Heidelberg." Nöldge to Derichsweiler, 2 December 1935, RSFWü V*2 α 567.

[96] "German Student Corps—Not for Hitler Youth," *Manchester Guardian*, 8 July 1935.

[97] Cf. "Die Richtlinien des NSDStB vom 25. Juli 1935," *Deutsche Corps-Zeitung: Amtliches Mitteilungsblatt des Kösener SC-Verbandes* 52, no. 4 (July 1935).

[98] Protokoll Reichstagung NSDStB, 11/12 May 1935, RSFWü II*2 φ 319.

quite competent to give basic instruction in National Socialism without having to undergo special training courses; and in the second place, they feared that since the successful course participants were automatically to become NSDStB members and would thus fall under the disciplinary jurisdiction of the Students' Association, "the NSDStB Group Leaders would be all too easily tempted to extend their authority beyond the ideological and political to cover the whole of fraternity life."[99] Many fraternities were hesitant about registering their students for the projected courses, though those in Hamburg seemed willing at first, until the news came that those who were not members of the NSDStB would have to pay a course fee of 50 marks.[100]

Lammers's patience had already been exhausted before the announcement on the training camps. He dispatched a lengthy and stinging letter to Derichsweiler. He accused him of doing nothing to hinder the continual attacks of the local NSDStB leaders on the fraternities and furthermore of not justifying his right to exclusive control over political education. Lammers asked: "Do you really have such a splendid training staff at your disposal that you can afford not only to reject but even to forbid any help in this area?" His trump card was that he knew by daily contact the "will of the *Führer*" much better than Derichsweiler, and Hitler had assured him that he wished "the fraternities and fraternity associations to be made gradually . . . into valuable and valid members of the Third Reich." The openly destructive attitude of many NSDStB leaders thus stood in direct contradiction to "the highest authority."[101]

Clearly pleased with his confident and assertive letter, and wishing to give the ultimate snub to Derichsweiler, with his "youthful inexperience, lack of political insight and self-confessed impotence vis-à-vis the junior leaders," Lammers

[99] See n. 97.
[100] Semesterbericht Nöldge, 8 July 1935, RSFWü V*2 α 537.
[101] Lammers to Derichsweiler, 1 July 1935, BA R128/38.

arranged for the whole question of the fraternities to be brought before Hitler himself for arbitration. But when the day appointed for the meeting arrived, the Saxo-Borussia witch hunt was in full cry, and there were fears that it would weaken Lammers's case for upholding the fraternities, especially since the advisers summoned to confer with Hitler on the matter were "for the most part no friends of the fraternity students."[102]

The conference was finally held on 15 July 1935 in Berlin, and Hitler poured forth a two-and-a-half-hour monologue expounding his views on the student situation and surprising everyone present with his attitude toward the fraternities. He declared it useless to appoint political training instructors for them because there was no point in trying to pour new wine into old skins. Yet the fraternities were neither to be banned nor dissolved, for this would merely give rise to clandestine opposition. The police did not close down the known haunts of criminals, for then they would lose control of the whereabouts of these people; thus it was with all the refuges of reaction. The only decisive way to beat them was to set up something better in their place, and then they would automatically die out. Lammers was deeply shocked to discover for the first time that Hitler not only thought the fraternities worthless but even compared them with groups of criminals, and he announced his resignation as president of the Student Fraternity Association Group there and then. Hitler refused to accept this, pointing out that all the fraternity associations would then immediately guess

[102] Besides Hitler, Lammers, and Derichsweiler there were also present Hess, Bormann, Ley, Schirach, and Adolf and Gerhard Wagner. Cf. Vortrag Derichsweiler in der Reichsschule Bernau (Sonderkursus für den NSDStB), 17 July 1935, BA NS38/50. Derichsweiler mistakenly gives the date of the meeting as 16 July. Ley in his talk at the same place on the previous day had already mentioned it as having occurred on 15 July. Steinberg quite wrongly claims that Hitler spoke in person to the student leaders assembled in Bernau. Steinberg, "Sabres," p. 791.

his (Hitler's) attitude. Lammers was ordered to remain in office and say nothing.[103]

Lammers was bound by his promise of secrecy not to reveal actual details of the meeting, but he was able to indicate its results to the fraternity association leaders. He explained that there was no prospect of the fraternities' becoming National Socialist "affiliated organizations," and that the proposed political training of the fraternities would therefore no longer take place.[104] The troublesome *Deutsche Burschenschaft* believed that it would receive preferential treatment from the Party if it staunchly upheld its ambition to become a recognized ideological indoctrination unit and challenged Lammers's decision not to press the matter.[105] Lammers again asked Hitler's permission to resign on 6 August 1935, but once more it was refused. When the president of the *Deutsche Burschenschaft* expressed his views in print, Lammers decided to ban the association from the Student Fraternity Association Group.[106] Shortly afterward he also banned the important *Kösener* association for refusing to carry out his order to apply the Aryan membership requirements of the NSDAP to its own fraternities.[107] Having thus lost two of the largest associations, the Student Fraternity Association Group had no further justification as a representative body, and Lammers succeeded finally in resigning on 6 September 1935, whereupon the GStV folded up two days later.[108]

The following week Derichsweiler announced at the Nu-

[103] The account of this secret meeting owes much to the author's interview with Albert Derichsweiler, 12 March 1973. The details are either corroborated or made plausible by remarks of Ley and Derichsweiler at the time (see n. 102).

[104] Protokoll Verbändeführer-Sitzung, 24 July 1934, BA R128/14.

[105] Lammers to Derichsweiler, 9 August 1935, BA R128/39.

[106] Protokoll Sitzung GStV-Arbeitskreis, 23 August 1935, BA R128/16.

[107] The KSCV was excluded on 5 September, the DB already on 21 August 1935. Cf. Horst Bernhardi, *Frisia Gottingensis 1931-1956* (Heide/Holstein, 1956), p. 50.

[108] Text of Lammers's resignation in Stitz, *Der CV*, p. 344.

remberg Rally that freshmen would no longer be permitted to belong to both the NSDStB *and* a fraternity. They would now have to choose whether to become "warrior or philistine," for no political activity would be allowed in the fraternities.[109] Derichsweiler urged the fraternities and the fraternity associations to disband and hand over their houses to the NSDStB. Ahead of all the rest the *Deutsche Burschenschaft* clamored to submit itself to the control of the NSDStB, and on 18 November 1935 at a grandiose ceremony on the *Wartburg* handed over the tattered banner of the original *Burschenschaft* to the care of the NSDStB. The *Deutsche Burschenschaft* was declared to be incorporated intact into the National Socialist Students' Association.[110] The other fraternity associations soon disbanded as well in the realization that the representation of the interests of the fraternities at the national level had proved a signal failure.[111] They had not failed for want of effort or good will. They had been anxious to become accepted members of the Nazi community but had not fully realized the totality of the sacrifice that that entailed in renouncing their former way of life. "There is no longer any private life at the *völkisch* university," Ernst Krieck had proclaimed in 1933, ". . . now there is only life for the community."[112] But the fraternities' idea of National Socialism was for an NSDStB member to come and hold a lecture once a week and otherwise to leave them in peace.[113] The NSDStB could not rest assured of its absolute power, however, while these numerically superior and fi-

---

[109] Rede Derichsweiler (Reichsparteitag NSDStB-Sondertagung), 13 September 1935, BA NS38/1. Derichsweiler extended the ban on fraternity membership from freshmen to all NSDStB members on 6 December.

[110] Bernhardi, "Göttinger Burschenschaft," p. 223.

[111] No fewer than eleven major fraternity associations disbanded during the month of October. Stitz, *Der CV*, p. 350.

[112] Ernst Krieck, *Die Erneuerung der Universität: Rede zur Übergabe des Rektorats am 23. Mai 1933* (Frankfurt am Main, 1933), p. 4.

[113] Cf. Derichsweiler's comment in Protokoll Reichstagung NSDStB, 11/12 May 1935, II* φ 319.

nancially more secure organizations remained independently active.

The fraternity associations were destroyed, but the operation had not quite the end result that Derichsweiler had expected. The individual fraternities for the most part remained in existence, as did their supporting alumni associations. Even former *Deutsche Burschenschaft* fraternities that had been permitted to become NSDSTB *Kameradschaften* saw no reason to halt their traditional ceremonies. In the Hamburg DB fraternity *Alemannia*, other NSDSTB members were regarded merely as guests who enjoyed the privilege but not the right to conduct their training in the fraternity house.[114] Other fraternities were annoyed that *they* were not now recognized as *Kameradschaften*. The *Niedersachsen* fraternity wrote a bitter letter reminding the student leadership of their close involvement with the NSDSTB since before the seizure of power;[115] and the *Hegelingen* fraternity offered its house and members to the Hitler Youth in a fit of pique.[116]

The illusion that the *Deutsche Burschenschaft* had been especially favored was shattered at the end of January 1936 when Gerhard Wagner, the Party's Commissioner for Higher Education, declared the terms of incorporation null and void because they had been drawn up without his approval.[117] If this annoyed the *Deutsche Burschenschaft's* fraternities, general disillusionment spread when Derichsweiler banned "fraternity *Kameradschaften*" altogether on 22 February. From now on no fraternity could (in theory, at least) simply restyle itself a *Kameradschaft* in order to remain in existence.[118] A nationwide Gestapo inquiry was set in motion to report on the dissolution of the fraternities. It found that

[114] Behmke to Nöldge, 9 December 1935, RSFWÜ V*2 α 567.
[115] Reinstorff to Faust, 8 October 1935, ibid.
[116] Nöldge to Derichsweiler, 4 December 1935, ibid.
[117] Bernhardi, *Frisia Gottingensis*, p. 53.
[118] Reinhold Bässler, "Die deutsche Studentenschaft in ihrer verfassungsgeschichtlichen Entwicklung" (Diss.iur., Tübingen, 1941), p. 228.

". . . not a single fraternity has disbanded in the real meaning of the word. . . . Rather it is the case that all the disbanded fraternities have only dissolved the undergraduate section (first- to third- or fourth-semester students), whereas the alumni section continues to flourish as ever."[119] Indeed there was active antagonism between the fraternities and the NSDStB. When the former had placed their houses at the disposal of an NSDStB *Kameradschaft*, they had expected, as the owners, to be allowed to continue to live there and were shocked by the greed of the NSDStB leaders, who desired not merely the use but the deed of the house as well. For their part, the NSDStB groups were angry that the demise of the fraternities, which was what really affected them at the local level, had not automatically followed on from the disappearance of the national fraternity associations. In Bonn, Nazi students stole the flag of the *Corps Teutonia*;[120] in Jena the flagstaffs of two fraternities were sawed down;[121] and in Marburg a street battle was fought with iron bars.[122] The students in Tübingen, a bastion of fraternity life, had formed a sort of local fraternity association, the *Bund Tübinger Verbindungen*. Many NSDStB members there had refused to resign from their fraternity following Derichsweiler's ban on dual membership and had often preferred to leave the NSDStB (while often retaining NSDAP membership). The Tübingen students had shrewdly made a gift collection for 100 needy storm troopers in an attempt to play off one branch of the Party against another.[123]

[119] Bericht, "Entwicklung der Korporationsfrage," n.d. (May 1936?), ZStA REM 872.

[120] Gestapo Köln to Gestapa Berlin, 22 February 1936, ibid.

[121] Lagebericht Stapo Weimar, 18 March 1936, ibid.

[122] Hoffmann to Oberstes Parteigericht, 19 May 1936, BDC OP Derichsweiler/Hoffmann.

[123] Politische Polizei Tübingen to Landespolizeiamt Stuttgart, 25 February 1936, ZStA REM 872. Fraternities in Erlangen and six other towns sought to improve their image in 1935 by collecting money to feed a total of 135 poor children daily. The praise that they received angered Derichsweiler, who halted the scheme. REM to NSDStB, 11 December 1935, ZStA REM 907.

In short, although the supply of freshmen had now virtually dried up, the individual fraternities were still very much alive and refused to succumb to the bludgeoning of the Students' Association. Despite the official rejection of residential communities, the NSDStB groups still badly needed the fraternity houses as meeting places for the *Kameradschaften* and were shortsighted enough to expect the fraternities to hand over their valuable properties lock, stock, and barrel without the slightest wish for any further influence, let alone financial compensation. The fraternities' reluctance to surrender, even after the defeat of their national associations, was both incomprehensible and infuriating to the Nazis. The belief that further aggression would bring the fraternities into line was quite misplaced and served only to aggravate the situation. It contributed substantially to Derichsweiler's downfall.

Student Apathy and Political Education

The most insidious problem that the Nazi student leaders ever faced was the apathy with which their programs were met. Trained to see everything in terms of conflict, the leaders were prepared to deal with opposition. But this was not so much overt resistance as a kind of tacit dissent. It left them furious and disgusted and more disposed than ever to adopt a fighting stance in order to eradicate this weakness of character from the student body.

The troubles centering on the *Kameradschaft* House in Hamburg severely hampered the political education program of the NSDStB, but nevertheless a start was made in the training of members. The leadership initiative now shifted from the University to the District Student Leadership (*Gaustudentenführung*). As part of the reorganization of the NSDStB following Stäbel's dismissal, the regional grouping of NSDStB units in "Areas" (*Kreise*), corresponding to those of the German Students' Union, was shifted to "Districts" (*Gaue*), duplicating those of the Nazi Party. Hamburg was a particularly

186

cohesive District because all the constituent college units lay close together in the same city.[124] The University NSDStB group remained the most important unit of the District. Of 108 students who attended the ideological "study groups" in the winter semester 1934-1935, ninety-nine were from the University.[125]

The theme of these seminars, "*Volk* and Race," was intended to prepare the NSDStB students to lecture to the nonmembers during the following semester.[126] The topics discussed suggest that the course was a justification of anti-Semitic policies. The summer semester 1936 saw an expansion of the theme, as "*Volk* and Nation," to include more generally current political questions. There was a poor response from the students, who appeared overwhelmingly uninterested in the activities of the NSDStB. The head of the Press and Propaganda Department complained that "the Hamburg student is one of the most miserable figures who still run loose at the universities. Even at the big patriotic rallies which the Students' Union has put on here, the size of the audience was limited to the members of the NSDStB,

---

[124] The constituent members of the District Student Leadership were the student bodies at the University of Hamburg, the Hamburg College of Engineering, the Hamburg State Technical Institute, the Hamburg College of Fine Arts, and the Hamburg College of Civil Engineering (see Appendix 3 for membership figures). Much to the annoyance of the District Student Leadership, they never succeeded in gaining jurisdiction over the two groups at the Merchant Marine Schools in Hamburg and Altona, which fell to the *Gau Ausland*. After 1943, the District Student Leadership also embraced the students at the School of Fashion.

[125] Arbeitsberichte Nöldge, 26 and 28 January 1935, RSFWü V*2 α 537.

[126] Arbeitsbericht Nöldge, "Schulungsarbeit," 28 January 1935, ibid. The books to which the students were referred were Hitler's *Mein Kampf*, Alfred Rosenberg's *Der Mythus des 20. Jahrhunderts*, H.F.K. Günther's *Kleine Rassenkunde des deutschen Volkes*, and Martin Staemmler's *Rassenpflege im völkischen Staat* (possibly also his *Volk und Rasse*). A list drawn up in the summer of 1936 gives the titles of more than 100 books in the library of the district headquarters of the Hamburg NSDStB. Forst to Sill, 22 June 1936, RSFWü II* φ 182.

of the Party and its organizations."[127] Even at the peak of its popularity in the student government the NSDStB had never gained the votes of more than 28.5 percent of the Hamburg student body.[128] Part of the trouble now was that the student leaders were dissatisfied with anything less than total enthusiasm, but they did little to try to win it, imagining that they had every right to deserve it automatically. It was difficult to secure a high attendance at events even from the NSDStB members, since most of them were simultaneously active in the SA, SS, HJ, and so forth, and these organizations still often refused to give them time off for other commitments.

Yet two training camps held in the summer vacation marked an unqualified success for the start of the intensive training of the entire Hamburg student body. These were held especially for students born in 1914, who would probably be the first cohort for conscription and therefore stood in the most urgent need of Nazi indoctrination before coming under the influence of the army.[129] As so often, the Nazi "camps" were not held under canvas: the first, for technical college students, was held in a romantic, if somewhat dilapidated, old farmhouse, whereas the university students' "camp" was accommodated in a spacious and comfortable former convalescent home. The old Labor Service concept of the captive audience prevailed, and the isolation of the group well away from the city meant that all their attention was necessarily directed in the first place toward the formation of "comradeship" (*Kameradschaft*) with their fellow participants and leaders.

It would be a mistake to overlook the fact that the volunteers for these camps did, even within the strict discipline

---

[127] NSDStB Hamburg Hauptamt V. Tätigkeitsbericht für das Sommersemester 1935, n.d., RSFWü V*2 α 517.

[128] During the winter semester 1932-1933. See Appendix 1.

[129] Protokoll Reichstagung NSDStB (Referat Mähner, Amtsleiter Politische Erziehung), 11/12 May 1935, RSFWü II* φ 319.

imposed, have enormous fun together. When a friendly atmosphere had built up mutual respect and trust, they were all the more receptive and susceptible to the ideological persuasion to which they were subjected. The (enforced) *leisure* to study Nazi political writings stimulated minds entirely unused to this and directed it along the required channels. From the college students' camp the leader reported that "everything one put in front of them was completely new. . . . The only books which they had handled before were technical ones. Previously they had no interest in political books. I believe, however, that the camp has given them such a stimulus that most of them will take up the *Mythus* even now in the vacation for their intellectual improvement."[130] The university camp produced similar experiences: ". . . I gave them chapters of *Mein Kampf* and the *Mythus* to read. Many of them had never really *studied* even *one* chapter of these works. . . . But through the restricted choice of chapters every one of them really came to grips with Hitler and Rosenberg. Now many of them sit around reading. . . ."[131]

Many more leaders were now being systematically trained, but there was an embarrassing lack of students willing to be led. At the University of Hamburg the NSDStB membership (including probationers) increased from 412 in November 1933 (14 percent of the student body) to 514 in July 1936 (25 percent of the student body), but even then, not all were enthusiastically active members.[132] Work in the students' departmental groups (*Fachschaften*), whose task was to put a Nazi slant on scholarship, was sluggish and apathetic because it did not represent a prerequisite for examinations. If it proved difficult to awaken students' interest in projects

[130] Lagerbericht Bey, Gauschulungslager in Kollmar a.d. Unterelbe, n.d. (August 1935), RSFWü V*2 α 537.

[131] Lagerbericht (Ochsenius), n.d. (September 1935), RSFWü V*2 α 531.

[132] Figures in RSFWü II*146 α 79; and Bergmann to Sill, 8 July 1936, RSFWü II* φ 182. See also Appendix 2.

during term time (not least because of the students' many other commitments), it was even harder during the vacation. A scheme to take over the workplace of factory workers, in order to give them the opportunity for a holiday on full pay, found the support of only six students in the entire University.[133]

The student leaders were manifestly failing to politicize the university as they had hoped; nor could they engender even in the ranks of the NSDStB that tremendous activism that the end of the Weimar Republic had seen. Then they had formed a small and tightly knit cadre of students who had joined purely because they *were* politically committed, and those who did not show the requisite degree of engagement were simply dismissed. The Student Leader at the University of Hamburg feared for the future of universities if current conditions persisted. He perceived them as producing "academically trained experts but not leaders." Recognizing that Party leaders were drawn less and less from among university graduates, he gloomily foresaw the ultimate conversion of the universities into technical colleges.[134]

Rather than seeing this decline as the outcome of deliberate Nazi policy toward the academic classes, the student leaders viewed it as a sad result of the ideological apathy of the student body, which could be prevented by a redoubling of efforts to achieve the political university. It seemed, though, that Rector Rein had no radical solution to offer. An assembly of the University was assured by Rein, Senator von Allwörden, and District Student Leader Nöldge that "the Hanseatic University of Hamburg will be upheld at all costs,

---

[133] Jomka to Killer, 19 February 1936, RSFWü V*2 α 537. Another forty-six students were gathered from other units of the district for the "factory service." Cf. Stimmungs- und Tätigkeitsbericht Ochsenius, 5 March 1936, RSFWü V*2 α 542.

[134] Bergmann to District Student Leader, 20 March 1936, RSFWü V*2 α 546.

and that all rumors about its liquidation are groundless."[135] But nothing positive was undertaken to improve its political image beyond an effort to curb the expression of dissent: the syndic ordered a weekly report on new political graffiti in the University lavatories![136]

At other universities, too, attempts to force students out of their apathetic attitude did not work. Only half the students at the College of Agriculture in Berlin could be pressed into attendance at NSDStB training sessions. All those who had refused to participate were ordered to report for two full days of service to the community: eighty did respond, but ninety students still ignored the summons.[137] The student leaders at the University of Cologne were angry because only 200 students out of 3,000 turned up for their May Day celebration in 1935. They thereupon set up a swastika flag at the university's main entrance, hid themselves, and pounced upon students who did not salute the flag in passing, keeping a record of their names. A mandatory assembly of the entire student body was called, but even the student leader admitted that a pep talk under these circumstances would do little good: "Such compulsory rallies are of course not the way to improve the mood [of the students]. This is regarded

[135] Niederschrift Besprechung des Rektors mit den Dekanen, 28 May 1936, UniHH 0.30.6.; "Über den Ausbau der Universität," *Hamburger Anzeiger*, 11 June 1936.

[136] It does not appear that the staff were very cooperative in this strange quest. The head porter reported some months later, "No writing of any kind in the toilets has come to the attention of the janitorial management recently, and when it has, it has been immediately removed." The exasperated syndic repeated that the graffiti was to be copied down, not removed! Struve to Hellmann, 27 June 1936, UniHH T.8. The decision was probably prompted by the court proceedings against the student Helmut Roeske for derogatory remarks against the Nazi Party. In court he had testified that to judge by the graffiti in the university lavatories, one could only conclude that many students were opposed to the regime. He was sent to prison for eighteen months, and the University of Hamburg debarred him from university study for life. UniHH Di.R.3.

[137] Bericht Werner, 4 July 1935, ZStA REM 872.

as disagreeable force and pure chicanery. Their degree of success is diametrically opposed to their declared aim."[138]

The mishandling of the political education program, as perceived by broad sections of the student population, played a central role in the final removal of the leaders of both the German Students' Union and of the NSDStB. Attempts to oust Andreas Feickert from the DST leadership began almost immediately after the publication of the Feickert Plan, emanating first and foremost from Dr. Lammers's Reich Chancellery. One of his officials did his best to extract a sworn statement from Derichsweiler that Feickert had defamed Lammers. It was understood that Feickert had accused Lammers of having deliberately given Hitler false information about the Feickert Plan in order to elicit the *Führer*'s disapproval.[139] Derichsweiler was pleased to stoke the fire with the information that Feickert had allowed his membership in the Party to lapse in November 1932, in the crucial weeks when national support was slipping.[140] Lammers was quick to remind Rust how intolerable it was that such a person should hold high office, particularly as the (nominal) Deputy Leader of the NSDStB, a Party organization.[141]

When Rust withdrew any co-responsibility for political education from the DST, Feickert began to search out some positive task for his organization outside the extensive realm of ideological, political, and physical education. The departmental groups, theoretically embracing all students, came under the jurisdiction of the German Students' Union,

[138] Bericht, "Zur Stimmung unter der Studentenschaft," 17 June 1935, ibid.

[139] Aktenvermerk Nordmann to Lammers, 25 October 1934, BA R128/1008.

[140] Lammers to Rust (draft by Nordmann), 14 November 1934, ibid. The reason for Feickert's slip was clearly his preoccupation with preparations for the DST's Labor Service plans. See above, chap. 3.

[141] After their appointment, both Feickert and Derichsweiler had named each other as deputy leaders in their respective organizations, though any mutual consultation quickly ceased. Erlass Hess, "Aufgaben der neuen Studentenorganisation," 30 July 1934, UniHH 0.30.6.

and it was to these and the nazification of scholarship that Feickert now turned his attention in his attempt at reassertion. He hoped to use a much-publicized DSt "Spring Conference" (*Frühjahrshochschule der DSt*) as a base on which to build. This was to be a much grander version of the informal gatherings of Professor Rein on the island of Sylt.[142] The focus would be placed on the reform of various disciplines. When the plan fell through, ending the only positive work Feickert seemed to be doing, the German Students' Union stood in danger of collapse. Indeed it was now widely recognized that "the NSDStB is the decisive organization at the university, whereas the DSt exists in name only."[143] Even student leaders began to call for Feickert's departure.[144]

At the beginning of 1935 Derichsweiler proposed a new constitution for the student body to replace those issued only a year before. He claimed that neither the German Students' Union nor the German Technical Students' Union had any purpose, since all their tasks were ideological in nature and therefore should fall to the NSDStB.[145] Although the Reich Education Ministry continued to protect the German Stu-

---

[142] Feickert had enlisted the support of Ernst Krieck as the codirector of the conference. Rundschreiben Drescher to Student Leaders, 23 January 1935, ZStA REM 890. For Krieck's role in the attempted reforms of higher education, see Gerhard Müller, *Ernst Krieck und die nationalsozialistische Wissenschaftsreform: Motive und Tendenzen einer Wissenschaftslehre und Hochschulreform im Dritten Reich* (Weinheim, 1978), esp. chap. 5.

[143] "Vertrauliche Mitteilungen der Deutschen Landsmannschaft," *Beilage zur Landsmannschafter-Zeitung*, 29 April 1935, p. 26.

[144] Erich Pempeit, an assistant of Feickert, was arrested at 4:30 A.M. by the Berlin police on suspicion of participation "in a secret plot to engineer the downfall of *Reichsamtsleiter* Derichsweiler." His opinion was sought under interrogation about the demands for Feickert's resignation by the Student Leaders Diederichs and Scheel. Bericht Pempeit, 25 April 1935, RSFWü I*00 φ 30/2. Scheel's name seems to crop up wherever trouble was brewing: it appears that he was at the same time defaming Derichsweiler, claiming that NSDStB headquarters was riddled with Catholics. Cf. Derichsweiler's opening speech in Protokoll Reichstagung NSDStB, 11 May 1935, RSFWü II* φ 319.

[145] Derichsweiler to Kunisch, 19 February 1935, ZStA REM 909.

dents' Union, its higher education officials began to acknowledge that neither Derichsweiler nor Feickert was entirely suitable as a student leader. For the first time, Professor Bachér noted in a memorandum for Rust the idea that student leaders should not be students: "The 'genuine students' have long been fed up with being 'led,' schooled and commanded by 'student bigwigs.' . . . They desire leadership by older persons who live and act in an exemplary fashion, who are more capable than they."[146]

Feickert's credibility and authority crumbled, and doubt filled DSt headquarters concerning its proper tasks in the student body. Frustrated at Rust's repeated refusal to see him in order to discuss the problems of the DSt or even to send him positive indication of support, Feickert offered his resignation on 11 March 1935 and made his own proposals for the strengthening of the Student Unions against the NSDStB. He suggested that DSt headquarters be dissolved and the leadership built into a department of the Education Ministry, which would have direct jurisdiction over the individual Student Unions.[147] The plan was ignored, though Rust did issue on 25 April 1935 a rejoinder to a circular of Derichsweiler's to the effect that the student departmental group work remained the task of the DSt. Undaunted, Derichsweiler issued another memorandum stressing that it certainly was not. The Ministry parried with a seven-point list of the tasks claimed for the DSt.[148] Rust called all the

---

[146] Vermerk Bachér to Rust, 18 February 1935, ibid.

[147] Feickert was particularly annoyed to have been excluded from the Party's Higher Education Commission, to which Derichsweiler had been appointed on 21 February. Rust hedged as usual, signifying that his plans for the DSt were "not yet sufficiently developed to allow the possibility of a fruitful discussion." Feickert to Rust, 11 March 1935, RSFWü II*A29 α 477.

[148] The tasks of the DSt concerned (1) Departmental groups, (2) Labor Service, (3) Frontier areas (including the Rural Service), (4) International topics, (5) Press and film, (6) Student Sport, and (7) Female students. Eil-Rundschreiben Derichsweiler, 30 April 1935, ibid.; Erlass Rust, 15 May 1935, UniHH 0.10.2.8.

194

local leaders of students' unions to the Ministry on 26 May 1935 for a conference. His intended encouragement was more a testimony to his own weakness. His advice to the students' union leaders amounted to little more than "grin and bear it": "Something or other is bound to crystallize out of this gradually. A complete reformulation of the student code in the very year of the creation of the student code would not have made a very pleasant impression on the outside world. In the presence of the *Führer* and in his name, the Reich Minister of the Interior proclaims a new student code and in the same year this student code is rescinded: *ordre, contreordre, désordre!*"[149]

At the local level, this vacillation indeed resulted in confusion, for the holders of DST and NSDStB posts were more often than not one and the same person. The struggle between state and Party organs was by no means peculiar to the student world. In the autumn a confidential circular was prepared for junior leaders in all branches of the Nazi movement, reminding them that "never must a lack of agreement or the incidence of difficulties reach the public ear. Both sides should be clear that otherwise each of them, the state and the Party, are the losers, because the reputations of both suffer."[150] Hess followed this with an edict insisting that press announcements on student affairs should in the future be censored by Gerhard Wagner in order to avoid "the ugly picture of contradictory decrees."[151]

Having seen in Hitler's attitude to the fraternity associations an endorsement of Derichsweiler's policies and thus of his overall leadership, Rust was now willing to let Feickert go. The latter had been thoroughly trounced by Derichs-

---

[149] Protokoll Konferenz Studentenschaftsführer, 26 May 1935, ZStA REM 868.

[150] Rundschreiben Bormann, 12 October 1935, RSFWü II*A29 α 477. The circular consisted of extracts from a speech by Hess to Party functionaries at the recent Nuremberg Rally.

[151] Anordnung Hess, 223/35, 19 November 1935, MicAlex T-81/237/5022862-63.

weiler and had practically spent himself in the struggle. Not only was he on the verge of a nervous breakdown, but he was facing charges arising from a car accident in which he was apparently drunk.[152] Feickert and the Ministry approached four student leaders (among them Gustav Adolf Scheel), all of whom turned down the offer of the DST leadership, seeing, like Feickert himself a year earlier, no chance of success as long as the NSDStB leadership remained separate.[153] And so Feickert was obliged *malgré tout* to soldier on in a position that no one wanted.

The beginning of the year 1936 saw the NSDStB strong and aggressive and delighting in the steady weakening of the fraternities and the DST. Derichsweiler's headquarters moved from three small rooms in the Brown House at Munich to its own building in the *Karlsstrasse*.[154] On 26 January 1936 the tenth anniversary celebrations of the NSDStB's foundation were held in Munich with much fanfare. Hitler himself came to make a speech (albeit of little relevance to student affairs),[155] and Derichsweiler triumphantly proclaimed the NSDStB's imminent takeover of the German Students'

[152] The drunken driving charge was the ostensible excuse for Rust's suspension of Feickert the following February, though he had in fact known about it for months. Vermerk Heinrich, 9 August 1935, ZStA REM 868.

[153] Vermerk Bachér, 14 August 1935, ibid. Herbert Guthjahr, the Berlin Student Leader, was mentioned again the following winter as a possible successor along with Waldemar Müller, who eventually took the post. Vermerk Weinrich to Rust, 7 February 1936, ZStA REM 907.

[154] The move to Karlsstrasse 16 took place during the week 10-16 February 1936. Not wishing to be outdone, the German Students' Union moved into larger headquarters on 12 October 1936.

[155] Hitler caused a diplomatic upset by "his thundering proclamation . . . of the (apparently divine) destiny of the white race to rule the world and the right of European nations to colonize backward areas." *Japan Times*, 29 January 1936. The Foreign Office was particularly worried that large orders from India with the Krupp firm would be canceled, and it dispatched cables to India and Japan denying that Hitler had implied any of the sentiments attributed to him. Vermerk Stutterheim to Lammers, 19 February 1936, BA R43II/991a.

Union.[156] Powerless to speak at these Party celebrations himself, Feickert took immediate steps to make a speech in Munich in order to point out that the DST had no intention of surrendering. A telegram from Rust forbade him to do so.[157] The Minister had apparently given up the struggle and suspended Feickert from office a fortnight later.[158] Feickert formally resigned on 2 April 1936. A note in the Ministry files reveals that he was to be sentenced with seven months' imprisonment for his drunken driving offenses.[159] It appears that he avoided this on appeal, for on 23 April he was advised by the Ministry to study abroad for eighteen months to two years until the affair had blown over and was promised a scholarship to finance this face-saving operation.[160]

One of Feickert's assistants, Waldemar Müller, was given temporary charge of the DST. Within a week Derichsweiler had extracted a statement from Müller, requesting Hitler to permit only a single Reich Student Leader, to be appointed *"by the Party* [emphasis added], with the consent of the Reich Education Minister."[161] Clearly Derichsweiler saw himself as the new leader.[162] Dr. Heinrich, the Education Ministry's official for student affairs, spread the view, however, that Derichsweiler was not an idealist but a pure schemer. In order to prevent Derichsweiler from usurping the post of DST leader, Heinrich began collecting evidence from university rectors on student dissatisfaction with Derichsweiler and the NSDStB. His own superior, Professor Bachér, also recorded that the rector of Königsberg University had "again confirmed to me that the students want to

---

[156] Feickert to Derichsweiler, 13 February 1936, RSFWü II*A29 α 477.

[157] Telegram Rust to Feickert, 6 February 1936, MicAlex T-81/236/5021297.

[158] Rust to Feickert, 21 February 1936, BDC Partei-Korrespondenz Feickert.

[159] Feickert to Heinrich, 6 February 1936, and marginal comments by Heinrich, ZStA REM 868.

[160] Heinrich to Feickert, 23 April 1936, ibid.

[161] Derichsweiler and Müller to Hitler, 28 February 1936, RSFWü II*A29 α 477.

[162] Vermerk Kunisch to Rust, 5 March 1936, ZStA REM 907.

hear *nothing* more of their so-called 'leaders,' who in reality act like shop stewards."[163]

Until a settlement was reached, Müller, seeing no reason to halt projects already underway, did his best to uphold the organizational framework of the DST. Derichsweiler kept up his crippling attacks: on 2 April 1936, he forbade NSDStB members to accept posts in the DST without his own prior permission.[164] Above all, he attempted to sabotage the DST's "Rural Service" (*Landdienst*). This extension of the Labor Service idea, based on the farms of the German frontier areas in the East, was fully recognized by the NSDStB as one of the few exclusive prerogatives of the DST while student support for it remained poor. As soon as interest in it began to grow, and its propaganda value came to be realized, Derichsweiler declared the Rural Service to lie after all under the jurisdiction of the NSDStB, despite the firm protests of the Education Ministry.[165] Although the NSDStB's takeover of the German Students' Union now seemed only a matter of time, Derichsweiler kept up his provocations. He could hardly have weakened his opponents any further, but he made them less ready to accept the reunion.

At the beginning of September Müller wrote to Rust, suggesting that the Minister confer with Hess at the forthcoming Nuremberg Rally over the question of a successor.[166] The subject was indeed discussed at the Rally, but the Party suggested the apparent compromise of allowing Derichsweiler the joint leadership for three months until a successor could be found. Rust would have agreed, but other ministerial representatives counseled him against this solution. Above all, the former leader of the *Deutsche Burschenschaft*, Hans Glauning, who had just been drafted into the Ministry, managed to persuade Rust of the absolute unacceptability

---

[163] Vermerk Heinrich to Rust, 21 April 1936, and marginal comment by Bachér, ibid.

[164] Rundschreiben Schmauser, 2 April 1936, RSFWü II*A42 α 479.

[165] Stellungnahme zur Frage des studentischen Landdienstes (Müller), 18 March 1936, RSFWü II*A29 α 477.

[166] Müller to Rust, 8 September 1936, MicAlex T-81/236/5021200-205.

of Derichsweiler even as temporary joint leader to the tens of thousands of present and former fraternity members.[167]

The deadlock remained unresolved, and local student leaders continued to be assailed by opposing orders from DST and NSDStB headquarters. One leader, of both an NSDStB group and his Students' Union, stood up at a conference in October 1936 to complain of "the petty war between the student leadership in Berlin [DST] and Munich [NSDStB]" and pointed out that it had been quite impossible for some time to comply with the wishes of both, "since their orders directly contradict each other." Declaring that the NSDStB was the worse offender, he angrily left the conference in protest, refusing to serve in the NSDStB under Derichsweiler's leadership.[168]

The attention of SS Chief Heinrich Himmler was drawn to the impasse in the student world by his Security Service (SD). This secret police branch of the SS, flourishing under Reinhard Heydrich, had since 1934 attracted many university graduates and undergraduates, among them the Baden District Student Leader Gustav Adolf Scheel.[169] The SD regarded itself as the think tank of the NSDAP and hoped, with

[167] Cf. Protokoll DST-Amtsleiterbesprechung, 24 September 1936, RSFWü II*A29 α 477.

[168] Stender to DST-Reichsführung, 24 October 1936; Stender to Reichsstudentenbundsführung, 24 October 1936; Müller replied to this student leader of the Technical University at Stuttgart: "I admire your manly behavior." Müller to Stender, 29 October 1936, RSFWü II*80 α 23.

[169] Müller believes that several students at Heidelberg besides Scheel were recruited by Reinhard Höhn, a lecturer in law. Müller, *Ernst Krieck*, p. 118. One of Feickert's assistants, Helmut Knochen, left DST headquarters in the summer of 1936 to work full time for the SD. Cf. Protokoll DST-Amtsleiterbesprechung, 24 September 1936, RSFWü II*A29 α 477. Knochen later played a part in the SD's preparations for the invasion of Poland and went on to become head of Group H (Investigation of ideological enemies abroad) in the International Department of SD headquarters. Alwin Ramme, *Der Sicherheitsdienst der SS: Zu seiner Funktion im faschistischen Machtapparat und im Besatzungsregime des sogenannten Generalgouvernement Polens* (Berlin, 1970), p. 107 and Anlage zu Schema 2; and cf. Michael H. Kater, *Das "Ahnenerbe" der SS 1935-1945: Ein Beitrag zur Kulturpolitik des Dritten Reiches* (Stuttgart, 1974), p. 192.

its ss backing, to play the role of watchdog of the Party. It was deeply concerned with ideology and with making National Socialism palatable to the intelligentsia, and thus it had a close interest in the universities and the ideological training that was carried on there. Indeed, some of Himmler's own fondest memories were of his work in student government.[170]

The SD now realized that the students' rejection of Derichsweiler was being extended to National Socialism as a whole.[171] Himmler was persuaded to intercede personally with Rust and Hess on behalf of Scheel, who was now SD chief of the whole of South-West Germany (at this time one of only seven *SD-Oberabschnittsführer*). Scheel, although no longer a student, had a long record as an agitator on behalf of National Socialism: he had been disciplined by the University of Heidelberg in 1932 for his part in demonstrations against the Jewish professor Emil Gumbel.[172] The Education Ministry had already offered him the DST leadership once. Hess had no better candidate and so, reluctant though he was to lose Derichsweiler, he agreed to the new appointment. Scheel submitted to Rust and Hess on 2 November 1936 the SD plan for the new Reich Student Leadership (*Reichsstudentenführung* or RSF). He made the adoption of it by both Party and Ministry a precondition of his acceptance of the post.[173] There was no time to quibble, for the new semester was beginning, and Scheel was hastily ap-

[170] "The single most frequent entry in Himmler's diaries during his years in school was in all probability '*Akten studiert*,' referring to his favorite pastime of working in the files of the student government. Here he could be happy in the obsessional world of rules and regulations." Peter Loewenberg also comments on Himmler's participation in a dueling fraternity in his article, "The Unsuccessful Adolescence of Heinrich Himmler," now reprinted in Peter Loewenberg, *Decoding the Past* (New York, 1983), p. 232.

[171] Brandt to Herff, 22 September 1944, BDC SS Derichsweiler.

[172] Faust, *Studentenbund*, 2: 57ff.

[173] Denkschrift Scheel, "Die Neuordnung des deutschen Studententums," 2 November 1936, ZSTA REM 894.

pointed Reich Student Leader (*Reichsstudentenführer*) three days later.

The Nazi students had so far only proved adept at destructive tasks, and even then they faced difficulties in the face of opposition from the fraternities or professors. When it came to constructive measures they had little to offer that could attract the students. In the absence of a coherent ideological program the NSDStB came more and more to rely, like the Nazi state itself, on a "permanent state of emergency" as a justification for its rule. The fight against a common enemy, in this period largely the "reactionary" fraternity students, and the search for new enemies helped to embellish the void that the so-called training program and ideology could not fill. The failure of the student leadership to assert itself fully among the students was, however, seen in terms of the confusion resulting from the constant stream of contradictory decrees from the two separate national headquarters rather than any intrinsic shortcomings. Yet at the local level the student leaders could not hope to inspire confidence and to impress the students with their unity so long as they tended to be more concerned with their personal authority than with the pursuit of their political goals. Their pettiness was unlikely to win over new followers. Even the Party's District Leadership in Hamburg recognized the absurdity of the NSDStB's racial zeal in attempting to oust the able director of the University's Chemical Institute, Professor Schlubach, on the grounds that his paternal grandmother had been a princess of Tahiti.[174]

[174] Clausen to NSDStB, 18 September 1935, RSFWÜ V*2 α 573.

CHAPTER SIX

The Consolidation of Control

It had appeared in 1933 that the complete nazification of the student body was imminent. No one foresaw during that spring just how disruptive the internal squabbles would prove to be. By the end of 1936 everybody believed that the blame for such limited progress should be laid at the door of the double-headed student leadership. When Gustav Adolf Scheel created a single, supreme body in its place, that explanation (or excuse) had to be set aside. Now there seemed to be no reason why the ideal, Nazi university, at least at the student end, should not come to fruition very rapidly.

This chapter examines the NSDStB in the last three peacetime years, when it was at its peak. Its enrollments rose, the number of *Kameradschaften* grew, and it generally settled down to greater acceptance by the faculty. Yet the picture was not perfect, nor Scheel's control complete, although this has often been assumed to be the case. Scheel's first and most pressing task was the institutional underpinning of the Reich Student Leadership, within both the Party hierarchy and the student body. In the latter the perceived problem was the continued existence of the last surviving remnants of the fraternities, their alumni associations. Scheel's handling of this question reveals the true nature of the apparently more conciliatory student leadership: there was still an iron fist inside the velvet glove.

Two further areas of concern for the student leaders are also examined here. The provision of higher education for all who could qualify, regardless of financial capability, had been one of the original planks in the Nazi program, when Hitler first drew it up shortly after the First World War. The neglect of this point nationally contrasted unfavorably with the policy instituted at Hamburg. This is seen in the context of other developments in that city, which show the University using the resources of the Nazi regime to enhance its position, especially in relation to its great rival, Berlin.

Finally, the old aim of nazifying scholarship, which had seemed so crucial to many in the NSDStB during the Weimar Republic, had still not been accomplished. Here was another area where Scheel could earn much praise if he made it a top priority. Once again, however, ideological work was pursued in a lukewarm fashion, as more urgent political tasks seemed to keep cropping up. Certainly the Reich Student Leadership made considerable progress in many areas and lost no time in publicizing it. But beneath the braggadocio of Scheel and his associates there was still a sense of frustration, which from now on they attempted to assuage by increasing their controls over all German students.

The Reich Student Leadership and the Growth of the Kameradschaften

Scheel assumed office as Reich Student Leader on 5 November 1936, and addressed his junior student leaders five days later in the impressive surroundings of Schloss Solitude at Stuttgart.[1] The very location was suggestive of a new style of leadership. Whereas the more down-to-earth Andreas Feickert had literally paved Scheel's way to the palace with pick and shovel,[2] the new Reich Student Leader clearly wanted to restore the bruised authority of the student leadership. His very first measure was to forbid the "unsuitable familiarity" of the customary *du* form of address in correspondence between student leaders, which he considered

---

[1] Rede Scheel, Schloss Solitude, 10 November 1936. Text in Institut für Hochschulkunde, Würzburg (IfH) B/P 33 (Pressedienst Reichsstudentenführung). Dibner, "History," p. 233, gives the date of Scheel's appointment as 7 November, but cf. Chef-Befehl, no. 1, 16 November 1936, RSFWü I*06 φ 56.

[2] See above, chap. 3, n. 38.

"entirely undesirable."[3] Scheel had gained wide respect as a student leader. Baden was almost the only district where there were no clashes between NSDStB and German Students' Union factions between 1934 and 1936, and he was given credit for this.[4] Since Scheel was the person who mobilized SS Security Service agents against the "Heidelberg asparagus eaters," his success may have been achieved through coercion, not charisma.[5]

Scheel was in the forefront of the Security Service's efforts to restore visible order to the Nazi state after the initial random violence. He was appointed at the age of twenty-six as director of the SD School in September 1934. He rose to become the head of the SD's southwest district in 1936, and this remained his chief job even after he became Reich Student Leader. Derichsweiler had seen the very strength of the NSDStB headquarters staff in the fact that he and his dozen department chiefs formed an intimate group who met daily and gathered over beer in the evening to make plans and discuss problems. Scheel was a mere bird of passage in the offices of the Reich Student Leadership.[6]

General fears arose that the student leadership would now be simply an adjunct of the SS. The Jena Student Leaders were summoned to the Reich Student Leadership in Munich on the mere suggestion that they held this view.[7] Although

---

[3] Chef-Befehl, no. 1, 16 November 1936, RSFWü I*06 φ 56.

[4] Clashes with the fraternities were kept to a minimum, too. Scheel's influence was said to have led altogether to "a much greater and more satisfactory success than in the rest of the Reich." Gestapo Karlsruhe to Gestapa, 16 April 1936, ZStA REM 872. Also Clemens Zimmermann, "Die Bücherverbrennung am 17. Mai 1933 in Heidelberg: Studenten und Politik am Ende der Weimarer Republik," in Leonhard, Bücherverbrennung, p. 65.

[5] See above, chap. 5.

[6] Dickerhof to RSF-Amtsleiter, 5 January 1938, BDC Partei-Korrespondenz Dickerhof.

[7] A letter of thanks to Derichsweiler for his leadership was immediately interpreted as opposition to the new leadership! RSF-Stabsamt, Niederschrift Anhörung Keppel, 20 November 1936, RSFWü II*156 α 87.

Scheel repeatedly denied the crucial nature of the ss link, he did little in practice to counter this impression. He never, for example, wore or even possessed the uniform appropriate to his position as Reich Leader of the NSDStB, but he appeared without exception in ss uniform.[8] Although he showed no favoritism toward any single Party Formation in his distribution of appointments, the SD, with its interest in ideology, controlled those sections concerned with scholarship.[9] Fritz Kubach headed the office for education and science, and Franz Six controlled the students' Reich Vocational Contest. Both of them were SD officers who had served under Scheel in the student leadership at Heidelberg. Like Scheel, they had already obtained a doctorate, as had six of the original eighteen members of the Reich Student Leadership. Scheel drew on the ranks of the SD once more when appointing the Regional Commissioners (*Gebietsbeauftragte*, later *Bereichsführer*), whose job was to watch over the Districts for signs of dissidence or nonconformity. As a step toward restoring the confidence of the faculty in the NSDStB, Scheel ordered all "objectively unjustified attacks against professors" to cease.[10]

In order to prepare for a purge of the student body, the SD approached the university authorities. Agents in Hamburg requested information on faculty or students who had been

[8] Scheel requested instructions from Heydrich on the acceptance of honors from other Party Formations. He stressed that "even on the acceptance of honorary ranks, it goes without saying that my uniform would continue to be only that of the ss." Scheel to Heydrich, 23 December 1937, MicAlex T-81/246/5033361-62. Scheel confirmed this during the author's interview with him on 11 April 1973.

[9] Following the separation of the functions of the SD and the Gestapo through the so-called *Funktionstrennungserlass* of 1 July 1937, the SD gained sole responsibility for the surveillance of education and science. Cf. Heinz Boberach (ed.), *Meldungen aus dem Reich: Auswahl aus den geheimen Lageberichten des Sicherheitsdienstes der SS 1939-1944* (Neuwied/Berlin, 1965), p. 12.

[10] Scheel to Hess, 11 May 1937, RSFWü II*114 α 58.

"enemies of the NSDAP before the seizure of power."[11] Far from releasing the files or even the names of former left-wing student group members, many of whom had already been disciplined in 1933, Rector Rein embroiled the SD in a tortuous correspondence. His bureaucratic pettifoggery persisted for almost a year, until the SD authorities simply threw up their hands. Rein claimed variously that ministerial permission must first be sought, that only the head of the SD subdistrict might inspect the files, and that the files could under no circumstances be removed from the University.[12] He was particularly adept at this game of legalism, shielding the University behind the decrees of one agency in order to protect it from another. The Reich Education Ministry gave him much ammunition, with its constant stream of unclear and often contradictory directives. Rein disliked any external meddling with his leadership of the University and particularly resented the interference of a police organization. Above all, he knew that he could rely on the protection of *Gauleiter* Kaufmann (who was no friend of Himmler's), and this especially allowed him to be so confidently assertive in the face of an ostensibly sinister intrusion.

Despite the very close ties, the Reich Student Leadership was not working entirely hand in glove with the Security Service. There was, for example, sufficient distance between the two for the latter to publish an ill-timed, critical, and sarcastic article in the SS newspaper, *Das Schwarze Korps*, about the alumni branch of the NSDStB without any prior consultation with the Reich Student Leadership. The initial embarrassment was bad enough, but when it was learned that other press organs were eager to print the story, the Reich Student Leadership hurried to urge the Propaganda Ministry to halt any further publication.[13]

[11] Aktenvermerk Capelle, 8 August 1937, UniHH A.1.6.

[12] Rein to SD-Unterabschnittsführer Hamburg, 3 September 1937; Bothe to SD-Unterabschnittsführer Hamburg, 12 March 1938, UniHH 0.30.2.

[13] A student leader in Hildburghausen had tried to encourage membership in the alumni association by pointing out that the buttonhole badge to

The influence of the SD or SS on the student leadership was almost never in the form of direct orders but in more general terms, inasmuch as Scheel's attitude pervaded policy making.[14] Scheel's SS mentality led him to demand two basic things of the Reich Student Leadership: the maintenance of the strictest discipline and, by the reliability and orthodoxy thus created, the development of an image of elite excellence.[15] The maintenance of discipline was laid down in new disciplinary codes for the NSDStB and the German Students' Union.[16] The latter body remained formally in existence within the new Reich Student Leadership, which theoretically consisted of the combined headquarters of the NSDStB and the DST. This measure ensured that the student leaders had disciplinary jurisdiction over the entire student body—as NSDStB leaders they only controlled the members of that organization. In drawing up the disciplinary codes Scheel took the SS code for his model, which, by its very vagueness concerning punishments and offenses, could conveniently sanction almost any punitive action.[17]

---

which one became entitled looked similar to that of the Party. "Beinahe Parteiabzeichen," *Das Schwarze Korps*, 5 May 1938; Tipke to Stephan, 17 May 1938, BA NS38/29. See also Giles, "Verbändepolitik," pp. 147-48.

[14] Dibner claims that with the very appointment of Scheel, "it followed that from now on Himmler had a large influence on the student groups and was greatly responsible for their future policies." Dibner, "History," p. 237. She offers no evidence of direct intervention on the part of Himmler. In fact, he concerned himself only infrequently with student affairs: during the war instructing Heydrich to have a few draft-dodgers among students of medicine shot *pour encourager les autres*, and giving instructions to contain the potential scandal of the "White Rose" resistance. In other words, he intervened for the most part only to ensure the maintenance of order. He did not closely monitor the political work of the Reich Student Leadership. Cf. Helmut Heiber (ed.), *Reichsführer! . . . Briefe an und von Himmler* (Stuttgart, 1968), pp. 69 and 183.

[15] The SS mentality is discussed fully in Hans Buchheim, "Command and Compliance," in *Anatomy of the SS State*, ed. Helmut Krausnick et al. (New York, 1968), pp. 319ff.

[16] "Dienststrafordnung des NSD-Studentenbundes" and "Dienststrafordnung der Deutschen Studentenschaft," *Verordnungsblatt des Reichsstudentenführers*, no. 14, 22 June 1937, UNIHH 0.30.6.

[17] Scharfe to Scheel, 7 April 1937, RSFwü II*82 α 24.

Scheel seems to have adopted a similar attitude regarding a constitution for the student body. One of his first priorities was the replacement of the outdated 1934 constitution of the German Students' Union with one clarifying the extensive powers of the new Reich Student Leader. A committee that included Ernst Krieck was formed in December 1936, but the work of drafting was delayed again and again.[18] The committee considered it axiomatic that "the main object of law-making [was] not to constrict a living growth between fixed regulations but to develop and arrange a new order of life organically."[19] When a draft was finally drawn up in November 1938, the Reich Education Ministry privately raised a number of objections. Officials were reluctant to give the unification of the leadership a constitutional finality, fearing that Scheel's successor might not be acceptable to them but would be imposed on the German Students' Union by the Party.[20] They were firmly opposed to the granting of direct, personal access to the Minister, as Scheel had demanded, knowing how pliable Rust could be in such confrontations if his advisors were not present to support him. So they simply sat on the proposals for several months and only agreed to preliminary discussions at the end of August 1939.[21] After the outbreak of the war, negotiations were halted. Scheel preferred to obtain the control that he wanted over the student body through police powers and not through a probably restrictive constitution.

"It is a fact," Scheel reported to Hess in March 1937, "that the importance of the work of the Reich Student Leadership is still not fully recognized by numerous sections of the Party."[22] Although prevaricating over the constitution, Scheel was annoyed that others did not observe certain for-

[18] Gerhard Miller stresses Krieck's strong influence on the thinking of the committee. Müller, *Ernst Krieck*, p. 505.

[19] Bässler, "Die deutsche Studentenschaft," p. 231.

[20] Vermerk Huber, 16 January 1939, zstA REM 909.

[21] Protokoll Besprechung Sandberger and Huber, 21 August 1939, ibid.

[22] Scheel to Hess, 9 March 1937, RSFWü II*114 α 58.

malities. The NSDStB was not accorded the respect due to it as a Formation (*Gliederung*) of the Party. This stemmed partly from the ambiguous position of the former. Officially the NSDStB was one of the seven Formations of the Party, and therefore Scheel, as Reich Leader, should have been of equal rank with *Reichsführer-SS* Himmler, or Reich Youth Leader Baldur von Schirach.[23] The DST, however, continued to exist nominally as a "supervised organization" (*betreute Organisation*), and the Party's control implicit in this was extended to the Reich Student Leadership as a whole (embracing both the DST and the NSDStB). The Reich Student Leadership itself was incorporated into the Party structure as a mere "Head Office" (*Hauptamt*).[24] Reich Organization Leader Ley treated the NSDStB as a dependency rather than a constituent part of the Reich Student Leadership, and as such made it liable to the ultimate control of *his* office.[25] Accordingly, Scheel was not given the rank of *Reichsleiter* in the Party hierarchy but only that of *Hauptamtsleiter*, the third rank down.[26] He discovered to his chagrin that he was not permitted to fly a rectangular standard on his official car like the other Formation Leaders but had to be content with the inferior triangular one.[27]

Such symbolic snubs hurt. It remains unclear whether this

[23] "Durchführungsverordnung zum Gesetz zur Sicherung der Einheit von Partei und Staat vom 29. März 1935," *Reichsgesetzblatt* 1, no. 39 (9 April 1935).

[24] Anordnung Ley no. 8/37, 19 April 1937, RSFWü I*06 ɸ 56.

[25] Aktenvermerk Paasche, "Besprechungsgrundlage Bormann: NSDStB als Gliederung," 25 February 1938, BA NS38/1.

[26] Although the Reich Student Leadership was declared to be a *Hauptamt der NSDAP* in April 1937, Scheel was not accorded the Party rank of *Reichshauptamtsleiter* until 30 January 1939. Cf. "1939 im Rückblick," *Die Bewegung*, 2 January 1940. A photograph of Scheel in uniform in 1944 shows him with a strange collar insignia, which looks like the *Reichsleiter* symbol superimposed over the *Gauleiter's* oak leaves, but I could find no announcement of his promotion to the Party's highest rank. Photograph as frontispiece of Reichsstudentenführung (ed.), *Zehn Jahre Langemarck-Studium Königsberg (Pr.)* (Königsberg, 1944).

[27] Schmauser to Horn, 10 December 1937, RSFWü II*98 α 43.

situation was ever formally resolved to Scheel's satisfaction, but no practical weakening of his position resulted from it. When, for example, Schirach, a close ally of Ley's, claimed the right to conduct the political education of students in the teacher training colleges, Martin Bormann came to Scheel's aid with a Party Chancellery ruling that this was unquestionably the Reich Student Leadership's task.[28] The whole question reflects the jostling for power of Nazi leaders rather than suggesting a reluctance to accord status and relative autonomy to a section of the intelligentsia.

One of the disadvantages of the German university system, from the point of view of the NSDStB, was the freedom of the students to move from one university to another at will. This made control by the student leaders extremely difficult and a coordinated program of political education almost impossible. Scheel solicited the initial consent of Rust that each student should be compelled to spend his first three semesters, the length of the NSDStB basic training program, at the same university.[29] There would then be much less likelihood of students slipping through the NSDStB's net. Typically, the Reich Education Ministry changed its mind. It wished to keep students at the same college for only two semesters, with a mere recommendation to stay for a third. The ministry now defended mobility, believing it to be an important means of destroying north-south provincialism, of boosting support for the beleaguered institutions in East Prussia, and of generally strengthening the importance of the Reich in the face of federal particularism.[30]

As it was, many students did not report to the Student

[28] Bormann also overturned Schirach's ruling that HJ members might not at the same time join the NSDStB. Bormann to Scheel, 19 August 1938, BA NS38/55.

[29] Denkschrift Scheel, "Neuordnung des deutschen Studententums," 2 November 1936, ZStA REM 894.

[30] REM to Sandberger, 5 February 1937 (though a note reveals that it was not actually sent), ibid.

Leader's office on matriculation as instructed. Only some 40 percent of the Hamburg freshmen filled out a compulsory questionnaire for the NSDStB in the winter semester 1936-1937. Many refused to do so because they believed that it would lead to automatic membership in the NSDStB.[31] Scheel wished to have a personnel file kept on each student, containing reports on his political reliability.[32] Again the Education Ministry took sides with the students with the clever argument that Scheel's proposal stood in contradiction "with the efforts of the Four-Year Plan to reduce the use of paper to a minimum." More to the point, the official remarked that unmerited, negative reports would unfairly damage the career prospects of students.[33]

A better organizational framework for controlling the students was a major goal for Scheel, but the real problem lay in making the activities of the *Kameradschaften* attractive to the students at large. The NSDStB's training under Derichsweiler had still carried the air of militarism that had characterized the SA University Office, with outdoor maneuvers and drill. Though this by no means ceased under Scheel, who valued training in discipline, he was instructed to play down this type of activity by Himmler, who remarked forthrightly: "I regard it as a catastrophe when, as was the case in the last few years, the work of the [National Socialist] Students' Association . . . consisted in packing a fine rucksack and going on exercise. I don't need a Students' Union for that. I spoke to the new Students' Association Leader recently and I said to him: 'My dear Scheel, if ever I catch you drilling with your *Kameradschaften*, you will have me as your absolute enemy. In Student Houses you're meant to work intellectually and lead intellectually and put society

[31] Bergmann to Rein, 23 November 1936; Rein to students who had failed to complete questionnaire, 2 December 1936; and replies, UniHH 0.30.6.

[32] This attitude is typical of the SD. For Heydrich's dream of bringing "every single individual in Germany under continuous supervision," see Krausnick et al., *Anatomy*, p. 167.

[33] Kunisch to RSF-Stabsleiter, 28 October 1937, UniHH 0.30.6.

in order.' "[34] But at least rucksack-packing had given the *Kameradschaft* leaders *something* with which to fill the program. Scheel and his assistants toured Germany in their first months of office visiting *Kameradschaften*, and during the 1937 summer vacation they sat in conference for three days, pooling their experiences. They reached the sad conclusion that the average *Kameradschaft* leader had "very little idea of our proper political task" and was often at a loss for what activities he should undertake with the *Kameradschaft*. This was hardly designed to convince the majority of students of the justness of the NSDStB's claimed right to take up so much of the students' valuable time.[35] And in fact the *Kameradschaften* had not come very far with recruitment. During the winter semester 1936-1937, an average of 14 percent of the male students belonged to one. In the winter semester 1930-1931, more than twice that proportion had belonged to fraternities.[36] In the summer of 1937 the NSDStB could still only fill two out of every three places in the few residential *Kameradschaft* houses that it had acquired. The financial loss was considerable, as Table 5 shows.

A Hamburg student leader admitted that the real problem was the serious lack of capable leaders able to inspire the students. He added that the situation was in no way helped by the total absence of guidance from the Reich Student Leadership on the programming of *Kameradschaft* activi-

[34] The remarks were made in the context of a speech about homosexuality, to the increase of which Hitler feared that the marked *Vermännlichung* of life in the Third Reich would lead. Rede Himmlers anlässlich der Gruppenführer-Besprechung in Tölz, 18 February 1937. Text in Bradley F. Smith and Agnes Peterson, *Heinrich Himmler: Geheimreden 1933 bis 1945 und andere Ansprachen* (Frankfurt am Main, 1974), here pp. 99-100.

[35] Protokoll Arbeitstagung Reichsstudentenführung, 11-13 August 1937, RSFWü II*83 α 25.

[36] RSF-Organisationsabteilung, "Korporationen—Kameradschaften: Eine statistische Gegenüberstellung," 9 February 1937. RSFWü II*450 α 353. The table gives details for thirty-five college towns. As so often, the arithmetic of the Nazi student leaders is faulty, and I have corrected the percentages in reproducing the table in Giles, "Verbändepolitik," pp. 142-43.

TABLE 5. Underutilization of *Kameradschaft* Houses, 1937

University town	Maximum accommodation	Occupants summer semester 1937	Financial loss 1936-1937 in RM
Berlin	(rented to NSV)		20,277
Bonn	80	66	2,000
Charlottenburg	143	105	5,872
Darmstadt	100	49	6,830
Dresden	37	37	209
Düsseldorf	5	5	225
Erlangen	40	29	658
Frankfurt	40	35	1,307
Freiberg*	30	11	(several thousand)
Göttingen	65	59	3,360
Halle	80	37	16,284
Hannover	30	30	0
Heidelberg	25	20	252
Jena	100	25	64
Kiel	50	35	1,569
Köln	—	—	2,855
Königsberg	28	25	2,873
Marburg	39	30	2,933
Rostock	32	22	—
Total	924	620	67,568

Note. The dash indicates data not available.
* Possibly an error for Freiburg, since most of the others are major university towns.
Source: Streit to REM, 30 October 1937, ZSTA REM 893.

ties.[37] It was to this task that Scheel and his assistants turned their attention at their conference in August. Scheel and his colleagues agreed that "the *Kameradschaft* meetings suffer from a lack of content and therefore usually degenerate very quickly into general merrymaking."[38] The Reich Student Leadership hoped to solve this problem by producing for the *Kameradschaft* leaders a set of written guidelines explaining their tasks in detail. In order to boost their importance, it

[37] Tätigkeitsbericht Killer, 28 May 1937, RSFWü V*2 α 539.
[38] Protokoll Arbeitstagung Reichsstudentenführung, 11-13 August 1937, RSFWü II*83 α 25.

was announced in the autumn of 1937 that membership of the NSDStB could in the future be gained only through successful service in a *Kameradschaft*.[39] Admission was to remain voluntary, but any student not joining would henceforth be required to justify his refusal at length and in writing. He would then be summoned to appear in person before the local Student Leader, who would attempt to persuade him to change his mind.[40]

This bold effort to coerce almost every student into joining a *Kameradschaft* has once again led scholars to assume the success of the policy. Steinberg dates the perfection of the Nazi machine even earlier, stating that "by the summer of 1935, the lives of Germany's students had been carefully regimented," and that "by 1936, regimentation was complete." He believes that even before Scheel took office, "the majority of students were required to spend at least their first three semesters in communal living quarters." He offers no thoughts on why only some were obliged to do so and who they were.[41] Franze writes of "obligatory *Kameradschaft* training for all students," claiming that "in practice it was scarcely possible for the freshmen to refuse membership."[42] Adam reaches a similar conclusion. Although conceding that "admittedly enrollment in a *Kameradschaft* was not compulsory for freshmen," he goes on to postulate that since the NSDStB in Tübingen embraced 82 percent of the student body in the summer semester 1938, therefore "nearly every student also belonged to a *Kameradschaft*." His source for the size of the NSDStB, namely the Nazi stu-

---

[39] Anordnung Horn, "Mitgliedschaft im NSD-Studentenbund," text in *Die Bewegung*, 5 October 1937.

[40] RSF-Amt Politische Erziehung (ed.), *Richtlinien für die Kameradschaftserziehung des NSD-Studentenbundes* (Munich, n.d.) (page proofs in RSFWü II* φ 216), p. 19.

[41] Steinberg, *Sabers*, pp. 152 and 180.

[42] Franze, *Erlanger Studentenschaft*, pp. 330-91 and 393.

TABLE 6. Percentage of Male Student Body in *Kameradschaften*, Including Students Beyond Third Semester, Summer Semester 1938

Universities	Percentage	Universities (cont.)	Percentage
Berlin	13.0	Marburg	31.7
Bonn	18.7	München	13.6
Breslau	35.9	Münster	10.8
Erlangen	22.5	Rostock	28.1
Frankfurt	30.4	Tübingen	28.1
Freiburg	13.2	Würzburg	26.1
Giessen	33.6		
Göttingen	45.5	*Technical Universities*	
Greifswald	19.2	Aachen	44.2
Halle	20.9	Berlin	22.4
Hamburg	16.2	Braunschweig	34.0
Heidelberg	22.8	Breslau	54.7
Jena	18.4	Darmstadt	32.4
Kiel	22.7	Dresden	28.9
Köln	17.5	Hannover	42.5
Königsberg	57.0	Karlsruhe	26.7
Leipzig	32.2	München	18.1
		Stuttgart	48.8

Source: Numbers of *Kameradschaft* members in RSF-Organisationshauptstelle, "Zusammensetzung der Kameradschaften und Gliederungszugehörigkeit der Kameradschaftsmitglieder," n.d., RSFwü II*450 α 353; overall student numbers in *Statistisches Handbuch für Deutschland 1928-1944,* ed. Länderrat des Amerikanischen Besatzungsgebiets (Munich, 1949), pp. 625ff.

dent press, is highly questionable.[43] Statistics do exist from that same semester (not used by Adam) that show that a mere 16.5 percent of the male students at Tübingen were active members of a *Kameradschaft* (28 percent of the male student body, if one includes former members beyond their third semester). Table 6 shows the real extent of the *Kameradschaft* program. It will be noted that many universities had an even smaller proportion involved in the scheme. Admittedly the percentage of students attached to *Kameradschaften* rose until the outbreak of the war. There are no

---

[43] Adam, *Hochschule,* p. 103.

membership figures for 1939, but there is a record of 232 *Kameradschaften* at universities (not including technical universities) for the summer semester 1939, as opposed to 197 a year earlier.[44]

The published figures of the Reich Student Leadership are misleading. It claimed, for example, that in the summer semester 1938 there were 18,356 students in 875 *Kameradschaften*, whose members represented 70 percent of students in their first three semesters.[45] Yet only a third of these students were in institutions of higher education. The figure includes the *Kameradschaften* in the technical colleges (*Fachschulen*), a sector for which there is little detailed statistical data, and which the Reich Student Leadership considered to be of secondary importance. These colleges were certainly more numerous than those in the higher education sector. By 1936 there were 1,015 of them, of which by far the largest number (717) were agricultural colleges.[46] Many of them were very small, and at these especially the proportions of members were allegedly even higher. At teacher training colleges, 90 percent of the students in their first three semesters were said to belong to a *Kameradschaft*.[47]

Internal statistics of the Reich Student Leadership show that at universities and technical universities there were 6,676 students in 301 *Kameradschaften* in the summer semester 1938.[48] Forty-eight percent of the freshman intake

[44] List of numbers of *Kameradschaften* by town in RSFWü II*450 α 353.

[45] Martin Sandberger, "Das Nationalsozialistische Deutsche Studententum," in *Grundlagen, Aufbau und Wirtschaftsordnung des nationalsozialistischen Staates*, ed. Hans-Heinrich Lammers and Hans Pfundtner, vol. 1, group 1, 7d (Berlin and Vienna, n.d. [1939]), p. 17.

[46] Theodor Vahlen, "Wissenschaft, Erziehung und Volksbildung im nationalsozialistischen Staate," in Lammers and Pfundtner (eds.), *Aufbau*, vol. 1, group 2, 21 (Berlin, n.d. [1936]), p. 43.

[47] Sandberger, "Studententum," p. 17.

[48] RSF-Organisationshauptstelle, "Zusammensetzung der Kameradschaften und Gliederungszugehörigkeit der Kameradschaftsmitglieder," n.d., RSFWü II*450 α 353.

for that semester enrolled in a *Kameradschaft*.[49] Although at that time only a small proportion of the student body had experienced the NSDStB's political education program, as Table 6 indicates, the improvement in freshman enrollment held much promise for the future. It is difficult to judge how representative of future trends this figure is. There are no statistics for the following autumn, when the main freshman enrollment took place. Perhaps students coming fresh from their Labor Service duties were less enthusiastic about the NSDStB: of the previous autumn's freshmen (representing twice the number of those in the summer semester 1938), only 35 percent were persuaded to join a *Kameradschaft*.[50] Excitement over the Austrian annexation may also have caused the increase in the summer of 1938. No firm conclusion may be drawn from the figure for the NSDStB group at the University of Hamburg (Table 6), for Hamburg had an untypically poor recruitment of freshmen in the summer semester 1938.

In a sense, the real problem was not winning members in the first place, although that had to be done. It was the retention of the students' interest and loyalty, without which the political education program could not advance very far. Like his predecessors, Scheel was less successful in this area. The backbone of Scheel's new, revitalized *Kameradschaften* was to be the "Ten Commandments" that he promulgated at the Nuremberg Rally in September 1937. Thirteen were drafted originally but then trimmed, no doubt with biblical precedents in mind. What positive effect this collection of bombastic phrases ever had is unclear. Although they might have offered inspiration to dewy-eyed freshmen, they were certainly not very original. Some were taken from the favorite Nazi author, Hanns Johst, others

---

[49] Calculated from ibid. and a table of freshman enrollment figures from 1931-1939, "Die Neuzugänge (1. Semester) zu den Hochschulen der reichsdeutschen Studierenden," UNIHH C.10.16.

[50] Ibid.

from Fichte and Nietzsche.[51] It is difficult to judge how much notice students took of the commandments. There is no subsequent mention of them even in the correspondence of the student leaders.

Likewise the guidelines issued for the *Kameradschaft* leaders were too vague to be of much practical help in enlivening these groups.[52] The range of activities was supposed to include the following events. A weekly, two-hour "political evening" served to prepare students for their vacation service on a farm or in a factory. Topics such as "The *völkisch* struggle in the East," or a detailed study of the particular area in which the *Kameradschaft* would be serving, were chosen to try to arouse interest in this work. In addition, a short review of current events was to be presented every two weeks. A fortnightly "community hour" was intended to familiarize students with their German historical and cultural heritage. The *Kameradschaft* leader was instructed to choose, in particular, themes that showed Germany in its most difficult and decisive struggles for existence and the great men that these periods produced. Concerts and theater visits formed part of this task, not, it was stressed, for pleasure or entertainment but for the serious business of learning respect for the great, German artistic geniuses. A weekly instruction period covered the Student Code of Honor, the history of student movements, and questions of etiquette. A singing session was held once a fortnight. Considerable emphasis was placed on physical fitness. There were to be exercises twice weekly before breakfast, and fencing on at least two other mornings. One afternoon each week was set aside for group sports with all the *Kameradschaften* of the university, together with the semi-active older members of the *Kameradschaft* (with three semesters' service behind them).

---

[51] "Die Gesetze des deutschen Studenten," *Die Bewegung*, 14 September 1937.
[52] See n. 40.

At the beginning and end of the semester the *Kamerad-schaft* would act as hosts to its alumni and other guests. A talk of general interest would be given during the first part of the evening, though political themes were to be avoided on these occasions, as the main purpose of the gathering was social. Following the custom of the former fraternities, the participants would be seated at a long table and the main part of the evening devoted to the consumption of beer, though not to the traditional excess: the new ideal student was to be measured not by his capacity for alcohol but by the degree of his sobriety.[53] The *Kameradschaft* leader was empowered to hold further social evenings as the need arose. Those to which the opposite sex was invited, however, were not permitted more than twice a semester. If the *Kame-radschaft* held a dance, its members were to understand that it was "not a matter of the personal pleasure of the individual" but rather an exercise in etiquette with ladies.[54]

This last point was typical of the tone of the whole booklet: niggling and overly serious about inconsequential subjects, yet skimming over the real issues. In the tradition of the fraternities, which had sometimes issued instructions on acceptable colors for socks, the guidelines were filled with painstaking advice on such subjects as visiting cards, dress for the theater, and table manners. Yet they remained vague on all but the bare outline of the actual programming of the meetings. This was done deliberately, for fear of otherwise curbing the putative creative talents of the individual leaders through the imposition of a rigid, stereotyped program.

There remained at the local level the same degree of confusion as before as to exactly what the leaders were meant to do with their students at meetings. Not surprisingly, the latter voted with their feet: while the Hamburg State Technical Institute, for example, boasted of a nominal NSDStB

[53] This oft-repeated cliché originated from a rare article by Hitler on student affairs. "Um die Zukunft der Deutschen Studentenschaft: Studenten und Politik," *Völkischer Beobachter*, 13/14 February 1927.

[54] RSF-Amt Politische Erziehung, *Richtlinien*, p. 39.

membership of 264, the highest attendance ever reached at meetings was forty-three (thirty-two of whom were office-holders anyway). Even when the frustrated leaders then tried to *force* all freshmen to join a *Kameradschaft* (disregarding the official policy of the Reich Student Leadership), no more than 75 percent bowed to their wishes.[55] The University of Hamburg presented a similar picture of apathy: of forty-eight freshmen summoned to an introductory camp for prospective *Kameradschaft* members, only thirteen appeared.[56] Now that students who had suffered the strictures of both Labor Service and military service were beginning to arrive at the university, traditional student freedom looked more attractive than ever.

This apathy toward the activities of the NSDStB was not restricted to Hamburg. At Münster a ceremony marking the anniversary of the Nazi seizure of power was attended by only 600 students out of 2,250, and 400 of them were students of Catholic theology (who always tried to give the student leaders as little cause for recrimination as possible). At another rally at which the *Gauleiter* held the main speech, only 220 appeared. A mere eighty students turned out for a celebration, welcoming students who had completed their military service.[57] There were always ways of avoiding such "duties." Otto Roegele relates how he was excused from an NSDStB training camp in 1938 because he claimed that he could not afford to buy a pair of jackboots.[58]

It was not so much hostility as indifference toward the NSDStB. The *Kameradschaften* were simply not attractive in the way that the fraternities had been. Without their own

[55] Hanne to Ochsenius, 13 April 1938, RSFWü V*2 α 560.

[56] Schützendorf to Ochsenius, 2 May 1938, RSFWü V*2 α 539.

[57] Remarks made by Rector Mevius at the 1939 rector's conference. Stenographischer Bericht Rektorenkonferenz, March 1939, zStA REM 708.

[58] Paradoxically, he also claimed that there was no escape from the NSDStB or SA. Otto Roegele, "Student im Dritten Reich," in *Die deutsche Universität im Dritten Reich: Eine Vortragsreihe der Universität München* (Munich, 1966), pp. 146-47.

houses they found it difficult to build up a corporate identity. It was all the more tiresome that huge fund-raising drives had been conducted to provide the Hitler Youth with meeting places. "A simple Hitler Youth house is a palace compared with the rooms in which the student work has to be carried on," the Hamburg District Student Leader lamented. The local alumni associations of former fraternities had indeed offered fraternity houses to the NSDStB, but they had demanded such high rents that the District Student Leadership had been unable to accept.[59]

The continued existence of these alumni associations remained one of Scheel's major worries. Considerable holdings of money and property remained in their hands after the dissolution of the fraternities themselves. Scheel desperately wanted to harness this wealth to his own political education program, especially as the NSDStB's own alumni association was proving a dismal failure. As early as March 1931, a sponsors' organization for the NSDStB had been called into being by Hitler, and the dormant body had been revived on 14 May 1936 by Hess as "Aid for the Students' Struggle" (*NS-Studentenkampfhilfe*).[60] By May 1937 it had gathered a mere 5,118 members from some 180,000 fraternity alumni.[61] Scheel, himself a former fraternity student, was anxious not to alienate the alumni from the start, and he hoped to repair the ill-feeling caused by Derichsweiler. At a rally for the *Studentenkampfhilfe* on 13 May 1937, he actually praised the past work of the fraternities and their tradition of political engagement. He tried to win over the alumni by assuring them that he was not simply interested in their monthly subscriptions but in their active involvement with the *Kameradschaft* of their choice.[62] By apparently promising them

[59] Ochsenius to Staatsverwaltung Hamburg Abt. I, 25 July 1938, StA Uo5.
[60] Erlass Hess, 14 May 1936, MicAlex T-81/236/5020962.
[61] List of membership figures by District, "Stand der NS-Studentenkampfhilfe am 15. Mai 1937," RSFWü II*62 α 16.
[62] Gustav Adolf Scheel, *Tradition und Zukunft des deutschen Studententums: Die Rede des Reichsstudentenführers bei der Grosskundgebung*

direct influence on student life again, and by proclaiming once more that the *Studentenkampfhilfe* was the only society of alumni that would be officially recognized by the Party, Scheel hoped that the fraternity alumni associations would promptly disband.

In fact, support for the *Studentenkampfhilfe* was given only grudgingly. The leader of the Hamburg branch, Senator Richter, started on entirely the wrong note by publicly attacking the Hamburg faculty for not having joined (in fact, application forms had not yet been sent out). This brought protests from the rector and from the dean of the Medical Faculty, who was particularly angered that the insults came from a senior official, who did not have "youth and ignorance" to excuse him.[63] One of the professors found it strange that he should now, in a letter soliciting his support, be addressed as "Dear Old Comrade" (*Lieber Altkamerad*) by a student leadership that had constantly deplored how hopelessly "fossilized" and unsuitable the professors were for the education and leadership of academic youth.[64] Rector Rein reported to the District Student Leader that although a large number of faculty were indeed willing to support the *Kameradschaften*, many would find it absolutely out of the question to pay the 24 marks' annual subscription expected by Scheel. Even if specially low rates were allowed to these professors, Rein saw the further danger that "if a substantial percentage has to be forwarded to Munich, then in actual fact very little will remain for the support of the *Kameradschaften* at our University."[65]

Although by the start of the winter semester membership

---

des NSD-Studentenbundes und der NS-Studentenkampfhilfe München, 13 Mai 1937 (Munich, 1937).

[63] Keeser to Rein, 19 February 1937, UniHH 0.30.7.

[64] Rose to NSDStB Hamburg, 11 March 1937, ibid. -

[65] Rein to Gaustudentenführung Amtsleiter NS-Studentenkampfhilfe, 27 May 1937, ibid. Rein had noted that over 9 marks was to be siphoned off by the Reich Student Leadership to cover administrative costs and "particularly urgent tasks within the student body as a whole."

of the *Studentenkampfhilfe* was approaching 15,000, this did little more than scratch the surface of the fraternity alumni associations.[66] Scheel decided to step up propaganda for the scheme and arranged for Himmler and other dignitaries to write open letters of support and applications for membership.[67] By February 1938, Scheel's patience was exhausted, and he delivered a clear ultimatum to the alumni associations: those that did not give a "binding written declaration" by 15 May 1938 of the willingness of all their members to support the *Studentenkampfhilfe* would be excluded from any further active participation in student life.[68] Almost immediately after the publication of this decree, the Austrian *Anschluss* occurred. The intensely nationalistic dueling fraternities decided, officially in a wave of patriotic fervor but probably also in recognition of the hopelessness of their future existence, to disband and transfer to the *Studentenkampfhilfe*.[69] The attitude of the *Verein Alter Bremenser* was typical: it realized that the student leadership was now so anxious for support that the alumni would be welcomed under virtually any conditions, even if they attached themselves *en bloc* to a particular *Kameradschaft*. They strongly suspected that, despite an initial softening, the Reich Student Leadership would quickly deny them any effective influence on the students. Yet this was their goal: the alumni did not simply want to live on their reminiscences but were interested in current undergraduates. Therefore they opted to go along with the new scheme, since it seemed the only way of preserving any real connection with student life.[70]

[66] "Stand der NS-Studentenkampfhilfe am 15. November 1937," RSFWü II*62 α 16.

[67] Scheel to Uhlmann, 25 October 1937, MicAlex T-81/246/5034025-26.

[68] "Hochschulnachrichten: Altherrenbund der Deutschen Studenten," *Hamburger Nachrichten*, 3 March 1938.

[69] "NS-Altherrenbund der Deutschen Studenten," *Völkischer Beobachter*, 6 May 1938.

[70] Rundschreiben von der Decken, 16 May 1938, RSFWü V*2 α 545. It appears that a copy of this "strictly confidential" circular reached the Hamburg District Student Leader via the SD.

Ignoring the continued existence of the large Catholic alumni associations,[71] Scheel now had Hess proclaim the complete unification of alumni associations within the *Studentenkampfhilfe*, in celebration of which the latter was renamed the National Socialist Alumni Association of German Students (*NS-Altherrenbund der deutschen Studenten* or NSAHB).[72] Meanwhile, the Reich Student Leadership had submitted to Himmler, as Chief of Police, a large dossier on the alleged treasonable activities of Catholic fraternities, including confiscated correspondence between Austrian fraternities and their German counterparts over the previous five years.[73] Himmler responded as anticipated by banning them. He declared all student or alumni associations other than the NSDStB and NSAHB to be "politically intolerable."[74] Where persuasion had failed, police intervention seemed the easiest solution.

In fact, some alumni associations had been doing rather well. The *Verein Alter Landsmannschafter* in Hamburg had blossomed under the aegis of Senator Richter, the local *Studentenkampfhilfe* leader who was himself a member. The association was among the first to encourage all its members to join the *Studentenkampfhilfe*, and its future seemed secure to them. Having taken the precaution of adding political lectures to their program, the members were soon pursuing the old, familiar activities much as ever, such as a monthly

[71] Steinberg asserts that all organizations of a confessional nature had already been banned in February 1934 by the constitution of the German Students' Union. All the constitution in fact mentions is the *intention* to exclude any denominational divisions within the student body that might hinder its unity (sec. 4). The DSt had no authority to ban private student corporations. Steinberg, *Sabers*, p. 158, and Frick, *Student*, p. 21.

[72] Anordnung Hess, 30 April 1938, BA NS38/29.

[73] Alleged extracts from the dossier in "Die Staatsfeindlichkeit katholischer Studentenverbände," *Die Studentische Kameradschaft*, no. 10, January 1939, pp. 58-64.

[74] Sandberger, "Studententum," p. 22.

hike through the countryside with the undergraduates.[75] The *Landsmannschafter* were the only group of alumni in Hamburg to place a fraternity house at the disposal of the NSDStB.[76] The thirty members of *Kameradschaft* 1 took over the house of the former *Hammonia* fraternity, albeit under the watchful eye of 100 *Landsmannschafter* alumni, who were permitted to affiliate themselves *en bloc* to the *Kameradschaft*.[77] Although the *Landsmannschafter* could not be faulted for their apparent willingness to help, the house turned out to be a mixed blessing for the NSDStB. Not only did the fraternity alumni relieve the NSDStB of 15 marks in monthly rent for each member of the *Kameradschaft*, but the house was so completely dilapidated that it proved to be a grim and barren meeting place. *Kameradschaft* 4 lent a hand in the summer semester 1938 in an attempt to redecorate the place, but funds ran out after just two rooms had been wallpapered.[78] In response to the pleas of District Student Leader Ochsenius, the *Gauleiter* provided the handsome sum of 10,000 marks to improve the facilities of the *Kameradschaften*.[79] Until now they had been meeting in classrooms or in restaurants and bars. The local branch of the student aid organization, the *Reichsstudentenwerk*, the chairmanship of which Scheel had successfully struggled to gain, purchased a house at about this time for the use of the *Kameradschaften*. The city paid 10,000 marks for furniture

---

[75] "Aus der Arbeit der VAL Hamburg," *Landsmannschafter-Zeitung* 51, no. 3 (March 1937).

[76] Monatsbericht Schützendorf, December 1937, RSFWü V*2 α 539.

[77] "Aus der Arbeit der VAL Hamburg," *Landsmannschafter-Zeitung* 52, no. 8 (March 1938).

[78] Ochsenius to Staatsverwaltung Hamburg Abt. I, 25 July 1938, StA Uo5.

[79] Protokoll Ochsenius, "Sitzung am Dienstag d. 1. Oktober 1938 bei Staatssekretär Ahrens," RSFWü V*2 α 549. Ahrens promised to urge Governor Kaufmann to approve the payment of another 10,000 marks. There is no evidence that Kaufmann did so. Ahrens also agreed (apparently for the first time) to make available for the Hamburg student leaders 1,800 marks per annum from Party funds to cover their personal expenses.

TABLE 7. Hamburg University Male NSDStB Membership According to Students' Semesters

Semester	1st semester students			2d semester students			3d semester students			Students beyond 3d semester		
	NSDStB freshmen	All male freshmen	%	NSDStB members	All male students	%	NSDStB members	All male students	%	NSDStB members	All male students	%
WS 1937-1938	46	144	31.9	24	—	—	24	—	—	216	942	22.9
SS 1938	23	97	23.7	56	135	41.5	23	60	38.3	111	965	11.5
WS 1938-1939	92	139	66.2	36	71	50.7	73	127	57.5	337*	877	38.4
SS 1939	68	103	66.0	91	135	67.4	40	72	55.5	156	845	18.5
2d T 1940	43	97	44.3	108	169	63.9	17	17	23.9	115	426	27.0
SS 1941	17	28	60.7	35	115	30.4	71	135	52.6	106	324	32.7
WS 1941-1942	8	393	2.0	23	39	59.0	26	123	21.1	59	396	14.9
SS 1942	0	117	0	16	80	20.0	11	40	27.5	74	523	14.1
WS 1942-1943	40	259	15.4	37	142	26.1	26	123	21.1	114	626	18.2
SS 1943	24	117	20.5	34	178	19.1	22	130	16.9	210	705	29.8

Note. WS = winter semester. SS = summer semester. T = trimester. Dash = data not available.
* This unusually high figure probably includes the alumni of the *Kameradschaften.*
Source: Calculated from statistics in RSFWü V*2 α 560. Overall freshman enrollments corrected from Charlotte Lorenz, *Zehnjahres-Statistik des Hochschulbesuches und der Abschlussprüfungen* (Berlin, 1943), 1, p. 320ff.

and promised a further 6,000 marks for the upkeep of the building.[80]

The acquisition of their own exclusive meeting places or dens did improve the initial attractiveness of the *Kameradschaften*. Enrollments rose sharply during this semester, and initiates were pledged to remain active for three consecutive semesters. The accompanying table is more revealing about support for the NSDStB than the overall membership figures because it is able to show how far the NSDStB succeeded in winning over the students in their first three semesters, at whom the main thrust of the political education program was aimed (see Table 7). It can be seen that a few extra students were picked up each semester to add to earlier cohorts. Thus the 46 initiates of the winter semester 1937-1938 became 56 by the following summer, and 73 by their third semester. Similarly, the freshman cohort of the summer semester 1938 rose in eighteen months from 23 to 36 and finally 40. The greatest success came with freshmen during the academic year 1938-1939, of whom two out of three signed up for NSDStB membership. A persuasive factor for them may have been the active encouragement of the new rector, Professor Gundert, during the autumn matriculation ceremonies in 1938. He made a point of urging students to join the NSDStB. This rate of enrollment was impressive enough. Although the Reich Student Leadership regarded it as unacceptably low, it does seem to represent a sort of natural limit. Even Hitler's diplomatic triumphs and the annexation of Austria did not convince one-third of the students of the need to support the NSDStB.

The wartime figures present an altogether sorrier picture, the reasons for which will be explored in the following chapter. Some of the blame can be attributed to external factors, with the military situation imposing an annoying fluidity on the comings and goings of students. But local variables played their part as well. The drop in enrollments of fresh-

[80] Ibid.

men that Table 7 shows for 1941 coincided with the replacement of Rector Gundert by Professor Keeser, who was less enthusiastic about the NSDStB. Also at this time the city administration ceased its subsidies for the *Kameradschaften* because they were not "in the urgent interest of the defense of the Reich."[81] These do seem to have been important factors. If the provision of a real "home" for the *Kameradschaften* had such a marked effect, it is remarkable that Scheel did not throw all his weight behind the acquisition of funds for this purpose. But where was he to find the money? In the case of Derichsweiler's budget, Party Treasurer Schwarz believed that the Reich Education Ministry should pay the vast sums of money involved because political education was something intended for all students. The Ministry's view was that *political* education should be financed by the Party, since it insisted on exclusive control of this area. The stalemate continued.

Yet money alone could not provide the answer to the problems of the *Kameradschaften*. Fraternity alumni had brought a necessary stabilizing element into the constantly fluctuating student sector. A certain lack of continuity in the student leadership was an inevitable fact of student life; the alumni formed a bridge between successive generations of undergraduate members. The NSDStB realized this and genuinely wanted alumni—but not *these* fraternity alumni. Several years would elapse before it would be possible to have entire alumni associations composed of ex-NSDStB members, so for the moment the fraternity alumni had to be tolerated. If they were denied all influence in the *Kameradschaften*, they were useless as alumni, yet the Nazi student leaders were not sufficiently trusting to give them much influence. As usual, the NSDStB leaders wanted the best of both worlds. They led badly yet expected everyone to follow without a murmur. They expected others to give unstintingly of their time, money, and experience but insisted on retaining a strict control over the giving, lest the donor should appear more important or competent than the NSDStB leaders themselves.

City Pride and Hamburg's Initiatives

If the Reich Student Leadership continued to view parts of academe with distaste, the faculty were well aware that others in government and Party shared this view. In Hamburg the professors believed that the best way to overcome attacks was by marching forward. They found an unlikely candidate as their standard-bearer. *Gauleiter* and Governor Karl Kaufmann had grandiose visions of the city under his command, which those around him sought to reinforce with every means. In 1937 he embarked upon a program of expansion with the promulgation of the Greater Hamburg Law, by which the city's area was increased to include suburbs formerly belonging to Prussia.

At this time rumors persisted that certain universities might be closed down in the light of dwindling student numbers. The foundation of a College for Foreign Studies (*Auslandshochschule*) in Berlin was especially painful to the Hamburg professors, since they had always considered their great port city, "Germany's gateway to the world," as the proper center for this college. Indeed, Hamburg University had been founded specifically as an expansion of the old Colonial Institute. A particular snub was felt by the holder of the Chair for Colonial and Overseas History, none other than Rector Rein, who regarded Berlin as flagrantly trespassing on territory that Hamburg had been developing for the last thirty years. Rein's dreams of bringing to Hamburg the Diplomats' Training College being mooted at this time were checked by Berlin's coup. He gained the *Gauleiter*'s sympathetic ear and described in vivid terms the distinct possibility of "severe damage to the cultural image of Hamburg."[82] Kaufmann himself sent a letter to Education Minister Rust, asking for a clear statement of intent, which Rein followed up with a personal visit to the Ministry in order to sound out policy there.[83] He was able to return with a guarantee that support for Hamburg University would continue. But during an interview with the ministerial adviser on medical education, he was informed that, although Hamburg was acknowledged as *the* place for an Institute for Marine and Tropical Diseases, the rest of the Medical Faculty might well be closed down, since "Hamburg had enough overseas academic tasks without it."[84] The prospect of losing such a large portion of the student body (and medical students formed nearly half the student body that year) was equally displeasing to the rector and to the *Gauleiter*, for the city's main hospital was run by the University Medical Faculty.

Rein used the threat to the University to persuade Kaufmann to pour money into a new campus that would make Hamburg one of the finest (and thus institutionally safest) universities in the country. The *Gauleiter* included the University in the redevelopment scheme for the north bank of the Elbe. The project was on a vast scale typical of Nazi architecture, and Hitler himself followed it with interest. Architects' plans were drawn up for a quite splendid university campus in the Jenisch Park, where the existing mansion would be used as a clubhouse for the professors and brand new *Kameradschaft* houses and sports grounds constructed on the site for the District Student Leadership. The war eventually led to the abandonment of the whole scheme, although it was not halted until the middle of 1941.[85] Plans

[82] Besprechungsgrundlage, "Universität und wissenschaftliche Einrichtungen in Hamburg" (Streng vertraulich), February 1937, UniHH F.80.4.1.

[83] Aktennotiz Rein, "Besprechungen in Berlin am 9. und 10. März 1937 im Zusammenhang des Briefes des Herrn Reichsstatthalters vom 16. Februar 1937 an den Herrn Reichserziehungsminister," ibid.

[84] Ibid. Cf. also Rust to Kaufmann, 4 May 1937, UniHH C.51.1.

[85] A number of architect's sketches and plans in UniHH F.80.4.3. See also

were also energetically pursued in the spring of 1938 for the resurrection of the former Colonial Institute so that Hamburg should not lag behind Berlin. These, too, occupied Rein's attention and interest greatly at this time.

Adolf Rein was elevated to the title of Honorary Alderman (*Ratsherr*) of the City of Hamburg in February 1938, and on 7 March the *Gauleiter* opened discussions with the NSDStB and NSDDOZB on the appointment of a new rector.[86] In the light of the excellent relations Rein enjoyed with Kaufmann, it seems highly unlikely that the latter was trying to ease him out of office against his wishes at a time when he was performing such sterling work toward the improvement of the status of the University. Neither can the Reich Education Ministry's decree limiting rectorships to a period of three years be seen as the prime cause of his resignation, for this was only issued on 22 March and was never successfully enforced.[87] Rein's own subsequent claim that he was dismissed from office through the machinations of the NSDDOZB, which he used during denazification proceedings in 1945 as proof of opposition to National Socialism, cannot be believed.[88] It is out of the question that the *Gauleiter* would have allowed himself to be influenced by the District

---

Bernhard Löschenkohl, *Die deutschen Gaue seit der Machtergreifung: Hamburg* (Berlin, 1941), pp. 19ff.

[86] District Student Leader Nöldge suggested the NSDDOZB leader, Professor Irmscher. Nöldge to Kaufmann, 10 March 1938, RSFWÜ V*2 α 546.

[87] It is possible that there was advance knowledge of the decree. Ministerial representatives were in Hamburg, for example, for Scheel's speech on 28 January. For the failure to enforce the decree, see Seier, "Der Rektor als Führer," pp. 128ff.

[88] To the question "Have you ever been dismissed from the civil service, the teaching profession or ecclesiastical positions for active or passive resistance to the Nazis or their ideology?" Rein answered: "Left the office of rector of the University because of opposition and protests of the NS-Dozentenbund." Addendum to Personal Questionnaire, Military Government of Germany, 8 November 1945, HB personnel file Rein. In 1953, Rein claimed unequivocally that Rust had forced his resignation as a direct consequence of Gundert's and Irmscher's complaints about the Vaughan Williams affair. Interview Schottelius/Rein, 26 February 1953, AFGNH Box 3752.

Lecturers' Leader Irmscher, with whom he stood on very bad terms.[89] Nor was Irmscher very popular in the Reich Education Ministry at this time: he had opposed the promotion of Professor Schlubach by describing him, among other things, as "a completely decrepit cripple." Unfortunately for Irmscher the autobahn chief, Fritz Todt, was a mountaineering partner of Schlubach's and was able to expose the lies with the news that at that very moment the alleged cripple was up in the Alps![90]

During the summer of 1938 there was an incident that Irmscher seized upon in an attempt to discredit Rein and undermine his relationship with the *Gauleiter*. In 1937 the Hamburg businessman, Alfred Toepfer, had anonymously donated 10,000 marks for each of three annual awards to be made by the University, among them the Hanseatic Shakespeare Prize for the arts in Great Britain. Not bothering to summon a panel of judges, Rein had decided personally, as head of the University, to give the prize in the first instance to the composer Ralph Vaughan Williams. The award was announced on 20 October 1937 and the formal presentation ceremony set for June 1938.

One month before the ceremony, District Lecturers' Leader Irmscher began to spread rumors that Vaughan Williams was a Communist sympathizer. District Student Leader Ochsenius was shown a conference program of the British "Society of the Friends of Soviet Russia," on which the name of Vaughan Williams was included as a participant. The document was passed to the SD. When Ochsenius received his invitation to the presentation ceremony he therefore returned it to Rein, feeling obliged to dissociate himself, as he put it, from the honoring of "a British Communist." By 3 June 1938, the matter had been brought to Kaufmann's

[89] Kaufmann was extremely angry to discover that Irmscher was seeking political reports on his (Kaufmann's) nominee for the rectorship behind his back. Ochsenius to Irmscher, 26 April 1938, RSFWü V*2 α 546.

[90] Todt to Wacker, 5 March 1938; Todt to Mentzel, 5 March 1938, BA R21/rep 76/216.

attention by the SD, and the *Gauleiter* at once imposed "absolute silence" on all who knew of the document.[91] A cancellation of the prizegiving at this stage would cause acute embarrassment and probably damage Anglo-German relations. The British Ambassador Henderson had already been invited to the ceremony. The District Student Leader was persuaded that "the reputation of the Reich and of the city of Hamburg demands that the ceremony be held. In that case, the student body must also be represented." Ochsenius himself, however, still declined to attend and refused any official participation by the NSDStB, extricating himself from the embarrassing dilemma by suggesting that students should appear without uniforms, in their role as members of the German Students' Union.[92] It was to this diplomatic solution that the *Gauleiter* agreed, and the event took place as planned on 15 June 1938.[93]

Needless to say, the dust that Irmscher had raised did not endear him any more to the *Gauleiter*. He did his utmost, as Ochsenius scornfully noted, to dodge responsibility for the affair.[94] Ochsenius himself, who had acted almost too properly, was told: "You have shot at sparrows with cannons!"[95] Kaufmann was not, then, well disposed toward the nomination of Professor Knoll for the rectorship by Irmscher

[91] Aktenvermerk Ochsenius, "Zum Shakespeare-Preis 1938," 3 June 1938, RSFWü V*2 α 546.

[92] Aktenvermerk Ochsenius, "Betr. Shakespeare-Preis (Letztes Konzept, benutzt bei Gauleiter am 7. Juni 1938)," 7 June 1938, ibid.

[93] Vaughan Williams did not actually receive the money until after the war. His daughter writes: "The prize was rather in the nature of fairy gold, for he could not take it out of the country. When they first heard of it, he and Adeline had thought of buying pictures or a splendid car or even diamonds, but he could not have taken these out of Germany any more than the cash. Nor was he allowed to give it to the Quakers for relief work, so it had to be left in the bank." Not surprisingly, Vaughan Williams was quite oblivious to the background drama to the "cordial reception" that he was given. Ursula Vaughan Williams, *R.V.W. A Biography of Ralph Vaughan Williams* (London, 1964), pp. 221-22.

[94] Ochsenius to Kubach, 23 July 1938, RSFWü V*2 α 573.

[95] Ochsenius to Schmidt, 11 June 1938, RSFWü V*2 α 546.

and Ochsenius, and he relied instead on Rein's suggestion of Professor Goerttler, an acquaintance at Heidelberg.[96] Ochsenius alerted Reich Student Leader Scheel, who still maintained close links with Heidelberg University, his *alma mater* (of which he was an Honorary Senator). Scheel wrote back that Goerttler was "impossibly reactionary" and that everything possible must be done to block the appointment; he reminded Ochsenius that "it is particularly important that from now on a real National Socialist occupies the Hamburg rectorship."[97] Scheel's protests did not prevent Kaufmann from nominating Goerttler for endorsement by the Reich Education Ministry. But in the end the combined opposition of both Scheel and Reich Lecturers' Leader Schultze made it impossible for the Ministry to carry through the appointment.[98] Nonetheless, Kaufmann was at least able to topple Knoll, the favorite of the NSDStB and NSDDOzB. Ochsenius himself had to admit that high praise could not be accorded to this professor of sports medicine in terms of his scholarship. The University Student Leader warned that even politically Knoll was "not the ideal solution," since his leadership would be impaired by strong opposition in his own Faculty.[99]

When Irmscher then tried to block the appointment of Dr. Hans Peter Ipsen to a chair of law, Kaufmann would have no more to do with him. As one of the chief architects of the Greater Hamburg Law, Ipsen was well acquainted with the Governor and enjoyed his support. Kaufmann regarded as inexcusable meddling the fact that Irmscher, disciplinarily

[96] Ochsenius to Scheel, 11 June 1938, ibid. Goerttler was the man fetched by Rein from Zurich to fill the chair of anatomy, in the face of student pressure that the Hamburg Nazi Lecturers' Leader Blotevogel be given the post. In the autumn of 1935, Goerttler had left to take up another post at Heidelberg. See above, chap. 4.

[97] Scheel to Ochsenius, 16 June 1938, RSFWü V*2 α 546.

[98] Scheel to Ochsenius, 15 September 1938, ibid.

[99] Ochsenius to Scheel, 11 June 1938; Seiler to Ochsenius, 23 September 1938, ibid.

a subordinate of his, had sent without his knowledge a negative report on Ipsen to the Reich Education Ministry. Worse still, he had quite falsely claimed that the information derived from the District Student Leadership, thus bringing Ochsenius into disfavor. On 7 November 1938, Irmscher was obliged to resign "for health reasons."[100]

After many weeks of negotiations Professor Wilhelm Gundert, dean of the Philosophical Faculty, was appointed as the new rector. Gundert had traveled to Japan in 1906 as a missionary and had become a schoolteacher and eventually in 1927 the director of a German-Japanese Cultural Institute. He did not return to Germany until 1936, as Hamburg's Professor of Japanese Studies. Gundert had grown enthusiastic about National Socialism, following exposure to gramophone records and films of Hitler's speeches. Party pamphlets had won him over completely.[101]

Although lacking the strong qualities of leadership of an Adolf Rein, Gundert would certainly be a faithful servant to his Party superiors, and perhaps this very lack of independence made him acceptable to them. Rein had no confidence in him whatever and refused to serve as prorector under Gundert, as would have been the normal procedure for the retiring rector.[102] Yet Rein remained in the forefront of academic affairs by becoming head of the Political Faculties Group and of the Colonial Institute, which he regarded as the two most important segments of the University.[103]

Since its formation, the work of the Political Faculties Group had focused on four main tasks. It had organized one or two annual "camps" for Hamburg faculty and students,

[100] Protokoll Ochsenius, "Besprechung beim Gauleiter," 1 September 1938, RSFWü V*2 α 549. Irmscher to rector, 7 November 1938, UniHH T.10.7.

[101] Gundert to Landahl, 15 November 1945, HB personnel file Gundert.

[102] Protokoll Ochsenius, "Sitzung am 1. November 1938 bei Staatssekretär Ahrens," RSFWü V*2 α 549.

[103] Each of these positions gave him *ex officio* membership of the University senate, which now met again regularly under Rector Gundert.

held at Schloss Kalkhorst, a remote estate in Mecklenburg.[104] A second area of activities centered on international studies. Whereas the camps mainly stressed Rein's concern to promote history as the premier discipline, here Rein's old preoccupation with foreign affairs in his Political Round Table had become institutionalized. An important function of this group was the provision of classes for the general public on the language, literature, and culture of other countries.[105] A third section of the Political Faculties Group, dealing with area studies, looked closer to home. It examined the geographical, economic, cultural, and political importance of both the Hamburg region and the wider area of the North Sea.[106]

The main core of the Political Faculties Group remained the fourth section, which concerned itself with political, or politicized, science. Since it did so in a far too abstract and unpolitical way from the NSDDOZB's point of view, it was dragged into the campaign against Adolf Rein during 1938. The meetings of this section had become highly specialized faculty seminars. It was even beginning to split up along Faculty lines: the natural scientists held their own separate sessions, for example.[107] Without attempting to halt this development, the dean of the Political Faculties Group, Professor Raethjen, did make an effort to revert to the stated purpose of the whole Group, that of bringing together faculty from all disciplines, by creating a new study group called *"universitas"* to consider problems of common interest to professors in the natural sciences and humanities.[108] This forum was warmly supported by a number of scholars,

---

[104] The estate was owned by Alfred Toepfer, the donor of the Shakespeare Prize. Details of the camps in UniHH C.51.4.

[105] UniHH C.51.2. and C.51.5.11.

[106] UniHH C.51.6.

[107] Miscellany from the *Naturwissenschaftliche Arbeitsgemeinschaft* in UniHH C.51.3.

[108] Rundschreiben Raethjen, "Politische Wissenschaft," 8 November 1937, ibid.

though the NSDDOZB leader, Irmscher, felt that his own role was insufficient.[109] Dr. Ernst Schrewe, head of Hamburg's community college (*Volkshochschule*), recalled that the idea of the whole Political Faculties Group was "an affirmation of the idea of the *'universitas,'*" and he questioned the need for the latter. This set him musing on the wider implications of the work of the Political Faculties Group, and he concluded that it possessed "no proper political authority" for its concern with the political foundation of academic work. Since this was the job with which the NSDDOZB had been charged, perhaps the faculty would be better advised to continue their efforts under the auspices of the Nazi Lecturers' Association. This remark provoked the marginal comment from Rein, to whom the letters were forwarded: "No, because nothing happens!"[110] Apart from his well-known low opinion of the NSDDOZB, Rein would never have consented to the subjugation of the Political Faculties Group to a Party organization because one of the founding ideas of his institution was the reassertion of professorial leadership in the face of intrusions from the outside, nonacademic world.

If the Political Faculties Group had somehow failed to become the outstanding model that he had hoped it would be, Rein was now convinced that the promotion of colonial studies would raise Hamburg University to a special status within Germany.[111] Indeed his heart seemed to be in this new task above all else. In December he was commissioned by the senate to examine all the courses taught at Hamburg with a view to directing the curriculum wherever possible

[109] Irmscher also found an invitation to Professor Wilhelm Flitner to read a paper quite inappropriate because Flitner was a former supporter of the Social Democratic Party. Raethjen to rector, 31 May 1938, ibid.

[110] Rundschreiben Raethjen, "Die Arbeitsgemeinschaft 'universitas,' " 12 April 1938, ibid. Schrewe to Raethjen, 28 April 1938, and other replies, ibid.

[111] Professor Gundert likewise agreed (albeit in denazification proceedings) that the Political Faculties Group lost its concern with politicization and served at this time purely "for the scholarly exchange of ideas, with the aim of resisting specialist encapsulation." Gundert to Landahl, 15 November 1945, HB personnel file Gundert.

toward colonial and international interests.[112] By 1939, Rein had become disillusioned with the Political Faculties Group and allowed its activities to dwindle.[113] He no longer saw it as a unifying force for the professoriate (students had been excluded from its main seminar long ago). When the NSDDOZB began scheming to set up a rival body that would exclude Rein altogether, he resigned as dean, noting bitterly: "I hope that the time will come again when the university will form a true community; if this goal is not reached, then the German university, in my opinion, is destined for ruin."[114]

From the point of view of the student leaders, the university atmosphere improved under Gundert's leadership. The NSDStB was given more recognition, to the delight of its leaders.[115] The NSDStB was now allowed to play a major role at the matriculation ceremony, during which the entire hall was draped with its flags.[116] The University Student Leader participated regularly in meetings of the University Senate, albeit only for that part of the agenda that concerned student affairs. He was even given a limited voice in the appointment of assistant lecturers (*Assistenten*), although there is nothing to show that the rector was ever influenced by the opinions of the NSDStB.[117] The master-scholar attitude persisted. Och-

[112] *Mitteilungen des Rektors der Hansischen Universität*, Winter semester 1938-1939, no. 18, UniHH C.51.3.

[113] In a circular to the faculty, Rein excused the lack of meetings with his other commitments. Rundschreiben Rein, 28 February 1939, UniHH C.51.3.

[114] Rein to Anschütz, 19 July 1939, UniHH C.51.1.

[115] "At the University we have in Prof. Gundert for the first time since the seizure of power a rector who (makes it clear) on the occasion of the matriculation ceremony that he expects active involvement in the NSDStB from his students. Gundert seeks his own support from us." Gaustudentenführung Hamburg, "Politischer Lage- und Tätigkeitsbericht," 8 May 1939, RSFWü V*2 α 532.

[116] Vermerk Korte, "Allgemeine Ausführungsbestimmungen zur Immatrikulationsfeier am 23.11.1938," UniHH A. 170.140.1.

[117] The student leaders had wanted a voice in the appointment of higher ranks, but this appears to have been denied them. There is only talk of

senius was not too shortsighted to recognize the continuing importance and power of Professor Rein within the University and went out of his way to heal any lingering ill-feeling and to destroy the prejudices against the District Student Leadership that Rein had formed in the days of his predecessors, Dansmann and Nöldge. When the *"Kameradschaft Formel"* proposed Rein as its Alumni Leader, Ochsenius did not withhold his support.[118]

Karl Kaufmann probably did not always have a keen personal interest in higher education: he had never attended college. Once he became governor of the City of Hamburg, he showed an increasing and conscientious desire to govern responsibly, that is, in a way in which the Hamburg "Establishment" might consider responsible (while remaining an absolute National Socialist above all else). It was also his ambition to create within his district shining examples for the rest of Germany.[119] The more Adolf Rein stimulated his interest in the plans for the University, the more eager Kauf-

---

their involvement where assistant lecturers (*Assistenten*) are concerned. The procedure agreed upon was that if no objections were received from the student leader a fortnight after he had been notified of a pending appointment, it would be assumed that he had approved. Ochsenius to Kubach, 21 January 1939, UniHH C.20.4.

[118] Ochsenius had admittedly been put under pressure by Hamburg's State Secretary Ahrens to give his endorsement. Cf. Protokoll Ochsenius, "Sitzung am 1. November 1938 bei Staatssekretär Ahrens," RSFWü V*2 α 549. Rein assured Ochsenius that he had "not taken cover behind Ahrens in order to become an Alumni Leader." Protokoll Ochsenius, 16 December 1938, RSFWü V*2 α 546. In a footnote to this memo, Ochsenius noted that Vaughan Williams had recently signed a declaration of protest in London about "the measures against the Jews in Germany." This is the only reference in the Hamburg student files to the *Reichskristallnacht*, apart from a minute by Ochsenius on the *Gauleiter's* New Year's speech to the 400 members of the Hamburg Party's *Führercorps*, in which he reiterated Göring's praise for the relatively moderate and disciplined "Jewish campaign" in Hamburg. Protokoll Ochsenius, "Der Gauleiter am Abend des 5.1.39 im kleinen Saal der Musikhalle," RSFWü V*2 α 549.

[119] Hüttenberger sees Kaufmann as "the embodiment of a more urbane, Hamburg version of the NSDAP." This might lead one to expect above-average support from the students. Hüttenberger, *Gauleiter*, p. 50.

mann became to have a guiding hand himself in developments. The inefficacy and petty squabbling of the NSDStB and NSDDozB can only have strengthened his belief in the desirability of his own governance, whereas the persuasive, *positive* suggestions of Rein amid the total absence of ideas from the Party organizations convinced him that Rein was the right man to be entrusted with University development plans.

On ridding himself of Irmscher as District Lecturers' Leader, Kaufmann attempted to place the District Student Leadership under his thumb by attaching its various departments (e.g. Press and Propaganda, Political Education) to the corresponding offices of the Party's District Leadership. This demanded a certain stretching of the constitutional position, for although the District Student Leader came under the disciplinary jurisdiction of the *Gauleiter*, the latter was not meant to exercise any practical control over the affairs of the Student Leadership. In this respect, the Reich Student Leadership saw the clear possibility of territorial trespassing and a dangerous precedent for other Districts, and it took steps to have the order withdrawn.[120] But whatever the theoretical constitutional situation, within the *Gau* Karl Kaufmann ruled the roost. Ochsenius was impressed with the way that the authority of the *Gauleiter* brought the cooperation, without any friction, of all the Formations of the NSDAP in Hamburg as well as the Armed Forces.[121] In the spring of 1939, Kaufmann began to take his own personal initiative in the field of higher education. He did this in accordance with sound Party principles.

Paragraph 20 of the 1919 Program of the NSDAP had stated the Nazis' demand that higher education be made available to all talented young people, regardless of their parents' income or position. Yet this was never borne out by the prac-

[120] Reich to RSF-Personalhauptstellenleiter, 18 November 1938, RSFWü II*64 α 17.

[121] Politischer Lage- und Tätigkeitsbericht Ochsenius, 31 January 1939, RSFWü V*2 α 532.

tice of the Nazi regime. During the last years of the Weimar Republic, the proportion of students from working-class backgrounds rose only insignificantly (from 3.7 percent in the summer of 1928 to 5.9 percent in the summer of 1931). Table 8 shows the changes under the National Socialists. For the purposes of comparison, I have used the same categories as those employed by Michael Kater for the Weimar Republic.[122] Lower civil servants, among whom were some manual laborers, are included in the working-class figures.

In order to highlight the regime's social policies more sharply, Table 8 gives the numbers of male freshmen rather than of the whole student body. If the National Socialists were serious about opening up avenues of higher education to lower income groups, one would expect to find significant changes here. Because the government merely tolerated rather than encouraged women in universities, they cannot be expected to reflect any positive policy and have therefore been left out of consideration. Their exclusion makes the working-class enrollments look slightly better, but the percentages still do not suggest a radical change in admissions policies. The two highest figures are not evidence of policy. The 9.9 percent working-class enrollment in the summer semester 1934 occurred at a time of record-low male freshman matriculations (almost half those of the previous and following semesters, and not to be equaled till the war). This temporary disruption of the regular, entering cohort was brought about by the inauguration of the general student Labor Service scheme as a prerequisite for admission. When these students did finally arrive at college in the fall, the normal social profile of the student body resumed.

Likewise, the dramatic 11.3 percent working-class enrollment of the winter trimester 1941 is not as encouraging as it looks. If women are added to this, then working-class representation shrinks to 6.3 percent of the freshman cohort. Moreover, in absolute numbers, there were a mere 171 male

[122] Kater, *Studentenschaft*, pp. 60 and 208.

TABLE 8. Social Composition of German Male Freshman Cohorts During the Third Reich

Semester	Upper middle class (%)	Lower middle class (%)	Working class (%)	Working class (N)
SS 1933	35.3	57.3	7.4	773
WS 1933-1934	36.1	58.8	5.1	305
SS 1934	30.9	59.2	9.9	332
WS 1934-1935	35.5	57.8	6.7	441
WS 1937-1938	41.0	53.6	5.4	347
SS 1938	42.4	53.8	3.8	176
WS 1938-1939	38.6	54.8	6.6	419
SS 1939	41.7	53.7	4.6	306
WT 1941	27.5	61.2	11.3	171

Source: Calculated from figures in Charlotte Lorenz, *Zehnjahres-Statistik des Hochschulbesuchs und der Abschlussprüfungen* (Berlin, 1943), 1: 372.

freshmen in this category, fewer than in any peacetime year in Nazi Germany. All in all, the social background of Nazi students did not deviate noticeably from that of their Weimar predecessors. If anything, a slight shift in favor of upper middle-class enrollment can be detected. Similarly, an increase in the number of students with graduate fathers occurred between 1933 and 1939. Lorenz's statistics also reveal that Party functionaries were not sending their children to college. A measure of the degree of Nazi anti-intellectualism may be seen in the fact that among a freshman intake of 7,310 in the summer semester 1939, only eight students were the sons or daughters of Party officials (*Partei-Beamte*).

Scholarships for poor students did not demonstrate Nazi commitment to a meritocracy. Admittedly, there was an extension of the grant-aid program in 1933 for "politically reliable" students, but by 1937 the money set aside for awards for remission of university fees had been cut by almost 50 percent.[123]

Derichsweiler had tried to obtain scholarships for work-

[123] Cf. "Gebührenfreies Studium," in *Kurzberichte aus der Arbeit des Jahres 1937*, ed. Reichsstudentenwerk (Berlin, 1938), p. 8.

ing-class students from the German Labor Front. He believed that the scheme, despite labor leader Robert Ley's enthusiastic support, was killed at Party headquarters by Martin Bormann.[124] Since 1934 there had been a program of pre-university cramming for students from poor families who, having only undergone elementary school training, were not qualified for university entrance. This functioned on an almost negligible scale and was expanded under Scheel in 1937 to embrace the still very modest number of seventy would-be students.[125] The entry of these students as freshmen in the fall of 1938 would entirely account for the higher working-class enrollment that Table 8 shows. Although by December 1938 the Reich Student Leader proclaimed publicly a target of 1,000 students, the figure he in fact aimed for in his budget projection for 1939 as head of the *Reichsstudentenwerk* was a mere 200 men.[126] That June the scheme had been renamed "Langemarck Study," in honor of the students killed in battle in the First World War at Langemarck in Belgium. The press lauded the program as a measure of true socialism by the Reich Student Leadership.[127] Of course, a combination of talent and poverty was not sufficient to secure a place in the eighteen-month courses: short-listed candidates were further scrutinized in a six-day selection camp to determine their ideological, political, physical, and racial suitability.[128]

[124] Interview Giles/Derichsweiler, 12 March 1973.

[125] "Vorstudienförderung," in Reichsstudentenwerk, *Kurzberichte 1937*, p. 28.

[126] Erläuterungen zum Haushaltsplan des RSW für das Rj. 1939, Anlage 3, ZStA REM 895. The Reich Ministry of Finance did not approve the necessary funds. Aharon F. Kleinberger, "Gab es eine nationalsozialistische Hochschulpolitik?" in Heinemann, *Erziehung und Schulung*, p. 20.

[127] One study claims that 800 students were selected in 1940, but this is probably based on a Nazi press report. R. H. Samuel and R. Hinton Thomas, *Education and Society in Modern Germany* (London, 1949), p. 133.

[128] Rundschreiben Boetel, "Bewerbung von SA-Angehörigen für das Langemarckstudium der Reichsstudentenführung," 4 April 1939, BDC SA Ulrich Gmelin.

Although *Gauleiter* Kaufmann praised the idea of Lange-marck Study, he criticized its scale as a "pitiful gesture" and censured the Reich Education Ministry for its total lack of involvement in the question of support for the education of the working class. He gathered together a group of leading Hamburg businessmen and set about forming a colony of hostels for poor students from the Hamburg area. An ideal campus was available in the pleasant grounds of the former Eilbecktal Mental Hospital, and in a remarkably short time Kaufmann succeeded in finding the necessary funds.[129] Both the initial cost of structural alterations and the estimated running costs each equaled almost double what the *Reichs-studentenwerk* spent on Langemarck Study for the entire country in 1938.[130] Kaufmann's admission that he hoped to set an example for the rest of the Reich reveals again the pride that he felt for his District's higher education facilities. Kaufmann also saw a reliable source of future Party leaders in the Eilbecktal students.[131] Only convinced Nazis would be admitted in the first place, and those lucky enough to be selected would feel bound to the Party with especial loyalty because of the unique educational opportunity with which it had provided them. This in itself was a step away from the normal practice of the Party, which tended to shun grad-uates as leaders.[132]

[129] ". . . in these rooms in which lives worthless to the community were formerly preserved, worthy young men, financially deprived students are now to be able to live and eat without cost, in order to carry out their studies in peace." There is no record of the fate of the patients. Karl Kaufmann, "Der Marschallstab im Tornister," *Hamburger Tageblatt*, 23 May 1939.

[130] In 1938 only RM 140,000.—was spent nationally on Langemarck Study. The Eilbecktal renovations cost RM 250,000.—, and annual expenses of RM 263,000.—were budgeted. Cf. Haushaltsplan des RSW für das Rj. 1939, ZStA REM 895; Protokoll Ochsenius, "Erste Sitzung des Kuratoriums der Studentensiedlung Eilbecktal am 6. März 1939," RSFWü V*2 α 549.

[131] Aktenvermerk Ochsenius, "Rede des Gauleiters im Rathaus vor Kreis-leitern und Gauamtsleitern," 22 May 1939, ibid.

[132] Schoenbaum, *Social Revolution*, pp. 236-37.

TABLE 9. Proportion of NSDAP Members Among All Hamburg University Students

Semester	Absolute numbers of male NSDAP members	Percentage of all male students	Absolute numbers of female NSDAP members	Percentage of all female students	Total NSDAP student members	Percentage of all students
SS 1938	561	43.8	52	21.8	613	40.3
WS 1938-1939	403	33.3	17	7.2	420	29.0
SS 1939	426	37.0	14	6.0	440	31.8
2d T 1940	244	32.8	60	23.5	304	30.4
SS 1941	283	47.8	—	—	—	—
WS 1941-1942	582	59.9	122	32.1	704	52.1
SS 1942	31	4.2	32	6.3	63	5.1
WS 1942-1943	136	11.8	70	10.5	206	11.3
SS 1943	163	14.4	190	22.9	353	18.0

Note. NSDAP membership includes probationary members (*Anwärter*). WS = winter semester. SS = summer semester. T = trimester. Dash = data not available.
Source: RSFWü V*2 α 560.

It is not clear whether the Eilbecktal scheme actually increased student applications to the Party. The absolute numbers of Party members among the students increased only marginally. The outbreak of the war intervened before real results could have shown up. Table 9 gives the available data on Party membership among the students. It is unfortunate that the figures do not cover a sufficient span of the peacetime years to indicate a trend. What is immediately striking is the limited nature of Party involvement. This refutes Kater's assertion that as early as 1935, "70 percent of the entire school and university pupils in the Reich were found to have been members of the NSDAP."[133] He has now retracted this

---

[133] This represents a misreading. The source in fact shows that among the schoolboy and student members in the Party, 70 percent had joined since January 1933. Michael Kater, "The Reich Vocational Contest and Students of Higher Learning in Nazi Germany," *Central European History* 7 (September 1974): 247; Reichsorganisationsleiter der NSDAP (ed.), *Partei-Statistik: Stand 1. Januar 1935 (ohne Saargebiet)* (Als Manuskript gedruckt), 1: 132-35. For his retraction, prompted by an earlier draft of my

in his stimulating book on the Nazi Party. He points out there that a smaller proportion of the new Party initiates after 1933 were students, as the Party broadened its base, but that a greater percentage of students became members. This is not surprising in a career-minded group of young people, especially when viewed in reference to their previously dismissive stance before the seizure of power, when only 1.5 percent of Hamburg students had joined up (by 1 December 1932, at a time when joint membership of both Party and NSDStB was required of existing members of one organization—see Appendix 2).

Kater's concern is to explain the weak, overall presence of students in the NSDAP, and he gives plausible reasons for the progressive decline of interest between 1933 and 1939. It must be remembered, however, that he is making a projection from sets of samples of Party members, not on actual membership figures from individual universities. The data from Hamburg in Table 9 do not fit his picture of the elite "sharply turn[ing] its back on the National Socialist movement after the war started." It can be seen that the numbers remained fairly stable at the beginning of the war and then rose in almost a surge until 1942. They then evaporated overnight, with only sixty-three Party members remaining that summer out of 704 in the winter semester. The low percentages thereafter call into question Kater's assertion that as many as 40 percent of all students were Party members at the end of the Third Reich. Yet this sudden drop in Party members should not be taken to reflect disillusionment with the Party or the war on the Russian front: the sudden drafting of huge numbers of students all over Germany directly into the war effort is the more likely cause of these local fluctuations. Perhaps Party membership was viewed in the early part of the war as a safeguard against this. It is especially interesting to note that for much of the

---

book, see Michael H. Kater, *The Nazi Party: A Social Profile of Members and Leaders 1919-1945* (Cambridge, Mass., 1983), p. 332 n. 111. For his interesting remarks on student Party members, see pp. 97-100 and 126-28.

TABLE 10. Proportion of NSDAP Members Among Hamburg University NSDStB Members

Semester	Absolute numbers of male NSDAP members in NSDStB	Percentage of all male NSDStB members	Absolute numbers of female NSDAP members in NSDStB	Percentage of all ANSt members	Total number of NSDAP members in NSDStB	Percentage of all NSDStB members
SS 1938	162	—	15	—	177	—
WS 1938-1939	267	49.6	12	12.0	279	43.9
SS 1939	271	76.3	11	18.0	282	67.8
2d T 1940	113	39.9	34	27.0	147	35.9
WS 1941-1942	103	88.8	85	43.6	188	60.4
WS 1942-1943	76	32.9	39	17.6	115	25.4
SS 1943	91	31.4	76	12.9	167	19.0

Note. NSDAP membership includes probationary members (*Anwärter*). WS = winter semester. SS = summer semester. T = trimester. Dash = data not available.
Source: RSFWü V*2 α 560.

period between 1938 and 1942 the men at least preferred to join the Party rather than the NSDStB (cf. Table 9 with Appendix 2). If hopes of favorable treatment did exist, then 1942 dashed them.

Table 10 separates the female section (ANSt) from the male members of the NSDStB in order to show that they were not usually the prime source of Party recruits. The generally low proportion of NSDStB members who thought it worthwhile to apply is rather surprising. In the summer semester 1938 only 2 percent of the *Kameradschaft* members held rank in the Party as a leader (*Politischer Leiter*). Most still served in other Formations and evidently felt that this was sufficient demonstration of their loyalty. Yet in that same semester there were 18 percent of the active *Kameradschaft* members (first through third semesters) who did not bother to serve in any Nazi organization other than the NSDStB. Among the remaining, older NSDStB members, the proportion was almost one-third.[134]

[134] RSF-Organisationshauptstelle, "Zusammensetzung der Kameradschaften und Gliederungszugehörigkeit der Kameradschaftsmitglieder," n.d. (summer semester 1938), RSFWü II*450 α 353.

In short, there was less activity in all the National Socialist organizations than the Hamburg student leaders would have liked. Only about one student in every three belonged to the Party or the NSDStB in the spring of 1939. The Eilbecktal scholarship scheme would certainly bring closer ties and, as a measure of genuine socialism, would do much to enhance the image of the National Socialist movement in Hamburg.

Selection of the students was carried out in two camps, in April and May 1939. The candidates had to provide among other tests, written comments on twenty-seven questions such as the following:

1. Are there born criminals or are criminals products of their environment?
2. For what reasons was the Führer *forced* to take Bohemia and Moravia under the protection of the Reich?
3. How are events of recent months compatible with the Führer's statement: "We have no more territorial claims in Europe"?
4. What is the attitude of the Führer toward scholarship?
5. Which daily newspaper do you regard as the best and why?[135]

The quiz examined the assimilation both of the standard ideological points of National Socialism as well as the propaganda explanations of current events. Each candidate also underwent an interview with District Student Leader Ochsenius, with whom Kaufmann had entrusted the selection. One hundred and forty students were immediately found to occupy the new hostels on their opening in May, and the intention was to increase this figure to 250 by the following Easter. The dispatch with which the whole operation was accomplished—a mere eleven weeks between the first meeting of the fund-raising board of trustees and the grand opening of Eilbecktal—shows how speedily such a measure *could* be implemented if desired. But at the national level nothing

[135] Copy of test paper in RSFWü V*2 α 549.

similar had been attempted in over six years since the seizure of power.[136] Ochsenius believed that Scheel had deliberately delivered a snub to Kaufmann by sending neither a representative to the opening ceremony nor even the usual congratulatory telegram for this sort of occasion.[137] Scheel was evidently not interested in the success of the scheme and thought that Kaufmann was encroaching again on the territory of the Reich Student Leadership. The only concern he showed at all in the matter was that, however many students the individual bedrooms were designed to accommodate, they should on no account be occupied as double rooms because of the risks of homosexuality, a problem that was causing him undue worry at this time.[138]

The truth was that a significant increase in the number of working-class students was not a plan that appealed to Scheel as it clearly did to the more socialistic Kaufmann. The student body remained for Scheel an elite and, not least because of parsimonious grant-aid policies, virtually the same upper middle-class elite that it had formerly been. Scheel did not attempt to tear down barriers but if anything tried to strengthen them and erect more. In 1939 he wanted to change the NSDStB uniform from "the simple brown shirt," claiming that "damage to health, in some cases even pneu-

---

[136] At the Reich Student Leadership it had become official policy that financial need was no longer a central consideration in the awarding of grant aid to the politically reliable: "The complete exclusion of the criterion of need is being striven after as a matter of principle." "Wer wird gefördert?" *Frankfurter Zeitung*, 25 June 1938.

[137] Aktennotiz Ochsenius, 5 May (*sic*: June) 1939, RSFWü V*2 α 549.

[138] Protokoll Ochsenius, "Eilbecktal-Besichtigung des Gauleiters," 19 March 1939, ibid. Recently the rector of the University of Munich had been arrested on charges concerning homosexual offenses, and Scheel announced that he was determined to "eradicate this evil" from the universities. His student leaders were ordered to ensure that student offenders who were apprehended shot themselves! *Informationsdienst der Reichsstudentenführung*, 17 May 1939, RSFWü V*2 α 568. Scheel's misgivings were evidently ignored in Hamburg, for a photograph of the Eilbecktal hostel plainly shows the interior of a bedroom for *two* students. "Hier werden 250 Studenten wohnen," *Hamburger Anzeiger*, 24 May 1939.

monia, is the inevitable consequence of the present uniform regulations of the Students' Association."[139] Scheel also felt that jackboots and riding breeches were out of place at the theater or a concert. He was anxious to adopt something comparable to the going-out uniform (*Gesellschaftsanzug*) of the ss as the standard NSDStB uniform, thereby underlining the growing importance of "social events" for the NSDStB. Forcing a student who was faced with some of the highest university fees in Europe[140] to spend his limited resources on an ostentatious uniform might increase the elitist pride of the student, but it was hardly a sign of solidarity with lower income groups. Status was what really counted in Scheel's world.

The Nazification of Scholarship

The social composition of the student body still, then, gave scope for improvement, though nationally there was little real concern to change things. There was, in addition, another area of the NSDStB's early program that remained unresolved. As early as 1928, Baldur von Schirach had called for the reworking of scholarly thought in the various disciplines according to National Socialist principles. The re-

---

[139] Scheel to Lutze, 31 July 1939, BA Sammlung Schumacher 279. "Not good enough any more?" was the SA Chief's comment in the margin. In the old days before the seizure of power, the insubstantial uniform was regarded as part of the toughening process, despite its frequent unsuitability: "As I went through the streets of Schwabing, I really felt in the early morning cold just how thin the Brown Shirt was. . . ." Hikad, *Studenten im Braunhemd* (Berlin, 1933), p. 21. The outbreak of the war halted Scheel's plans for a new uniform. A dress uniform for NSDStB leaders had already been designed in 1937. Cf. "Reichsarbeitstagung 1937," *Die Bewegung*, 29 June 1937; also the illustration in Peter Krause, *"O alte Burschenherrlichkeit": Die Studenten und ihr Brauchtum* (Graz, 1979), p. 180.

[140] Hans Huber, *Der Aufbau des deutschen Hochschulwesens: Vortrag gehalten auf der dritten fachwissenschaftlichen Woche für Universitätsbeamte der Verwaltungsakademie Berlin am 30. Januar 1939* (Berlin, 1939), p. 46.

sults of such efforts hitherto in the Third Reich left much to be desired.

Intellectuals knew that the Party had little time for them and that they were scorned for their independent thinking. Scheel attempted to heal the rift, to repair the propaganda image of the politically irresponsible scholar, and to lead the appeased academic toward greater engagement for the Party through "Nazi scholarship."[141] His efforts were periodically spoiled by Hitler's own rantings against intellectuals. Such an occasion was the annual rally of veterans of the 1923 Putsch on 9 November 1938. In his speech to them, Hitler blamed the German collapse of 1918, as he frequently did, on the "intellectuality" of the leaders of the state, ridiculing the view that "so-called, alleged knowledge" was a more valid quality of leadership than character and manly bearing. He favorably compared the "instinct" of the masses with the intellectuality of the "eternal critics." The intellectuals, according to Hitler, were "not bearers of faith, not unshakable, and above all, they do not stand fast in moments of crisis and danger. For while the broad, healthy mass of people does not hesitate to forge itself together into a *Volksgemeinschaft*, [the intellectuals] scatter like hens in a chicken run. And therefore one cannot make history with them, they are useless as supporting elements of a society."[142] These remarks caused so much embarrassment to the Reich Student Leadership that it devoted the whole front page of its newspaper the following week to persuading students that the *Führer* had not been referring to academics as such but

[141] "We do not want scholarly National Socialism," Scheel stressed, "but National Socialist scholarship." The last thing he wanted was a scholarly and critical examination of Nazi doctrine; what Scheel sought was the subjection of all branches of scholarship to rigid Nazi preconceptions. Dibner translates this quotation inside out and misinterprets it accordingly: "As Scheel pointed out, 'We are not interested in a national socialistic science but in a scientific National Socialism.'" Dibner, "History," pp. 255-56.

[142] "Adolf Hitlers Rede an Grossdeutschland," *Völkischer Beobachter*, 10 November 1938.

to dubious characters "with long hair and broadly padded shoulders."[143]

The low esteem in which intellectuals were held contributed to the drop in student numbers as much as the quotas restricting freshman intake, which often were not even met. Higher education was no longer viewed as the road to career success. The best Nazis, the very people whom the Reich Student Leadership would have liked in the ranks of the student body, tended to stay away. Within the universities academic standards fell as National Socialist activities took up more and more of the students' time. This tended to increase worries about graduate placement. Professorial complaints about the negative effects of compulsory sport, SA service, and Labor Service had been voiced all along.[144] By the time the officials connected with the Four-Year Plan began to take stock in 1936, the situation had become extremely serious. On the fourth anniversary of the seizure of power, Professor Becker, president of the Reich Research Council, wrote a sobering memorandum on the shortage of engineers and technical workers. In January 1937 there were indeed only 1,000 unemployed university graduates, as opposed to 50,000 when Hitler became chancellor. Yet the *Luftwaffe*, for example, had only 10 percent of the engineers, technicians, and mechanics that it needed. Becker lamented the fact that the deliberate restriction of student numbers had been all too successful and had indeed turned out to be "a serious error." He placed much blame on the Hitler Youth for its highly effective, negative propaganda about the academic professions, which kept many school-leavers away from college study. Extramural activities, he noted, were leading to severe delays in graduation: over 25 percent of all students were in or beyond their ninth semester. Had they completed their studies in the prescribed time, at least another 2,000 diploma-level engineers would have been avail-

[143] "Die Organisation der intellektuellen Feigheit," *Die Bewegung*, 15 November 1938.
[144] See above, chap. 4, nn. 111-113.

able for 1937.[145] Complaints continued from the Bureau of the Four-Year Plan. In August another of its advisers, Dr. Kraus, was quoted in the *Daily Telegraph* as saying that "by 1942 Germany would be faced with a shortage of 35,000 engineers."[146]

Nothing was done to alleviate these problems. The attempts to make scholarship respectable again by its thorough nazification were a dismal failure. If the students were apathetic toward the *Kameradschaften* in which they were meant to participate until their fourth semester, they were even less interested in the NSDStB's departmental study groups that were supposed to be their concern thereafter.[147]

Little enthusiasm was shown for the amateurish pursuits of these groups, for the leaders were often quite out of touch even with Party doctrine on certain matters. This was particularly evident in the natural sciences. An academic debate on glacial cosmogony was raging in the mid-thirties, its advocates claiming that it alone was compatible with Nazi ideology. The battle was terminated by the official ideological arbiter, Alfred Rosenberg, who stated in a rare moment of rationality that the Party could not take a dogmatic ideological standpoint on such purely scientific questions.[148] Yet similar squabbles continued: Einstein's theory of relativity was held to be a Jewish doctrine, and as such to be rejected out of hand, even though scientists themselves found it "difficult to do without some of its concepts and

[145] Denkschrift Becker, "Zur Frage der Ingenieur- und Facharbeitermangels," 30 January 1937, ZStA REM 896/1.

[146] *Education in Nazi Germany*, by Two English Investigators, with a Foreword by Sir Norman Angell (London, 1938), p. 45.

[147] Cf. Monatsbericht Schlag, 29 April 1937, RSFWü V*2 α 539. Professor Niedermayer at Berlin noted in 1940 that "the departmental study groups have suffered a total shipwreck, though nobody has had the courage to say it. They are considered burdensome and as an inadequate, indeed ridiculous copy of proper instruction." Hellmut Seier, "Niveaukritik und partielle Opposition: Zur Lage an den deutschen Hochschulen 1939/40," *Archiv für Kulturgeschichte* 58 (1976): 238.

[148] Erlass Rosenberg, "Freiheit der Forschung," 7 December 1937. Text in *Nationalsozialistische Monatshefte*, no. 100 (July 1938), p. 655.

approaches in present-day atomic physics." Professor Raethjen at Hamburg saw a greater danger in identifying scientific concepts with ideologies, since scientific knowledge
might at any time be essential in a practical or technical
way for the national interest. He noted pointedly that "no-
one would dream of destroying all the artillery devices which
in some way made use of the results of ballistics experiments
published by the Jew Schwarzschild." Far from drawing the
logical consequences from this and acknowledging that the
natural sciences (apart from biology) had no connection with
ideology, the NSDStB in Hamburg set about examining the
theory of relativity "with a view to isolating the Aryan elements."[149]

The scant interest in such ludicrous pursuits was roused
no further when they were linked with the Reich Vocational
Contest of German Students, an academic project competition. This had been started in 1935 by Feickert in an attempt to strengthen the role of the German Students' Union,
when he hitched onto the Reich Vocational Contest proper
a section specifically for students. The contest had first
taken place in 1934 as a nationwide apprentices' competition
embracing some 250 trades, with the aim of boosting self-
confidence, standards, and output.[150] The declared goal of
the student sector was "to prove before the whole world that
the talk of a drop in achievement in the Third Reich is
merely an empty phrase," that Nazi scholarship, inasmuch
as it existed, was not poor scholarship.[151]

Although NSDStB Leader Derichsweiler promised support

[149] Raethjen to Rust, 2 December 1938, UniHH A.1.6.
[150] Artur Axmann, *Olympia der Arbeit: Arbeiterjugend im RBWK* (Berlin,
1936), pp. 10ff. I would dispute Kater's claim that the inclusion of the
students demonstrated that they were "not an elitist group" but were in-
tegrated into the broad *Volksgemeinschaft*. Kater, "Vocational Contest," p.
227. The reverse conclusion seems more apt because the students alone
were cordoned off in their own special subsection.
[151] Derichsweiler's words in the publicity brochure, *Reichsleistungskampf* (ed. Hauptamt für Presse und Propaganda der DSt), p. 4, UniHH
0.10.2.9.

for the scheme in the first instance, he suddenly changed his mind in mid-September, probably at the behest of Gerhard Wagner.[152] During the following months, the issue became central in the power struggle between Feickert and Derichsweiler, as the latter set about creating his own project contest. Having insisted that the DST change its original disciplinary classification of themes to a handful of commonplace headings, the NSDStB proclaimed its own parallel competition with the attractive title "Olympia."[153] In this the art students who designed the best trophies would see them actually presented at the Olympic Games in Berlin the following summer; the prizewinning works of music students would be performed in public during the Olympics. Whereas Feickert's applicants had little incentive other than the possibility of meeting Hitler at a reception for the winners, Derichsweiler was able to secure cash prizes to the value of 10,000 marks. As a competition, "Olympia" was an almost complete failure: it only drew a paltry 500 contestants. The standard of entries was so low that it proved difficult to justify the distribution of the prize money (the judging had not been completed before the prizegiving anyway), and the winners were largely forgotten beside other Olympic-inspired competitions in Germany at that time.[154] Nonetheless it was a useful tactical weapon and provided Derichsweiler with a constant aggravation to the DST throughout this period, as each tried to win over the students.

In terms of public relations the Reich Vocational Contest

[152] Feickert to Kreisführer, 7 October 1935, RSFWü III*A-1.1.2.

[153] Kater notes both versions of topic headings but does not explain the reason for the modification or mention the NSDStB's rival "Olympia" contest. Kater, "Vocational Contest," p. 229. The Education Ministry's officials knew full well that Derichsweiler was trying to sabotage the DST's competition and were extremely uncooperative toward him. They drafted a letter for Rust to send to Hess, complaining about the pointlessness of the NSDStB's "Olympia" contest. Derichsweiler to Heinrich, 9 December 1935; Draft Kunisch for Rust, 28 January 1936, ZStA REM 907.

[154] Bericht Derichsweiler, "Die Ergebnisse im Reichswettbewerb 'Olympia,' " RSFWü II*264 α 181.

was more successful, and until the Reich Student Leadership was set up, the NSDStB tried hard to seize control of it. It too failed, however, to attract many entrants: only 3,728 students (5 percent of the student body) took part during the first year; since the official figure was 5,000, it is likely that the official figures for subsequent years were also exaggerated.[155] Though some of the more practical contributions, dealing with problems of textiles, raw materials, and energy, were allegedly put to good use, many of the papers presented were of little scholarly merit.[156] One of the Hamburg entries that found favor with the judges in 1937, for example, was a superficial essay titled "Spare time activities for sailors on board and in port," which, though it represented a whole semester's work by a team of seven students, was only nine pages long.[157] Nor was the world likely to be convinced of the high standards of Nazi scholarship by another Hamburg entry of the same year on the "Decoration of Sagebiel Hall for a rally of Hamburg students with *Gauleiter* Kaufmann."[158] Even entries with greater pretensions to scholarship usually did not live up to expectations: a fifty-page entry

[155] The actual number of participants may be calculated from the lists in Franz Six, *Studenten bauen auf! Der 1. Reichsleistungskampf 1935/36: Ein Rechenschaftsbericht* (Marburg and Berlin, n.d.), pp. 163-68. The official figure in ibid., p. iii. The figure 4,000 is given in Wilhelm Kaffl (ed.), *Wille und Weg der nationalsozialistischen Studenten: Bericht von der ersten Reichsarbeitstagung des NSD-Studentenbundes und der Deutschen Studentenschaft, Heidelberg, 22. bis 25. Juni 1937* (Munich, n.d. [1937]), p. 85. Cf. also the figures for the first three years in Fritz Kubach, *Studenten bauen auf! Der 3. Reichsberufswettkampf der deutschen Studenten 1937/38: Ein Rechenschaftsbericht* (Deutsche Arbeitsfront [DAF]-Zentralbüro, n.d.), p. 28.

[156] Details of the implementation and publication of entries in 1937 by subject in "Das Ergebnis des Reichsberufswettkampf im Bilde der Statistik," *Die Bewegung*, 15 June 1937. Cf. also "Bewertung und Verteilung der Arbeiten auf die einzelnen Sparten beim 3. Reichsberufswettkampf der deutschen Studenten," *Die Bewegung*, 5 July 1938.

[157] Copy of paper by students of the Merchant Marine School at Hamburg in RSFWü III*B-2.

[158] Copy of paper by students of the Hamburg College of Fine arts, ibid.

examining the "History of the State Institute of Chemistry
and Physics of the Hanseatic University with special reference to the Jewish question" could, despite the tendentious
promise of its title, only draw from the judges the disappointed comment: "The paper merely gives a set of biographical sketches."[159]

Such otiose pursuits were not viewed favorably by professors, and at the 1937 Rectors' Conference the delegates
discussed the "primitive and dilettante" nature of the Reich
Vocational Contest and the harm it did by diverting students
from their "proper" studies.[160] This was an exaggeration,
since relatively few university students did participate. The
proportion was greater in the technical colleges (and complaints came from them, too), since many of the themes
offered were more likely to suit these students than those
at universities. In 1938, 56 percent of the entries were from
nonuniversity colleges (i.e. excluding universities and technical universities), although such institutions accounted for
only 24 percent of the student body.[161] Kater concludes that
the Reich Vocational Contest demonstrates "a high degree
of ideological infection within the student body even in the
prewar phase," yet it is self-evident that competitors writing
specifically for Nazi adjudicators would pay appropriate ideological lip service if they entertained any hope of winning.[162] Indeed, it seems that all entrants in Hamburg had
to pass an ideological test in order to participate.[163] Given

[159] Copy of paper by Hamburg University students, ibid.

[160] Protokoll Eisfeld, "Rektoren-Konferenz in Marburg am 15. Dezember
1937," UniHH C.10.8.

[161] Calculated from lists of entries in Kubach, *Der 3. Reichsberufswettkampf*, passim, and student figures for winter semester 1937-1938 in *Statistisches Jahrbuch für das Deutsche Reich*, ed. Statistisches Reichsamt,
vol. 57 (Berlin, 1938), pp. 602-603.

[162] Kater, "Vocational Contest," p. 237.

[163] Mentioned in correspondence relating to an article published in the
Berner Tagwacht (16 May 1938) that ridiculed the nature of the questions
in an ideological test of Hamburg students. The syndic wondered if this
were the test taken in connection with the Reich Vocational Contest. Ac-

the relatively poor support for the contest, generalizations about the whole student body go too far.

The students of Hamburg University showed little interest in the contest. The Reich Student Leadership took the University's Student Leader to task in the autumn of 1937 because a headquarters representative had met with an attendance of only 200 students (out of a possible 1,500) at the opening rally for the Reich Vocational Contest; even worse, Student Leader Seiler himself had not bothered to attend, on the grounds that he was preparing for an examination.[164] That year it had been necessary to offer prizes in order to attract more applicants. The offer in the previous contest of payment of a semester's college fees for the winners had brought little benefit because most of the winning entries came from senior students. Of the 273 winners, 112 had already graduated by the time the results came out and were thus unable to profit from their prize.[165] During the first year of the war, the War Propaganda Service replaced the contest, and after a sorry attempt had been made to reestablish it in 1941, it was abandoned altogether.

Since the nazification of scholarship was a central task of the student leadership, why was it that the Reich Vocational Contest received such scant support from university students? An indication of the answer lies in the Nazis' attempts to maintain, as a cover for the ideological void, a "permanent state of emergency." In addition, students were being urged by student leaders as well as professors to complete their studies as thoroughly as possible so that their expertise might be harnessed to the Four-Year Plan, and

cording to the student leadership, not wishing to admit to absurd examinations, this could not be so. Bothe to Gaustudentenführung, 3 June 1938; Ochsenius to Bothe, 15 June 1938, uniHH A.1.5.

[164] This almost made Scheel cancel his visit to Hamburg, planned for the end of January 1938, for he evidently feared the embarrassment of speaking to rows of empty seats. Stellvertretender Reichsstudentenführer to Richter, 13 December 1937, MicAlex T-81/246/5033482. Keppel to Seiler, 26 November 1937, MicAlex T-81/246/5033691.

[165] Erläuterungen zum Haushaltsplan des RSW für das Rj. 1939, Anlage 8, ZStA REM 895.

many were wholly immersed in university study proper. The NSDStB placed greater urgency on its *political* than on its *ideological* tasks. The consolidation of the *Kameradschaf-ten* in order to embrace all the freshmen was a political necessity and a prerequisite of subsequent uniform ideological indoctrination. The hope was to gain the students' support more readily with concrete "politically necessary" tasks where ideological persuasion had clearly failed. An example of this that gained in importance at the end of the thirties was Rural Service.

The voluntary Labor Service scheme had been nurtured with particular pride in Hamburg in the early thirties, and the national student leadership kept up a tradition of vacation work, especially on the farms of East Prussia. Yet this had never become a fully accepted and welcomed part of student life. Under Scheel's leadership there evolved two types of rural service: the so-called harvest help program (still common in Eastern Europe today) in which students were sent to bring in the harvest, and second, the rural service proper (*Landdienst*). The latter was restricted to *Kameradschaft* members, as the emphasis lay not merely on providing a supplementary labor force but on participating in the political life of villages and boosting the work of local units of the Party in frontier areas.[166] For example, in 1939 the Hamburg District Student Leadership undertook a diverse selection of projects in its "foster villages": female students set up kindergartens; students from the College of Art gave weaving demonstrations in an attempt to promote cottage industry among the womenfolk, and another group drew up plans for a "Strength Through Joy" anglers' resort; a study of drainage problems was made, and yet other students busied themselves with surveying and mapping the land.[167]

In short, National Socialism made itself felt through the

[166] Eberhard Potratz, "Studentischer Einsatz," in *Hamburger Studentenbuch 1938/39*, ed. Karl Graak (Hamburg, 1939), p. 76.

[167] Studentischer Landdienst, Kreisführung Schlochau, "Kreisbericht des Frühjahrseinsatzes 1939," n.d., UniHH 0.10.2.10.

259

students' activities in a thoroughly impressive and agreeable way in these outlying areas—at least most of the time: one NSDStB member was murdered at Easter 1938 by villagers in Posen, following an altercation over a local girl.[168] On the whole, though, this direct contact with workers and peasants in their home setting was considered extremely beneficial. Students gained greater insights into the way of life than when working-class men had simply been attached to their isolated Labor Service camps.[169] Although the scheme was supposed to be voluntary, ever greater pressure was applied, as the political situation demanded it, to ensure the necessary level of participation. Hess entreated Scheel in July 1938 that "as a matter of principle, no force of any kind whatever should be applied to bring about participation after the third semester."[170] Yet he turned a blind eye to Scheel's coercion of *Kameradschaft* members. It still proved impossible to engender sufficient enthusiasm to ensure a good turnout for the harvest help. In 1937, the Hamburg Student Leader managed to drum together a mere ninety students, many of whom must have been *Kameradschaft* members. This fell short of the target of 12 percent of the student body, which other universities failed to meet as well. Many students simply had to get a job during the vacation in order to help finance the following semester's study.[171]

In 1939, chances of a half-hearted response could not be taken. International tension made the speedy gathering of the harvest of the utmost importance, and in April a letter went from ss headquarters urging the Ministry of the Interior to provide extra subsidies for the Reich Student Leadership's program. It underlined the fact that "this year especially the task falls to the Student Rural Service of acting as a certain

---

[168] "In Erfüllung seiner Pflicht ein Student im Landdienst ermordet," *Die Bewegung*, 5 April 1938.

[169] Remarks to this effect by Professor Bachér, Protokoll Konferenz Studentenschaftsführer, 26 May 1935, zsta REM 868.

[170] Leitgen to Scheel, 28 July 1938, RSFWü II*363 α 269.

[171] Semesterschlussbericht Seiler, 5 July 1937, RSFWü V*2 α 539.

counterbalance to the dangers which are bound to crop up more than before, in the light of frontier-policing measures which have become necessary on the German-Polish border."[172] Without hesitation, the Ministry doubled its intended subsidy to 30,000 marks.[173] Meanwhile, Scheel decided to apply "considerable moral pressure": he threatened that any student without a valid excuse, who did not volunteer, would be excluded from re-registration at college the following autumn—a piece of pure bluff, as only the Reich Education Ministry had the power to order such a measure.[174] Rector Gundert discovered on telephoning to Berlin, however, that the Ministry wished at all costs to keep the scheme voluntary.[175]

Scheel's next ploy was to have Himmler write him an open letter stressing the absolute necessity of providing 25,000 students.[176] There was panic at the Reich Student Leadership when it was discovered that students were rushing to draft offices to volunteer for a short spell of vacation military service in order to exempt themselves from the back-breaking harvesting.[177] This escape route was blocked, and sufficient numbers of students were ultimately prevailed upon

[172] Greifelt to Vollert, 24 April 1939, RSFWü II*363 α 269. The Party press contrasted the land-oriented socialism in the service of peace that German students were performing with a picture showing Etonians drilling as reserve officer candidates. "Die Erntehilfe der deutschen Studenten," *Völkischer Beobachter*, 19 July 1939, quoted in Schoenbaum, *Social Revolution*, p. 68.

[173] Kracke to Fähndrich, 29 April 1939, RSFWü II*363 α 269.

[174] Kracke to Fähndrich, 13 May 1939, ibid.

[175] Aktennotiz Gundert, 16 June 1939, UniHH 0.10.2.10.

[176] Himmler to Scheel, 27 May 1939, RSFWü II*363 α 269. Scheel had good reason to be anxious, for in 1937 it was officially admitted that only 10,000 students had participated (in reality probably fewer). "Die Rede des Reichsstudentenführers," *Die Bewegung*, 14 September 1937.

[177] A circular distributed by a group calling itself the "Revolutionary Students (of) Berlin" urged students not to participate in the "Harvest Help" or any other of the NSDStB's activities and ceremonies "that make us the laughing stock of the world." RSF-Dienststelle Berlin to Kracke, 21 July 1939, RSFWü I*00 φ 38.

to take part.[178] At Hamburg, Rector Gundert supported the scheme warmly and donated 300 marks from the University's funds toward expenses.[179] To testify to his own enthusiasm, Gundert toured the villages in person, visiting the Hamburg students at their work in Pomerania.[180]

But if, in this quarter at least, there was some awareness of the seriousness of the political situation, some of the student leaders appeared positively naïve. One of the *Kameradschaften* had long been planning a trip to Flanders for the summer of 1939 and incredulously refused to heed a sudden ban on "any further contact with Belgium and Holland" by the Political Education Department of the Reich Student Leadership.[181] The incensed *Kameradschaft* leader, Wilhelm Formel, angry at the thought of wasted months of preparation, deliberately left unanswered the letters from the Reich Student Leadership. He gained the wholehearted support of both District Student Leader Ochsenius and the leader of the Reich leadership's Area Office North (which was in Hamburg), who also rejected the intrusion into these praiseworthy and valuable international overtures.[182] It took a stern threat of disciplinary action before the Hamburg leaders finally acknowledged the ruling from Munich and ac-

[178] Arrangements were made with the draft offices to turn away these student "Wehrfreudigen," RSF-Amt Politische Erziehung, Bekanntgabe PE 15/39, 15 June 1939, RSFWü II*378 α 457. The student press later claimed that 45,000 students had participated in the "Harvest Help" in 1939. "1939 im Rückblick," *Die Bewegung*, 2 January 1940. Scheel increased the claim to 47,000: quoted in Dibner, "History," p. 254.

[179] Ansprache Gundert beim Pflichtappell der Studentenschaft zur Verkündung der Erntehilfspflicht, 21 June 1939, UniHH 0.10.2.10.

[180] Some 350 Hamburg students participated in the Harvest Help, and 120 Kameradschaft members in the Rural Service. *Mitteilungen des Rektors der Hansischen Universität*, summer semester 1939, no. 9, 1 September 1939.

[181] The ban had come from the same official of the Reich Student Leadership (Kracke) who was coordinating the deployment of students in the Polish border areas. Kracke to Ochsenius, 8 May 1939, RSFWü V*2 α 568.

[182] Schuster to Bauersfeld, 8 June 1939, ibid. Also Ochsenius to Kracke, 17 May 1939, ibid.

cepted that their presence in the Lowlands that summer was not desired.[183]

It is not possible to judge just how aware of war preparations the Reich Student Leadership was. One can assume with some degree of certitude that since the coordinator of the SD's preparations for the Polish attack was Scheel's close friend, *SS-Standartenführer* Professor Franz Alfred Six, Scheel at least understood the pressing necessity of his students' mission in the frontier areas.[184] The degree of direct involvement, however, is not the central point. The fact is that the student leadership had been "defense-minded" (as it was euphemistically called), had been promoting paramilitary training and intensive sport, since the early thirties. In this respect the student body had been well prepared for war. Moreover, the desire for freedom from the yoke of Versailles and for the return of colonies was an accepted tenet. But this was precisely the problem: it was just generally accepted; there was nothing peculiarly National Socialist about these views, nothing to win over the students to National Socialism.

The relative neglect of ideological matters was due in part to more pressing political tasks. Yet it had always been claimed from the start that the very special concern of the NSDStB was with ideology. Even with the backing of the SD "think tank," the Reich Student Leadership was unable to produce a workable blueprint for the *Kameradschaften* in order to make the political education program attractive to students. This suggests that the SD officers had not quite the intellectual ability and imagination that they believed they possessed, although in the SD, too, political matters tended to push ideological theorizing into the background. The failure in this area may be contrasted with the increasing emphasis on the elitism of the NSDStB, which sought, as it were,

---

[183] Bauersfeld to Aussenstelle Nord der RSF, 23 June 1939, ibid.

[184] Six was by now one of the three department heads at SD headquarters (Amt Inland). Ramme points to SD initiative behind the students' work in the frontier areas. Ramme, *Sicherheitsdienst*, pp. 94 and 105.

to prove its worth by the mere insistence on it. The less successful the NSDStB was in its tasks, the more the self-importance of its members and their activities was encouraged.

The question of status was an important one. Universities did still enjoy prestige, despite frequent harassment from the Party. Even *Gauleiter* Kaufmann wrote of his Eilbecktal scheme under the title: "The field marshal's baton in the knapsack" ("Der Marschallstab im Tornister").[185] But the elite that Kaufmann envisaged had a sounder and more attractive basis than that of the NSDStB. Instead of promoting a corps of leaders apparently *in vacuo* (for it was seen that the Party did not turn extensively to the NSDStB for recruitment of leaders), he had the clear goal of enhancing the standing of Hamburg and building it up as a great colonial center. The hoped-for colonies would open up a massive job market for *trained* personnel (much more than for political leaders). If Hamburg could be set up as a sort of clearinghouse as well as a training center for these positions, it would enjoy immense prestige in the Reich.[186] This demanded a center of academic excellence of the type Adolf Rein strove unflaggingly to maintain and expand. The cry for the return of Germany's colonies was so constant that it must have appeared only a matter of time before she was allowed to regain them. In such an atmosphere, it is not surprising that the students, in probable awareness that most of them would never be chosen as political leaders, devoted themselves to their studies in order to be in the foremost ranks of skilled graduates when the colonial market opened up.

Kaufmann indeed *hoped* for political leaders (particularly from the Eilbecktal men), but political training could not be the primary task of the university and had always to take

[185] "Der Marschallstab im Tornister," *Hamburger Tageblatt*, 23 May 1939. The phrase is Napoleon's.

[186] For the University's part in this, see Marlis Lüth, "Hamburg und die Kolonialpolitik im Dritten Reich," *Zeitschrift des Vereins für Hamburgische Geschichte* 59 (1973): 55-87, especially pp. 79ff.

second place. Rein realized the implications of this for the independence of the university; the NSDStB and NSDDOZB leaders invariably did not. After 1939, the severe shortages of manpower dictated the necessary priorities even more: the state simply could not afford to emphasize political education to the neglect of academic training. As will be seen, the low actual priority of political training (in contrast with its high declared priority) led to acute embarrassment in the Reich Student Leadership during the war, and Scheel set out to increase the extent of his controls over the students so that he might conceal his ineffectiveness and maintain the external picture that he was making steady progress in the politicization of the student body.

CHAPTER SEVEN

The University at War

The final period of the NSDStB's history was its most unsettled. The problems of continuity of the leadership, inherent in any student organization, were magnified, but even the membership was now subjected to alarming and unforeseeable fluctuations in size from one semester to the next. War disrupted institutions of higher education all over Europe, and the effect on students was generally to make them more conscientious in the brief time that was available to them for study. This attitude prevailed for the most part in Germany, too. Because of the emphasis that the Reich Student Leadership placed on conspicuous political activity, however, it was not enough simply to study harder. The NSDStB expected students to show greater interest in its ideological programs as well. Anything less than wholehearted enthusiasm came under suspicion of promoting sabotage of the war effort. Given the widespread current of impatience with the NSDStB, the student leaders remained very nervous for most of the war. On the other hand, the war offered real fulfillment for many of the members in the propaganda tasks that came their way. At long last they were able to put their academic training to practical use in the service of National Socialism. They were, however, in the minority. What characterized the NSDStB during the war was not the spirit of voluntarism and satisfaction but a sense of frustration and the need for tighter controls.

War Service Duties

The invasion of Poland began during the university vacation, just one week after the last students had returned to

Hamburg from their Rural Service.[1] The Reich Education Ministry decided to suspend teaching activities at all but a few universities for the duration of the war, since a large proportion of the student body had been called up by the armed forces. Of those in the age groups that had not been drafted, the foremost volunteers were the loyal members of the National Socialist Students' Association. The NSDStB very nearly collapsed overnight. By the end of August 1940, five of the eighteen department heads in the Reich Student Leadership were dead, and the student leaders of ten colleges had been killed. Although 95 percent of the student leaders at all levels were reportedly at the front,[2] Scheel himself did not enter the military until June 1940, when "despite a serious heart ailment" he was finally accepted into the *Luftwaffe*. Although he had worked hard to be admitted, he emphasized that he would be needed for other, more important tasks in the future, having been promised the command of a security police "task force" (*Sipo-Einsatzgruppe*) "in future areas still to be occupied."[3]

Every one of the *Kameradschaft* leaders in Hamburg joined the armed forces. The University student leadership folded up completely and was taken over by the District Student Leader. The Eilbecktal Student Hostels, the pride and joy of that summer, were evacuated for use as a military hospital, though they reverted to students' use on 1 February 1940 because there were no patients.[4] Apart from the NSDStB volunteers, students were far less eager to enlist than in 1914,

[1] *Mitteilungen des Rektors*, 1 September 1939, UniHH C.10.1.2.

[2] Rede Kubach, Studentenführertagung München, 29 August 1940, LC CGD RSF 488. One student leader in Hamburg was not so enthusiastic: Meinert Hansen did his utmost to avoid active military duty by claiming that he was indispensable for the operation of the compulsory sports program of the students. "So this is the spirit of Langemark!" the University Student Leader noted in disgust. Carstensen to Ochsenius, 20 November 1939, RSFwü V*2 α 570.

[3] Scheel to Rust, 3 June 1940, ZStA REM 896. Scheel did not in fact become the head of one of the SD task forces.

[4] Tätigkeitsbericht Carstensen, 10 February 1940, RSFwü V*2 α 532.

which provoked critical comments from Party Treasurer Schwarz about the failure of the NSDStB in its task of political education: ". . . there was much too much talk, and nothing done."[5]

Although Hamburg had its first air raid on 3 September 1939 in the form of leaflets dropped over the city by the Royal Air Force, it remained on the whole fairly quiet. The rector seemed almost exuberant to announce that one of the student leaders, Werner Seiler, had been shot "already during the first attack on Poland," and the first Hamburg student death, in the course of the assault on Brest-Litovsk in the third week of September, received pride of place in the University newsletter.[6]

The universities that had been allowed to stay open quickly became hopelessly overcrowded. The German High Command ruled that soldiers eligible to study medicine could be released from active service in order to do so. A large number of them opted to spend what promised to be a short war in this way. Hess's office noted that the Catholic church had been dropping hints about this possibility of escaping front-line duty.[7] Despite the closures of universities, there were still 48,182 college students by the end of the winter trimester 1939 (compared with 73,455 students in the summer semester 1939).[8] An announcement that all school-leavers under the age of twenty would be released from their compulsory Labor Service, if they wished to study, aggravated the situation even further. Scheel was horrified by these "catastrophic" measures, which had been taken, to his annoyance, "without any consultation with the Reich

[5] Chef des SS-Hauptamtes to Himmler, 2 July 1941, IfZ NO-029.

[6] *Mitteilungen des Rektors*, 1 October and 1 November 1939, UniHH C.10.1.2.

[7] Stab Stellvertreter des Führers to Rust, 16 January 1940, ZStA REM 897.

[8] Statistisches Reichsamt (ed.), *Statistisches Jahrbuch für das Deutsche Reich 1939/40*, vol. 58 (Berlin, 1940), p. 615. Another publication gives significantly smaller figures: 36,934 and 56,667 respectively. Länderrat des Amerikanischen Besatzungsgebiets (ed.), *Statistisches Handbuch von Deutschland 1928-1944* (Munich, 1949), p. 622, which is based on Lorenz, *Zehnjahres-Statistik*.

Student Leadership." According to the SD, the sixteen- and seventeen-year-old students were behaving more like immature schoolboys. Scheel claimed that in some cases grandmothers were having to accompany freshmen incapable of completing the paperwork for matriculation. This is a clear case of Scheel's generalizing from one particular instance. A subsequently released SD report, though also prone to exaggeration, describes just *one* grandmother in Breslau.[9] Scheel was "dismayed" to think that such students, reported to be disrupting lectures with peashooters, might be fully qualified doctors by the age of twenty. Apart from the fact that they did "not represent a physical and racial elite," he was above all shocked to hear that many of those who refused to join the NSDStB openly admitted that they did so "for ideological reasons."[10]

Scheel enlisted the help of SD headquarters, which, picking on a variety of small incidents, printed in its secret situation reports a disturbing general picture of students caring little about work and spending much of their time in bars and dance halls. This helped substantially to pave the way for Scheel's tightening of controls over the student body.[11] The schoolmasterly Rust was almost certain to be shocked by the reports, and Scheel had no difficulty in persuading the Minister that the "boozing and silly pranks" of these stu-

[9] Meldungen aus dem Reich, 5 January 1940, BA R21/724. Although they were "embarrassingly frank," as Gordon Craig describes them, they were also exaggerated for effect. Gordon A. Craig, *Germany 1866-1945* (Oxford, 1978), p. 662.

[10] Scheel calculated their graduation date on the basis of the three-trimester year introduced in the autumn of 1939. The Education Ministry reverted to semesters at Easter 1941. Scheel to Hess, 16 December 1939, BA R4311/940b.

[11] Berichte zur innenpolitischen Lage, "Unwürdige Haltung der jungen Studenten," 24 November 1939, BA R58/145; Meldungen aus dem Reich, 5 January 1940, BA R21/724. The recipients of these reports on "public opinion" and the reaction to various measures taken during the war were the ministers of state and the Party's *Reichsleiter* (not apparently Hitler himself). Other top civil servants received only those reports relevant to their department. Boberach, *Meldungen*, pp. xvii-xviii.

dents were responsible for "the frequently mentioned drop in standards." Rust instigated the formation of watchdog committees (composed of the rector, a professor, and the Student Leader) that would investigate all cases in which complaints about a student had been made "from whatever quarter," "even if the [university] disciplinary code does not appear to provide grounds for action."[12] But Scheel was not content with the banishment of recalcitrant students from the university. In a secret decree he expounded further on the measures to be taken by the student leaders. If a student did not fulfill the duties required of him by the Reich Student Leadership, he was to be questioned by the Student Leader and given a written reprimand. If a subsequent reprimand were to prove necessary, the student would be handed over to the Gestapo for further "interrogation." Scheel, now an Inspector of the Security Police and the Security Service, made arrangements to have the police files on students forwarded to him for his personal decision on the appropriate punishment, which would be "in serious cases a concentration camp."[13] Moreover, he expanded his network of "special agents" (i.e. SD spies within the student body) for the specific purpose of "establishing which students have proven especially unworthy."[14] Under the terms of Rust's decree the rector was obliged to institute disciplinary proceedings whenever the SD demanded.

Once this control framework had been established to Scheel's satisfaction, the SD reports quickly became more favorable toward students at large: "The reports from university towns concur in the observation that the student's attitude has generally improved, and keenness to work has

[12] Geheimerlass Rust, 10 January 1940, RSFWÜ V*2 α 568.

[13] There is no evidence that any action was taken at Hamburg on the basis of these decrees. K-Befehl Scheel, 1 February 1940, ibid.

[14] Meldungen aus dem Reich, 5 January 1940, BA R21/724. The report also suggested the introduction of a certificate of political reliability as a prerequisite of matriculation.

increased."[15] The university situation still received attention, but the emphasis lay more on the conditions of study. The almost universally condemned cramming of eighteen months' work into twelve was dropped in favor of the old two-semester year at Easter 1941.[16] Complaints continued about the freshmen's lack of even basic general knowledge. One SD reporter asked: "When, for example, a student holds Leonardo da Vinci to be an Italian film star . . . , how can such people become the intellectual leaders of the new Reich?"[17] With the matriculation figures soaring after all universities had opened their doors once more at the beginning of 1940, Scheel was eager to seize every opportunity in order to exclude would-be opponents of the NSDSTB who might damage his good name as its leader by their uncooperative attitude. He chose to interpret offhanded remarks made by Rust in conversation with him at Strassburg as a firm mandate to begin a "special campaign for cleansing the atmosphere of the universities" at the end of November 1940, in order to "remove hostile, immature, opportunistic, and criminal elements."[18] Awareness of this did not penetrate the Reich Education Ministry until the operation was already underway, but the Ministry at once declared itself "100% against such campaigns," knowing the behavior of the students to be not nearly as blameworthy as the Reich Student Leadership suggested. Although it was not possible to halt the campaign completely, the Ministry insisted on reserving for itself the final decision on whether a student should be disciplined.[19]

[15] Meldungen aus dem Reich, 5 February 1940, MicAlex T-175/258/2750759.

[16] "It is uniformly reported from all parts of the Reich that the announcement of the suspension of the trimester division (of the academic year) . . . has been unanimously greeted by university teachers, students, and members of the academic professions in general." Meldungen aus dem Reich, 25 March 1941, MicAlex T-175/260/2753493.

[17] Meldungen aus dem Reich, 5 October 1942, BA R58/176.

[18] Schulz to Huber, 19 December 1940, BA R21/Rep 76/937.

[19] Aktenvermerk Huber, 14 January 1941, ibid.

During the war, those students who were neither soldiers nor members of the NSDStB were obliged to join so-called Service Groups of the German Students' Union (*Dienstgemeinschaften*) so that the Reich Student Leadership could boast that everyone was making a contribution to the war effort. Scheel feared that the universities might not otherwise be kept open. All youths were obliged to participate in service duties such as harvesting, though during the war there was a greater emphasis on the premilitary training of the sixteen- to eighteen-year-olds.[20] Scheel was adamantly determined that at no time must the impression arise that the students were having an easy life in wartime Germany.[21] At first the "service groups" were active during term time. In the autumn of 1940, some 300 Hamburg students acted as tram conductors, missing all their afternoon classes for a fortnight at a time, which brought firm protests from the faculty.[22] These tasks were small, however, compared with the vacation duties that came to be required of the students.

In the summer of 1941, for the first time, every student not in the armed forces had to spend the greater part of the summer at the disposal of the Reich Student Leadership. Many of the students were put to work in armaments factories, some 15,500 as unskilled and 3,900 as skilled laborers. Others worked on the railways and the roads, some brought in the harvest, 1,200 helped on their parents' smallholdings, and several hundred female students looked after evacuated children in the countryside.[23] Work in the factories was particularly unpopular and was resented throughout the war by students and parents alike, who considered, particularly dur-

[20] Brandenburg, *Geschichte der HJ*, pp. 228ff.

[21] Scheel to Mentzel, 2 October 1943, BA R21/Rep 76/951.

[22] Aktenvermerk Cramer, "Über dem bisherigen Einsatz bei der Strassen- und Hochbahn," n.d. (October 1940); also press cuttings, UniHH 0.10.2.18. Lütgens to Raethjen, 25 October 1940, UniHH 0.10.2.19.

[23] Übersicht zum Kriegseinsatz der RSF für die Zeit vom. 1. September 1939 bis zum 31. Dezember 1942, Hoover Institution Stanford (HIS), Microfilm Collection, NSDAP-Hauptarchiv, Reel 20, Folder 375.

ing the frenzied period of the three-trimester year, that the already short breaks should be free for study.[24] Dr. Lammers later told Rust that he held the vacation War Service to be absolutely irresponsible in the light of the blatant drop in academic standards.[25] Scheel insisted on maintaining it "for political and psychological reasons."[26] The often chaotic organization of duties, not planned locally but in distant Berlin, led to further complaints.

The Acting District Student Leader at Hamburg reported that students were being assigned to firms that had no use for them. There was no attempt to correlate the geographical position of the students' home and his place of work, so some were faced with a daily journey of three or four hours. One student whose home was in Cuxhaven, for example, was sent to a firm 150 kilometers away.[27] In subsequent years, the feeling grew that the students' special skills were being wasted: one Hamburg engineering student complained bitterly at having to clear bomb rubble with foreign prisoners of war.[28] For the summer of 1943, the Acting District Student Leader took pains to ensure that students would be employed only in skilled work. He determined that this time "there was no question of service for pure propaganda reasons" and made plans to draft the students into schools and hospitals and to act as research assistants in departments of the University.[29] He proposed the latter "partly in disagreement with the Reich Student Leadership," but he earned the keen support of the Hamburg professoriate.[30]

A number of students were to be sent to schools in the

[24] Bericht Reinecke, 10 October 1941, RSFWü V*2 α 532.

[25] Lammers to Rust, 1 September 1943, BA R21/Rep 76/951.

[26] Scheel to Mentzel, 2 October 1943, ibid.

[27] Tätigkeitsbericht Potratz, 14 September 1942, RSFWü V*2 α 532.

[28] Merkel to Potratz, 7 October 1942, RSFWü V*2 α 565.

[29] Protokoll über die Verhandlungen am 27. Mai 1943, RSFWü V*2 α 563.

[30] Reinecke to Keeser, 5 May 1943, and numerous requests for assistants from departments of the University, UniHH N.20.2.11. The plans were never carried out because of the air raids on Hamburg that summer.

conquered Polish areas. The work programs here, carried out first in the summer of 1940 by some 800 students from all over Germany, were conducted under the aegis of the ss Settlement Staff (*SS-Ansiedlungsstab*). That first year three Hamburg medical students had traveled to Lodz (Litzmannstadt) for their clinical practice and wrote a glowing report on the insights they had gained "into the many, often unsolved questions of modern mass migration." The students viewed the Jewish ghetto with interest and worked in a clinic in the town and later in a nearby transit camp for new German "settlers."[31] The promotion of this form of service was intended to encourage the participants to move permanently to settlement areas themselves after graduation to become doctors, teachers, and administrators. In 1942, 1,200 German college students took part, and the following year 2,500 spent their vacation in the east. Although the majority of students were favorably impressed by what they were shown, there was "a considerable number of critical and disconcerted comments" from students whose skills had been wasted here, too, in routine and dull secretarial work. The sd warned that this was not the way to encourage them to make their careers in the eastern outposts.[32]

On a much more modest scale, female students were also sent to France. In 1941, for example, 260 of them traveled to the west (whereas 2,000 were sent to the east).[33] The tasks allotted them in France were so poorly supervised that many of the girls seized the opportunity to have a good time with locally stationed soldiers. The Hamburg girls were particularly reproached for their "conspicuous make-up, hair, and

[31] "Studentischer Facheinsatz Ost," *Hansische Hochschul-Zeitung*, January 1941, pp. 5-9.

[32] sd-Berichte zu Inlandsfragen, "Stimmen zum studentischen Osteinsatz," 21 February 1944, ba R58/192.

[33] Übersicht zum Kriegseinsatz der rsf für die Zeit vom 1. September 1939 bis zum 31. Dezember 1942, his nsdap-Hauptarchiv, Reel 20, Folder 375.

dress" and for spending more than just their leisure time driving around in officers' cars.[34]

A more academic activity was the War Propaganda Service, initiated soon after the outbreak of war by Scheel, with the warm approval of Goebbels, who requested that the students "devote particular attention to the question of Churchill."[35] The goal of the project was to assemble propaganda material against England, ideally in the form of short quotations from English texts. Obscurity did not seem to matter, as long as the passages were absolutely genuine and accurate so as to "serve as a scholarly contribution to the destruction of the nimbus of English respectability in the world."[36] Social questions stood in the center of inquiries, viewed from two aspects: "1. The British upper class: its plutocratic capitalism, its social ruthlessness, its thirst for wealth, and its intended financial exploitation of the masses of its own country and of the conquered nations. 2. The lower classes in Britain and the Empire: their powerless existence, their social defenselessness, their desolation, their distress, the wretched conditions of their lives."[37]

Within this framework for all colleges the specific tasks assigned to Hamburg were the systematic combing of *Hansard* from the year 1900 onward and the collecting of satirical cartoons from *Punch*. Some forty students were engaged in these tasks during the first half of 1940.[38] The Reich Student Leadership even hired a secretary for them, in a departure

[34] Kalb to Ochsenius, 29 May 1941; Bericht Conrad, "Über die Hamburger Studentinnen," 19 May 1941, RSFWÜ V*2 α 540.

[35] Rundschreiben Bähr, 9 December 1939, RSFWÜ V*2 α 564.

[36] Gundert to Sauer, 26 April 1940, UNIHH 0.10.14.2. Extracts from an army colonel's talk in Jersey Town Hall in April 1857, culled from the local newspaper, the *Jersey Independent* were by no means too obscure to be used. Cf. Propagandaamt der DAF und der RSF, *Sonderdienst*, April 1940, p. 6.

[37] Merkblatt Bähr, "Studentischer Kriegspropagandaeinsatz," 30 January 1940, UNIHH T.20.5.

[38] Jäger to Eckert, 22 August 1940, RSFWÜ V*2 α 564.

from its usual parsimony.[39] By the end of the year, students throughout Germany had reportedly examined 6,000 scholarly works and scoured the entire British press over the past forty years for material. The fruits of this immense labor were put to use in pamphlets published by the Reich Student Leadership and in two elaborate volumes that the Propaganda Ministry brought out.[40]

Not only did this bring welcome aid to the Ministry, but it also appealed to the students who opted for this project. District Student Leader Hans Ochsenius was also involved in propaganda work. He was drafted into a "Propaganda Company" of the army after completing the oral examination for his doctorate in October 1939. In many ways, Ochsenius was the perfect choice for a propagandist. He had been enthusiastically involved with the National Socialist movement since the age of fifteen, having joined the National Socialist Schoolboys' Association in Hamburg in November 1929. On reaching the University, he rose quickly in the ranks of the NSDStB and was placed in charge of political education during his freshman year.

Ochsenius's father, a retired lieutenant-colonel, gave him

[39] Bähr to Graak, 9 April 1940, ibid.

[40] Wilhelm Ziegler (ed.), *Ein Dokumentenwerk über die englische Humanität* (Berlin, n.d. [1940]) and *Ein Dokumentenwerk über die englische Demokratie* (Berlin, 1940). One of the co-editors of these works was Wolff Heinrichsdorff, the former Hamburg NSDStB Leader, now a prominent official in the Propaganda Ministry. In Hamburg, the latest results of the hunt for quotations were published regularly in the student newspaper under the heading "The mask falls!" A whole special edition was published on Britain (*Hansische Hochschul-Zeitung*, June 1940) with the title, in English, "Enough of all This!" which had come from a *Picture Post* article (April 1939) denouncing the slum areas of London. The German Foreign Office also published work based on the students' research in a series of pamphlets, the so-called Black and White Books, which dealt with the iniquities of British domestic and foreign policies. Cf. "Aus dem Studentischen Kriegsleistungskampf: Ein Rechenschaftsbericht über die bisherige Arbeit," *Die Fachgruppe* (Organ des Amtes Wissenschaft und Facherziehung und Mitteilungsblatt der Reichsfachgruppen der Reichsstudentenführung), no. 3, September 1940, p. 9.

a conservative outlook on life, but not a narrow one. His home was a cosmopolitan one: a Professor Hudson from Cambridge was a guest or lodger for extended periods during the twenties, as was Miss Burton, a niece of Lord Northcliffe who studied singing in Hamburg.[41] It is tempting to think that it was from this relative of Britain's former propaganda chief that Hans Ochsenius developed his own interest in this area. From early days, he had grown up with a fierce anticommunism. The Marburg philologist, Professor Maass, a friend of the family, filled the youth with admiration for the patriotism of the Marburg Students' Company, who had murdered a number of Communists. The articles that Ochsenius later wrote for the NSDStB and as a war reporter are highly articulate. They are at their best when he is attempting to convey enthusiasm for the German cause or for National Socialism or optimism about the future: his idealism comes across more convincingly than his ideology, which is understandable, given the inner contradictions of National Socialist doctrines. Traveling as a war reporter on the Western front in June 1940, he was thrilled to see Hitler in person three times in one day near Lille, and his account is filled with almost childlike excitement.[42]

In general, those War Service activities that utilized the specialist knowledge or ability of the students, giving them the feeling that they were contributing to "intellectual warfare," were much better received and more keenly pursued than those involving purely manual labor. Factory jobs were often left to the female students, who were regarded in Nazi Germany as second-rate citizens in other ways.

[41] Biographical details taken from a memorial written by his father with a number of extracts from articles and private letters. Karl Ochsenius, "Sol invictus! Denkschrift für meinen Sohn Hans-Karl Ochsenius, Gaustudentenführer Hamburgs, Dr. phil., Leutnant der Reserve, durch Freitod aus dem Erdenleben geschieden am 13.5.1945," typescript in AFGNH. For the former Miss Burton's portrait of Ochsenius, see her autobiography: Christabel Bielenberg, *Ride Out the Dark* (New York, 1971), pp. 20-21.

[42] Ochsenius to parents, 2 June 1940, RSFWü V*2 α 562.

Women Students and the NSDStB

Little has been said so far in this book about women students. The reason for this is the paucity of archival material, and that in turn results from the scant attention accorded to women in the plans of the student leadership. During the war they could not be ignored, as their numbers approached those of male matriculants for the first time ever. Yet the essential antifeminism of the Nazi student leadership was by now so deeply ingrained and well rehearsed that attitudes did not fundamentally change. They had been firmly established back in the Weimar Republic.

University study had always been considered a largely male domain, and this attitude was reinforced by Nazi doctrine, which saw the woman primarily as the bearer of children, the mother. In the summer of 1930, Baldur von Schirach intended to rid himself of the women members of the NSDStB altogether, but he met with such strong protest from the individual groups that he was obliged to revise his plans. In order to exclude them from the NSDStB groups yet still retain their support, above all in AStA elections, he set up the National Socialist Women Students' Group (ANst) as a separate organization.[43] The Hamburg branch, formed in November 1930, differed little in its program of lectures and discussions from the NSDStB, though first-aid courses usefully took the place of the street brawls of the men.[44] Talks in the summer semester of 1931 covered such subjects as "Purpose and Aims of ANst," "Race Hygiene," and "The Program of the NSDAP."[45]

[43] Announcement of the foundation of the group in *Die Bewegung*, August 1930. As this book goes to press, a book by Jacques Pauwels, devoted to women students in the Third Reich, is about to be published.

[44] Antrag Koppitke auf Eintragung in das Korporations- und Vereinsregister bei der Hamburgischen Universität, 28 November 1930, UniHH 0.30.5.328. On women in the early NSDStB, see Michael H. Kater, "Krisis des Frauenstudiums in der Weimarer Republik," *Vierteljahrsschrift für Sozial- und Wirtschaftsgeschichte* 59 (1972): 247ff.

[45] Arbeitsbericht ANst Hamburg, n.d. (July 1931), RSFWü V*2 α 510.

From a membership of nine at the beginning of May 1933, numbers had trebled by the end of the month, thus rising substantially but not as dramatically as the NSDStB membership. The program that month consisted of three evenings of discussion on the "political university" and a combined trip with the local League of German Girls (BDM) to a large storm troopers' rally in Kiel on 7 May. The ANSt members also hiked through the woods to a Hamburg Students' Union Women's Labor Camp and decided to hold their own camp in order to give the members a taste of life as a settler.[46] By the winter semester 1934/1935, ANSt work had settled into a pattern of civil defense activities covering first aid, air-raid precautions, and communications.[47]

On Derichsweiler's assumption of office as NSDStB Leader in July 1934, the ANSt was dissolved as an independent body and given the status of a mere subdepartment at NSDStB headquarters.[48] It lost its independence partly because of the fear that it did not have the strength to survive alone between the "two great lionesses," the Leaders of the BDM and the *Deutsche Frauenschaft*, both of whom wanted to incorporate the ANSt women as junior leaders of their respective organizations.[49] It split up into *Kameradschaften* like the NSDStB, and by the summer semester 1939 there were at least four in Hamburg. The women were meant to have a politically slanted program, but they appear to have received even less advice than the male *Kameradschaft* leaders. Hamburg's ANSt-*Kameradschaft* 4, for example, was "given" the themes "The East (Rural Service)" and "Colonies" for the summer

[46] Monatsbericht ANSt Hamburg, summer semester 1933, MicAlex T-81/237/5022156-61.

[47] "Die Arbeit des Hauptamtes VI für Studentinnen im Wintersemester 1934/35," *Hamburger Universitäts-Zeitung*, 19 January 1935. The work seems to have been neglected, however, in the following semester; cf. Niederschrift Besprechung des Rektors mit den Amtsleitern der Studentenschaft, 31 May 1935, UniHH 0.10.2.2.

[48] Rundschreiben Derichsweiler StF 5/34, "Anordnungen und Richtlinien für den Neuaufbau des NSD-Studentenbundes," RSFWü II* φ 312.

[49] Protokoll Reichstagung NSDStB, 12 May 1935, RSFWü II* φ 319.

semester 1939. After watching a film, "German Land in Africa," the students merely settled down to plough through literature on the colonial question. The leader came to the conclusion that the women "ought perhaps to concentrate more strongly on ideological, literary, and cultural tasks than on political training."[50] At the same time, her colleague in *Kameradschaft* 2 lamented the "alarming ignorance of our poetry" by some of the women and suggested this should be given more attention.[51]

As with the NSDStB, scholars have taken contemporary published accounts at face value and assumed that the ANSt was numerically stronger than was in fact the case. Thus Jill Stephenson accepts that in 1936 some 65 percent of all female students were members, as were 75 percent a year later.[52] Available figures from Hamburg—15.4 percent of female students in the winter semester 1935-1936 and 22.1 percent in the winter semester 1937-1938—suggest that this was not the case.[53] Coercion in some places may have raised the average, but as so often, Nazi press accounts were either exaggerated or downright false. A Hamburg newspaper report in January 1940 stated the following: "The 'ANSt,' that is the National Socialist Women Students' Group, formerly a volunteer organization, has been extended all over the Reich from the beginning of the first Trimester 1940 to become a Formation of the NSDAP, to which every female student must belong."[54] It is interesting to note that the newspaper felt it necessary to explain to readers just what the ANSt was. In fact, there is no evidence that the ANSt was raised to Formation status in the Party hierarchy or that membership was ever made generally compulsory. This was probably a

[50] Arbeitsbericht Walther, summer semester 1939, RSFWü II*532 α 431.
[51] Semesterbericht Clausen, summer semester 1939, ibid.
[52] Jill Stephenson, "Girls' Higher Education in Germany in the 1930s," *Journal of Contemporary History* 10 (January 1975): 62.
[53] See Appendix 2.
[54] "Studentinnen im Frauendienst," *Hamburger Fremdenblatt*, 26 January 1940.

piece of bluff in order to increase enrollments, and indeed it seems to have had some effect: 49.4 percent of the female students at Hamburg belonged to the ANSt in the second trimester 1940. For the first trimester 1941 a 100 percent enrollment was reported to NSDStB headquarters; if this is correct, then it represents the only time that force was used in Hamburg. By the summer, membership had trailed off to 28.4 percent.[55]

After the summer of 1941 membership of the ANSt was at least proportionately higher than that of the NSDStB itself. Sizable groups of people with first-aid training could be mobilized in the event of an attack. This practical training began to take precedence over political training, for it was far easier to teach straightforward gas-mask drill than dubious eugenic doctrine. Because of the acute shortage of leaders, women now began for the first time to fill some of the posts in the student leadership, though in Hamburg at least they were restricted to the purely administrative jobs of student records and accounting. One cannot speak of "(the recognition of) a role of equal status" with the men, which Franze postulates for Erlangen at this time.[56]

The fact that by the summer semester 1942 there were twice as many ANSt groups as male *Kameradschaften* in Hamburg says little about status.[57] Scant attention was paid even now to the political education of women at Hamburg. The District ANSt Leader, Elisabeth Schröder, admitted in 1942 "that she had not been at all active in ANSt work during the last few semesters, because she was preparing for her final examinations and was also ill for a time."[58] Nor did matters improve with the appointment of her successor, Marianne Hohn, who turned out to be "too heavily com-

[55] See also above, Tables 9 and 10.

[56] Franze, *Erlanger Studentenschaft*, pp. 363-64.

[57] A list of Hamburg student leaders in May 1942 shows seven NSDStB *Kameradschaften* and thirteen ANSt groups. UniHH 0.10.3.4.

[58] Kottenhoff to Carstensen, BDC Partei-Korrespondenz Arnold Carstensen.

281

mitted to her job at the Labor Office to devote vigorous attention to student affairs."[59] Since at this time women accounted for some 40 percent of the Hamburg student body, this represented a serious neglect.[60] It underlines the essential National Socialist belief that women had better not concern themselves with political affairs.

The Reich Student Leadership was anxious for as many women as possible to wed, or at the very least to produce babies. A leading article in the NSDStB newspaper in August 1942 praised the merits of a "student marriage" and announced new financial concessions for soldier-students who married.[61] Two years later, the ANSt's role as a sort of marriage bureau was even more strongly urged: soldier-students on leave from the front line were finding it difficult to meet girls informally, and the ANSt groups were exhorted to hold mixed activities with the NSDStB, in an atmosphere, of course, of "the conscientious earnestness and tact which this question demands."[62] One assumes that such meetings were not, in the event, so stuffy as the Reich Student Leadership's guidelines typically tried to make them.

The Instability of the Wartime University

The student body was very different in complexion during the war, if only because of the presence of so many women. The catchment area of the *Kameradschaften* was further reduced quite drastically by the large number of soldier-students who remained under military command. They thus

[59] Bericht Reinecke, "Studentische Führung und studentische Arbeit in Hamburg (Dezember 1941 bis Ende Dezember 1943)," 30 January 1944, RSFWü V*2 α 571.

[60] The proportion of women in Hamburg rose from 17.6 percent in the first trimester 1940 to a peak of 46.8 percent in the summer semester 1944. Calculated from lists of enrollment in Statistisches Landesamt der Freien und Hansestadt Hamburg (ed.), *Die Universität Hamburg im Spiegel ihrer Hörerzahlen* (no. 12 in the series Hamburg in Zahlen, 1958), pp. 180-81.

[61] "Studenten-Ehe?" *Die Bewegung*, 22 August 1942.

[62] "Student und Heirat," *Die Bewegung*, June 1944.

TABLE 11. Proportion of Hamburg Students in Military Service by Faculty, Winter Semester 1942-1943

Faculty	Number of soldier-students	Percentage of all male students in Faculty
Medicine	86	13.3
Law	83	59.8
(and economics)	116	
Arts	47	61.0
Natural Sciences	59	59.6

Source: Reinecke to RSF Referent für Wehrmachtsfragen, 10 March 1943, RSFWü V*2 α 532.

represented a particular irritant to the student leadership, since they fell outside the jurisdiction of the NSDSTB altogether. Soldiers who had been released from active service received every inducement to study: they were exempt from all university fees and received in addition a maintenance grant, with extra supplements for wounded soldiers.[63]

Of the 1,130 male students at Hamburg in the summer semester 1943, for example, 833 were soldiers (73.7 percent).[64] Most had been seconded to the University to complete their interrupted studies. Although during the war at least 50 percent of the Hamburg students were studying medicine, soldier-students were released to study other subjects as well. During the winter semester 1942-1943, the soldier-students were distributed among the Faculties as listed in Table 11. The low proportion in the Medical Faculty probably reflects the past policy of giving priority to the release of medical students who were near the completion of their studies. By the autumn of 1942, there were simply very few soldiers left who had not been given this opportunity already. Although they were at liberty to join a *Kameradschaft* and were indeed encouraged constantly by the student leaders to do so, most soldiers remained unmoved by these appeals. After their long enlistment in the strictness

[63] "Sonderförderung der Kriegsteilnehmer," June 1941, UniHH 0.40.10.1.
[64] Aktenvermerk, n.d. (summer semester 1943), RSFWü V*2 α 560.

of military life, they wanted to plan their own affairs again, to devote themselves to their studies and have the rest of the time to themselves.[65] Although the Student Companies did hold regular parades, their members enjoyed a large amount of free time in which they could have participated in *Kameradschaft* life. Their lack of interest in the Students' Association was not surprising when many of the NSDStB members who had been at the university long enough to advance to positions of leadership were youths physically unfit for military service who had come there straight from school. Soldiers back from harsh realities of front-line fighting felt scant respect for these youngsters and were not inclined to accept them as their ideological teachers.[66] When enthusiasm for the *Kameradschaften* was aroused it was not always uniform: the commander of the Army Students' Company at Hamburg inspired some of his soldiers to join in the work of the NSDStB in the spring of 1943, whereas the Air Force Scholars' Company displayed complete apathy.[67] Even where soldier-students were won over, they did not remain at the university for any predictable length of time, being called up and released in mid-semester entirely as the military situation demanded. This more than anything hindered the accomplishment of a continuous and coordinated program of political training.[68]

In the opinion of *Gauleiter* Kaufmann, the Reich Student Leadership did not have a clear conception of its task anyway. Kaufmann believed that the NSDStB ought to be working

[65] Meldungen aus dem Reich, 16 Feburary 1942, MicAlex T-175/262/2755905-6. Sometimes even NSDStB members were not blameless in this respect. Hans Blaschke was expelled from the group at the University of Hamburg in August 1944 for persistent disorderly behavior. His comrades objected when he noisily brought male and female acquaintances into the *Kameradschaft* house at all hours of the night. Vermerk Formel, 11 August 1944, RSFWü V*2 α 570.

[66] Ochsenius to Thomas, 31 March 1943, RSFWü V*2 α 532.

[67] Reinecke to RSF Referent für Wehrmachtsfragen, 10 March 1943, ibid.

[68] Rundbrief RSF-Stabsführer Thomas no. 6, 5 June 1942, RSFWü V*1 γ 600.

toward the creation of "a sort of *esprit de corps,* as the fraternities formerly set out to do."[69] And indeed the *Kameradschaften* moved increasingly during the war back to the traditions of the fraternities. By 1942, the "*Kamerad*" was being referred to by the old fraternity term "*Bursch,*" and drinking evenings with the alumni were actually encouraged.[70]

In Hamburg, the Acting District Student Leader went so far as to allow a committee certain rights of governance, "as in the old days (of the fraternities)," alongside the *Kameradschaft* Leader.[71] Frustrated by the sorry lack of attention paid to the *Kameradschaften,* he tried to make membership compulsory for the first three semesters from the autumn of 1942, but given the small proportion of male civilian students at the University he could not achieve an impressive result.[72] The central dilemma remained the lack of good leaders, but the old problem of a lack of suitable meeting places persisted to aggravate matters.[73] While Ochsenius was away in France the one *Kameradschaft* Room at the College of Fine Arts lost all the furniture and fittings he had worked hard to have installed and was turned into an exhibition room.[74]

In response to difficulties experienced generally, the Reich Student Leadership expanded the 1942 version of the *Kameradschaft* "Guidelines" into a much more comprehensive

[69] Aktennotiz Ochsenius, "Besprechung mit dem Gauleiter," 24 September 1940, RSFWü V*2 α 549.

[70] Reichsstudentenführung-Amt Politische Erziehung (ed.), *Grundsätze der Kameradschaftsarbeit des NSDStB (Ausgabe Oktober 1942),* pars. 30ff. and 98.

[71] Potratz to Gehring, 9 November 1942, RSFWü V*2 α 561.

[72] Membership of the *Kameradschaften* doubled, but from only 11.4 percent to a mere 22.1 percent. See above, Table 7.

[73] "Work as a whole in all the *Kameradschaften* suffers from matters concerning personnel, and from the absence of replacements for those comrades called up for the forces." Tätigkeitsbericht Potratz, 28 May 1942, RSFWü V*2 α 532.

[74] Ochsenius to Wiedemann, 23 September 1940, RSFWü V*2 α 571.

edition in April 1943. Now there were quite detailed instructions for the wooing of freshmen, all of whom were invited to a *Kameradschaft* open meeting. Here they would receive individual attention from a member who would be assigned to each person for the evening.[75] Most surprising was the call of the Reich Student Leadership for the reintroduction of the "big brother" role of the "*Leibbursch*," previously shunned by the NSDStB for fear of promoting homosexual relations. Each *Kameradschaft* freshman would now choose from among the older members someone to act as his special mentor.[76] The Reich Student Leadership had considered this in 1939, but had not taken up the idea, owing to Scheel's constant fears. Ochsenius had come out warmly in favor of a more personal note in the *Kameradschaften*, as a balance to frequent regimentation elsewhere.[77] This traditional feature of the life of the fraternities had contributed much to their strength as communities, but it could do little to inject new life into the *Kameradschaften* while the external factors of the war remained so trying.

The centerpiece of the *Kameradschaft* program, the fortnightly (if possible, weekly) "political evening," was meant to run as follows: "Each 'Political Evening' must be conducted in a lively, absorbing and stimulating way. All that is boring, verbose and superficial is to be left out. There is no place here for long-winded lectures and dilettante talks."[78] But it was no use asking for this, when skillful speakers were often just not to be found. A weekly set of instructions for the *Kameradschaft* leaders was promised but failed to materialize, despite the real necessity for these. Scheel, busier than ever as *Gauleiter* and Governor of Salz-

[75] Reichsstudentenführung-Amt Politische Erziehung (ed.), *Dienstanweisung für die Kameradschaft vom 20.4.1943*, par. 48b.

[76] Ibid., pars. 64-65.

[77] Reich to Ochsenius, 14 January 1939; Ochsenius to Reich, 23 January 1939, RSFWü V*2 α 568.

[78] Anordnung Bässler no. PE 11/43, 30 November 1943, RSFWü I*01 φ 250.

burg, and attending to student affairs in a staff conference only once a week,[79] happened to remember this in April 1944, and reminded his director of political education to produce this "utterly essential" publication.[80] The gazette never appeared, and the *Kameradschaft* leaders remained without the help they so badly needed.[81]

It is scarcely surprising, therefore, that the National Socialist student leaders rarely produced their model student. Nevertheless, they expected the public to perceive students as paragons of ideological perfection. There was a flurry of activity in the Reich Student Leadership during the summer of 1941, when the plot of a projected film, *"Young Hearts,"* became known. The Ufa company planned to depict a scholarship student at Berlin falling for two girls on a cycling tour. After buying a yacht in order to impress them, and being seduced by one of the girls, he would be seen to take up a life style quite beyond his means. The Reich Student Leadership's Cultural Department held the view that no German student would ever go astray like this. The release of the film, it was felt, would certainly damage the credibility of the Reich Student Leadership as the guardian of student morals: "The film must under all circumstances be suppressed, even if there is a danger of a row with Ufa."[82] Scheel's associates could never look at the student world lightheartedly.

Not only were the *Kameradschaft* leaders inadequate; sometimes the Student Leaders themselves were scarcely

[79] Interview Giles/Scheel, 11 April 1973.

[80] Scheel to Bässler, 5 April 1944, BDC Partei-Korrespondenz Reinhold Bässler.

[81] A new journal did commence publication in 1944, titled *Sieg der Idee: Führerorgan der Studenten Grossdeutschlands*. It was filled with articles of general cultural interest and can have done little to help. IfH B/S 13.

[82] Schulze-Berghof to Gmelin, 10 June 1941, BDC Partei-Korrespondenz Ulrich Gmelin. The efforts of the Reich Student Leadership were to no avail: the film was made and released on 30 November 1944. It does not appear that any copies have survived. David Stewart Hull, *Film in the Third Reich: Art and Propaganda in Nazi Germany* (New York, 1973), p. 250.

better. In 1941 a sudden wave of drafting caused a complete vacuum in the student leadership in Hamburg.[83] In order to prevent the total collapse of the NSDStB at the University, Rector Gundert asked a law student, Achim Freiherr von Beust, to take over as Student Leader. Von Beust had had some contact with the NSDStB before as a writer of cinema reviews for the student newspaper, but because of his delicate health he had never been obliged to join any Party organizations. He was not even a member of the NSDStB before he became its leader at Hamburg University, and then he did not progress during his short term of office beyond probationary status.

Although it appeared that the District Student Leadership was really scraping the bottom of the barrel, von Beust's undistinguished political record would have been overlooked had not another detail come to light. His fiancée was already expecting a baby by him at this time, and though illegitimacy was no question for moral reproach in the Third Reich, she also chanced to have a Jewish parent. When this fact became known, there were fears of a scandal of the first magnitude. Von Beust resigned and promised to leave Hamburg at the request of the Acting District Student Leader. Yet even though the affair was quite successfully hushed up, the SD was brought in to try to concoct charges against him. Von Beust was accused of making the remark, "I am closer to an English aristocrat than to a German worker," and of having ties with "Swing" groups. In the end nothing could be proved, but the undeniable reality of his "affair with a half-Jewess which did not remain without consequences" was quite sufficient to justify his dishonorable discharge from the NSDStB.[84]

[83] All students born between 1919 and 1921 were called up at the same time. Wehrersatz-Inspektion Hamburg to Schulz, 5 April 1941, UniHH 0.1.6.

[84] Author's interview with Achim Freiherr von Beust, 19 April 1972. Carstensen to RSF-Rechts- und Gerichtsamt, 7 May 1942; RSF-Rechts- und Gerichtsamt, Beschluss in Sache Beust, 23 May 1942; Beust to RSF-

Von Beust's successor as Student Leader at the University, Ernst Hüttmann, lasted in office for a month. Again the limited choice had fallen unfortunately on someone whose personal life was far from exemplary, and it was likely to cause a scandal if made public. For Hüttmann was having an affair both with his landlady, a thirty-six-year-old widow with children, and with a fourteen-year-old friend of the landlady.[85]

At the beginning of 1941, Rector Gundert announced his intention to resign from office. Although not running the full three years now allowed by the REM, he wished to return to his academic work. He proposed as his successor Professor Eduard Keeser, a pharmacologist.[86] This time there was no behind-the-scenes appointment in an office in the City Hall but a grandiose ceremony, as if to emphasize that Gundert was leaving of his own free will. The presence of Minister Rust himself was secured, though *Gauleiter* Kaufmann fell ill (perhaps diplomatically) at the last moment.[87]

Keeser had been mentioned as a possible candidate for the rectorship as long ago as January 1935 by the District Student Leader.[88] Although Keeser's relations with the NSDStB were not unfriendly, there was now little direct contact between the student leadership and the rector. This represented a

---

Rechts- und Gerichtsamt, 18 June 1942, BDC Partei-Korrespondenz Beust. For discrimination against students married to a *"Mischling,"* see Albrecht Götz von Olenhusen, "Die 'nichtarischen' Studenten an den deutschen Hochschulen: Zur nationalsozialistischen Rassenpolitik 1933-1945," *Vierteljahrshefte für Zeitgeschichte* 14 (April 1966): 197.

[85] Bericht Justin, 19 November 1941, RSFWÜ V*2 α 570.

[86] Protokoll Fakultäts-Ausschuss der Philosophischen Fakultät, 18 January 1941, UNIHH Phil. The Faculty decided that it could not really offer any objection to Gundert's nomination of Keeser, since most of the professors did not know the man. The medical school was located at a distance from the main campus, and there was less contact than between the professors of the other Faculties.

[87] Numerous press cuttings in UNIHH A.170.14.4.

[88] With the notation: "Not a Party member, but on the whole good." His other suggestion was Professor Walther Matthes, who taught ancient history. Dansmann to Feickert, 11 January 1935, RSFWÜ V*2 α 516.

tendency that had been growing since the outbreak of war. It was difficult enough, without the added burden of following the work of the NSDStB, to accomplish the ever more complex task of administering the University in wartime; picking one's way through the labyrinth of lengthy, verbose, and confusing decrees from the Reich Education Ministry; and trying to create a semblance of orderly governance. Keeser had much less time than Gundert for his duties as rector, for he continued throughout the war his high-priority research for the military on the toxic effects of the chemicals used in munitions factories. Keeser's own health suffered considerably as a result.[89]

The prevailing conditions of study and the peculiar composition of the student body during the war demanded a student leadership little short of ideal if the NSDStB was to achieve its aim of ensuring that all students graduated as convinced National Socialists. Yet never was the leadership weaker and more inexperienced, often applying quite inappropriate solutions to problems whose nature was barely perceived. Ochsenius, thought of by many as "the only great and honest man" in the Hamburg District Student Leadership, had shown both insight and ability as a leader.[90] Yet he was away for most of the war, though an infection of the jaw allowed him to stay in Hamburg for the winter of 1940-1941 to complete his dissertation. Such measures as the compulsory membership in the *Kameradschaften* ordered by his deputy, Eberhard Potratz, ran quite contrary to Och-

[89] His request for permission to use an automobile to facilitate his several daily trips from the University to his laboratory failed because no tires were available for nonmilitary vehicles. Keeser to Ahrens, 13 May 1941; Reichsstelle für Kautschuk und Asbest to Keeser, 24 June 1941, UniHH personnel file Keeser.

[90] Bericht Justin, 19 November 1941, RSFWü V*2 α 570. Contemporary accounts and later recollections center on strict fairness and unflinching idealism as the chief characteristics of Ochsenius. In interviews with the author, Scheel recalled him as having "great decency," and Achim von Beust remembered Ochsenius's surprising concern and sympathy with him over his misdemeanor.

senius's belief in the necessity for free choice, which he came more and more to espouse. Unseasoned by experience, he had originally held the opposite view. Thrust into the post of *Kameradschaft* leader during his freshman semester in the midst of a mass walkout, he had regretted that he could not use force to keep the house full.[91] His frustration at the impending collapse of the only *Kameradschaft* at the time was understandable. *Gauleiter* Kaufmann may well have influenced him on this question. At the Nuremberg Trials in July 1946, Kaufmann claimed to support wholeheartedly "the principle of volunteer work in the *Gau* under all circumstances because . . . I did not expect any political success from forced cooperation."[92]

Ochsenius, and others in Hamburg, came to put the blame for the students' frequent lack of interest in the NSDStB on a certain miseducation in the Hitler Youth. Scheel, on the other hand, never ceased to urge that only boys with a satisfactory Hitler Youth service record should be permitted to study in the first place.[93] The latter, as Ochsenius well realized, was far from being a guarantee of excellence. Indeed, he thought that experience in the Hitler Youth often stifled any inclination for subsequent voluntary activity in the National Socialist movement.[94] The University Student Leader reported how much more eagerly the young *Kameradschaft* members responded to training when they felt "that they were not being forced from outside." The freshmen invariably felt the need to let their hair down after the constraints of Hitler Youth and Labor Service discipline and "reacted

[91] Arbeitsbericht Ochsenius, 22 January 1935, RSFWü V*2 α 537. See also above, chap. 5, n. 45.

[92] International Military Tribunal, *Trial of Major War Criminals before the International Military Tribunal at Nuremberg*, vol. 20 (Nuremberg, 1948), p. 27.

[93] Cf. *Meldungen aus dem Reich*, 5 January 1940, BA R21/724.

[94] Ochsenius to SD-Leitabschnitt Hamburg, 18 November 1940, RSFWü V*2 α 568.

against 'being organized' with their conception of 'student freedom.' "[95]

These students were to some extent making up for their lost youth and were probably the better for it. The die-hard Nazis who never deviated from the rigid path prescribed for them were all the duller for their unimaginative passivity. Ochsenius once made the astute comment that the latter had "never really been young." They had never enjoyed the spontaneity of childhood fantasy and adventures but had been drilled in Nazi organizations almost from the cradle. They would never grow into inspiring men, full of imagination, who would be able to lead others. This greatly disturbed Ochsenius because he believed that the NSDStB would be called on to provide vast numbers of leaders after the war to set up the new German order in Europe.[96] He feared that if the university graduates were not equal to the task, this would signify the end of the universities themselves and of the NSDStB. For this reason, he was particularly anxious that the former student leaders now serving in the armed forces should eventually return to their NSDStB posts to provide the solid leadership that he thought beginning to crystallize by 1939. Ochsenius thought that the war had "come three years too early" for the NSDStB. Given the extra time, he felt sure that it would have been able to set the *Kameradschaften* on their feet effectively and would have refined leader training methods so as to withstand disruptions.[97] He attached great value to the maintenance of contacts among former colleagues through a regular newsletter.[98]

Ochsenius made these comments, which have just been discussed, in the earlier part of the war, before the mere

[95] Bericht Schulz, "Stimmung und Haltung der Studenten an der Hansischen Universität im Trimester 1941 (unter besonderer Berücksichtigung der letzten drei Kriegstrimester)," 16 April 1941, RSFWÜ V*2 α 560.

[96] Ochsenius to Kubach, 19 February 1941, RSFWÜ V*2 α 568.

[97] Ochsenius to SD-Leitabschnitt Hamburg, 12 March 1943, RSFWÜ V*2 α 532.

[98] E.g. Feldpostbrief Ochsenius, 29 November 1940, RSFWÜ V*2 α 566.

suggestion of defeat had surfaced. By 1943, it did not appear that victory was going to be so easy after all. The loss of Stalingrad was deeply felt and was regarded by many as the turning point.[99] Public feeling ran against what was seen as the luxury of studying, and this view prevailed in certain Party circles also. *Gauleiter* Giesler had told the women at Munich that they would do better to "present the *Führer* with a baby" than to sit around studying.[100]

When Goebbels proclaimed "total war" on 18 February, then, there were general fears once more that student numbers would be reduced drastically and whole universities closed down. Concern was heightened when members of the White Rose resistance group were arrested in Munich on the same day as Goebbels's speech.[101] Scheel requested Bormann and Himmler to treat the whole question not as a student or academic matter but as an affair involving "former members of the Armed Forces," and he hastily expelled the accused from the German Students' Union before the sentence was carried out four days later "so that they should not be executed as students."[102]

On 16 March 1943 the Education Ministry announced that the universities would remain open, and that students would be exempt from general wartime labor duties, on the con-

[99] Professor Burchard of the Faculty of Medicine had been an SA member since August 1932, a Party member since January 1933, and an enthusiastic propagator of National Socialist ideals. Yet it was said of him, even by his critical colleagues: "After Stalingrad there followed his inner alienation from National Socialism." Berichterstattung des Senats der Universität Hamburg in der Entnazifizierungssache Professor Dr. Burchard, 12 July 1946, HB personnel file Burchard.

[100] Giesler continued: "If some of the girls are not pretty enough to find a boy friend, I will gladly direct them to one of my adjutants . . . and I can promise them a pleasurable experience." At this point a number of female students tried to leave the meeting in protest against these vulgarities. Christian Petry, *Studenten aufs Schafott: Die Weisse Rose und ihr Scheitern* (Munich, 1968), pp. 98ff.

[101] See below.

[102] Vermerk Gmelin, "Vorfälle in München: Vergehen von drei ehemaligen Studierenden," 20 February 1943, BA R21/rep 76/922.

dition that they devoted themselves to a thorough, yet above all speedy, completion of their studies in order to fill as rapidly as possible the now serious gaps in the professions.[103] The president of the German Physical Society, Carl Ramsauer, stressed again at this time that 3,000 fewer soldiers would not harm the army, whereas 3,000 more physicists might decide the war.[104] Similar arguments on the military advantages that the universities could provide had long been put forward. The trouble was that no one outside the educational sector believed in the importance of the academic world until the military reverses of 1942 and after caused them to reconsider. The decision now meant, in effect, that the universities ceased to be regarded as centers of education and became mere training institutions.[105] Any student unable to keep pace with the new demands for greater diligence was to be suspended from further study, a measure that the Reich Student Leadership saw as a welcome opportunity to settle old scores with the "little groups of troublemakers at most of the universities."[106] The Education Ministry instructed universities to expel students who were not studying hard enough, but Hamburg found only six whom it could justifiably reproach.[107]

This first campaign for the elimination of unsuitable students (*Ausmerzeaktion*) was not regarded as a success by either the Reich Student Leadership or the Ministry. Only 250 students (0.5 percent of the student body) were turned

[103] Scheel to Gaustudentenführer, 22 March 1943, UniHH N.20.2.11.

[104] Alan D. Beyerchen, *Scientists under Hitler: Politics and the Physics Community in the Third Reich* (New Haven, 1977), p. 187.

[105] "Nicht Bildungs-, sondern Ausbildungsstätten." Phrase taken from the paper read to the Rector's Conference in Salzburg on 28 July 1943 by Regierungsdirektor Kock: "Überprüfung der Studierenden, Meldung zum Arbeitseinsatz." Text with Rundschreiben REM WJ 2325, 16 September 1943, UniHH N.20.2.11.

[106] "The elimination campaign gives us . . . the legal basis for stern action." Vertrauliches Rundschreiben Thomas to Gaustudentenführer, 21 April 1943, quoted in Petry, *Weisse Rose*, pp. 222-23.

[107] Protokoll Universitätssenat, 12 May 1943, UniHH C.20.4.

away from all the universities. The Ministry found it difficult to believe that 99.5 percent of the students were models of diligence and urged the rectors to be "rather too strict than too lenient" in the future.[108] If there were suspicions about the student body as a whole, this was even more true of foreign students. They had been under observation since the outbreak of war and had already given cause for concern. In October 1941, the SD claimed that Bulgarian Communists were studying at Munich. Even more disturbing was the widespread predilection of German girls for southern and exotic-looking men. A dawn police raid on the Berlin lodgings of foreign, male students found most of them, in apparent ignorance of Nazi racial teachings, in bed with Aryan admirers.[109] The Education Ministry inclined to the view that the women were the more to blame (the non-German men were not bound to Nazi doctrine in the first place), and it did not accept the reputed need for tighter controls over foreign students.[110]

Scheel, however, decided by 1943 that it was necessary to conduct "the essential and exact, systematic observation of all foreigners at German universities . . . to a still wider extent than before." Painting a picture of the spies and saboteurs everywhere, he ordered the setting-up, in close collaboration with the Gestapo and SD, of "Societies of German and Foreign Scholars." These were to embrace all foreigners within a university so that they might more easily be watched and controlled.[111] In Hamburg, foreign students

[108] Kock, "Überprüfung der Studierenden," REM WJ 2325, 16 September 1943, UNiHH N.20.2.11. The sentiment was echoed in SD-Berichte zu Inlandsfragen, 24 January 1944 ("Stimmen aus Hochschulkreisen zur Ausmerze ungeeigneter Studierender"), BA R58/192.

[109] Meldungen aus dem Reich, 23 October 1941 ("Verhalten ausländischer Studenten im Reich"), BA R21/Rep 76/922.

[110] Aktenvermerk Kock, 17 November 1941, ibid. The same comment was made by Goebbels in his staff conference of 5 March 1941. Willi A. Boelcke (ed.), *The Secret Conferences of Dr. Goebbels, October 1939-March 1943* (London, 1967), p. 124.

[111] Streng vertrauliches und geheimes Rundschreiben Scheel, RSF-Befehl

were lured into membership of the society with a reception at the plush Hotel Atlantik, at which "by an ample provision of vermouth and spirits, as well as a plentiful supply of cigars and cigarettes, the atmosphere was exceptionally lively."[112] The success of the evening was even greater than expected, for there were calls for days afterwards from foreign students—whose presence in Hamburg had been unknown—begging to be invited to the next event. This again gives the lie to the assertation of the NSDSTB's omniscient efficiency, even as a "police" organization. There were always ways of escaping its range of vision: one was to change one's place of study every semester. Von Beust did this several times after his dismissal from Hamburg, and by the time his papers had caught up with him at the next place, he had already moved on to yet another university.[113] Though this solution was not available to students in their first three semesters after Scheel's deliberate steps to stop the practice in 1936, it was widespread among the younger students before then for just this purpose.[114]

The bombings of Hamburg did not seriously affect the work of the University until 1943. In the autumn of 1940, some eight o'clock lectures were shifted to a later hour in order to allow extra sleep after the nighttime air-raid alarms, but the University itself remained unscathed.[115] An incendiary bomb dropped into the offices of the District Student Leadership during a raid in July 1942, but the damage was

---

11/43, "Ausländer im Reich" (date illegible), RSFWü V*2 α 568. Already a year earlier the District Student Leadership had appointed a student, on the instructions of the SD, to spy on foreigners studying at the University of Hamburg. Bescheinigung Potratz, 1 July 1942, RSFWü V*2 α 570; Potratz to Staatspolizei Hamburg, 2 July 1942, V*2 α 568.

[112] Bericht Akademische Auslandstelle Hamburg, "Empfang für ausländische Studenten im Hotel Atlantik," 24 May 1944, RSFWü V*2 α 532. It was subsequently proposed that a special bar be set up to serve as a gathering place for foreign students. Dickhaut to Amt für Raumbewirtschaftung Hamburg, 19 January 1945, UniHH P.1.10.

[113] Interview Giles/Beust, 18 April 1972.

[114] Cf. Roegele, "Student im Dritten Reich," p. 146.

[115] Protokoll Dekansbesprechung, 11 September 1940, UniHH C.10.15.2.

patched up during the summer vacation.[116] At the end of July 1943, however, Hamburg was subjected to some of the most terrible bombings of the war, resulting in the death of some 45,000 people and the destruction of 277,000 homes.[117] So horrifying was the success of "Operation Gomorrah" in Hamburg that Goebbels, fearing a similar attack on Berlin, ordered the evacuation of all nonessential civilian personnel from there on 6 August 1943.[118]

The Student Leader at the Engineering College in Hamburg had already drawn up contingency plans for an emergency some six weeks beforehand. When an attack came, trained squads would be instantly available to deal with water and gas mains, electricity supplies, and a variety of other repairs and salvaging operations. The college itself was the assembly point, but it was in the event totally destroyed by bombs, creating difficulties in getting the emergency squads together. When they were finally ready several days later, they made a considerable contribution to the mopping-up operations and received much local publicity. Special attention was given to the work of a team of "safe-breakers" who rescued secret documents and armaments blueprints from safes stranded both in flooded cellars and dangling precariously from high walls in bombed-out buildings.[119]

The University did not suffer quite so badly. Worst hit was the University Clinic, where practically every building received some damage, and about one third of the Medical School campus was totally destroyed. Fortunately not one of the 1,800 patients received any injury, thanks to Rector

[116] Feldpostbrief Gaustudentenführung no. 29, 13 August 1942, RSFWü V*2 α 566.

[117] Martin Middlebrook, *The Battle of Hamburg: Allied Bomber Forces Against A German City in 1943* (New York, 1981), offers a detailed account.

[118] Andreas Hillgruber and Gerhard Hümmelchen, *Chronik des Zweiten Weltkrieges* (Frankfurt am Main, 1966), pp. 95-96.

[119] Bericht Börstling, "Einsatz der Studentenschaft der Ingenieurschule der Hansestadt Hamburg während des Grossangriffes vom 25. Juli bis 30. Juli 1943 und der nachfolgenden Einsatzzeit," 18 March 1944, RSFWü V*2 α 573.

Keeser's construction of shelters in recent years.[120] In the rest of the University, only six departments were destroyed, among them the Historical Seminar and the Institute of Japanese Studies.[121]

After the first night's raid, hundreds of injured and homeless people assembled in the *Moorweide* Park adjacent to the University. The student refectory in the District Student Leadership building was turned into a first-aid station on the initiative of the student leaders. The smallness of the building meant that only a few students could be employed here, but considerable numbers were engaged in evacuating the crowds that were gathering. A *Waffen-SS* officer issued the District Student Leadership with a warrant authorizing the students to commandeer motor vehicles, and in a variety of buses, lorries, and private cars, they transported over 63,000 evacuees to some fifteen neighboring suburbs and towns in two weeks.[122] In addition, students of the College of Civil Engineering assisted in a cartographic survey of the damage, and the Students' Company of the Army set up the first-aid stations on the roads leading out of Hamburg for the benefit of the stream of refugees leaving the city. The Air Force Scholars' Company meanwhile assisted in the emergency surgery that was performed day and night in what remained of the University Clinic.[123]

The "terror attack," as it was called, did nothing to check the size of the Hamburg student body.[124] The winter se-

[120] "Convinced of Hitler's bellicose intentions, I pursued the construction of bunkers so vigorously that Eppendorf became the best protected hospital in Germany." Denazification statement Keeser, n.d., HB personnel file Keeser.

[121] Both former rectors Rein and Gundert lost their departmental libraries and their homes and private libraries in these raids.

[122] Voss to Reinecke, 12 January 1944, UniHH T.1.3.

[123] Bericht Reinecke, "Studentische Führung," 30 January 1944, RSFWü V*2 α 571.

[124] Goebbels banned the use of the word "catastrophe" because of its "unfortunate psychological and political effects." He ordered the substi-

mester saw at the University only a hundred students fewer than the 1,960 of the summer semester. With the continuing incidence of serious air raids, students now tended to continue writing examinations in an air-raid shelter, if interrupted by an attack, rather than postponing completion until the next day, when their university department might no longer be standing.[125] Arrangements were made to evacuate the Engineering College students to Breslau and Konstanz, but the students refused to leave Hamburg because they wanted to help rebuild the College.[126] If anything, then, the horrors of the summer led to an increase in solidarity among the students and devotion to the duties (academic and extramural) that they were called on to fulfill. But the worsening situation also led a few students to crystallize their feelings into opposition to the Nazi regime.

The White Rose Resistance Group

Already in November 1942, a leaflet critical of the regime, written by the student group calling itself the "White Rose," had been brought from Munich to Hamburg and circulated among a few friends. Hans and Sophie Scholl were apprehended while distributing these at the University of Munich on 18 February 1943, and were tried, condemned to death, and executed together with Christoph Probst four days later.[127] At Easter 1943, another student brought to

---

tution of the phrase *"Soforthilfe"* for the term *"Katastropheneinsatz."* The word *"Terrorangriff"* seems to have become common parlance at this time also. Goebbels to Governors, "Wunsch des Reichsmarschalls auf Beseitigung des Wortes 'Katastrophe,' " n.d. (copy forwarded to University on 10 January 1944), UNIHH R.1.14.

[125] Eisfeld, *Aus fünfzig Jahren*, p. 151.

[126] Other temporary accommodation was found. Bericht Reinecke, "Studentische Führung," 30 January 1944, RSFWü V*2 α 571.

[127] The best critical account of the activities of this well-known group is Petry, *Weisse Rose*. An extensive bibliography of the numerous writings about the group is in Ursel Hochmuth, *Candidates of Humanity: Dokumentation zur Hamburger Weissen Rose anlässlich des 50. Geburtstages*

Hamburg news of the downfall of the Munich group. Although there was indeed a definite offshoot of the group here, it is incorrect to speak of *a* White Rose group at Hamburg; rather there were a number of informal circles, comprising perhaps fifty people in all, sometimes overlapping but often with little or no contact with or knowledge of each other.

Whereas the Munich students composed inflammatory leaflets, in Hamburg there was little initiative for action beyond duplicating the Munich messages. It is true that some of the Hamburg students concerned themselves more with political ideology than did those at Munich, partly because they knew of a ready source of Marxist and other forbidden literature, but the main group grew out of a literary circle. After her dismissal from the Lichtwark School at Easter 1935, the progressive teacher, Erna Stahl, held literary soirées at her home for some of her former pupils. Many of the Hamburg White Rose members came from this group, and indeed their activities remained largely confined to discussion and reading.[128] In any case, they had no clear alternative to the Nazi regime they disliked and did not go so far as to espouse communism. What these students really wanted was a greater measure of personal freedom, much like the majority of students arriving at the university, particularly after the introduction of compulsory Hitler Youth service. As one of them put it, "Essentially the problem was not that we were against the Nazis, but that the Nazis were against us."[129] Resistance as such found expression mainly in small, symbolic ways: the men, for example, as a sign of their anglophilia, adopted the un-German habit of carrying

---

von Hans Leipelt (Hamburg, 1971), pp. 69ff.

[128] Ursel Hochmuth and Gertrud Meyer, *Streiflichter aus dem Hamburger Widerstand 1933-1945: Berichte und Dokumente* (Frankfurt am Main, 1969), pp. 387ff. Albert Krebs points out that a substantial number of the first members of the National Socialist Schoolboys' Association came from the same school, but that it provided even more supporters of the Communist Party. Allen, *Infancy*, p. 92.

[129] Thorsten Müller, quoted in Petry, *Weisse Rose*, p. 80.

furled umbrellas with them everywhere.[130] Above all they liked to listen to jazz music and dance the "swing."

The campaign against jazz was one of the more resented measures of the Nazi regime, which did little to destroy the popularity of the music among young people and much to raise it to the level of symbolic opposition. In Hamburg the *Gauleiter* forbade members of any Nazi organization to dance the swing.[131] The local SD viewed it conclusively as the root of all degeneracy, attributing to the "swing dancers" a pervasive, treasonable attitude, not to mention interracial sexual offenses, prostitution, homosexuality, and burglary.[132] At the University, an announcement of the syndic caused amusement: "I draw your attention to the fact that, according to German sensibilities and German conceptions, the so-called 'swing' and similar 'dances' are unaesthetic and therefore un-German. I do not expect any student of the Hanseatic University to be so disreputable as to imitate this sort of 'dance.' " The notice had to be removed when students scribbled an ironic "Bravo!!!" and "Idiot!" on it.[133] The Reich Student Leadership even went to the trouble of including relevant instructions in the *Kameradschaft* regulations: "Jazz music, as well as the swing and the Lambeth Walk are unworthy of a National Socialist community and are therefore forbidden."[134] Thus it was particularly distress-

---

[130] Author's interview with Dr. Albert Suhr, 17 December 1971.

[131] Rundschreiben Ochsenius, 12 January 1939, RSFWü V*2 α 528.

[132] Extracts from a Hamburg SD report in Vorlage für Bormann, "Staatsfeindliche Einstellung von Swing-Tänzern," MicAlex T-81/675/5484196-200.

[133] Anschlag Bothe, 2 February 1939, UniHH 0.10.3.5.

[134] Reichsstudentenführung-Amt Politische Erziehung (ed.), *Dienstvorschrift für die Kameradschaften des NSD-Studentenbundes im Kriege* (Munich, 1940), p. 23. The campaign against jazz had begun with the front-page article in the students' newspaper: "Wir schämen uns," *Die Bewegung*, 6 December 1939, showing contrasting photographs of jazz dancers and tribal Africans. It reminded readers that they would not want to be associated with the type of men who indulged in this sort of dance, "with their hair as long as possible, often perfumed and lightly powdered, with broad shoul-

ing for the student leadership to find that even an official *Kameradschaft* in Hamburg was dancing to English gramophone records.[135] Close cooperation between the District Student Leadership and the SD and a mutual exchange of information led to the dismissal of known swing devotees from the universities and temporary peace of mind for the student leaders.[136]

Some of the Hamburg students did actually plan to express their opposition in acts of direct sabotage. The possibility of contaminating the Hamburg water supply with tetanus bacteria was discussed, as was the detonation of the city's Gestapo headquarters.[137] These ideas were eventually rejected in favor of the destruction of the railway bridge outside the main station. This would be directly disruptive to the war effort and beneficial to the welfare of many people, since it was over this bridge that troop trains constantly transported the youth of Hamburg to the Front, and often to their deaths. The contact in Munich, however, from whom it had been hoped to obtain nitroglycerine for the bomb, proved uncooperative, and the plan was dropped, possibly due in part to the alarm raised by the unexpected arrest of one of their number, Albert Suhr, on 13 September 1943.[138] Unknown to them all, one of the participants in their soirées was in the pay of the Gestapo.[139] In the following weeks some thirty

---

ders and the walk of an affected, vain ladies' man." For good measure, it added that this type of *Niggertanz* had of course been popularized by the Jews.

[135] Bürger to Ochsenius, 27 November 1940, RSFWÜ V*2 α 568.

[136] Tätigkeitsbericht Potratz, "Zusammenarbeit mit dem SD," 14 September 1942, RSFWÜ V*2 α 532.

[137] Petry, *Weisse Rose*, p. 141.

[138] Interview Giles/Suhr, 17 December 1971.

[139] Maurice Sachs-Ettinghausen was introduced to the circle in August 1943 as a former secretary of André Gide and friend of Jean Cocteau. With naïve openness and considerable pride the students related to the Frenchman the activities of their group. In March and April 1944 he was placed consecutively as a cellmate with Dr. John Gluck and then with Albert Suhr, where the still unsuspecting prisoners talked of even more details of the

other arrests followed, including that of Professor Degkwitz on 22 September 1943 for "defeatist" remarks he had made in private letters.[140] Thanks to the Gestapo spy, whose integrity no one suspected, almost all the members of the groups were behind bars by the end of the year.[141]

The defendants were not all brought to trial before the end of the war, and they suffered unspeakable deprivations and brutality in prisons and concentration camps. Of those whose trial was completed, three were executed and another five lost their lives in captivity (one through suicide). This, more than anything, has won them a place in the annals of the German Resistance.[142] With all due respect for their intellectual independence, one must remember that these students were not standing alone against an unflinching phalanx of enthusiastic National Socialists. The majority of

---

group's members. Albert Suhr, "Maurice Sachs und die Hamburger 'Weisse Rose,' " *Die Andere Zeitung*, 21 November 1968; Hochmuth, *Candidates*, pp. 23-24 and 42ff.

[140] Although found guilty by the notorious People's Court, Degkwitz had his death penalty commuted to seven years' imprisonment by Freisler, who noted that the measles serum developed by Degkwitz had saved the lives of well over 40,000 German children. As Freisler put it: ". . . a whole division of German soldiers stands at the front, which would not be standing there able to fight selflessly, were it not for Degkwitz. These soldiers march up, as it were, as petitioners for the life of Rudolf Degkwitz." Urteil Volksgerichtshof, 24 February 1944, HB personnel file Degkwitz. After the war, Degkwitz denied altogether his early association with the Nazi Party (see above, chap. 4, n. 62). He was embarrassed by testimonies that he was identifiable in a well-known early photograph of Hitler and his followers and in 1948 emigrated to the U.S. in protest against the reinstatement of "almost all the former Nazis" at German universities. Niederschrift Sitzung Vorstand des Zentral-Ausschusses, 17 January 1947, ibid.; "Rücktritt aus Prinzipien," *Die Welt*, 24 June 1948.

[141] The dates of the main arrests are given in Hochmuth and Meyer, *Streiflichter*, p. 414.

[142] Not only an epic poem but even a full-scale opera has been composed about the "White Rose" (which had its première in Dresden in 1967). Klaus Drobisch (ed.), *Wir schweigen nicht! Eine Dokumentation über den antifaschistischen Kampf Münchener Studenten 1942/43* (Berlin, 1968), pp. 161 and 171ff.

students did not have the good fortune of contacts with suppliers of banned books, but by their noncompliance, for example in staying away from the lectures arranged by the Political Faculties Group, they might be considered to have demonstrated "passive resistance" like the White Rose members.[143] Many lecturers and most students no longer gave the Hitler salute inside the University.[144] The point is that none of this so-called opposition was really effective. The White Rose group could have been severely damaging, but no bridges were ever blown up in the end. Petry, the only author to attempt a sober judgment of the group, speaks of the lingering feeling of regret that it did not appear possible "to bring idealism and moral engagement under the control of political rationality." Perhaps it is better to call the White Rose members dissenters rather than members of the Resistance. This is not to detract from their courage: as Ian Kershaw has recently shown very persuasively, even dissent was a limited phenomenon in the Third Reich.[145]

The effect of the execution of the Munich students was negligible, even on their fellow students. Far from inaugurating the mass protests that the Scholls were convinced would accompany their deaths, the Munich students roundly cheered the university porter who had apprehended them.[146] A stray leaflet was still circulating in Germany at the end of 1943 under the title of "The Scholl Campaign," but it had little to offer in the way of information or proposals.[147] Concern about the arrests in Hamburg seems to

[143] The rector had occasion to complain to the Student Leader about this matter. Keeser to Gundert, 10 June 1941, UniHH C.51.3.

[144] One student reportedly claimed that ". . . the Hitler salute had not been used for a long time among the students in Hamburg. The students were in agreement with the professors on this point." Oberreichsanwalt beim Volksgerichtshof, Anklageschrift gegen den Studenten der Volkswirtschaft Jens Hansen, no. 4 J 342/44, 14 January 1944, UniHH Di.H.9.

[145] Petry, *Weisse Rose*, p. 151, and Kershaw, *Popular Opinion*.

[146] Petry, pp. 121-22.

[147] Spengler to REM, 2 November 1943, BA R21/Rep 76/922. The leaflet, which seems to have escaped the attention of the chroniclers of the group,

have been shown by few people apart from *Gauleiter* Karl Kaufmann, who was acutely embarrassed that this should have happened in his District and was scathing in his criticism of Scheel's inability to inspire the students.[148] To make matters worse, the Acting District Student Leader reported to Kaufmann, in the presence of Rector Keeser, that "about a third of the Student Companies were not only opposed to the regime, but inferior and debauched in their character and morals."[149]

The Collapse of the NSDStB

By 1944, Hamburg, more badly bombed than most German university cities, presented a sorry background for academic meditation. Large numbers of students were still in the city, at least in the early part of the year, and they required the attention of the NSDStB. The appointment of Wilhelm Formel to deputize for District Student Leader Ochsenius in Hamburg, however, brought a considerable deemphasis of expressly political activities. He saw his task primarily as that of ensuring peace and quiet.[150]

Formel had long been active in the NSDStB, first in the *SS-Mannschaft* House and later as a *Kameradschaft* Leader.[151] Having been enlisted in the Army at the outbreak of the

---

is dated April 1943, Munich. It was seized in Frankfurt am Main sometime after this.

[148] Author's interview with Dr. Wilhelm Formel, 7 March 1972.

[149] Rector Keeser intended to take Formel well and truly to task for this indiscretion but was held back by Dr. Ernst Schrewe, the acting head of the Hamburg Education Authority, who "asked (him) to refrain from taking steps against (Formel), in order to prevent the creation of tensions between the NSDStB and the Student Companies (or the army), such as already existed in the rest of the Reich." Formel had successfully patched up relations between the two. Aktennotiz Keeser, 12 February 1944, UniHH 0.10.3.4.

[150] As he argued plausibly in his interview with the author.

[151] Formel was turned down for full membership of the SS because of what was described as a "non-hereditary physical defect"—he was too short! RSF-Personalbogen Formel, RSFWü V*2 α 570.

war, he was transferred from front-line duties at the end of 1940 for the "political supervision of French prisoners of war," following a recommendation from the Hamburg District Student Leader.[152] Returning to the Front again, he was taken out of active service because of a serious leg injury from the fighting around Lake Ladoga near Leningrad. He received the news of the loss of Stalingrad during his fifth month of hospitalization, and although it must have been a crushing blow to him, he bolstered his morale by drinking in Goebbels's propaganda. "I have never thought," he wrote to Ochsenius, "that history makes a gift of an empire to any race; it must be fought for! By the whole race—tough and hard." He convinced himself that the tragedy of Stalingrad was a good and necessary thing, for it would make everyone sit up and realize that extra resources of strength had to be applied by everyone in order to win the "last round" of the war.[153]

Here, then, was in one man a soldier with front-line experience and a solid National Socialist, the combination that the largely absent Ochsenius had long been seeking in his quest for a deputy who could bridge the gulf between the military groups and the NSDStB. He wrote immediately to Formel, whom he knew to be just undergoing a second amputation in the hospital, begging him to accept the post so that at last "one of us old-timers" could be permanently in the District Student Leadership again.[154]

It was not unusual for injured soldiers to fill NSDStB posts. In the Munich District, for instance, all the positions were held by wounded students.[155] A soldier with fighting expe-

---

[152] Geheimes Rundschreiben Bähr to student leaders, "Sondereinsatz für das OKW," 13 September 1940; Ochsenius to RSF-Stabsamt, 26 September 1940, RSFWü V*2 α 568. In accordance with OKW (Oberkommando der Wehrmacht) instructions, Formel never discovered to whom he owed his sudden transferral. His Company at the Front was almost entirely wiped out a few weeks later. Interview Giles/Formel, 7 March 1972.

[153] Formel to Ochsenius, 5 February 1943, RSFWü V*2 α 561.

[154] Ochsenius to Formel, 24 February 1943, ibid.

[155] Doerfler to Giesler, 26 March 1943, BDC Partei-Korrespondenz Julius Doerfler.

rience was often chosen by preference, since it was considered that he would more easily command general respect. The incumbent Acting District Student Leader at Hamburg, Georg Reinecke, was regarded from the start by Ochsenius as a temporary and rather unsatisfactory deputy. Permanently crippled in the knee as a boy during Hitler Youth training, he was prevented in Ochsenius's eyes "from sharing in that *esprit de corps* so absolutely necessary for young people." He exhibited an exaggerated *Geltungsbedürfnis* and a schoolmasterly attitude toward the students.[156] To the annoyance of Ochsenius, who refused to give his endorsement in all cases, Reinecke gathered over half a dozen posts within the student leadership in his own person, including that of Student Leader at the University *and* the Teachers' Training College, as well as Acting District Student Leader. Although instructed to step down completely in favor of Formel, he persistently attempted to demonstrate how indispensable he was, despite the relative lack of success of his two years in office, and he was still trying to recoup his losses a year later.[157]

When Wilhelm Formel took office in December 1943, the work of the NSDStB was failing in a number of important ways. In his own words, "(a) the *Kameradschaften* had collapsed completely and dissolved; (b) no corps of leaders existed; (c) cooperation with the Party and its Formations had lapsed; (d) the wounded students were left out of student life [i.e. the *Kameradschaften*] completely, just as the student body as a whole was utterly uninterested. . . ."[158] On top of this, the District Student Leadership's office had suffered further bomb damage on 13 December 1943.[159] Formel re-

[156] Aktennotiz Ochsenius, 7 September 1944, RSFWü V*2 α 572.

[157] Ibid. Also Formel to Rother, 8 March 1944, RSFWü V*2 α 568; Formel to Keeser, 12 April 1944, UniHH 0.10.3.4.

[158] The picture is largely accurate, but as in the case of many reports, Formel was striving to contrast his own achievements with the previous muddle. Some allowance for exaggeration must be made. Semesterbericht Formel, 7 September 1944, RSFWü V*2 α 532.

[159] Addendum to Feldpostbrief Gaustudentenführung no. 42, 14 Decem-

garded his prime task as winning back the confidence of the soldiers and took positive steps toward this by filling all the posts within the student leadership with soldier-students alone. At the same time, he restored its standing with the Party's district leadership to its prewar position and with the University, where student representatives once more took part in senate and Faculty meetings.[160]

It is difficult to judge just how successful Formel's attempt to revitalize the *Kameradschaften* was. Membership statistics no longer exist for his period of office, but he claimed to have put the six *Kameradschaften* at the University back on their feet, refounded a seventh, and created an eighth. Formel's report for the Reich Student Leadership on the summer semester 1944 was far more positive and self-congratulatory than the Political Education Leader's report for Formel (on which it was based). The latter spoke of personality clashes characterizing the life of three of the eight, and another failed utterly to win any new members.[161] Despite the changes in the student leadership, it remained as difficult as ever to persuade the soldiers to join in the work of the NSDStB.

The projected pampering of the soldier-students through the provision, under the auspices of the Reich Student Leadership, of preparatory refresher courses and a whole series of booklets surveying various courses of study was a failure from the start. The printed material invariably arrived late, due to escalating postal difficulties and, in Hamburg at least, in insufficient quantities.[162] Reich Lecturers' Leader

---

ber 1943, RSFWü V*2 α 566. The Berlin Liaison Office of the Reich Student Leadership was gutted on the night of 22 November 1943. Rundschreiben Braune, 24 November 1943, UniHH 0.10.2.1.

[160] Reinecke had started attending senate meetings on 30 March 1943 as soon as he began to hear of Ochsenius's intentions to replace him. There had been no student representative since 7 February 1940.

[161] The eighth *Kameradschaft* had only three members. Semesterbericht Fuchs, 5 August 1944, RSFWü V*2 α 532.

[162] *Mitteilungen und Bekanntgaben des Soldatendienstes des Reichsstudentenführers*, January and April 1944, UniHH M.50.14.4.

Schultze complained bitterly to Bormann that he had not been consulted about the study guides. He believed some of the recommended reading to be completely unsuitable: for example, a philosophy booklist contained works by "notorious opponents of National Socialism" such as Karl Jaspers.[163]

In the autumn of 1944, the universities received their biggest upset since September 1939. The work of the NSDStB was violently disrupted and never really regained any momentum afterward. Many universities made preparations to close down, at least partially. The cause was the so-called Second Decree concerning "Total War" of 25 July 1944. Its effect on the education sector was not outlined until 1 September, and even then it was not finalized for one subgroup, the female medical students, until 24 October 1944.[164] The universities realized that they would in any case have to suffer large cutbacks. Hamburg was told that it would have to close down its Law Faculty and send the students in question to Greifswald. Frenzied negotiations took place behind the scenes, and a letter was obtained from the Mayor of Greifswald certifying that it would be impossible to find accommodation for the extra students in the town.[165] The Arts Faculty, destined to lose its students to Göttingen, conceived a subtler method of self-preservation that received the blessing of the head of the Higher Education Department of the Ministry, Professor Mentzel, who told Rector Keeser "that he could not alter anything of the formal content of the decree concerning the closure of the universities and Faculties, but that he would consent to our helping our students 'by illegal means' if possible."[166] Thus it was settled

[163] Schultze to Partei-Kanzlei, 4 January 1944, zstA Dienststelle Reichsleiter Rosenberg 13715.

[164] Rundschreiben Rust, 1 September 1944, uniHH N.20.2.11.

[165] Bescheinigung Oberbürgermeister von Greifswald, 21 October 1944, stA Uo8/4.

[166] Keeser to Rektor Universität Göttingen, 26 October 1944, uniHH N.1.22.

between the two rectors that the applications for matriculation at Göttingen would be brought *en bloc* by courier from
Hamburg, but that the students themselves would remain
in Hamburg. The teaching of the Hamburg students would
be delegated by the Göttingen heads of departments to Hamburg lecturers, who were to hold in Hamburg classes corresponding to those announced in the Göttingen lecture
list.[167]

Just as Hamburg and doubtless other universities had completed such complex preparations for the changes due in the
winter semester, the Reich Education Ministry issued a brief
telegram on 1 November 1944 ordering that the modifica-
tions would not, after all, be put into effect.[168] It was realized,
at this late hour, that a concentration of several similar faculties and research institutes in one place would, in the light
of the inadequate air-raid defenses, be "a positive support to
the enemy." The universities therefore remained open wherever possible, but with drastically reduced student numbers.
Of the 85,517 students of the summer semester in 1944, 54
percent were lost at one blow: 15,560 soldier-students were
recalled to active service; 26,403 women and 4,393 male
civilian students were called up for civilian war duties,
mainly in the armaments industry.[169] Hamburg's student
body shrank from 2,156 students to 959 (of whom 607 were
in the Medical Faculty), the previous semester's peak of 46.8
percent female students now dropping to 26.6 percent.[170]

The situation in the District Student Leadership became
critical as Formel lost his best leaders and most of the important positions fell vacant. He was greatly disappointed

[167] Göttingen University was to issue attendance certificates at the end
of the semester. Niederschrift Snell et al., "Betreuung der von der Hansischen Universität Hamburg zur Philosophischen Fakultät der Universität
Göttingen kommenden Studenten," 28 October 1944, ibid.

[168] Telegram Mentzel to rector, 1 November 1944, ibid.

[169] Rundschreiben Mentzel, WA 1960, 30 December 1944, N.20.2.11.

[170] Statistisches Landesamt Hamburg, *Die Universität Hamburg im Spiegel ihrer Hörerzahlen*, pp. 180-81.

that his hard work of restoration had to "suffer such blows. As so often in student work, we are faced in the coming semester with yet another fresh start."[171] There was, however, an even greater disruption to come. Hardly had the semester started than it was decided that all students would be mustered in the people's militia, the *Deutsche Volkssturm*, although at least as a separate battalion under the command of Formel.[172] At first the professors were assigned to groups in the locality of their homes, but Formel succeeded in having them transferred to the student battalion in order to maintain the impression of a unified university.[173] The NSDStB Assistant Leaders became Formel's staff officers, and their time was now completely taken up with civil defense training.

The files of the District Student Leadership were hastily bundled together and sent off to the archives of the Institute for German Student History at Würzburg.[174] The District Student Leadership itself now virtually closed down. The business of the Reich Student Leadership was practically brought to a standstill by the total destruction of its Munich headquarters in an air raid on the night of 17-18 December 1944.[175] As the military situation worsened in 1945, fewer and fewer classes were held, and the students were increas-

[171] Semesterbericht Formel, 7 September 1944, RSFWü V*2 α 532.

[172] Gaustabsführer Deutscher Volkssturm to University, 23 November 1944, UniHH 0.1.6.

[173] Interview Giles/Formel. Eisfeld relates that one morning after an air raid, it took him four hours to pick his way through the rubble to the spot where he had been assigned to help build a tank barricade. Eisfeld, *Aus fünfzig Jahren*, p. 152.

[174] It comes as no surprise that the very last document in the files of the District Student Leadership concerns the continuing petty intrigues of the NSDDOZB. Formel to Kubach, 5 October 1944, RSFWü V*2 α 573.

[175] Scheel himself had been operating from Salzburg with a small staff for some time. I could not locate at Salzburg or elsewhere the files of this office, and they were presumably burned. The headquarters of the NSDDOZB in Munich, which Scheel headed since 1944, was bombed on 7 January 1945. Its office also moved to Salzburg. Rundschreiben Kubach, 12 January 1945, ZStA Dienststelle Reichsleiter Rosenberg 13715.

ingly summoned for *Volkssturm* duties. The Student Battalion was responsible for the defense of the Hamm area, near the city center. On 27 April 1945, the *Gauleiter*, hearing that ss troops were standing by near Hamburg to arrest him if he should announce the surrender of the city, threw a double barbed-wire cordon around his official residence by the Alster and called in the students to protect him. Another group was detailed to guard the wireless transmitter at Moorfleet, where postcapitulation messages, recorded with the utmost secrecy by Kaufmann and Armaments Minister Speer, lay ready for broadcast. Formel himself was on duty here and successfully hindered an ss attempt to enter the radio station.[176]

The war ended for most Hamburg students on 3 May 1945, when the British entered the city for Kaufmann's formal capitulation in the City Hall. Only the staff officers of the Student Battalion remained at their posts for a few days more. Concerned about the effects for them as Nazi leaders of a mass release of political prisoners from the concentration camps, they wished to ensure that the weapons that the battalion possessed were delivered safely into the hands of the Allies.

For Hans Ochsenius, more ardently idealistic than most of his colleagues, the German defeat was a crushing blow. He believed too much in his own propagandistic writings of the inevitable German victory until the very last moment. On going to wake him on Sunday morning, 13 May 1945, his mother found that he had committed suicide. He evidently expected harsh treatment at the hands of the Allies and had written about the vindictiveness of the enemy in his last articles in 1945. His suicide note revealed that he had already toyed with the idea of killing himself two months earlier in the Barbarossa Tower in the Palatinate,

---

[176] Interview Giles/Formel. Kurt Detlev Möller, *Das letzte Kapitel* (Hamburg, 1947), provides a poignant account of the last months of the war in Hamburg. Also Middlebrook, *Battle of Hamburg*, p. 314.

where the crown jewels of the old empire had been kept in medieval times. But he had wanted to see his parents once more. Having done so, he could no longer face the desolate future he foresaw for himself and for Germany and decided to end his life "in dignity and honor" rather than "clinging doglike to existence until they take me away to torments without end."[177] Like Education Minister Rust, who had committed suicide five days earlier, District Student Leader Ochsenius held an exaggerated view of his importance in the National Socialist state.

[177] Extracts from suicide note in Karl Ochsenius, "Sol invictus!" pp. 3 and 40, AFGNH.

CONCLUSION

The constant fluctuation of the size and membership of the student body placed all kinds of hindrances against the organization of a definite program of political education. Properly trained leaders might have helped, but all those who had been chosen to lead were away fighting. The wartime student leaders had not risen to their positions through the exhibition of special qualities, or through the successful accomplishment of training courses, but were all too often just students who were willing to lend a hand. Had the Party been genuinely concerned with the political education of the student body, it ought to have realized the importance of keeping at least some of the prewar leaders out of the military in order to serve the state at their NSDStB posts. Ochsenius frequently lamented this loss, and Rector Gundert was not unsympathetic toward the problem. He even considered asking the Education Ministry to secure Ochsenius's release from military service, but the ministry was hardly likely to persuade the Army to relinquish its officers by stressing what good leaders they made.[1]

One cannot accept Ochsenius's view that all would have been well if only the war had not come in 1939. War was bound to break out during the Third Reich and whenever it did, the most reliable Nazis would always be the first to volunteer for the Army in order to set an example for the other students, even if they were not immediately called up. Without a directive from Party headquarters to keep the student leaders at their posts, the latter would never risk being accused of shirking their responsibilities to the mili-

---

[1] Gundert to Rust, October 1940, draft in UniHH 0.30.6.II; a second draft in 0.13.3.5.

tary war effort by doing so.[2] And yet NSDAP headquarters never gave much attention to the students unless it needed them for a specific job, such as supplementing the labor force in munitions factories. It was very much a one-way relationship: when the Party wanted something from the student leadership, it expected it to be provided, but never was any well-considered advice or more tangible support given regarding the special problems of the student sector. This derived from the style of leadership in the Nazi state: the top leaders made the broad decisions, but the problems of implementation were left entirely to the junior leaders, all the more so if they were fraught with apparently insuperable difficulties.

To a certain extent, the Reich Student Leadership was to blame for the lack of concern: it attempted to gloss over its problems in dealings with higher agencies. If Scheel repeatedly requested outside help or even admitted failure, then his damaged reputation might halt his flourishing career. As a member of an espionage organization (the SD), he was in turn alarmed at the thought of any reports about the NSDStB reaching higher authorities except through the filter of his own office. A satirical show by the participants of a training course for *Kameradschaft* leaders in 1944 gave Scheel a sleepless night because of the inclusion of political jokes. Scheel held that "the *Kameraden*, as a result of their usually deficient political education, do not have sufficient insight nor above all the right to make apparently humorous remarks in this field. If the *Führer* were to hear just once of merely one of the sketches that were performed yesterday, it would signify with certainty the end of our *Kameradschaften*."[3] The success of the NSDStB stood and fell with

[2] The SD reported the derisive remarks of freshmen about uniformed Party members in the street, such as "Make way, here comes a member of the Inner Front!" Meldungen aus dem Reich, 8 December 1939, BA R58/146.

[3] Scheel to Bässler, 11 April 1944, BDC Partei-Korrespondenz file Bässler. The sort of sketches presented are hinted at in Scheel's next letter to Bässler, which recalls the following: "The story about the bug and about Bässler,

these *Kameradschaften*. Wartime difficulties are understandable, but even beforehand, in the last peacetime semester and the sixth of Scheel's term of office, they were far from being the smoothly running units that he had envisaged. A typical report from Göttingen spoke of good intentions but uninspired leadership: "All measures ordered from above are indeed carried out, but their execution lacks spirited, political will and logical, National Socialist perception."[4]

"Measures," "orders," were carried out, but otherwise the leaders were at a loss for what to do. They were not necessarily unintelligent. Certainly in the Reich Student Leadership after 1936 there were no academic failures. Scheel made a particular point of excluding the "professional student" type of leader in favor of those who had often already proved their academic respectability with a doctorate. He gave every encouragement to filling the local posts with bright students. But a high IQ is no guarantee of an original mind, and even where Scheel did find academically successful students, they exhibited overwhelmingly, like the staff of the national leadership, a sad poverty of fresh ideas. The most that the Reich Student Leadership seemed to be able to provide were the broad "guidelines" for *Kameradschaft* training, which differed little from fraternity models and grew more and more like them as time went on. Scheel made no secret of this: if in Derichsweiler the Party had chosen the right man to destroy the fraternities, then in Scheel it had found a good person to pick up the pieces, despite his lapses of impatience with the alumni.

As highly successful creators of a nationalistic, patriotic, self-confident upper class in the student world, the fraternities had aroused feelings of jealousy in the NSDStB lead-

---

who is indeed no bishop, but draws a bishop's stipend, shook me deeply." Scheel to Bässler, 8 May 1944, ibid.

[4] RSF Amtsleiter Presse und Propaganda Wolff to Horn, "Bericht über Inspektion der Studentenführung Göttingen," 12 July 1939, BDC Partei-Korrespondenz file Ernst Horn.

ership. The fraternities represented a firmly entrenched elite, and the NSDStB wanted to be that elite. It set about this by trying to step almost literally into their shoes. Yet the increasing return to the outward forms of fraternity life, which old fraternity members hailed as proof of Scheel's fundamental sympathy with their ideals and traditions, was not recognized as the paucity of ideas that it really signified. For the NSDStB's espousal of fraternity thinking advanced in direct proportion to the decrease in the effectiveness of the *Kameradschaften*. It seemed to be falling back on tried and proven forms when its own efforts at experimentation miscarried.

If the NSDStB represented an elite, why was it not an attractive one to the majority of students, whatever its activities? One of the main threads running through the experience of the student leaders was the overwhelming apathy of the students. Successive leaders put on military-style exercises to attract the defense-minded students, subsidized cultural visits for theater- and concert-goers, ran academic competitions for the studious, yet still the students shied away from the thick end of the carrot: political education. Even the most pertinent appeal of all, that of financial aid, did not have quite the expected effect. Although monetary grants became available only to those willing to participate in NSDStB activities, many of those students who did need assistance still often preferred to earn their money during the vacation rather than put up with the NSDStB for the duration of the semester.

Only in part did the cause of this general apathy lie in the uninspiring nature of the NSDStB leadership. Of decisive importance in shaping student attitudes were the increasing obligations of all young people to Party and state before they ever arrived at the universities: first, they had to perform their labor service, then military service, and by 1939 membership in the Hitler Youth was made nominally compulsory. Traditionally freedom had played a central part in the role expectations of the German student, and the yearning for this became all the greater as the Nazi state made more and more demands on the spare time of young Germans. It was not so much the enjoyment of freedom per se that was sought so avidly—most students did not radically disagree with an authoritarian regime; rather the uncooperative attitude of many students was simply the expression of a normal youthful urge for a little self-assertive independence, in this case heightened into a feeling of necessity for at least a temporary respite from rigid regimentation.

In view of the reported enthusiasm of previously indifferent students toward the NSDStB after attendance at their first camp, the question arises: why was membership in the NSDStB not made compulsory for all students, as was the Hitler Youth for all schoolchildren? If the NSDStB leaders were convinced that they had something worthwhile and attractive to offer, why not force the students to sample the fare? The answer would appear to be given by Stäbel's decision in February 1934, followed by Hess's definitive statement in July that the NSDStB would revert from being a mass organization to an elite one, embracing no more than 5 percent of the student body. Yet subsequent leaders were concerned with more than this tiny minority. Scheel's declared aim that "the political-ideological education of the NSDStB will embrace every student up to the end of his third semester" does not conflict with the elite view because of the category of probationary membership.[5] The NSDStB wished indeed to accept only the select few to full membership, but it aimed to have the maximum possible number of students as probationers, both to facilitate the screening process and as a source of extra income through subscriptions.

Although Scheel, on taking office, seemed prepared to force all students to undergo the political indoctrination of the NSDStB, he soon backed down. In his speech at the Nuremberg Rally in 1937, he looked forward to the time when

---

[5] Denkschrift Scheel, "Die Neuordnung des deutschen Studententums," 2 November 1936, ZStA REM 894.

there would no longer be "free students" (*Freistudenten*) outside the NSDStB training program, but he added that no one need fear that he would be forced to join.[6] It was uncharacteristic of Scheel to move toward a more liberal position without some prompting. Perhaps the realization that the *Kameradschaften* were not yet sufficiently developed to cater satisfactorily for all the freshmen was the reason for it. It seems more likely that it was his nominal superiors, Rust and Hess, who remained adamant about the voluntary nature of the NSDStB.

They were both concerned to a surprising degree with public and foreign opinion, and Rust was probably permanently frightened by the furor over the compulsion of the Feickert Plan. When the Berlin press announced in November 1936 that only members of the Formations of the Nazi Party would be accepted as students at the university, Rust hurried to issue an emphatic disclaimer.[7] Despite the urgency of providing as large a task force as possible for the harvest in 1939, and applying the "moral pressure" that Scheel considered necessary, the Education Ministry insisted on the retention of the voluntary character of the program. The Reich Vocational Contest was set up specifically to counter foreign accusations of a drop in German academic standards.

Scheel had no legal means of forcing all students through the *Kameradschaft* mill. The Reich Student Leadership never produced a constitution, which Scheel initially felt would merely hamper him. And so Scheel's constitutional base remained the manifesto he had submitted prior to his assumption of office. Although almost all the DST and NSDStB offices were combined in the Reich Student Leadership, the plan had made a point of retaining the Department of Political Education strictly within the NSDStB, thus denying

---

[6] "Die Rede des Reichsstudentenführers," *Die Bewegung*, 14 September 1937, p. 3.

[7] Rust to DST, 3 November 1936, RSFWü II*A46 α 481.

the Education Ministry any influence that it might have brought to bear on a DST officeholder. This now meant, however, that the Reich Student Leadership had no disciplinary powers over the entire student body (DST) in the realm of political education and could only force NSDStB members to join the *Kameradschaften*. Even after the outbreak of the war, Scheel was unable to increase his powers openly in this respect, and his request to Hess to secure a better intake of students through the prerequisite of a certificate of political reliability was not met.[8] In the end Scheel as *Gauleiter* got around this in his own Salzburg district by refusing the school-leaving certificate to those without a satisfactory Hitler Youth service record "on grounds of immaturity."[9]

In the last resort Scheel was reluctant to paint a picture of student apathy that was black enough to persuade his superiors of the need for compulsory NSDStB membership, for fear of testifying to his own inefficacy. Instead, he set up the undercover "special campaigns" to identify dissidents and made secret provisions to send the uncooperative ones among them to concentration camps. As long as Scheel kept up the facade of orderly progress in the task of political education, neither Party nor Ministry would acknowledge the necessity for compulsion, seeing only the success of voluntary policies as a further benefit in the selection process: the putative minority of students who did not volunteer for the NSDStB were not worthy of attention in any case and would be passed over when seeking jobs after graduation in favor of more ardent supporters of the state. This was all very well at the beginning of the Third Reich, when there was a surplus of graduates. By 1939 a steady drop in student numbers had begun to reveal a serious shortage in the academic professions. Qualified graduates were badly needed, whether they were ideologically sound or not.[10]

[8] Meldungen aus dem Reich, 5 January 1940, BA R21/724.

[9] Persönlicher Referent des RSFers Dr. Renz to student leaders, 10 February 1944, RSFwü V*1 γ 600.

[10] Schoenbaum observes that "neither ideology nor long-term interests

A further reason for Rust's reluctance to turn the entire student body over to the NSDStB may simply have been that this would have constituted an admission of *his* failure to politicize the university from above. Rust did suffer serious qualms about his failure as Education Minister. His speech to the 1943 Rectors' Conference in Salzburg, delivered in a state of acute inebriation, was seen as "as public admission of his impotency." So devastating was Rust's behavior throughout the conference that one participant was moved to remark: "If we win the war, how shall we ever maintain our victory with such leadership? We don't even deserve the hegemony of Europe."[11]

Already in 1939, Ernst Krieck had written a confidential letter to Scheel lamenting the lost opportunities in the higher education sector that poor leadership had caused. Even Krieck, the Nazi scholar par excellence, could not bring himself to blame his colleagues entirely: ". . . even the sympathetic cannot always bridge the gap between their political attitude and their scholarship—for that demands a creative achievement of which not all are capable. . . . Leadership in the realm of scholarship and literature is almost anarchy, or reaction at least. One cannot put the blame for *that* solely on those who work down at the grass roots level." Krieck saw fully politicized scholarship as a vital yet underestimated "cornerstone of the future." Yet all around him professors sought "to tread again the old, familiar paths."[12] By this time, few of them were even pretending to be political activists. Academic promotion within the university came to depend again more on scholastic merit than on Party

---

seem to have guided [university admission] policy." Schoenbaum, *Social Revolution*, p. 273.

[11] Kaltenbrunner to Bormann, 16 November 1943, BDC Partei-Korrespondenz file Rust. For Rust's paralyzing moods of depression, see also Rolf Eilers, *Die nationalsozialistische Schulpolitik: Eine Studie zur Funktion der Erziehung im totalitären Staat* (Cologne and Opladen, 1963), pp. 112ff.

[12] Ernst Krieck to Scheel (Vertraulich), 8 May 1939, RSFWü I*06 φ 123.

involvement.[13] Even as early as 1935, it was noted that the only "political" professors had been those ousted in the faculty purges. Those remaining had for the most part never interested themselves in political matters and failed to do so now.[14] New appointments did little to change the overall picture.

What was the reason for the apparent neglect in such a major area? It is tempting to speculate that Hitler chose such a weak and unoriginal man as Rust for his Education Minister, knowing that the former schoolmaster would never gain the respect of academic circles, nor be able to nazify the universities, precisely so that he might have his prejudice against intellectuals confirmed.[15] This, however, is to imply too much subtlety on the part of Hitler, who did not require substantiation of his prejudices at such length but believed the universities to be moribund anyway. There was no place in Hitler's Reich for institutions that taught people to *think*. On the other hand, the young intellectuals of the SD did seek to point out that an uneducated corps of leaders, such as had existed in the early days of the NSDAP, was no longer satisfactory now that the Nazis were leading the state, and that therefore the Party really ought to draw more heavily on the universities for its leaders.[16] Although Himmler was himself squarely *professorenfreundlich* (unlike Hitler), the view did not gain wide currency. When Gerhard Wagner and Hess were fantasizing in 1934 about "a sort of intellectual ss,"[17] the academic National Socialist elite that the NSDStB might

[13] Richard Zneimer, "The Nazis and the Professors: Social Origin, Professional Mobility, and Political Involvement of the Frankfurt University Faculty, 1933-1939," *Journal of Social History* 12 (1978): 148-58.

[14] Nockemann to Gestapa Berlin, 17 June 1935, ZStA REM 872.

[15] Maser reports that Hitler first offered the post of Education Minister to his acquaintance, Karl Alexander von Müller, the distinguished Munich Professor of History, who declined it. His evidence for this interesting assertion is, however, typically unsound. Maser, *Adolf Hitler*, p. 370.

[16] Kater, *Ahnenerbe*, pp. 130-31.

[17] See above, chap. 5, n. 55.

produce, they were thinking largely in terms of people able to give smart answers to the criticisms of National Socialism at home and abroad. Not even the loquacious Goebbels had succeeded in concealing the brutalities of the first eighteen months of the Third Reich behind optimistic talk of the achievements of the regime.

University-trained experts loyal to the Party needed to be recruited for public relations purposes in order to make authoritative pronouncements on the superiority of National Socialist thought in all fields and give scholarly respectability to National Socialism. Most members of the Party leadership, however, had no great respect for learning. Very few of them were university graduates. A number had attended a university but dropped out during the course of their studies.[18] It may have been the stigma of failure that kept their backs turned to higher education in the years to follow and that made them refuse to acknowledge the importance of learning. University was an embarrassing memory best erased. Scheel himself was by no means indifferent toward the fate of the universities. Yet he, too, and his staff suffered from a fundamental misconception of education.

First, the student leaders completely misunderstood the nature of the fraternities. The NSDStB attempted to be, in supposed emulation of them, both a social and an educational organization (a *"Lebensgemeinschaft"* and an *"Erziehungsgemeinschaft"*).[19] There was a failure to recognize that the fraternities had not been overt educational groups. The nationalistic ethos they had produced had not been imparted by direct teaching but rather by example: within these communities the senior members passed on certain codes of behavior, standards, and attitudes casually and gradually to their juniors. The subtler method was the more effective

[18] Bracher, *Dictatorship*, p. 274, and Daniel Lerner, *The Nazi Elite* (Stanford, 1951), pp. 89-90.
[19] Befehl Scheel RSF 56/37, 1 October 1937, RSFWü II*62 α 16.

323

because it was quite painless. The Nazis did not comprehend this and clung to a preference for formal teaching of ideological matters, with compulsion to receive that training if need be. They badly needed scientific and technological excellence for the international power struggle but set too high a premium on political reliability.

Excessive rote learning stifles the imagination. A. N. Whitehead once noted that "necessary technical excellence can only be acquired by a training which is apt to damage those energies of mind which should direct the technical skill. This is a key fact in education, and the reason for most of its difficulties."[20] How much truer this is of indoctrination, which deliberately sets out to dull the mind into inert receptivity. Leaders noticed already during the war that the students, after years of exposure to Nazi ideology and propaganda, frequently lacked all originality and agility of mind. Their thinking had always been done for them; they had been brought to accept "official" dogma unquestioningly. The Hamburg student leader Ochsenius saw that these people would never make inspiring leaders; they would never be able to teach well to others what they now believed in but could only pass it on in the same dull manner in which they had received it, and thus badly and probably unsuccessfully. The net result of the slowly advancing totalitarian sweep of the National Socialist indoctrination program seemed to be a sterility of mind in the ranks of the NSDStB that would have led in time to an ever greater paralysis of German scholarship and science.

The NSDStB was born as a revolutionary group; it nourished itself on the struggle with an enemy. It is much easier to destroy quickly than to achieve speedy progress through a constructive program. The NSDStB continued always to create the air of a "permanent revolution" by concocting imag-

[20] A. N. Whitehead, *The Aims of Education and Other Essays* (London, 1929), p. 144.

inary foes. They came in and went and were brought back again in the absence of fresh ideas: Communists, Jews, fraternity alumni, intellectuals, foreigners. The message of Scheel's head of Political Education, Dr. Reinhold Bässler, on Hitler's birthday in 1943 ran to the same familiar tune: "The *Kameradschaft* is not an end in itself, but the means to an end. Its goal is the completion of the National Socialist revolution in the student body and the university. Its enemies are always the same: philistines, bigwigs and priests, intellectuals, defeatists, crawlers, bureaucrats and good-for-nothings."[21]

As an organization that saw itself largely in terms of military metaphors, with the "political soldier" fighting the putative enemy, it was essential for the NSDStB both to increase its resources and, especially when so many other branches of the Party and state were competing for these, to have a strong and able commander. Scheel was successful in this respect, rising continually in the Party and state hierarchies to head the grant-awarding *Reichsstudentenwerk* in 1938, to become *Gauleiter* and Governor of Salzburg in 1941, and Reich Lecturers' Leader in 1944. As the final accolade he was named Reich Minister of Education in Hitler's testament. All that could be done to secure power for the Reich Student Leadership was accomplished by Scheel. Thanks to him his office became fully equipped to deal with enemies. There seems little doubt that as Education Minister he would have ordered every German student to undergo ideological indoctrination in the *Kameradschaften*. Yet the Reich Student Leadership was fighting the wrong battle. The enemies were for the most part imaginary. For all the potential power that Scheel wielded on paper by 1945, there was still no one in the student leadership with the insight

[21] Anordnung Bässler PE 8/43, 20 April 1943, reproduced in *Dienstanweisung für die Kameradschaften vom 20.4.1943*, ed. Amt Politische Erziehung der RSF, p. 3.

and imagination to understand and solve the vast problems of general apathy. Looking back on the struggles of the Weimar period, one Nazi student recalled: "Our greatest enemy was student apathy."[22] Twelve years later, for all the organizational authority that the NSDStB had achieved, the validity of this comment had not diminished.

[22] Peter H. Merkl, *Political Violence Under the Swastika: 581 Early Nazis* (Princeton, 1975), p. 133.

APPENDIX ONE

ASTA Election Results in Hamburg 1928–1933.
(The elections took place on or near February 10 each year.)

Year and List	Proportion (%) of students voting	Percentage of all students voting NS	Number of votes	Percentage of votes	Seats gained
1928	68.0	6.6			
Völkischer Ring (NSDStB)			151	9.7	1
Deutscher Korpora-tionen			585	37.7	5
Arbeitsgemeinschaft der deutschen Fin-kenschaft			177	11.4	1
Deutscher Studenten-bund (Deustubu)			627	40.5	5
Liste für Fachschafts-arbeit			10	0.6	0
1929	59.0	7.6			
Völkischer Ring (NSDStB)			199	13.0	1
Deutsche Korpora-tionen			545	35.6	5
Deutsche Finkenschaft			235	15.3	2
Deutscher Studenten-bund			485	31.7	4
Sozialistische Studen-tenschaft			68	4.4	0
1930	60.2	11.5			
NSDStB			366	19.0	2
Widerstandsblock (= fraternities)			627	32.6	5
Deutsche Finkenschaft			272	14.2	2
Hochschulpolitische Arbeitsgemeinschaft (remainder of Deus-tubu)			229	11.9	1
Sozialistische Studen-tenschaft			359	18.7	2
Revolutionäre Sozia-listen			70	3.6	0

327

Year and List	Proportion (%) of students voting	Percentage of all students voting NS	Number of votes	Percentage of votes	Seats gained
1931	62.7	24.8			
NSDStB			883	39.5	5
Widerstandsblock			525	23.5	3
Deutsche Finkenschaft			238	10.7	1
Sozialistische Studentenschaft			500	22.4	3
Revolutionäre Sozialisten			88	3.9	0
1932	65.1	23.0			
NSDStB			1,004	43.1	5
Nationaler Widerstandsblock			273	11.7	2
Grossdeutscher Ring			386	16.6	2
Demokratischer Studentenbund			189	8.1	1
Sozialistische Studentenschaft			348	14.9	2
Revolutionäre Sozialisten			132	5.7	0
1933	63.4	28.5			
NSDStB			981	44.9	6
Nationaler Widerstandsblock			299	13.7	2
Grossdeutscher Ring			270	12.4	1
Demokratischer Studentenbund			164	7.5	1
Sozialistische Studentenschaft			261	11.9	1
Revolutionäre Sozialisten			211	9.7	1

Sources: for 1928-1930, RSFWü V*2 α 507; for 1931, ZStA RMdI 26109; for 1932–1933, BA R129/122.

APPENDIX TWO

NSDStB Membership and Matriculation Figures for the
University of Hamburg

Semester	NSDStB membership	Male Hamburg students	ANst membership	Female Hamburg students	Total Percentage in NSDStB
WS 1926-1927	1	1,738	(2)[a]	393	0.1
WS 1927-1928	6*	1,925	—	480	0.2
SS 1928	11*	2,094	—	511	0.4
SS 1929	20	2,519	(5)[a]	682	0.8
WS 1930-1931	28	2,891	—	855	0.7
SS 1931	45	3,081	—	992	1.1
WS 1931-1932	60[b]	2,789	—	957	1.6
SS 1932	55	2,806	—	971	1.5
WS 1932-1933	43[c]	2,683	11	911	1.5
SS 1933	266	2,409	27	790	9.2
WS 1933-1934	412	2,219	63	735	16.1
WS 1934-1935	141	1,748	—	557	6.1
SS 1936	514*	1,556	—	509	24.9
WS 1937-1938	310	1,284	56	253	23.8
SS 1938	463	1,281	—	239	30.5
WS 1938-1939	538	1,211	98	236	44.0
SS 1939	355	1,150	61	235	30.0
2d T 1940	283	744	126	255	40.9
T 1941	—	826	408	408	
SS 1941	229	592	95	334	35.0
WS 1941-1942	116	971	195	380	23.0
SS 1942	101	730	212	510	25.2
WS 1942-1943	231	1,155	222	664	24.9
SS 1943	290	1,130	590	830	44.9

Note. WS = winter semester. SS = summer semester. T = trimester. Dash
= data not available. Blank space in last column indicates that a percentage
cannot be given because figures for male students were unavailable for the
1941 trimester.
*Including women—separate figures for female members not available.
[a] Female NSDStB members. ANst proper not formed until WS 1930-1931.
[b] Includes members from Hamburg State Technical Institute.
[c] On 1 December 1932.
Source: Pre-1938 figures from miscellaneous correspondence; figures thereafter from statistics in RSFWU V*2 α 560. Figures unavailable for other
semesters.

APPENDIX THREE

NSDStB Membership at Hamburg Colleges (other than
the University of Hamburg)

Semester	NSDStB members			All students			Percentage in NSDStB
	Male	Female	Total	Male	Female	Total	
Hamburg College							
of Engineering							
WS 1938-1939	151	1	152	841	1	842	18.0
SS 1940	212	1	213	648	1	649	32.8
SS 1941	190	0	190	425	0	425	44.7
WS 1941-1942	72	0	72	375	0	375	19.2
SS 1942	37	0	37	362	1	363	10.2
WS 1942-1943	210	0	210	406	1	407	51.6
Hamburg State							
Technical Institute							
WS 1938-1939	98	125	223	265	384	648	34.4
SS 1939	160	203	363	198	276	474	76.6
SS 1940	53	350	403	55	350	405	99.5
WS 1940-1941 to							
SS 1942			"In process of reformation"				
WS 1942-1943	28	49	77	28	49	77	100.0
Hamburg College							
of Fine Arts							
WS 1938-1939	43	19	62	62	54	116	53.4
SS 1939	41	13	54	56	44	100	54.0
WS 1940-1941	38	32	70	40	62	102	68.6
SS 1941	14	40	54	30	66	96	56.2
WS 1941-1942	16	44	60	34	62	96	62.5
WS 1942-1943	40	81	121	70	127	197	61.4
Hamburg College							
of Civil Engineering							
WS 1938-1939	32	0	32	313	0	313	10.2
WS 1940-1941	113	0	113	194	0	194	58.2
SS 1941	81	1	82	135	2	137	59.8
WS 1941-1942	56	0	56	147	1	148	37.8
SS 1942	30	1	31	97	3	100	31.0
WS 1942-1943	34	2	36	97	2	99	36.4

Source: RSFWü V*2 α 560.

SELECT BIBLIOGRAPHY

1. *Archival Material*

Archiv der ehem. RSF und des NSDStB, Würzburg (RSFWü):
    German Students' Union
    Hamburg Students' Union and NSDStB
    NSDStB headquarters
    Reich Student Leadership
    Reich Vocational Contest
Archiv der Forschungsstelle für die Geschichte des Nationalso-
    zialismus in Hamburg (AFGNH):
    Karl Ochsenius, "Sol invictus! Denkschrift für meinen Sohn
        Hans-Karl Ochsenius, Gaustudentenführer Hamburgs,
        durch Freitod aus dem Erdenleben geschieden am
        13.5.1945," Typescript Hamburg 1947
    NSDStB miscellany
    Records of interviews with Prof. Rein and Frau Heinrichsdorff
Berlin Document Center (BDC):
    Hauptarchiv der NSDAP
    NS-Lehrerbund
    NSDAP-Zentralkartei
    Party Correspondence
    Proceedings of the Oberste Parteigericht
    SA files
    SS Officers' personnel files
Bundesarchiv, Aussenstelle Frankfurt am Main (BAFM):
    Deutsche Burschenschaft
Bundesarchiv, Koblenz (BA):
    Deutsche Studentenschaft
    Gemeinschaft Studentischer Verbände
    "Meldungen aus dem Reich"
    Nachlass Dr. Albert Krebs
    Reichserziehungsministerium
    Reichskanzlei
    Reichsstudentenführung

Sammlung Schumacher
Institut für Hochschulkunde, Würzburg (IfH):
Student press and other published material
Institut für Zeitgeschichte, Munich:
Miscellaneous documents (inc. microfilms and photocopies)
Library of Congress, Washington, D.C. (LC):
Papers of Fritz Kubach, Eric Otto, and Arnold Brügmann
Staatsarchiv Hamburg (StA):
Hamburg NSDStB files 1927-1932
State Press Office—cuttings on student and University matters
University Authority
Universität Hamburg (UniHH):
Philosophical Faculty
Rector's office and university administration (now in StA)
University Authority personnel card index on academic staff
University Authority personnel files on academic staff
University personnel files on academic staff
University Registry personnel card index on students
Wiener Library, London (now at Tel Aviv):
Press cuttings on German universities
Zentrales Staatsarchiv, Potsdam (ZStA):
Dienststelle Reichsleiter Rosenberg
Reichministerium des Innern
Reichserziehungsministerium

2. *Periodicals and Serials*

Akademische Warte: Kampfschrift für den nationalen Sozialismus auf den Hochschulen. Beiblatt der Hansischen Warte, 1929-1930.

Akademischer Beobachter: Kampfblatt des NSDStB, 1929.

Der Altherrenbund. Amtliches Organ des NS-Altherrenbundes der deutschen Studenten, 1938-1943.

Die Bewegung: Zentralorgan des NSD-Studentenbundes, 1933-1945.

Burschenschaftliche Blätter, 1936-1939.

Deutsche Corps-Zeitung: Amtliche Zeitschrift des Kösener SC-Verbandes, 1926-1937.

Deutsche Hochschulstatistik, Sommerhalbjahr 1928-Wintersemester 1935-1936.

Der Deutsche Student: Zeitschrift der Deutschen Studentenschaft, 1933-1936.

Deutsche Studentenzeitung: Kampfblatt der deutschen Studenten. Amtliches Nachrichtenblatt des NSDStB, 1933-1935.

Deutsche Wissenschaft, Erziehung und Volksbildung: Amtsblatt des Reichsministeriums für Wissenschaft, Erziehung und Volksbildung und der Unterrichtsverwaltungen der Länder, 1935-1943.

DSt Akademische Korrespondenz, 1928-1933.

DSt Wissen und Dienst, 1933-1935.

Die Fachgruppe: Organ des Amtes Wissenschaft und Facherziehung und Mitteilungsblatt der Reichsfachgruppen der Reichsstudentenführung, 1940-1944.

Hamburger Anzeiger, 1926-1944.

Hamburger Echo, 1926-1933.

Hamburger Fremdenblatt, 1926-1944.

Hamburger Nachrichten, 1926-1936.

Hamburger Neueste Nachrichten, 1926-1933.

Hamburger Tageblatt, 1931-1945.

Hamburger Universitäts-Kalender, 1929-1931 (subsequently: Hamburger Hochschulführer, 1931-1933).

Hamburger Universitäts-Zeitung: Akademisches Nachrichtenblatt für Gross-Hamburg, 1919-1935.

Hamburgischer Correspondent, 1926-1933.

Hamburgisches Gesetz- und Verordnungsblatt, 1919-1945.

Hansische Hochschul-Zeitung: Das Blatt der Hansischen Hochschulen, 1935-1941.

Hansische Warte, 1929-1930.

Der Junge Revolutionär: Organ des NSDStB, 1927-1928.

Landsmannschafter-Zeitung, 1926-1937.

Mitteilungen des Rektors der Hansischen Universität, 1934-1945.

Die musische Erziehung (ed. RSF-Kulturamt), 1938-1942.

Nachrichtenblatt der Deutschen Studentenschaft, 1919-1931.

Nationalsozialistische Hochschulbriefe: Kampfblatt des NSDStB, 1926-1927.

Nationalsozialistische Monatshefte: Wissenschaftliche Zeitschrift der NSDAP, 1930-1939.

Nationalsozialistische Studentenkorrespondenz, 1932-1934.

Personal- und Vorlesungsverzeichnis der Hamburgischen Universität, 1919-1945.

Politische Wochenübersicht des NSDStB, 1935.
Pressedienst der RSF, 1938-1939.
Pressedienst des NSDStB, 1931-1932.
Reichsgesetzblatt, 1919-1945.
Schröders Allgemeiner Deutscher Hochschulführer, 1934/35-1938/39.
Das Schwarze Korps, 1935-1944.
Sieg der Idee: Führerorgan der Studenten Grossdeutschlands, 1944.
Statistisches Jahrbuch für das Deutsche Reich, 1926-1941/42.
Die Studentische Kameradschaft, 1938-1940.
Verordnungsblatt des Reichsstudentenführers, 1936-1944.
Verordnungsblatt und Mitteilungen des NSD-Studentenbundes der NSDAP, 1936.
Volk im Werden: Zeitschrift für Kulturpolitik, 1933-1945.
Völkischer Beobachter, 1926-1945.
Zentralblatt für die gesamte Unterrichtsverwaltung in Preussen, 1926-1934.

3. Interviews

Achim Freiherr von Beust (Student Leader, University of Hamburg, Summer Semester 1941), 18 April 1972.

Albert Derichsweiler (NSDStB Reich Leader 1934-1936), 12 March 1973.

Andreas Feickert (DSt Reich Leader 1934-1936), 27 September 1973.

Wilhelm Formel (Acting District Student Leader of Hamburg 1943-1945), 7 March 1972.

Gustav Adolf Rein (Rector of Hamburg University 1934-1938, Professor of Colonial and Overseas History), 30 November 1971.

Gustav Adolf Scheel (Reich Student Leader 1936-1945), 11 April 1973.

Rudolf Sieverts (Professor of Criminal Law, University of Hamburg), 7 December 1971.

Werner van der Smissen (Student Leader, University of Hamburg, Summer Semester 1945), 28 November 1971.

Bruno Snell (Professor of Classical Philology, University of Hamburg), 22 November 1971.

Albert Suhr (Member of the Hamburg "White Rose" resistance group), 17 December 1971.

4. *Books and Articles*

Adam, Uwe Dietrich. *Hochschule und Nationalsozialismus: Die Universität Tübingen im Dritten Reich.* Tübingen, 1977.

Allen, William Sheridan, ed. *The Infancy of Nazism: The Memoirs of ex-Gauleiter Albert Krebs 1923-1933.* New York, 1976.

Anschütz, Helga. "Die NSDAP in Hamburg: Ihre Anfänge bis zur Reichstagswahl vom 14. September 1930." Ph.D. diss., Hamburg, 1955.

Assel, Hans-Günther. *Die Perversion der politischen Pädagogik im Nationalsozialismus.* Munich, 1969.

ASTA an der Universität in Hamburg, ed. *Das permanente Kolonialinstitut: 50 Jahre Hamburger Universität.* Hamburg, 1969.

Bässler, Reinhold. "Die deutsche Studentenschaft in ihrer verfassungsgeschichtlichen Entwicklung." Diss.iur., Tübingen, 1941.

Baeumler, Alfred. *Männerbund und Wissenschaft.* Berlin, 1934.

Bauer, Helga. "Die studentische Selbstverwaltung und die studentischen Gruppierungen an der Universität Hamburg 1919-1933: Organisation und Entwicklung unter Berücksichtigung des Einflusses der wirtschaftlich-sozialen Verhältnisse der Freien und Hansestadt Hamburg." Master's thesis, Hamburg, 1971.

Baum, Rolf-Joachim et al., eds. *1582-1982: Studentenschaft und Korporationswesen an der Universität Würzburg.* Würzburg, 1982.

Beatus, Morris. "Academic Proletariat: The Problem of Overcrowding in the Learned Professions and Universities during the Weimar Republic 1918-1933." Ph.D. diss., University of Wisconsin, Madison, 1975.

Becker, Carl Heinrich. *Vom Wesen der deutschen Universität.* Leipzig, 1925.

Benz, Wolfgang. "Vom freiwilligen Arbeitsdienst zur Arbeitsdienstpflicht," *Vierteljahrshefte für Zeitgeschichte* 16 (October 1968): 317-46.

Benze, Edmund. *Erziehung im Grossdeutschen Reich: Eine Überschau über ihre Ziele, Wege und Einrichtungen.* Frankfurt am Main, 1939.

Bernett, Hajo. *Untersuchungen zur Zeitgeschichte des Sports.* Schorndorf/Stuttgart, 1973.

Bernhardi, Horst. *Frisia Gottingensis 1931-1956*. Heide/Holstein, 1956.

———. "Die Göttinger Burschenschaft 1933 bis 1945: Ein Beitrag zur studentischen Geschichte in der nationalsozialistischen Zeit." In *Darstellungen und Quellen zur Geschichte der deutschen Einheitsbewegung im neunzehnten und zwanzigsten Jahrhundert*, edited by Paul Wentzcke, vol. 1, pp. 205-48. Heidelberg, 1957.

Beyerchen, Alan D. *Scientists under Hitler: Politics and the Physics Community in the Third Reich*. New Haven, 1977.

Bielenberg, Christabel. *Ride Out the Dark*. New York, 1971.

Bleuel, Hans Peter. *Deutschlands Bekenner: Professoren zwischen Kaiserreich und Diktatur*. Berne, Munich, and Vienna, 1968.

———, and Ernst Klinnert. *Deutsche Studenten auf dem Weg ins Dritte Reich: Ideologien, Programme, Aktionen, 1918-1935*. Gütersloh, 1967.

Bolitho, Gordon. *The Other Germany*. London, 1934.

Bolland, Jürgen. "Die Gründung der 'Hamburgischen Universität.' " In *Universität Hamburg 1919-1969*, edited by the University of Hamburg, pp 17-105. Hamburg, 1969.

Bollmus, Reinhard. *Das Amt Rosenberg und seine Gegner: Studien zum Machtkampf im nationalsozialistischen Herrschaftssystem*. Stuttgart, 1970.

Bracher, Karl Dietrich. *Die Auflösung der Weimarer Republik: Eine Studie zum Problem des Machtverfalls in der Demokratie*. Villingen, 1955.

———. *Das deutsche Dilemma: Leidenswege der politischen Emanzipation*. Munich, 1971.

Brandenburg, Hans-Christian. *Die Geschichte der HJ: Wege und Irrwege einer Generation*. Cologne, 1968.

Carlsen, Ruth. "Zum Prozess der Faschisierung und zu den Auswirkungen der faschistischen Diktatur auf die Universität Rostock 1932-1935." Ph.D. diss., Rostock, 1965.

Carmon, Arye. "The Impact of the Nazi Racial Decrees on the University of Heidelberg," *Yad Vashem Studies* 11 (1976): 131-63.

Degkwitz, Rudolf. *Das alte und das neue Deutschland: Erfahrungen und Erkenntnisse eines deutschen Arztes und Hochschullehrers, niedergeschrieben während des Krieges*. Hamburg, 1946.

Derichsweiler, Albert. "Die rechtsgeschichtliche Entwicklung des deutschen Studententums von seinen Anfängen bis zur Gegenwart." Diss.iur., Munich, 1938.

————. "Student der Bewegung," *Volk im Werden* 3, no. 2 Sonderheft NSDStB (March 1935), pp. 80-84.

Der Deutsche Hochschulführer: Lebens- und Studienverhältnisse an den Deutschen Hochschulen, Studienjahr 1939, edited by Reichsstudentenwerk gemeinsam mit der Reichsstudentenführung, 21. Ausgabe. Berlin, 1939.

Die Deutsche Studentenschaft in ihrem Werden, Wollen und Wirken, edited by Vorstand der Deutschen Studentenschaft, n.p., n.d. [Berlin, 1928].

Deutsche Studentenschaft. *Wir fordern Rüstungsausgleich! Eine wehrpolitische Schulungswoche der DSt.* Berlin, 1931.

Deutsches Studentenwerk. *Kurzberichte aus der Entwicklung seit der nationalsozialistischen Revolution 1933/34*, Sonderdrucke der Zeitschrift *Der Deutsche Student*, August 1933 bis Januar 1934.

————, eds. *Deutsches Studentenwerk 1921-1961: Festschrift zum vierzigjährigen Bestehen.* Bonn, 1961.

Die Deutsche Universität im Dritten Reich: Eine Vortragsreihe der Universität München. Munich, 1966.

Deutsche Wissenschaft: Arbeit und Aufgabe. Leipzig, 1939.

Dibner, Ursula. "The History of the National Socialist German Student League." Ph.D. diss., University of Michigan, 1969.

Doeberl, Michael et al. *Das akademische Deutschland*, 3 vols. and 2 supplementary vols. Berlin, 1930-1931.

Döring, Herbert. *Der Weimarer Kreis: Studien zum politischen Bewusstsein verfassungstreuer Hochschullehrer in der Weimarer Republik.* Meisenheim, 1975.

Drobisch, Klaus, ed. *Wir schweigen nicht! Eine Dokumentation über den antifaschistischen Kampf Münchener Studenten 1942/43.* Berlin, 1968.

Düning, Hans Joachim. *Der SA-Student im Kampf um die Hochschule (1925-35): Ein Beitrag zur Geschichte der deutschen Universität im zwanzigsten Jahrhundert.* Weimar, 1936.

Education in Nazi Germany, by Two English Investigators, with a Foreword by Sir Norman Angell. London, 1938.

Eilers, Rolf. *Die nationalsozialistische Schulpolitik: Eine Studie zur Funktion der Erziehung im totalitären Staat.* Cologne and Opladen, 1963.

Eisfeld, Curt. *Aus fünfzig Jahren: Erinnerungen eines Betriebswirts 1902-1951.* Göttingen, 1973.

Erdmann, Karl Dietrich. *Wissenschaft im Dritten Reich.* Kiel, 1967.

Faust, Anselm. "Die Hochschulen und der 'undeutsche Geist': Die Bücherverbrennungen am 10. Mai 1933 und ihre Vorgeschichte." In *"Das war ein Vorspiel nur..." Bücherverbrennung Deutschland 1933: Voraussetzungen und Folgen,* edited by Hermann Haarmann, Walter Huder, and Klaus Siebenhaar, pp. 31-50. Berlin and Vienna, 1983.

———. *Der Nationalsozialistische Deutsche Studentenbund: Studenten und Nationalsozialismus in der Weimarer Republik,* 2 vols. Düsseldorf, 1973.

———. "Professoren für die NSDAP: Zum politischen Verhalten der Hochschullehrer 1932/33." In *Erziehung und Schulung im Dritten Reich. Teil 2: Hochschule, Erwachsenenbildung,* edited by Manfred Heinemann, pp. 31-49. Stuttgart, 1980.

Feickert, Andreas. *Studenten greifen an! Nationalsozialistische Hochschulrevolution.* Hamburg, 1934.

Flitner, Andreas. *Deutsches Geistesleben und Nationalsozialismus: Eine Vortragsreihe der Universität Tübingen.* Tübingen, 1965.

Franze, Manfred. *Die Erlanger Studentenschaft 1918-1945.* Würzburg, 1972.

Frick, Wilhelm. *Student im Volk: Völkische Aufgaben der Hochschulen.* Langensalza, 1934.

Füssel, Stephan. " 'Wider den undeutschen Geist': Bücherverbrennung und Bibliothekslenkung im Nationalsozialismus." In *Göttingen unterm Hakenkreuz: Nationalsozialistischer Alltag in einer deutschen Stadt. Texte und Materialien,* edited by Jens-Uwe Brinkmann and Hans-Georg Schmeling, pp. 95-104. Göttingen, 1983.

Gamm, Hans-Jochen. *Führung und Verführung: Pädagogik des Nationalsozialismus.* Munich, 1964.

Geissler, Erich. *Die Burschenschaft Primislavia 1877-1952.* Erweiterte, teilweise geänderte Ausgabe des Festschrifts von 1927. Berlin, 1953-1955.

Giles, Geoffrey J. "The Academic Ethos in the Face of National Socialism," *Minerva* 18 (Spring 1980): 171-79.

―――. "Die Idee der politischen Universität: Hochschulreform nach der Machtergreifung." In *Erziehung und Schulung im Dritten Reich. Teil 2: Hochschule, Erwachsenenbildung*, edited by Manfred Heinemann, pp. 50-60. Stuttgart, 1980.

―――. "National Socialism and the Educated Elite in the Weimar Republic." In *The Nazi Machtergreifung*, edited by Peter D. Stachura, pp. 49-67. London, 1983.

―――. "The National Socialist Students' Association in Hamburg 1926-1945," Ph.D. diss., University of Cambridge, 1975.

―――. *Der NSD-Studentenbund und der Geist der studentischen Korporationen*. Würzburg: Deutsche Gesellschaft für Hochschulkunde, 1975.

―――. "The Rise of the National Socialist Students' Association and the Failure of Political Education in the Third Reich." In *The Shaping of the Nazi State*, edited by Peter D. Stachura, pp. 160-85. London and New York, 1978.

―――. "Student Drinking and the Third Reich: Academic Tradition and the Nazi Revolution." Paper presented at the Social History of Alcohol Conference, Berkeley, January 1984.

―――. "University Government in Nazi Germany: Hamburg," *Minerva* 16, no. 2 (Summer 1978), pp. 196-221.

―――. "Die Verbändepolitik des Nationalsozialistischen Deutschen Studentenbundes." In *Darstellungen und Quellen zur Geschichte der deutschen Einheitsbewegung im neunzehnten und zwanzigsten Jahrhundert*, edited by Christian Probst, vol. 11, pp. 95-155. Heidelberg, 1981.

Gillis, John R. *Youth and History: Tradition and Change in European Age Relations 1770-Present*. New York, 1974.

Gmelin, Ulrich. *Das Langemarck-Studium der Reichsstudentenführung*. Grossenhain, 1938.

Goebbels, Joseph. *Der geistige Arbeiter im Schicksalskampf des Reiches: Rede vor der Heidelberger Universität am Freitag, dem 9. Juli 1943*. Munich, 1943.

Graak, Karl, ed. *Hamburger Studentenbuch 1938/39*. Hamburg, 1939.

Die Hansische Universität, edited by Landesbildstelle Hansa und der Hansischen Universität Hamburg; Text by Professor Dr. A. Rein. Hamburg, n.d. [1937].

Hartshorne, Edward. *The German Universities and National Socialism*. London, 1937.

Hasse, Heinrich. *Stellung und Aufgabe der Wissenschaft im neuen Deutschland*. Heidelberg, 1934.

Haug, Wolfgang Fritz. *Der hilflose Antifaschismus: Zur Kritik der Vorlesungsreihen über Wissenschaft und NS an deutschen Universitäten*. Frankfurt am Main, 1967.

Haupt, Joachim. *Neuordnung im Schulwesen und Hochschulwesen*. Berlin, 1933.

Hederich, Karl Heinrich. *Hochschulschrifttum: Verzeichnis von Dissertationen und Habilitationsschriften*. Berlin, 1942.

Heidegger, Martin. *Die Selbstbehauptung der deutschen Universität: Rede gehalten bei der feierlichen Übernahme des Rektorats der Universität Freiburg im Breisgau am 27.5.1933*. Breslau, 1934.

Heinemann, Manfred, ed. *Erziehung und Schulung im Dritten Reich. Teil 2: Hochschule, Erwachsenenbildung*. Stuttgart, 1980.

Hikad (pseudonym for Hans Hildebrandt). *Studenten im Braunhemd*. Berlin, 1933.

Hirschfeld, Gerhard and Lothar Kettenacker, eds. *Der "Führerstaat": Mythos und Realität. Studien zur Struktur und Politik des Dritten Reiches*. Stuttgart, 1981.

Hochmuth, Ursel. *Candidates of Humanity: Dokumentation zur Hamburger Weissen Rose anlässlich des 50. Geburtstages von Hans Leipelt*. Hamburg, 1971.

Hoppe, Ferdinand. *Was soll ich studieren? Ein Ratgeber für die akademische Berufswahl*. Würzburg, 1944.

Horn, Daniel. "The Hitler Youth and Educational Decline in the Third Reich," *History of Education Quarterly* 16 (Winter 1976): 425-47.

———. "The National Socialist *Schülerbund* and the Hitler Youth 1929-1933," *Central European History* 11 (December 1978): 355-75.

Huber, Hans. *Der Aufbau des deutschen Hochschulwesens: Vortrag gehalten auf der dritten fachwissenschaftlichen Woche für Universitätsbeamte der Verwaltungsakademie Berlin am 30. Januar 1939*. Berlin, 1939.

Hübinger, Paul Egon. *Thomas Mann, die Universität Bonn und die Zeitgeschichte: Drei Kapitel deutscher Vergangenheit aus dem Leben des Dichters 1905-1955*. Munich, 1974.

Jahnke, Karl Heinz. *Weisse Rose contra Hakenkreuz: Der Wider-*

stand der Geschwister Scholl und ihrer Freunde. Frankfurt am Main, 1969.

Jarausch, Konrad H. *Students, Society and Politics in Imperial Germany: The Rise of Academic Illiberalism*. Princeton, 1982.

Jochmann, Werner. *Nationalsozialismus und Revolution: Ursprung und Geschichte der NSDAP in Hamburg 1922-1933. Dokumente*. Frankfurt am Main, 1963.

Kaffl, Wilhelm, ed. *Wille und Weg der nationalsozialistischen Studenten: Bericht von der ersten Reichsarbeitstagung des NSD-Studentenbundes und der Deutschen Studentenschaft, Heidelberg, 22. bis 25. Juni 1937*. Munich, n.d. [1937].

Kahle, Paul. *Bonn University in Pre-Nazi and Nazi Times 1923-1939*. London, 1945.

Kasper, Gerhard, Hans Huber, Karl Kaebsch, and Franz Senger, eds. *Die Deutsche Hochschulverwaltung: Sammlung der das Hochschulwesen betreffenden Gesetze, Verordnungen und Erlasse*, 2 vols. Berlin, 1942-1943.

Kater, Michael H. *Das "Ahnenerbe" der SS 1935-1945: Ein Beitrag zur Kulturpolitik des Dritten Reiches*. Stuttgart, 1974.

―――. "Krisis des Frauenstudiums in der Weimarer Republik," *Vierteljahrsschrift für Sozial- und Wirtschaftsgeschichte* 59 (1972): 207-55.

―――. "Die nationalsozialistische Machtergreifung an den deutschen Hochschulen: Zum politischen Verhalten akademischer Lehrer bis 1939. In *Die Freiheit des Anderen: Festschrift für Martin Hirsch*, edited by Hans Jochen Vogel et al., pp. 49-75. Baden-Baden, 1981.

―――. "Der NS-Studentenbund von 1926 bis 1928: Randgruppe zwischen Hitler und Strasser," *Vierteljahrshefte für Zeitgeschichte* 22, no. 2 (April 1974), pp. 148-90.

―――. *The Nazi Party: A Social Profile of Members and Leaders 1919-1945*. Cambridge, Mass., 1983.

―――. "The Reich Vocational Contest and Students of Higher Learning in Nazi Germany," *Central European History* 7 (September 1974): 225-61.

―――. *Studentenschaft und Rechtsradikalismus in Deutschland 1918-1933: Eine sozialgeschichtliche Studie zur Bildungskrise in der Weimarer Republik*. Hamburg, 1975.

―――. "Die 'Technische Nothilfe' im Spannungsfeld von Arbeiterunruhen, Unternehmerinteressen, und Parteipolitik," *Vier-*

teljahrshefte für Zeitgeschichte 27, no. 1 (January 1979), pp. 30-78.

————. "The Work Student: A Socio-Economic Phenomenon of Early Weimar Germany," *Journal of Contemporary History* 10 (January 1975): 71-94.

Kelly, Reece C. "National Socialism and German University Teachers: The NSDAP's Efforts to Create a National Socialist Professoriate and Scholarship." Ph.D. diss., University of Washington, 1973.

Kersten, Ulrich. *Das deutsche Studentenrecht*. Berlin-Zehlendorf, n.d. [1931?].

Klemmt, Alfred. *Wissenschaft und Philosophie im Dritten Reich*. Berlin, 1938.

Kneller, George. *The Educational Philosophy of National Socialism*. New Haven, 1941.

Köhler, Henning. *Arbeitsdienst in Deutschland: Pläne und Verwirklichungsformen bis zur Einführung des Arbeitsdienstpflicht im Jahre 1935*. Berlin, 1967.

Kösener SC-Verband. *Neue Hochschule: Vorschläge für eine totale Hochschulreform*, edited by Hauptamt für Presse des Kösener SC-Verbandes und des Verbandes Alter Corpsstudenten. Frankfurt am Main, 1935.

Koshar, Rudy. "Two 'Nazisms': The social context of Nazi mobilization in Marburg and Tübingen," *Social History* (January 1982): 27-43.

Kreppel, Otto. *Nationalsozialistisches Studententum und Studentenrecht*. Königsberg, 1937.

Kreutzberger, Wolfgang. *Studenten und Politik 1918-1933: Der Fall Freiburg im Breisgau*. Göttingen, 1972.

Krieck, Ernst. *Die Erneuerung der Universität: Rede zur Übergabe des Rektorats am 23. Mai 1933*. Frankfurt am Main, 1933.

————. *Nationalpolitische Erziehung*. Leipzig, 1933.

————. *Wissenschaft, Weltanschauung, Hochschulreform*. Leipzig, 1934.

Kubach, Fritz. *Studenten bauen auf! Der 3. Reichsberufswettkampf der deutschen Studenten 1937/38: Ein Rechenschaftsbericht* (DAF-Zentralbüro, n.d.).

Leisen, Adolf. "Die Ausbreitung des völkischen Gedankens in der Studentenschaft der Weimarer Republik." Ph.D. diss., Heidelberg, 1964.

Leitner, Erich. *Politik und Hochschule: Der CV in der Steiermark 1918-1938.* Vienna, 1978.

Leonhard, Joachim-Felix, ed. *Bücherverbrennung: Zensur, Verbot, Vernichtung unter dem Nationalsozialismus in Heidelberg.* Heidelberg, 1983.

Lilge, Frederic. *The Abuse of Learning: The Failure of the German University.* New York, 1948.

Linse, Ulrich. "Hochschulrevolution: Zur Ideologie und Praxis sozialistischer Studentengruppen während der deutschen Revolutionszeit 1918/19," *Archiv für Sozialgeschichte* 14 (1974): 1-114.

———. "Studenten und Politik 1914-1939," *Archiv für Sozialgeschichte* 17 (1977): 567-76.

Lipset, Seymour Martin, and Philip G. Altbach, eds. *Students in Revolt.* Boston, 1970.

Loewenberg, Peter. "The Psychohistorical Origins of the Nazi Youth Cohort," *American Historical Review* 76 (1971): 1457-1502.

Lorenz, Charlotte, *Zehnjahres-Statistik des Hochschulbesuches und der Abschlussprüfungen,* 2 vols. Berlin, 1943.

Losemann, Volker. *Nationalsozialismus und Antike: Studien zur Entwicklung des Faches Alte Geschichte 1933-1945.* Hamburg, 1977.

Ludwig, Karl-Heinz. *Technik und Ingenieure im Dritten Reich.* Düsseldorf, 1974.

Lüth, Marlis. "Hamburg und die Kolonialpolitik im Dritten Reich," *Zeitschrift des Vereins für Hamburgische Geschichte* 59 (1973): 55-87.

McClelland, Charles E. *State, Society, and University in Germany 1700-1914.* Cambridge, 1980.

Mannhardt, Johann Wilhelm. *Hochschulrevolution.* Hamburg, 1933.

Mehrtens, Herbert, and Steffen Richter. *Naturwissenschaft, Technik und NS-Ideologie: Beiträge zur Wissenschaftsgeschichte des Dritten Reiches.* Frankfurt am Main, 1980.

Meinhof, Carl. "Hamburgische Universität." In *Das akademische Deutschland,* edited by Michael Doeberl et al., vol. 1, pp. 199-204. Berlin, 1930.

Miehe, Gudrun. "Zur Rolle der Universität Rostock in der Zeit des

Faschismus in den Jahren 1935-1945." Ph.D. diss., Rostock, 1968.

Milberg, Hildegard. *Schulpolitik in der pluralistischen Gesellschaft: Die politischen und sozialen Aspekte der Schulreform in Hamburg 1908-1935.* Hamburg, 1970.

Mosse, George. *The Crisis of German Ideology: Intellectual Origins of the Third Reich.* London, 1966.

Müller, Gerhard. *Ernst Krieck und die nationalsozialistische Wissenschaftsreform: Motive und Tendenzen einer Wissenschaftslehre und Hochschulreform im Dritten Reich.* Weinheim, 1978.

Nipperdey, Thomas. "Die deutsche Studentenschaft in den ersten Jahren der Weimarer Republik." In *Kulturverwaltung der zwanziger Jahre: Alte Dokumente und neue Beiträge,* edited by Adolf Grimme, pp. 18-48. Stuttgart, 1961.

NS-Lehrerbund, ed. *Bekenntnis der Professoren an den deutschen Universitäten und Hochschulen zu Adolf Hitler und dem nationalsozialistischen Staat.* Dresden, n.d. [1933].

Ochsenius, Hans. "Die Studentenschaft der Hansischen Universität zu Hamburg bis 1939 unter besonderer Berücksichtigung der gesamten studentischen Entwicklung im Altreich." Ph.D. diss., Hamburg, 1941.

————, ed. *Hamburger Studentenbuch 1941.* Hamburg, 1941.

————. *Hansische Soldaten-Briefe der Kameradschaften und der Altherrenschaften des NSDStB zu Hamburg.* Hamburg, n.d. [1943].

Olenhusen, Albrecht Götz von. "Die 'nichtarischen' Studenten an den deutschen Hochschulen: Zur nationalsozialistischen Rassenpolitik 1933-1945," *Vierteljahrshefte für Zeitgeschichte* 14 (April 1966): 175-206.

Ott, Hugo. "Martin Heidegger als Rektor der Universität Freiburg i. Br. 1933/34," *Zeitschrift des Breisgau-Geschichtsvereins* 102 (1983): 121-36.

Partei-Statistik: Stand 1. Januar 1935 (ohne Saargebiet), edited by Reichsorganisationsleiter der NSDAP (Als Manuskript gedruckt), 3 vols. N.p., n.d.

Pauwels, Jacques R. "Women and University Studies in the Third Reich 1933-1945." Ph.D. diss., York University, Toronto, 1976.

Pesta, Hans, ed. *Hochschulführer für die Hansische Universität Hamburg 1938/1939.* Darmstadt, 1938.

Petry, Christian. *Studenten aufs Schafott: Die Weisse Rose und ihr Scheitern.* Munich, 1968.

Popp, Emil. *Zur Geschichte des Königsberger Studententums 1900-1945.* Würzburg, 1955.

Rantzau, Otto Graf zu. *Das Reichsministerium für Wissenschaft, Erziehung und Volksbildung.* Berlin, 1939.

Reichsstudentenführung, ed. *Zehn Jahre Langemarck-Studium Königsberg (Pr.).* Königsberg, 1944.

Reichsstudentenführung (RSF)-Amt Politische Erziehung, ed. *Richtlinien für die Kameradschaftserziehung des NSD-Studentenbundes.* Munich, n.d.

———. *Dienstvorschrift für die Kameradschaften des NSD-Studentenbundes im Kriege.* Munich, 1940.

———. *Grundsätze der Kameradschaftsarbeit des Nationalsozialistischen Deutschen Studentenbundes, mit den Ausführungsbestimmungen des Amtes Politische Erziehung der RSF.* Munich, 1942.

———. *Dienstanweisung für die Kameradschaft vom 20. April 1943.* Munich, 1943.

Reichsstudentenwerk, ed. *Kurzberichte aus der Arbeit des Jahres 1934,* 2. Folge der Sonderdrucke der Zeitschrift *Der Deutsche Student,* Februar 1934 bis Dezember 1934. Breslau, 1935.

———. *Kurzberichte aus der Arbeit des Jahres 1937.* Berlin, 1938.

———. *Bericht über die Arbeit im Kriege: Zum zwanzigjährigen Bestehen des Reichsstudentenwerks.* Berlin, 1941.

———. *Ich studiere: Ein Überblick über die Arbeit des deutschen Studententums.* Berlin, 1940.

———. *Soldat und Studium! Wegweiser für Kriegsteilnehmer durch die akademischen Berufe und ihren Ausbildungsgang.* Neumünster, 1943.

Rein, Adolf. *Europa und das Reich: Betrachtungen zur Geschichte der europäischen Ordnung.* Essen, 1943.

———. "Das Gesicht der deutschen Universität: Die Hansische Universität zu Hamburg." In *Hochschule und Ausland* 13, no. 9 (September 1935), pp. 30-37.

———. "Die Gestalt der politischen Universität," *Hamburger Universitäts-Zeitung* 15, no. 2 (22 May 1933), pp. 17-20.

———. *Die Idee der politischen Universität.* Hamburg, 1933.

———. "Illusion und Politik," *Deutsche Politik* 4, no. 35 (August 1919), pp. 277-80.

Rein, Adolf. *Die Wahrheit über Hitler aus englischem Mund*. Berlin, 1940.

———. *Warum führt England Krieg?* Berlin, 1940.

Ringer, Fritz K. *The Decline of the German Mandarins: The German Academic Community 1890-1933*. Cambridge, Mass., 1969.

———. *Education and Society in Modern Europe*. Bloomington, 1979.

Ritter, Gerhard. "The German Professor in the Third Reich," *The Review of Politics* 8 (April 1946): 242-54.

Ritterbusch, Paul. *Idee und Aufgabe der Reichsuniversität*. Hamburg, 1935.

Roegele, Otto. "Student im Dritten Reich." In *Die deutsche Universität im Dritten Reich: Eine Vortragsreihe der Universität München*, pp. 135-75. Munich, 1966.

Rupp, Rupert. *Dokumente über die englische Plutokratie* (Kriegsschriften der RSF, vol. 1). Munich, 1940.

Rust, Berhard, and Ernst Krieck. *National Socialist Germany and the Pursuit of Learning*. Berlin, 1936.

Sandberger, Martin. "Das Nationalsozialistische Deutsche Studententum." In *Grundlagen, Aufbau und Wirtschaftsordnung des nationalsozialistischen Staates*, edited by Hans-Heinrich Lammers and Hans Pfundtner, vol. 1, group 1, 7d. Berlin and Vienna, n.d. [1939].

Sandfuchs, Uwe. *Universitäre Lehrerausbildung in der Weimarer Republik und im Dritten Reich: Eine historisch-systematische Untersuchung am Beispiel der Lehrerausbildung an der Technischen Hochschule Braunschweig (1918-1940)*. Bad Heilbrunn/Oberbayern, 1978.

Scheel, Gustav Adolf. *Die Reichsstudentenführung: Arbeit und Organisation des deutschen Studententums*. Berlin, 1938.

———. *Tradition und Zukunft des deutschen Studententums: Die Rede des Reichsstudentenführers bei der Grosskundgebung des NSD-Studentenbundes und der NS-Studentenkampfhilfe München, 13 Mai 1937*. Munich, 1937.

Schelsky, Helmut. *Einsamkeit und Freiheit: Idee und Gestalt der deutschen Universität und ihrer Reformen*. Reinbek bei Hamburg, 1963.

Schirach, Baldur von. *Ich glaubte an Hitler*. Hamburg, 1967.

————. *Wille und Weg des Nationalsozialistischen Deutschen Studentenbundes.* Munich, 1929.

"Als Baldur von Schirach den Studentenbund führte . . . ," *Wille und Macht, Führerorgan der nationalsozialistischen Jugend* 4, no. 21 (30 October 1936), pp. 16-20.

Schlömer, Hans. "Die Ära der Gleichschaltung: Das Deutsche Studentenwerk im Dritten Reich." In *Deutsches Studentenwerk 1921-1961*, pp. 63-79. Bonn, 1961.

Schoenbaum, David. *Hitler's Social Revolution: Class and Status in Nazi Germany 1933-1939.* New York, 1967.

Scholl, Inge. *Students against Tyranny: The Resistance of the White Rose (Munich, 1942-43).* Translated by Arthur R. Schultze. Middletown, Conn., 1970.

Schorer, Friedrich, and Heinz Riecke. "Nationalsozialismus als Geist und Organisation in der Hamburger Studentenschaft der Jahre 1930-33," *Hamburger Universitäts-Zeitung* 15, no. 7 (8 February 1934), pp. 113-22.

Schulte, Günther G. *Institut für Hochschulkunde an der Universität Würzburg: Werden und Wirken 1882-1982.* Würzburg, 1981.

Schwarz, Jürgen. *Studenten in der Weimarer Republik: Die deutsche Studentenschaft in der Zeit von 1918 bis 1923 und ihre Stellung zur Politik.* Berlin, 1971.

Seeliger, Rolf. *Braune Universität: Dokumentation mit Stellungnahmen*, 6 vols. Munich, 1964-1968.

Seier, Hellmut. "Niveaukritik und partielle Opposition: Zur Lage an den deutschen Hochschulen 1939/40," *Archiv für Kulturgeschichte* 58 (1976): 227-46.

————. "Der Rektor als Führer: Zur Hochschulpolitik des Reichserziehungsministeriums 1934-1945," *Vierteljahrshefte für Zeitgeschichte* 12, no. 2 (April 1964), pp. 105-46.

Six, Franz. *Studenten bauen auf! Der 1. Reichsleistungskampf 1935/36: Ein Rechenschaftsbericht.* Marburg and Berlin, n.d.

Spitznagel, Peter. "Studentenschaft und Nationalsozialismus in Würzburg 1927-1933." Ph.D. diss., Würzburg, 1974.

Spranger, Eduard. "Mein Konflikt mit der nationalsozialistischen Regierung 1933," *Universitas* 10 (May 1955): 513-26.

Ssymank, Paul. "Organisation und Arbeitsfeld der Deutschen Studentenschaft." In *Das akademische Deutschland*, edited by Michael Doeberl et al., vol. 3, pp. 363-84. Berlin, 1930.

Stachura, Peter D. *The German Youth Movement 1900-1945: An Interpretative and Documentary History.* New York, 1981.

——. *Nazi Youth in the Weimar Republic.* Santa Barbara and Oxford, 1975.

Stark, Johannes. *Nationalsozialismus und Wissenschaft.* Munich, 1934.

Statistisches Handbuch von Deutschland 1928-1944, edited by Länderrat des Amerikanischen Besatzungsgebiets. Munich, 1949.

Steinberg, Michael Stephen. *Sabers and Brown Shirts: The German Students' Path to National Socialism 1918-1935.* Chicago, 1977.

——. "Sabres, Books and Brown Shirts: The Radicalization of the German Student 1918-1935." Ph.D. diss., Johns Hopkins University, 1971.

Stephenson, Jill. "Girls' Higher Education in Germany in the 1930s," *Journal of Contemporary History* 10 (January 1975): 41-69.

Stitz, Peter. *Der CV 1919-1938: Der hochschulpolitische Weg des Cartellverbandes der katholischen deutschen Studentenverbindungen (CV) vom Ende des ersten Weltkrieges bis zur Vernichtung durch den Nationalsozialismus.* Munich, 1970.

Strätz, Hans Wolfgang. "Die studentische 'Aktion wider den undeutschen Geist' im Frühjahr 1933," *Vierteljahrshefte für Zeitgeschichte* 16 (October 1968): pp. 347-72.

"Studenten im Kampf: Beiträge zur Geschichte des NSD-Studentenbundes," *Die Studentische Kameradschaft,* special number (April 1938).

Universität Hamburg 1919-1969, edited by the University of Hamburg. Hamburg, 1969.

Die Universität Hamburg als politische Universität (Hamburg im Dritten Reich, Arbeiten der hamburgischen Verwaltung in Einzeldarstellungen, Heft 2). Hamburg, 1935.

Universität Hamburg, ed. *25 Jahre Hamburger Universität: Ein Gruss der alma mater an ihre Angehörigen im Felde zum 10. Mai 1944.* Hamburg, 1944.

Universitätstage 1966: Nationalsozialismus und die deutsche Universität. Berlin, 1966.

Vahlen, Theodor. "Wissenschaft, Erziehung und Volksbildung im nationalsozialistischen Staate." In *Grundlagen, Aufbau und*

Wirtschaftsordnung des nationalsozialistischen Staates, edited by Hans-Heinrich Lammers and Hans Pfundtner, vol. 1, group 2, 21. Berlin, n.d. [1936].

Wacker, Otto. *Wissenschaftspolitik und Nachwuchs: Rede gehalten auf der ersten grossdeutschen Rektorenkonferenz am 7. März 1939,* edited by Deutschen Forschungsgemeinschaft, n.p., n.d.

Webler, Wolff-Dieter. *Nicht von ungefähr. . . . Zur Geschichte der deutschen Hochschule im Nationalsozialismus.* Bielefeld, 1983.

Wende, Erich. *C. H. Becker—Mensch und Politiker: Ein biographischer Beitrag zur Kulturgeschichte der Weimarer Republik.* Stuttgart, 1959.

Wolf, Abraham. *Higher Education in Nazi Germany, or Education for World Conquest.* London, 1944.

Wortman, Michael. "Der Nationalsozialistische Deutsche Studentenbund an der Universität Köln (1927-1933)," *Geschichte in Köln* 8 (October 1980): 101-18.

Ziegler, Wilhelm, ed. *Ein Dokumentenwerk über die englische Demokratie.* Im Auftrage des Reichsministeriums für Volksaufklärung und Propaganda herausgegeben unter Mitarbeit des Amtes Wissenschaft und Facherziehung der Reichsstudentenführung. Berlin, 1940.

———. *Ein Dokumentenwerk über die englische Humanität.* Berlin, n.d. [1940].

Zneimer, Richard. "The Nazis and the Professors: Social Origin, Professional Mobility, and Political Involvement of the Frankfurt University Faculty, 1933-1939," *Journal of Social History* 12 (1978): 147-58.

Zorn, Wolfgang. "Die politische Entwicklung des deutschen Studententums 1918-1931." In *Darstellungen und Quellen zur Geschichte der deutschen Einheitsbewegung im neunzehnten und zwanzigsten Jahrhundert,* edited by Kurt Stephenson et al., vol. 5, pp. 223-307. Heidelberg, 1965.

———. "Student Politics in the Weimar Republic," *Journal of Contemporary History* 5 (1970): 128-43.

INDEX

Library of Congress Cataloging in Publication Data

Giles, Geoffrey J., 1947-
Students and national socialism in Germany.

Bibliography: p.
Includes index.
1. College students—Germany—Political activity—History—20th century.
2. National socialism. 3. Students—Germany—Societies, etc.—History—
20th century. 4. Nationalsozialistischer Deutscher Studentenbund—
History. I. Title.

LA729.G53 1985   378'.1981'0943   85-42686
ISBN 0-691-05453-3 (alk. paper)